Isaac Lindo Mocatta

Moral Biblical Gleanings and Practical Teachings

Illustrated by biographical sketches drawn from the sacred volume

Isaac Lindo Mocatta

Moral Biblical Gleanings and Practical Teachings
Illustrated by biographical sketches drawn from the sacred volume

ISBN/EAN: 9783337012991

Printed in Europe, USA, Canada, Australia, Japan

Cover: Foto ©Lupo / pixelio.de

More available books at **www.hansebooks.com**

MORAL BIBLICAL GLEANINGS.

MORAL
BIBLICAL GLEANINGS

AND

PRACTICAL TEACHINGS,

ILLUSTRATED BY

BIOGRAPHICAL SKETCHES DRAWN FROM
THE SACRED VOLUME.

PS. XLV, 1, "MY HEART IS INDITING A GOOD MATTER."

BY

I. L. MOCATTA.

LONDON:
TRÜBNER & CO., PATERNOSTER ROW.
1872.

T. RICHARDS, PRINTER, GREAT QUEEN STREET, W.C.

CONTENTS.

INTRODUCTION - - - - - Pages i—iv

I.—INDUSTRY.

The Creation—its Artificer. *Essay.*—Greatly conduces to man's happiness—cheerful reflections to gladden labour—baneful influence of idleness—considerations which should stimulate to exertion—duties and man's moral responsibility. *Precepts. Example*, EZRA - - - - - - - 5—10

II.—OBSERVATION.

The Creation—the Governor of the Universe. *Essay.*—Study of nature—benefit therefrom—endless source of delight to the observant man—duty to gather its golden fruits—the glorious truths it reveals—study of human nature, and of our inner selves—conclusion to which it leads. *Precepts. Examples*, DAVID, SOLOMON. 11—16

III.—MARRIAGE.

The Creation—the Gracious Overseer. *Essay.*—Helpmate, Heaven's gift—should be correspondingly valued—obligation it imposes—non-fulfilment source of much misery—wise discretion essential in choice of wife—responsibility of both sexes—important reflection, without esteem there can be no permanent affection—too often overlooked by tender-hearted women—consequent misery—importance of discernment before marriage—a loving spirit after—how to secure prize—how retain happiness at family hearth—affection an active principle, religion a powerful cement. *Precepts. Examples.* Several wives who influenced their husbands to evil, others to good —HANNAH - - - - - - 17—23

IV.—TEMPTATION.

Eve—her disobedience. *Essay.*—Man's freewill—thence responsibility—laws given for general good—pleasures, two distinct kinds—which we should choose—how to resist evil—sinful courses hollow and baneful—power of prayer. *Precepts. Examples,* SAMSON, SOLOMON.
24—30

V.—ENVY.

Cain—his envious and wrathful disposition. *Essay.*—Whence derives its birth—its baneful influence—works outwardly and inwardly—best method of curbing or uprooting it—wilful permittance is sinful—equality—worth preferable to wealth—true riches of this earth—easy of attainment—set heart on them and envy is no more. *Precepts. Examples,* RACHEL, Miriam, Daniel's enemies, SAUL.
31—36

VI.—VIRTUE.

Noah—the just and pious man—a corrupt people—the deluge. *Essay.*—To be just, as understood in its full comprehensive sense—three paramount duties—in what they consist—how true virtue may be distinguished—how attained—benefit it confers—to seek is to find. *Precepts. Examples,* HEZEKIAH, SAMUEL, JOB - 37—45

VII.—AMBITION.

Builders of Babel—their presumption—their sin—their dispersion. *Essay.*—Man's mission here—duty to fulfil it, wherein lies man's true glory—a boundary line and certain penalty on depassing it—a power for good or ill—proportion to be kept between desired end and means of attainment—goodness far preferable to greatness, and is open to all. *Precepts. Examples,* HAMAN, JOSEPH, DAVID, DANIEL, Jotham - - - - - 46—52

VIII.—FAMILY AFFECTION.

Abraham—his generous self-denial, true kindness, and devotion—*Lot*—his heartless behaviour. *Essay.*—Home, school of the affections—how best fostered—nature's voice—where to turn for love and sympathy—necessary to our happiness, and its most desirable cement—it tempers affliction and sorrow—holy bonds. *Precepts. Examples,* JOSEPH, Jacob, Esau, MOSES, Amnon, JOB 53—61

IX.—FAITH.

Abraham (biographical sketch continued).—His obedience, resignation, and holy trust. *Essay.*—How it may be made a fixed principle of action—influence of the past on the future—faith in ourselves, and belief in God's Gracious Providence—benefits they confer—despair sinful—future sealed book—gracious promises—religious trust. *Precepts. Examples,* DAVID, DANIEL'S THREE COMPANIONS, DANIEL, Eli, Jonah - - - - - 62—73

X.—BENEVOLENCE.

Abraham (biographical sketch continued).—His hospitality and philanthropy exemplified. *Essay.*—Not enough to appreciate, we must practise—in what it consists—never to be separated from hope and piety—its practice, a duty and prerogative—neglect thereof sinful —self-conquest often necessary—the true philanthropist. *Precepts. Examples,* NEHEMIAH, Rebecca, Boaz, ELISHA - 74—84

XI.—PARENTAL DUTY.

Abraham (biographical sketch continued)—his love of truth and duty —his teachings and their beneficial results—Rebecca and Isaac. *Essay.*—Duty incumbent on parents—they hold the key to the heart of their child—great and serious their responsibility—in what their duty consists—influence for good—much to achieve—fail through injudicious training—the spoilt child—partiality—example better than precept—dereliction of duty sinful and entails certain misery—reverse picture. *Precepts. Examples,* SOLOMON, Rehoboam, Amaziah, DAVID, ELI, JOB - - 85—102

XII.—INDIVIDUAL MERIT.

Abraham (biographical sketch concluded)—this noble-hearted patriarch's character contrasted with that of *Lot*—impotence of latter for good—his selfishness—in the one an example—in the other a warning. *Essay.*—Character is the great distinction between man and man—it is his insignia—force of principle, what it will accomplish—necessity of repeated endeavours without discouragement— pride impediment to progress—success greatly depends on individual qualities—freewill man's birthright—his responsibility—sin of omission—man's true greatness. *Precepts. Examples,* JOSIAH, Hannaniah, GIDEON, CALEB, JOSHUA, MORDECAI 103—125

XIII.—MORAL COWARDICE.

Lot (biographical sketch concluded)—his defective character exemplified by additional proofs—penalty we pay for errors, omissions, and neglect of positive duties. *Essay.*—"I cannot" and "I will not", significant words—the language of moral infirmity or moral courage—causes of irresolution—how to combat them—life has definitive objects—sinful to disregard them—belief in good and our power for good—reflections which will encourage and strengthen—hope no flatterer to the resolute—power of religion. *Precepts. Examples,* Disobedient Prophet, HEZEKIAH, JOSEPH, Reuben
   126—141

XIV.—MEDITATION.

Isaac—his calm reflective disposition, his truly pious spirit. *Essay.*—Reflection should precede action—life full of complexities—successful issue of undertakings greatly depends thereon—profitable direction for our thoughts—how to control thought—self-interest a powerful auxiliary—its teachings—worldly and spiritual benefits—distinction between meditation and mere musing. *Precepts. Examples,* DAVID and JOTHAM - - - - 142—155

XV.—PRAYER.

Isaac (biographical sketch concluded)—his truly pious spirit further exemplified—his fortitude—his childlike faith. *Essay.*—Alike a duty and a privilege—none exempt from former—none denied latter—doubt this is to err—consequent penalty—cause of doubt and certain cure—of prayer, and firstly when we should pray, secondly for what we should pray, and thirdly how we may best pray—importance of prayer—should have first place among life's duties—power of prayer—a panacea for every ill—a chain between earth and heaven. *Precepts. Examples,* HEZEKIAH, DANIEL   156—180

XVI.—DISCRETION.

Jacob—his early training—the spoilt child—his character exalted by adversity. *Essay.*—Of a compound nature—necessary to enlist mind and heart—what it requires of us—all-powerful for good when united to religion—though esteemed a high virtue is rarely attained—causes thereof insidious foes and powerful antagonists—its valuable teachings—benefits it confers when united to piety. *Precepts. Examples,* ABIGAIL, JEPHTHAH, SAUL - - 181—201

XVII.—CONTENTMENT.

Jacob.—(Biographical sketch concluded)—his pious spirit under adversity—his unselfish conduct—Israel, the loved servant of God. *Essay.*—Temper of mind most conducive to happiness—whence derived—how maintained—its direst foes—not always those supposed to be such—should be made a settled habit of mind—an inestimable boon—may be attained by all—ever proportioned to moral character—mind lends its colour to every object—equality. *Precepts. Examples,* SHUNAMMITE, JOB -   -   -   202—224

XVIII.—SELF-DISCIPLINE.

Joseph—his truly virtuous life—his piety—his fortitude—contrasted with *Joseph's brethren*—their conduct. *Essay.*—High moral obligation—what it has to effect—practice makes easy—temptation synonymous with danger—its powerful auxiliaries—its true province—benefits it confers—penalty to which its disregard exposes man. *Precepts. Examples,* DAVID, JONAH   -   -   -   225—244

XIX.—FILIAL AFFECTION.

Joseph—(biographical sketch concluded)—his loving, generous disposition—additional proofs of other exalted and estimable qualities—contrasted with *Joseph's brethren*—their acts. *Essay.*—A debt we should be ever discharging—a paramount duty—how most effectively fulfilled—also prerogative—should be valued—its certain reward—causes of filial defection—home, what it should be—parental obligation—unfilial conduct entails certain misery and after regrets. *Precepts. Examples,* RUTH, MOSES, ABSOLOM, ELISHA
245—265

XX.—THE SABBATH.

The *Israelites* under Moses and Joshua—their frequent disregard of its observance—their long apprenticeship to freedom, and their reform. *Essay.*—Its observance a sacred obligation—to keep it holy a direct command from God—may not be disregarded with impunity—its chief characteristics—its high purport—imposes none but pleasurable duties—prime causes of its infringement—covetousness, religious indifference, thoughtlessness—numerous benefits it confers—negative as well as positive advantages. *Precepts. Examples,* The ISRAELITES under their Judges and Kings   -   . 266—287

XXI. RELIGIOUS ZEAL.

The *Israelites* under Moses (historical sketch continued)—their moral progress—instances where gratitude became an animating principle—best exemplified by individuals, thus, PHINEHAS, JOSHUA, CALEB—reverse, KORAH. *Essay.*—In what it consists—co-operation with the Divine purpose—prerogative—demands some self-denial, self-sacrifice—duty to our fellow-creatures—why rather shunned than courted—perverted zeal—bigotry—intolerance—spiritual pride—extremes injurious—how to expound religion—benefits which flow therefrom—our reward. *Precepts. Examples*, the ISRAELITES under their Judges, Kings, and Prophets—OTHNIEL, ASA, ELIJAH
288—309

XXII.—RESIGNATION.

Aaron—his character—his trials and conduct—his weakness detrimental to moral character of the nation of which he was the spiritual head—defects to be accounted for—sinfulness of his sons, and penalty thereof—character strengthened and improved through trials and sorrows. *Essay.*—Adversity, like life, has a high purpose—gauges man's moral condition, also strengthens and improves it—important to distinguish between those trials which are of our own making and afflictions sent from heaven—not difficult, being generally well defined—defects of character most common causes of trials, and trials in their turn the surest cure of defects of character—their further beneficial and kindly effects—sickness—pain—pity—virtue—Heavenly dispensations, blessings in disguise—death—trials never negative in their effects—if not soften then harden the heart—discontent, its sinfulness—affliction the medicine of life—two classes of misfortunes—important to distinguish between them—most powerful auxiliaries to resignation—God's providence and justice—kindle lamp of faith. *Precepts. Examples*, JEREMIAH, JOB, ESTHER
310—343

XXIII.—OBDURACY.

The *Israelites* under Moses (historical sketch concluded)—their stubbornness of disposition—cause thereof—influence exercised by surrounding idolatrous nations—their moral training—after results. *Essay.*—Not easily detected—in what it consists—is antagonistic to firmness, and should not be mistaken for it—causes of it—infirmity of purpose—passion or principle—defective training of the heart of youth—prevention or cure—repentance—logic of vice—disobedience and its certain penalty—reform of conduct—the fruits of virtue and piety. *Precepts. Examples.* The ISRAELITES under Joshua—their Judges and their Kings   -   -   -   -   344—370

XXIV.—TEMPER.

Moses—the "meekest of men"—his life divided into three distinct epochs—the first rife with circumstances unfavourable to his moral training, and ending in an act of violence; the second, passed in exile, subserved to a course of self-discipline, and prepared him for the important change which marked the third epoch, wherein he so ably and manfully, yet so meekly, discharged his high and glorious mission—his self-control frequently and severely tested—exceptional instances of irritability and anger—his numerous excellent qualities—his holy temper of mind. *Essay.*—The practical expression of the inward disposition of the heart—causes of good temper and ill temper—their antagonism—safeguard against the latter—piety twin sister to gentleness and cheerfulness—the beneficial effects of good temper on ourselves and others—ill temper a distemper, and militates against our own and others' happiness—the power of the individual to benefit the social community—how to conquer ill temper—how best acquire good temper—of discontent—of self-discipline—religion and expediency speak to same effect—important difference between good temper and easiness of disposition—benefits conferred by piety. *Precepts. Examples*, Cain, Simeon, Nabal, Naaman, HAZAEL, SAUL, AHAB, Haman, BALAAM, JONAH
371—405

XXV.—DEATH.

Moses (biographical sketch concluded)—his long life, embracing varied incidents and subjected to many severe trials—the numerous perils he encountered when engaged in his strenuous and never-ceasing efforts to benefit his countrymen—his loving, self-sacrificing spirit—incidents which mark the close of his great life—his life and death alike eloquent—preparation for his final departure—his death bespoke immortality. *Essay.* An universal dispensation, therefore no evil—a messenger from heaven—state of our own minds with regard to it—viewed abstractedly will assuredly be recognised as a blessing—God's goodness and loving kindness to be traced through this mysterious agent—reflections on it will work to practical good—often set at defiance—true fortitude at the final hour only possible to the virtuous and pious—of death-bed repentance—act while we have life before us—our wilful blindness—causes thereof—belief in immortality—benefits it confers—spiritual joys it imparts—how regarded by the impenitent sinner and by the virtuous man—last hour of the one and of the other—the lesson each bequeathes to posterity. *Examples*, ELI, SAMUEL - - - - 406—437

XXVI.—LETTER ON IMMORTALITY.
438—443

BIOGRAPHICAL INDEX - - - - - 445

INTRODUCTION.

No known work has ever brought before the human mind such innumerable examples rife with instruction as the Bible. Plainly does it point out, through individual character, what is good for man, and what must prove to his detriment. Practical examples of high moral virtue and piety are presented to us in all their native simplicity, and highly should they be prized as models for imitation; while vice is exhibited in all its natural deformity, so that it may scare and terrify those prone to err or sin. Humanity is written on all its pages. The portraits which adorn this ancestral chamber are little dissimilar in mental or in physical features from those of the individuals who now are playing their part on this world's stage. The soul drew its inspirations from the same Divine fount, and the unshackled mind was left, as now, free to choose the good and eschew the evil. We need not read its inspired pages by other lights than those of our daily experience, our reason, and our conscience. Nature, or the outer world, the heart, or inner man, ever ringing changes on the dial of time, alike remain immutable in their laws, their essence, and their mutual relation. The human heart is ever guided by the same feelings and impulses, the mind is coloured through like agencies, while Nature varies but to assimilate again. All this the Bible teaches while representing scenes and actors by the light of that eternal truth which beams forth from its every page. This mirror is held up for the mental eye of all ages; therefore it is the imperative duty of man to scan and compare, then regulate his life and shape his course thereby.

From this faithful record may be drawn conclusions on every known subject in which man's interests are concerned, while *precepts* conjointly with *examples* stand in goodly array to guide and urge him onwards in that road which will most surely conduce to his well-being, his happiness here and hereafter.

But as this moral lesson is spread over a broad surface, the unmeditative mind or casual reader finds it hard to disengage those precepts and examples which have an immediate reference to moral conduct, from other matters with which they are so largely interspersed and closely blended.

Concentration may, therefore, be productive of good. By culling each important fact which bears on our duties and obligations as we proceed in our Biblical history, we secure an easy index to them; and, by elucidating the subject-matter by traits of individual character, adding thereto apt quotations taken from Psalms, Proverbs, and the Prophets, a force is imparted which may greatly tend to stamp a vivid and durable impression on even the least susceptible mind or heart. To further this purposed object, a general view of each subject will be added, with such arguments as may help to urge us on in the pursuance of duty, and conduce to strengthen our bias or partial belief into profound conviction; for the mind once imbued with sound practical truths, a firm, unflinching, and vigorous course of action in the path of all that is good and noble will naturally ensue.

Among numberless important conclusions which suggest themselves as we span the Sacred Volume, and bring into a focus its high moral inculcations, practical as preceptive, the following are worthy of the deepest consideration; viz., that the heart of man, as well as his mental organism, ever retains the same attributes; that the Holy Volume answers to every sentiment, every emotion that can arise in the human breast; and that it leaves no one failing unreproved, no one virtue unenjoined: thus should ever be resorted to and made the test of our moral conduct, while chosen as our infallible adviser and guide. Then by its light is clearly shown that man is a free agent, and that there is no thraldom in vice but what the will sanctions, no obstacle to virtue but that we ourselves have helped to raise and will not conjure down; that if exhortation and reproof fail to awaken the sleeping conscience, trials and sorrows will surely come to sting the sinner into repentance; while the good and holy, who bow at the shrine of duty, find present reward in the consciousness of well-doing, with the glorious certainty of ineffable bliss hereafter. Next, that we should never suffer our energies to lie dormant, but exert our best faculties with earnest zeal in the cause of the general good, thereby compassing that of the individual;

that it is not for finite man to do evil that good may come from it. Finally, that in all our doings we must consider the end, as few actions fail to bring forth either sweet or bitter fruits; while the grand fundamental rule of life runs like a silken thread through all the broad pages of the Bible, oft impressed by glorious examples, ever urged in all the felicity of language, but summed up thus concisely for the generation of man, "Fear God, and keep his commandments."

To illustrate these and other principles of action is the object of these MORAL BIBLICAL GLEANINGS.

MORAL BIBLICAL GLEANINGS.

INDUSTRY.

Genesis, chap. i, v. 1, "*God created the heaven and the earth.*"

GOD is here portrayed as the Framer and Artificer of those stupendous works which are known to us by the word "Creation". The first character in which the Sovereign Ruler has allowed Himself to be represented to us in His Holy Volume is as the "Worker". What an ennobling moral lesson is here unfolded. Nowhere is to be found a more potent argument in favour of labour, speaking alike to high and low. Thus all, all should earnestly aid in the cause of progress, and strive with head, hand, and heart, to further the development of good. Would we make life the boon which the Gracious Ruler intended it to be, we must quicken every right feeling into action, make each useful thought subserve some practical good, and, above all, marshal before us those duties which our situation in life demands, and unceasingly labour in their fulfilment.

And it is well to bear in mind that Industry in no way implies negation of pleasure; on the contrary, it is its greatest promoter. A brisk sense of delight never fails to attend such vigorous action as is prompted by a desire to work out some laudable end. Each fresh endeavour but serves as a stimulus and incentive to persevere and accomplish; the goal kept steadily in view, no spur is necessary to urge us on, the very nearing carries pleasure in its train, while the object of desire once attained is the more prized when felt to be the just reward of past labour and exertion. Assuredly labour fulfils a most beneficent office in the arena of life; and, far from being regarded as mere drudgery, should be considered as a profitable state of discipline and moral training. It is, indeed, every way calculated to develope our energies and strengthen our virtues, while it possesses the additional advantage of greatly swelling the sum of human enjoyment. Not only do we rarely prize those blessings which have cost neither mental nor bodily fatigue, but also the hidden springs of plenty are seldom opened to us without exertion. God has concealed innumerable beauties from the unobservant eye of the sluggard, whilst many are the gratifications and blessings He concedes to diligence and honest labour. But would we have a yet further stimulus to Industry, let us for a moment consider ourselves incapacitated therefrom. How truly deplorable should we then deem our position; to be willing yet powerless; solely to possess a nerveless arm or effete mind instead of the vigour of manhood, the prolific brain! Then, if not before, but then perhaps too late, should we appreciate labour itself as well as the numerous advantages which accrue therefrom.

But Industry, apart from its own intrinsic merit, must yet be rated high, if only as antagonistic to that giant Idleness, the scorned of all that is good and great, who dies a coward tyrant's death at the first sling from the hand of Industry. Surely, when the many blessings which attend on labour are recalled, and the baneful effects of Idleness are considered, a conviction of the necessity of the high moral duty of exertion much force itself on the most dormant mind and wake it up to action. Truly, the industrious have numberless cheering and invigorating reflections to gladden them in their toil and well doings; take as examples the following: that every right action is the fulfilment of God's holy will; that "the pinnacle of fame has Industry for its basis"; that "toil seldom fails to bear rich and precious fruits"; that "they who sow the good shall reap the same"; and that man in fulfilling moral duties, is fitting himself for a higher state of being and an eternal bliss. Then to the listless idler, who in defiance of God's immutable and gracious laws, fails to use the faculties and natural vigour with which he has been blessed, is content to slumber through existence, useless and profitless to himself and others, the following considerations may be offered as a stimulus to exertion; that, to stand still while all is progressing around is to retrograde; also, he but fulfils a sacred duty who gives cheerfully and lovingly his quota towards swelling the sum of human happiness; and again, he who in manhood neglects the workshop will have but the workhouse to look to in old age. And as a further incitement to shake off the trammels imposed by idleness, we should reflect that it is closely allied to vice, the lower passions ever sprouting vigorously in the listless mind.

But by those who wilfully waste their energies in the pursuit of deluding and ensnaring pleasures, utterly regardless of the misery a devious and sinful course necessarily entails alike on themselves and their co-partners in vice, such reflections as these should be taken seriously to heart, that if to lose a day in inaction and spend fast fleeting time in unprofitable pursuits be wrong and displeasing to the most High, criminal and worthless indeed must they be who pervert life and its lofty purposes, allowing the passing hours to pander to base appetites and unruly passions, despoiling all that is noble, fair, and beautiful—in a word, committing moral *felo-de-se*. They who thus act will surely on the great Judgment Day be "weighed in the balance and found wanting."

Thus let us give the heart to good and useful works, for

where it points the feet will be fast to follow; search with all diligence after the good, make it the business of life, bar the door to sin, and all will be health and happiness within.

The Holy Volume teems with many an injunction to labour and give to life a great moral purpose, while severe is the penalty pronounced upon its infraction. In Ecclesiastes is found one of the most forcible PRECEPTS, "Whatsoever thy hand findeth to do, do it with thy might." Then we have in the Decalogue the emphatic and positive command, Exodus, chap. xx, 9, "*Six days shalt thou labour,*" which, following immediately upon the enumeration of duties we owe to God, and heading those due to man, not only amply demonstrates its high importance in the economy of the world, but also proves that *no one individual* may, no one dare claim exemption from this universal law. Then we are told in Proverbs, chap. xiii, 4, "The soul of the sluggard desireth, but hath nothing"; again, chap. xii, 24, "The hand of the diligent shall bear rule, but the slothful shall be under tribute"; also, "the sleep of the labouring man is sweet," and "The labour of the righteous tendeth to life"; and again, ch. x, 4, "He becometh poor that dealeth with a slack hand, but the hand of the diligent maketh rich"; ch. xviii, 9: "He who is slothful in his work is brother to him that is a great waster;" and "an idle person shall suffer hunger." Then the idler is thus forewarned (ch. vi, 9): "O sluggard, when wilt thou arise out of thy sleep? yet a little sleep, a little slumber, so shall thy poverty come as one that travelleth, and thy want as an armed man." And that we may value this warning and justly estimate its importance, it is repeated word by word in the twenty-fourth chapter. Thus we see that on every score it behoves us to set ourselves honestly and with hearty energy to work out practical good, and when we shall be conscientiously discharging each duty with assiduity, then may we, with hopeful confidence, pray in the words of Moses, Psalm xc, "Establish Thou, O Lord, the work of our hands upon us, yea, the work of our hands establish Thou it."*

Few Bible characters offer a better EXAMPLE of industry wisely and profitably applied than that of EZRA, he "who prepared his heart to seek the law of the Lord, and to do it;" and who became "the chosen instrument of God for the restoration of the Temple." He rigidly fulfilled all the sacred duties of his office, curbed Israel, then prone to idolatry, and taught them innumerable statutes and judgments. He "opened the Book of the Law in the sight of the people, and caused them to understand the sense thereof." He corresponded with the treasurers of King Artaxerxes, obtaining from them his requirements, and repeatedly addressed that monarch himself. He set magistrates and judges over the land, superintended the rebuilding of the Temple, and urged on the holy work by word and deed through the long day and longer night. He defeated the machinations of enemies from without, and quelled internal dissensions, made many useful reforms, and brought his people over to repentance, so that they forsook their evil ways." Withal he was a "ready scribe in the Law of Moses."

* Should any reader of these pages consider the quotations under the heading of *Precepts* too numerous, the writer would yet venture to claim indulgence on the score that in those cases where especial reference to the subject-matter is required, the more ample the materials furnished, the better service will be rendered. And who may not occasionally desire to secure easy and speedy reference to Scripture verses, and thence acknowledge as a desideratum this summing up of *varied* quotations on any particular subject under consideration? Further, it may be observed that a verse or precept which takes firm hold on one mind, and thence receives all the attention it merits, will frequently fail in touching home or leaving any permanent impress on that of another; thus, where one quotation may have small weight and work little good, another, perfectly similar in its inculcations, but differently couched, will sometimes stamp itself so effectively on the mind as to rise spontaneously and be ready at first call. A positive advantage which can only be secured through number and variety of quotations.

Here is a beacon of light whereby the pilgrim of life may steer his bark till he reaches that final haven where all is glory, peace, and rest.

OBSERVATION.

Gen., ch. i, v. 25, "*God saw that it was good.*"

THE conclusion we may reasonably draw from these words of high import is that, although Omnipotence had planned and executed, yet this was not enough, Omnipotence proceeded to survey, and pronounced the work perfect. If any blemish could possibly have been discernible, the infallible Superintendent of the Universe would have considered it as a blot on creation. He who graciously "saw that it was good" will now and for ever see that all is good and tending to good. Never need we fear that He will mar His handiwork or allow His creatures permanently so to do. Once firmly impressed with this belief, man will dismiss all cavilling doubts, and in grateful accents re-echo the gracious words of his Maker, "all is good."

Excellence is inscribed on every page of Creation, and it is the imperative duty of all beings to note this diligently, whether in the works or in the workings of their Artificer and Ruler. Our highest gratification and greatest good must redound therefrom. The thinking and observant man truly has endless sources of delight, for to him a wise and benign Overseer is clearly discernible, in the moral as in the physical world; in the latter he will mark a great and gracious design, while in the former he will recognise with grateful adoration an ever controlling hand. As he walks through the world with open eye his faculties will awaken and expand, the beauties of nature will grow upon him, fresh combinations and ever renewing novelty springing up on every side will draw forth his unbounded admiration, and furnish him with a grand and elevating lesson, as well as a continuous stream of guileless pleasures. Now they who seek may easily obtain the golden key of observation, wherewith they can unlock the rich treasury of nature, and entering, cull the precious fruits within, while through its medium will also be opened those secret laboratories where sciences and arts are nurtured and matured. Thus, why imitate the mole in preference to the lynx? why burrow in the dark or slumber through existence when we may walk abroad at noonday, gathering the precious fruits of observation? To be unobservant or a mere looker-on is surely beneath the dignity of man; but to behold with keen and earnest interest the wonders around, striving each day to acquire more and more mental light, making experience subserve to knowledge, and, above all, seeking out fresh and lasting subjects of gratitude towards the gracious Bestower of every goodly gift, such, indeed, is the fit employment of a rational being. This is "to live."

But, while the habit of observation insures a juster appreciation of, and a deeper insight into, all that is passing around and within us, it further tends to imbue our mind with the profound conviction that "whatever is is right." Though the limited capacity of man can grasp but parts of the vast comprehensive whole, yet he who has bent his intellect to the appreciation of the marvellous works of God, will see that wisdom and goodness ever shine with lustrous splendour, and though, like the sun, they are at times invisible to the individual, like that glorious luminary, they are never, never absent. Indeed, we have only to reverse the order of nature in any one particular, and modify aught in the natural or physical world, to be fully convinced that all works together for good. Could we arrest a single law of nature but for an inappreciable second of time, this bright world would be a wilderness, the stupendous and glorious universe a chaos! Then, when we consider the condition of men, beneficial results are to be seen in the very clashing of their interests, and a meaning is to be recognised in each stirring incident, each varying circumstance which affects or governs their actions. Thus, the endeavour to modify a polity based on natural law, or to banish all jarring elements which disconcert or mar the desires and workings of mankind would evidently be futile for good. Devious and eccentric as men's actions at first appear, yet, like the comet when closely studied, they present nothing vague or undefined; but divert the meteor's course, and the world would be in flames. And lastly, when we scan the incidents of our lives, how discernible is the invaluable and gratifying truth that each one has been conducive to our well-being, and that in every evil we can trace a greater good. But, were all curb withdrawn and man allowed free scope in the indulgence of the boundless desires of his heart, evil would indeed infallibly accrue. Truly, Divine Bounty ever filling up the just measure of the cup to all his creatures, allotting to each such proportion of the cardiac as He in His wisdom deems best, requires of man only that he should promote to the best of his power the well-being of his fellow-creatures, and, by thus swelling the general store of happiness, find his own share proportionably increased.

Finally, let us impress this truth on our minds, that nature never preaches in vain. If we but avail ourselves of the giant power of observation, we shall find it all potent for good; high and ennobling conceptions will elevate our souls, an appreciation of God's marvellous works will draw us nearer to the fount of all goodness, and a knowledge of our inner selves will materially conduce to a happy and pious life. By looking from effects to causes, studying art, nature, and man, with the heart as well as with the head, not clipping too closely imagination's wings nor yet trenching on the high privilege of reason, great will be our profit. Indeed, we must infallibly arrive at such all-important conclusions as these; that the great Omniscient rules over and overrules everything, making all conduce to the ultimate benefit of His creatures; thence that we should feel it to be our highest delight, as well as our bounden duty to praise and glorify with grateful hearts the Wise, Beneficent Giver of every good; that as free-will agents it is imperatively demanded of us to mould our actions in accordance with the commands of the Supreme: and, finally, that we should consider no event in life, no scene in nature, no incident throughout creation, too trivial to lead the mind to the Governor of the Universe, that Great First Cause, who graciously inaugurated the world's era with the emphatic declaration that "all was good."

Precepts (and Examples).—No individual figuring in Scriptural History appears to have been more fully impressed with the importance of self-knowledge, of attention to the laws of nature and individual character, than DAVID, the sweet singer of Israel. This is clearly demonstrated in his admirable compositions, as also in the excellence at which his son and successor arrived, for this result could hardly have been attained except through the judicious training of a wise religious parent, one impressed with the conviction that such knowledge tends to make a man both great and good. Thus spoke the Royal Psalmist, "I meditate on all Thy works; I muse on the works of Thy Hand;" and "When I consider the Heavens, the work of Thy Hands, what is man that Thou visitest him?" Again, "I will praise Thee, for I am fearfully and wonderfully made; marvellous are Thy works, and that my soul knoweth right well." Indeed, thus looking "through Nature up to Nature's God" will ever be attended by a pious resignation to the All Wise dispensations of the Most High! and a zealous desire to do His will. This was especially manifested throughout David's chequered career, and how firmly he believed that our very welfare depends on this habit is clearly proved in the

28th Psalm, fifth verse, where he declares, "Because they—the wicked—*regard not the works of the Lord,* nor the operations of His hands, God will destroy them and not build them up." Culling next from the Book of Proverbs, Solomon therein admonishes us, "Go to the ant, consider her ways, and be wise." In Ecclesiastes he remarks that "the wise man's eyes are in his head, but the fool walketh in darkness;" then, as a practical illustration, he tells us that I, SOLOMON, "gave my heart to seek and search out wisdom concerning all things that are done under Heaven;" again, "I saw and considered it well, I looked upon it and received instruction," and he further adds, "I considered in my heart that the righteous and the wise and their works are in the hands of God." He who thus wrote had sought and found. Solomon had well conned the page of Nature ere he "spake of trees, also of beasts and of fowls, of creeping things and fishes." He had cultivated a keen relish for the beautiful and useful. Arts and sciences flourished throughout his kingdom. He had probed the human breast, delved deep into the secret recesses of the passions, closely watched their workings, and followed their mysterious and intricate windings. To all this he owed that power of discernment which especially displayed itself in the celebrated judgment passed in the case of the two mothers.

Now, to render these EXAMPLES truly serviceable, it is necessary to mark the difference which existed in one all important particular between father and son. Before the keen inquiring spirit of King SOLOMON, Nature and all the concerns of this earth were written in legible characters; his capacious mind grasped comprehensive views of all *worldly* matters; but it never passed these bounds, for while the present and past came out clearly, the future remained to him a sealed book. Not so, however, with the Royal DAVID, who, besides possessing well-developed mental powers, was also endowed with the pre-eminent gift of inspiration, and that in so high a degree as to admit of the saying concerning Saul being applied to him, "Verily is he among the Prophets." To account for this, it suffices to note the material dissimilarity which existed in the characters of the tried servant of the Lord and the spoilt child of fortune. David's heart, ever inspired by true devotion, turned alike in prosperity or in trials towards God as the needle to the pole; never swerving but to react speedily and settle yet more fixedly. With *him* observation kindled faith. His aspirations centred not in vain worldly desires, but soared upwards and onwards into the far future. There were his thoughts, and there lay his powers of discernment, for was not " God in all his thoughts ?" How far otherwise was it with Solomon, who at first wisely *used*, and then, his heart turning from his God, *abused* the blessings vouchsafed to him, so that they became of nothing worth, and "all was vanity." Comparing David's admirable Psalms, the 34th and 107th, replete with faith, humility, and devotion, to the first chapter of Ecclesiastes, full of captious murmurings and caustic remarks on the vanity of pleasure, of labour, of all earthly things, and the contrast is perfect.

With the lesson of their lives and writings before us, to David let us especially direct our attention, for as with him passion will occasionally obtain the mastery, and trials depress the spirits, so also, like him, we may turn to our indulgent Father in love and trust, walk by the light of His Holy Word, and give hand and heart to all that is good." Thus we shall be led with him to exclaim in grateful rapture, " How full is the earth of the goodness of the Lord; blessed art Thou, the Giver of all good."

MARRIAGE.

> Gen., ch. ii, 18, "*And the Lord God said, it is not good that the man should be alone; I will make him a helpmeet.*"

IN these words it is pronounced by God Himself that man, by his very nature, requires companionship; and assuredly the gracious gift of a sister of the soul vouchsafed by the Bestower of "all good" is ever fraught with a world of happiness, if sought, as all blessings should be, in a religious spirit, and, when obtained, held and valued as a heavenly boon. Then, to prove that conjugal affection should take precedence of every other feeling, however sacred and however strong, Scripture emphatically declares that "a man shall leave his father and his mother, and shall cleave unto his wife." And further, that the high import of the marriage tie may be fully recognised and indelibly engraven on the heart, it is solemnised in the sight of heaven. This tender and sublime bond is ratified before that Throne of love and justice where we shall surely have to render an account of duties accomplished or left unfulfilled. Woe, then, to those who enter the marriage state regardless of the moral obligation it imposes! To them alone the blame, when happiness smiles not on a union, either thoughtlessly formed, or originating in an interested motive or passing fancy. But sanguine may he be who has selected with a wise discretion the one who is to be the wife of his bosom and the mother of his children. When congeniality of tastes, pursuits, and disposition are made its groundwork, and religion its corner-stone—when the mind or heart, not the face or purse, is made the prize coveted, when judgment, solicitude, and care are employed to find out the one who has proved herself a good daughter, a fond sister, a devoted, sympathising friend, and, above all, a truly religious child of the Supreme—then will this gift assuredly prove the rich blessing it was intended by the Most High, or, in the words of Scripture, "the heart of her husband doth safely trust in her: she will do him good, and not evil all the days of her life."

Now, important as is this step in life with men, it is even more so with women. The weaker ever bows before the stronger will, and thus the wife generally becomes the reflex of the husband. Yet it behoves both sexes alike, ere the words are spoken which seal the indissoluble bond, to reflect seriously that habits, traits of character, and modes of thought are borrowed from those with whom we come most in contact; and thus we sink or rise after marriage, just in proportion as we make a judicious choice of our partner for life. How solicitous, then, should we be to ascertain the character of the one with whom we are so completely to identify our interests and desires—indeed, would we save ourselves much misery and after-regret, we must resolutely resolve to throw aside any vague feeling of love immediately we discover defects of character or want of religion; for where there is no esteem, there cannot possibly be any permanent affection. Too frequently, however, will the warm kind heart think to win to good, one with defects patent even to the eyes of love itself, and so tie the bands regardless of consequences. Fatal, fatal error! What but baffled hopes and vain regrets can attend such infatuation! Slaves of habit ourselves, how dare we so presume as to hope to mould another to our will, and think to resist or control feelings which have been the growth of years? But further, would we summon happiness to the new home of married life, it will not suffice simply to glance at actions; we must also sound the heart that prompts them; nor should we look upon the face but as the index to the mind; in a word, we must seek to wed with intellect, virtue, and religion, the only true bulwarks of esteem and love. All, however, is comparative; none are faultless. Thus, while we should use our best discernment before marriage, we cannot be too dim-sighted afterwards. This is, indeed, the more incumbent because the idol we raise up in our hearts during early love generally wants the reality of truth, and therefore must speedily meet its downfall. Truly much, very much, depends on our good sense and good feeling; guided by these, we shall not fail to recognise our own defects, and make allowances for those of our partner for life, we shall shut our eyes to all blemishes, and open them wide with a loving spirit to discern the many excellent qualities which flourish and ripen when warmed by devoted love.

But how is a prize to be secured, unless we be such ourselves? Fond hopes are best attained by deserts. Seldom, except by merit, is true love kindled in the breast of the wise and good. Thus it behoves us to strive sedulously to render our characters amiable and estimable. When firmly convinced that marriage makes or mars us, we shall rarely fail in choosing one of unblemished name and sterling worth. The deeply interested are keen-sighted. Yet judgment will not always avail; failing intentional deceit on the one side, and incaution on the other, unsuitable matches will still occasionally be made. Through the conventionality of society, the interested parties generally have little opportunity of discerning whether the true essence of conjugal happiness, conformity of tastes and principles, exists.

Now it is especially when such mistakes occur that the finer qualities of our nature find ample room for exercise. By making some self-sacrifice, and displaying a kindly forbearance, the first chill of disappointment will pass away, and a genial warmth spring forth, frequently ripening into the fondest affection. Nought but ill-temper and perverseness will mar, much less destroy, domestic happiness. Thus, if we firmly resolve ever to look on the bright side, reflecting that, though there be points of difference, there are yet many more of agreement, and that identity of interests far outweighs opposing inclinations, then the clashing which can but embitter existence will cease, and a close intercourse of mutual kindness soon make the marriage state a "continual feast." To drink jointly our daily portion from the cup of religion, and "walk to the house of God together," to pray for and with each other, unite in common acts of charity, and have a gentle word of kindness ever ready on the tongue, will surely bring connubial bliss. Habit will day by day assimilate any two characters, and blend feelings however dissimilar. But the harsh and angry word must be for ever hushed—" Can two walk together and they be not agreed?" The strong will must be tempered, for love flies at the breath of tyranny. We must confide, and, above all, avoid dissimulation, which is disloyalty to love; further, while we strive to give pleasure, we must also be ever ready to receive it. The heart warms as it imparts happiness. Now to act thus can surely be no very arduous task, while ample will be the reward. As affection becomes an active principle, selfishness will die out, and the sweet sacrifices made at the altar of love within our homes will send forth their rich perfume. Happiness generated at the hearth will seek for expansion, and soon diffuse itself by word and deed throughout the entire circle in which we move.

But if those means are neglected which conduce to our mutual welfare, then will a double penalty be imposed. When the day of trial comes, and sickness or death enters our abode, we shall deeply regret our broken vows, the past will rise up against us, and we shall have to suffer all the bitter pangs of an upbraiding conscience. Thus, ere the day of separation arrives, let us be kind, be fair, nor grieve the heart of the confiding one. Above all, let us beware of any breach of faith, which is perjury in the face of heaven. Only when the vow uttered on the nuptial day is religiously performed, and every sacred obligation gladly fulfilled, will joy smile at the hearth, each anxious care there find rest, and the blessing of true devoted love descend thereon.

Woman, by nature self-denying, generous, loving, will assuredly find in her marriage vow a fresh stimulus to fulfil life's duties: while man, whose nature calls for that help-meet, the sweet sympathizing spirit, will appreciate the boon, and tenderly return her affection; for happy he who loves, and happy she who is beloved. Two hearts linked together by love to God are safe, for then, prompted by gratitude to a gracious Providence, they will mutually endeavour to rejoice the heart and strengthen the soul in virtue of the partner of their life. Heart will respond to heart, and mind will influence mind for good. A halo of pure happiness will surround the domestic circle. Woman, cheerfully fulfilling her mission, will be ever shedding wide her useful and ennobling influence; while man, joyful in her love, will never suffer the idea to intrude that he could be better off without her, but taught by unvarying experience, will recognise this grateful truth—that with her all pain is divided, while she doubles every pleasure.

The Book of Proverbs teems with PRECEPTS which, attentively considered, are every way calculated to induce caution in the choice of a wife, and thence guide us to matrimonial felicity. All-important is the following verse, since it at once tells us the helpmeet we should desire, and where this treasure is to be sought. We read, "*A prudent wife is from the Lord;*" therefore we should ask Him to bless our choice, and, making our selection in this spirit, shall surely be led to declare, in the words of the same penman, "Whoso findeth a wife findeth a good thing." It is, however, to the last chapter of Proverbs we should especially direct our attention before contracting the solemn engagement which can terminate only with life. There we have described the virtuous woman, whose "price is far above rubies;" the woman "*that feareth the Lord.*" Of her it is said, "She stretcheth out her hand to the poor, she looketh well to the ways of her household, she openeth her mouth with wisdom, and on her tongue is the law of kindness." We may next observe that the marriage tie is a favourite figure in the writings of the prophets when denoting the high obligation of Israel to be faithful and loving towards their God, who will in return "cherish and protect the spouse of his adoption." Thus in Malachi, "The Lord hath been witness between thee, O Israel, and the wife of thy youth." In Isaiah, "As the bridegroom rejoiceth over the bride, so shall thy God rejoice over thee." Then, also, in Solomon's beautiful song, God's love towards his people is thus figuratively declared, "I am my beloved, and my beloved is mine." Finally, the same writer describes the power and intensity of holy affection and the bitterness of outraged feelings—considerations which should be uppermost in the minds of all those who are about to enter the state of matrimony. We read, "Love is strong as death, the flood of waters cannot drown it, but jealousy is cruel as the grave."

The Holy Volume offers many EXAMPLES which speak plainly in warning us against an ill-assorted match, as also in cautioning us with regard to that culpable weakness which tamely yields to corrupt counsels. It is related in the history of our first parents, "ADAM harkened unto his wife to do evil." Again, ISAAC, aware how the soft influence of woman moves man to good or ill, charged his son Jacob "not to take a wife from the daughters of Canaan;" whilst Rebecca, in the tenderest accents of a mother, implored her son to the like effect. Then in JOB we find the strong will of this pious sufferer resisting that criminal counsel of his wife to "curse God and die," replying thereto, "Thou speakest as one of the foolish women speaketh." But not unfrequently the wife's is the stronger will, and she bears rule, as in the case of that vile monster of iniquity JEZEBEL, who brought much misery on her country by "stirring up Ahab to work wickedness;" and again JEHORAM "wrought evil in the eyes of the Lord, *for he had the daughter of Ahab to wife."* While numerous instances are to be found of females biassing or enticing their husbands to evil, the Holy Volume affords but few illustrations of woman's beneficial influence in the opposite direction; for, as none but the unfeeling and corrupt despise the rich inheritance of love, or tamper with the marriage vow, the teachings of Scripture are mostly confined to warnings and admonitions which alone can touch such hearts. Yet we have in ESTHER, in the SHUNAMMITE, and HANNAH, admirable examples for imitation. In the case of the latter we find Elkanah, full of confidence and love, saying to his much-cherished and truly religious wife, "Do what seemeth thee good."* Truly, when we possess a dear companion, to whom we may at all times and under all circumstances safely address these self-same words, then may we also feel assured that a " blessing will accompany us to our homes."

* 1 Samuel, ch. i, 23.

TEMPTATION.

Gen., ch. iii, 3, " Eat not, touch not of the fruit of the tree."

SUCH was the strict injunction of the Lord to our first parents, nevertheless EVE took of the fruit and did eat, for "it was pleasant to the eye." Gifted with freewill, Eve found herself at liberty to obey or disobey, to follow her own imaginings or act in accordance with God's positive command. Now surely the rich blessings lavished around, if nought else, might have engendered a deep sentiment of gratitude and love towards the Gracious Giver, and prompted an implicit obedience to His will; but cravings after the forbidden warped her mind from all sense of duty. One wild desire sufficed to efface the remembrance of her beneficent Creator, and even blotted out the pure delights of Paradise itself! Here then is presented to us an all-important every-day lesson, and well does it teach us resolutely to shun enticements and unlawful desires.

Man became a responsible being when endowed with freewill, and his abuse of this high prerogative must ever be as fatal to his well-being as derogatory to his dignity. Unbridled passions and base appetites never go unpunished. No individual can be suffered to infringe with impunity those laws which were promulgated for general benefit, since the happiness and good of the whole would thereby be endangered. When the unerring Judge has signified His high will, it is surely not for man to set himself in opposition thereto, and indulge those gratifications which He has prohibited. Continually urged as we are in the Holy Volume to decide between good and evil, life and death, to choose God's service and abhor the slavery of sin, surely it should be our endeavour to shun the dangerous paths of vice, and strive to become dutiful children of the Most High.

Now, to resist evil desires effectively, we must ever keep a strict and vigilant guard upon our thoughts, resolutely turning from those which are unruly, since they form the first inlets to sinful propensities. Acts ever closely follow the channel in which they run, and dangerous indeed is it to trifle or dally with depraved or impure imaginings. Surely one dark or sinful thought, if not speedily dismissed, will dim all that is light and bright in our nature. Hence must we restrain undue indulgence, in thought or deed, and above all things seek to stifle inordinate desires at their birth. Next it behoves us to distinguish between innocent and siren pleasures. These latter are apt to palm themselves upon us in the shape of some virtue, and thus with stealthy and subtle step enter the citadel of the heart. But we must do more than merely mark their dissimilarity; we must so attach ourselves to the former as to enable us to repel the more insidious advance of vices. And to do this effectively we must make home the repository for those materials which conduce to pure healthy enjoyment, and furnish pleasant and ample recreation. Assuredly a keen relish for good and useful pursuits being once excited, all vain longings will be easily quelled, and restless impulses subdued. Gratification will not be sought abroad when home is made the magnet where centres all delight. Youth imperatively demands pleasurable excitement, and when the caterers to this requirement of man's nature abide under the roof which shelters all that is most dear to his heart, the basilisk Temptation will near that threshold only to meet with a repulse. Thus intellectual tastes and accomplishments should be cultivated, the varied beauties of nature be made a source of enjoyment, and an undergrowth of tranquil pleasures be carefully nurtured, in order to fill up every vacuum of the mind. As the full cup can hold no more, so in the well-stored brain there will be no room for the entrance of those lax and sinful desires which infallibly leave behind them a sense of shame and remorse.

But the real power of resistance to vain imaginings and turbulent passions is to be sought and found in prayer. In Psalms we read, " In all thy ways acknowledge Him, and *He will direct thy steps,*" words which should satisfy us that He who places obstacles in our path, to prove the strength of our virtue, is ever at hand to remove them or give us the necessary power to resist temptation if earnestly and prayerfully entreated. In Judges we find, " And the nations were left that they might *prove* Israel, to know whether they would hearken unto the commandments of the Lord." Now, as with the nations so with the individual. God in His good pleasure tests the sincerity and loving obedience of each of His creatures, and he who implicitly obeys the statutes of the Lord, and regulates his desires by God's Holy Word, will assuredly render himself worthy of the favour of the Supreme, and ensure a passport to eternal life. Moreover, we may feel confident that " He who knoweth our frame " will not try us beyond our powers of endurance, but witnessing our struggles, and cognisant of the degree of perfection we are capable of attaining, will grant us His aid when sincerely implored. It is this certainty which should enable us to baffle or conjure down every rising gust of voluptuous passion, it ·is this conviction which should induce us to avail ourselves of the talismanic virtue of prayer. Temptation cannot prevail when in heartfelt accents we appeal to Him who reigneth above, for we shall then find in the words of Scripture that " God will strengthen us, yea, He will help us, yea, He will uphold us with the right hand of His righteousness." But if we seek not " our Help and Shield" in supplication, nor give to conscience its just rights over our actions, then will the first emotions of baneful passion obtain entire mastery over our heart ; and nought but their dire effects will suffice to turn us back to virtue and to God.

Now, if we would only listen to the voice of reason and experience, which plainly speaks of the hollowness of degrading pleasures, and also bear in mind that their indulgence is in direct violation of laws both moral and Divine, while ever highly injurious to others and ourselves, then should we obtain a greater control over the evil promptings of the heart, and all impetuous impulses. As, however, it is scarcely possible *always* to check our wayward passions, we must not suffer ourselves to be discouraged thereat, but at once make fresh resolves, adopt greater precautions, and put on more heavenly armour, in order to secure new triumphs with their ever-increasing power. Further, it behoves us to keep constantly in view a just sense of what is right, hold all that is evil in utter abhorrence, seek to maintain an empire over our better nature through love of God and love of man, and on the first approach of a dark thought give our hearts to prayer, for "a word to God is always a word from God." Thus may we overcome temptations, and win for ourselves the heavenly crown reserved for those who follow the path of virtue and religion.

PRECEPTS.—Now, although we may feel assured of safe guidance through the shoals which beset the passage of life if we habitually consult our consciences, we should yet turn to the Holy Volume, and seek to derive strength and instruction from passages such as the following:—Prov. chap. i. 10, "If sinners entice thee, consent thou not." Psalm xcvii, 10, "Ye that love the Lord, hate evil." Isaiah, chap. xxix. 15, "Woe to them that seek to hide their counsel from the Lord, and say, Who seeth us?" Then those who are apt to go astray, and observe not God's commandments, are forewarned that what the Lord approveth alone can prosper, and that evil courses will surely produce distress and suffering. Thus in Prov., "Then shall they (sinners) call upon me, but I will not answer; they do not choose the fear of the Lord, they would none of my counsel, they despised all my reproof, *therefore shall they eat of the fruit of their own way.*" There is one verse in Ecclesiastes which especially demands the attention of youth; the experience of the wisest of men is embodied therein, and a disregard thereto must surely entail the most dire consequences, with many after regrets. Solomon declares, chap. vii. 26, "I find more bitter than death the woman whose heart is snares and nets, and her hands as bands; *whoso pleaseth God shall escape from her; but the sinner shall be taken by her.*" The following verse in Job also calls for serious reflection, chap. xxxiv. 21, "The eyes of the Almighty are upon the ways of man, and He seeth all his goings. There is no darkness where the workers of iniquity may hide themselves;" and once fully convinced of this truth, we shall assuredly bear in mind the admonition offered to us in Prov. chap. iv. 27, "Turn not to the right hand nor to the left, remove thy foot from evil."

Numerous as are the EXAMPLES in the Bible which should act as practical exhortations to abstain from debasing pleasures, and the violation of God's holy commands, there is possibly no one character which speaks more forcibly to warn us against temptation than SAMSON. The Philistines, finding that his miraculous strength of body rendered him invincible, sought to effect his downfall through the weakness of his heart, and well did they succeed. They said to Delilah, "Entice him," and yielding to her persuasions, he discovered too late that "By the wanton, strong men are slain,"* and that "her house is the road to the grave, going down to the chambers of death."† Truly little will bodily strength, or even a highly gifted mind, avail if sensual indulgence induce a departure from the following sterling

---

* Prov., ch. vii, 26. † Prov., ch. vii, 25.

words of friendly counsel :—" Let not thine heart decline to her ways, go not astray in her path."

And for a practical illustration of this latter fact, we now turn to the life of SOLOMON, which indeed affords a convincing proof that mere worldly wisdom, devoid of godliness, is utterly powerless to save in the hour of temptation. If knowledge or understanding were, of itself, capable of keeping a man in the right path, that monarch would certainly never have erred so greatly, for are we not told, "And Solomon's wisdom excelled the wisdom of all the children of the east of Egypt?"* Neither did he greatly sin in his youth, for *then* was this high gift conjoined with piety, as we read, " Solomon loved the Lord, walking in the statutes of David his father."† Thus, at this period of life, when the passions must have been strongest, he held them under subjection, curbed his inclinations, resisted the allurements of sense, and sought to do God's high will. But in his latter years a sad change occurred; his vast possessions, his power, even his wisdom, elated his heart with undue pride, and he became forgetful of the gracious Giver of these numerous choice blessings. We are told that " he loved many strange women, and when he was old his wives turned away his heart after other gods; he built high places, and sacrificed to idols." His heart being "no longer perfect with the Lord his God," what availed his wisdom? Though he had urged his people to seek the Lord, and counselled them to observe His law, he himself departed therefrom, giving reins to his sinful passions and wickedly forsaking the Living God. His conduct was indeed highly culpable; for, though conscious of what was right, he yet wilfully disobeyed the Word of the Most High. Now had Solomon in the first moment of temptation sought God in prayer, and stood before His throne in humbleness of spirit, he would never have succumbed to those very vanities against which he

* 1 Kings, ch. iv. † 1 Kings, ch. iii.

had so strongly declaimed. Certain it is he would not in his old age have yielded to those temptations which he had piously resisted in the heyday of his youth.

Thus let us derive instruction from his grievous backsliding, keeping the love and fear of God so perpetually in our hearts that we may hold temptation at bay, and through pious devotion check every sinful propensity and triumph over each evil, each unruly passion.

ENVY.

Gen., ch. ix, 5, "*But unto Cain and to his offering God had not respect, and he was very wroth.*"

WHAT a deplorable temper of mind is here displayed. Though CAIN'S "countenance fell" on finding he had incurred the displeasure of the Most High, yet he repented not of his doings, nor sought to regain the favour of the Lord, but "was very wroth." And even when the All Just expostulated with him, saying, "Why is thy countenance fallen? if thou doest well shalt thou not be accepted?" still he evinced no disposition to amend his ways and serve the Lord in a pure and holy spirit. Overweening pride rendered him totally oblivious of God's equity; and thus the reward accorded to his brother Abel for his virtuous conduct, but withheld from him, wounded his self-love, and, rousing within his breast all the rancour of envy, in a fit of revenge he " rose up and slew his brother." Dire passion, that could make of a man a murderer and a fratricide! Nor did its baneful effects cease here. Envy and its concomitants, presumption and discontent, had so hardened the heart of Cain, that though he was brought to exclaim in the bitterness of his anguish, "My punishment is greater than I can bear, for from Thy face shall I be hid," he nevertheless could find no words of prayer or supplication to offer before the throne of justice and mercy, without which there can be no hope of pardon. Greatly had he offended; thus, great was his chastisement.

The degrading and self-tormenting passion of envy generally owes its birth to presumption and self-conceit, while its growth is stimulated by cupidity and unruly desires.

Pride arrogantly claims every privilege as a presumptive right; self-love egotistically demands every gratification; and as these feelings gain ascendency, so the spring of enjoyment becomes tainted, and a morbid state of mind is engendered. Everything is then necessarily viewed through a perverted medium. Selfishness and discontent conjoin to distort the vision of the envious, so that they can fix their gaze upon those points alone which lie beyond their reach. By under-estimating their own blessings, and over-rating those of others, they foster cravings which can never be fully gratified. Such is their egotism that they never have enough while there are others who possess more. Thus every good gift is obscured, and all power of enjoyment numbed.

But the baneful influence of envy works outwardly as well as inwardly, and much social evil is to be traced to this base and sordid passion. Openly it dares not show itself; of coward spirit, it seeks to wound in the dark, and cautiously masks the deadly malice and hatred which rankle within. Where goodness and worth flourish, there will it lurk to work evil, for envy knows no compunction, nor has esteem a place in its vocabulary. Even that prosperity or happiness which has attained its full proportions through merit is not safe from its poisoned fangs; a sworn foe to all that is good and fair, it knows no rest till the best and noblest are brought before its shrine as victims for immolation. Dark and sinful indeed is that mind which finds its own night in another's sunshine; and thus, by a just recoil, are gloom and misery stamped on every envious heart.

Now, as it is only in the vacant mind and selfish breast that this ignoble and malignant passion can permanently harbour, would we but strive to acquire through persevering industry that which we covet, and cultivate a kindly feeling towards our fellow-creatures, its power over us must assuredly cease, for goodness can wish no ill. But to preclude the possibility of its finding a seat within the heart, we must value and enjoy the blessings vouchsafed us, without regard to the state of others, which, indeed, we are apt greatly to miscalculate; or, if we must compare lots, let it be with the *less*, and not the apparently *more* favoured. This will surely tend to restrain immoderate desires, and render us happy and contented. Further, if we esteem virtue as the supreme good, and earnestly strive after excellence, at the same time casting from us any overweening ambition to excel, we may hope to soar to an eminence which petty envy will be powerless to reach.

Next, let us consider that He who "sees with equal eyes" can recognize no distinction between His creatures, except such as the presence or absence of virtue confers; and we rebel against the All Wise, tacitly accusing Divine justice, when we envy others those worldly possessions or that happiness which they have culled from the general fund, and contrived to retain fresh and unfaded. But when once happily convinced that infinite wisdom knows what is best for us, nor withholds aught which will prove to our ultimate advantage, and, further, that we must give the vigour of will to attain such things as we desire to obtain, without, however, presumptuously assuming that all we may set our hearts upon should be ours, then shall we readily believe that if our wishes remain ungratified we are but grasping at the shadow, not the substance. May we, then, ever seek God's favour, and be humbly grateful for the manifold blessings He vouchsafes, since thus we can best guard our hearts against the base passion of envy, and save ourselves from the many crimes which it but too surely engenders, as also from the condign punishment which infallibly attends its indulgence.

Now, as no one, whatsoever his station in society, and howsoever fortunate his lot, is exempt from crosses and trials, from woes and calamities, who will pretend to read on the apparently prosperous and joyful surface of a man's outer life the true state of his heart, the temper of his mind, and say with sincerity, "That lot is more enviable than mine, and I would gladly exchange"? Though much privation and sorrow may indeed have come home to us, they will not necessarily last; a change may be at hand, and, in any case, it is probable that we know the worst; but can we thus reason with regard to another? The prosperous man often dreads some reverse, while the lowly in estate need fear no fall. It is not, however, in general the whole lot of another we would seek to exchange for our own, but simply the temporal possessions; and as these are more and more coveted, so the real prizes of this earth become undervalued or despised. Yet what treasures are comparable with virtue, good temper, and religion? Surely it is towards these we should turn our attention, and, when once attained, let the tide of events flow as it may, and let the lot of others, viewed relatively to our own, seem howsoever prosperous, we shall still feel ourselves rich indeed. None could we envy, for none could have more rare and valued treasures. Contentment would then be our opulence, rectitude our nobility, a pious, humble, and satisfied heart our prosperity, and intercourse with a kind and gracious Father in heaven our supreme joy. These are the true riches of this earth, and never are they denied to prayer. To covet them only tends to make us more exalted beings, more worthy of Divine favour. These once possessed, envy is no more.

Although Proverbs offer but few PRECEPTS with regard to this most malignant passion, such a mild form of admonition being little adapted to touch this corroding disease of the heart, yet its dire effects are powerfully set forth in ch. xiv, 30, "Envy is the rottenness of the bone," whence may be gathered how fatal it is to man's individual wellbeing; while the baneful influence it is calculated to exert on others could not be better shown than in the following verse, ch. xxvii, 10: "Wrath is cruel, anger is outrageous, but who can stand before envy?" Then in Psalms we are warned that envy will oftentimes vent itself in words, and pour forth those ill-suppressed feelings of hate which rankle at the heart, as we read, "They (the envious) sharpen their tongues like a serpent; adders' poison is under their lips." Next, Asaph practically points out to us the fatal influence it is calculated to exercise over us. Thus he narrates of himself in Ps. lxxiii: "*My steps had well-nigh slipped, for I was envious when I saw the prosperity of the wicked.*" Then in Job we are told, "Wrath killeth the foolish man, and envy slayeth the silly one." Finally, we are emphatically bidden in the tenth commandment not to set our hearts on what belongs to another; that is to say, not to envy or covet the worldly possessions of our neighbour; an injunction which it will be well for us ever to retain in vivid remembrance.

Turning next to EXAMPLES, it is sad to find that RACHEL, the beloved wife of Jacob, was envious of her sister, the slighted Leah. Truly unjust, even to cruelty, was any such sentiment, and thence mark the consequences; the gall which flowed from this virulent passion poisoned the cup of her enjoyments, and in no small degree marred the happiness of her married life. Gloom spread over Jacob's household as envy entered his abode; and to this sinful passion was also due the banishment of Joseph from his father's roof, as well as the proposed act of his brothers, the consummation of which would have rendered them fratricides. Again, we may remark how severe was the penalty MIRIAM had to pay for allowing a spirit of envy to rise up against her brother's wife, which even envenomed her otherwise kindly feeling towards Moses himself. Then the enemies of DANIEL offer a like warning against the indulgence of this sinful passion. That able minister having been promoted to the highest dignity by King Darius, "because an excellent spirit was in him," the Presidents and Princes endeavoured to effect his ruin; but, by a just recoil, the same cruel death which, in their malice and envy, they had sought to bring on him, befel them and their families.

The history of SAUL affords ample proof that envy is far more easily roused by those below us in station and wealth, if they but throw a shadow over our path, than even by such as have attained the highest distinctions or greatest opulence. Early in David's history, we are told, Saul "greatly loved him," but when, at a later period, relationship and gratitude might well have promised an increase of kindly affection, envy stood in the way, the King viewing with jealous eye David's success over the Philistines. And this criminal feeling gained additional intensity when the women were heard to sing "Saul has slain his thousands and David his tens of thousands." What availed rank, power, or wealth, while a lowly subject had eclipsed him in valour? Nothing could bring a balm to Saul's wounded spirit but the death of his servant, and it was this base and senseless passion which goaded him on to those unjustifiable acts whereby he incurred God's displeasure, and finally brought about his own fatal end. Thus we see that even the most exalted in rank are not, as a natural consequence, exempt from this dire infirmity of mind, and this should lead us, whatsoever be our walk of life, to guard our hearts "with all diligence," and beware both of a covetous disposition and of a spirit of envy.

VIRTUE.

Gen. vi, 9, "*Noah was a just man and perfect in his generation. He walked with God.*"

WHAT a volume of moral ethics is comprised in these few words. To be just and to be perfect are here coupled together, and assuredly the man who uniformly makes justice the basis of his actions will not fall far short of perfection. Nor will he fail to " walk with God", for ever associating the attribute of justice with the Supreme—" the Judge of the whole earth, shall He not be just?"—and, clearly discerning its workings throughout the moral world, will endeavour to make his own line of conduct conform therewith. Certain it is that, just in proportion as man recognises this glorious attribute in the Great Disposer of Events, so will his faith in God grow firm and exalted, his practice of this God-like virtue become fixed and determined. And thus do we find it in the case of the righteous NOAH. No historic incident speaks more plainly of God's strict justice, tempered withal by mercy, than does this one about to be considered, and in which that righteous patriarch took so prominent a part. The Lord declared, " All flesh has corrupted itself; the world is filled with violence: thus I will destroy them from under heaven; all shall die." But the just man found grace in the eyes of the Lord, and God said unto Noah, "Make thee an ark, and thou shalt come into it; with thee will I establish my covenant." Now it is evident time was required for the work—indeed, the ark is supposed to have taken ninety-nine years in construction, and during that period much occurred which was well calculated to open the eyes of this corrupt generation, and forewarn them of the approaching crisis: for instance, the progress and completion of the ark itself, and the necessary preparations openly made by Noah, with the assembling of the animals; yet all was disregarded, and no symptom of reform was visible in the sight of the Omniscient. It was then only the Lord said unto Noah, "Come thou and all thy house into the ark, for thee have I seen righteous before me in this generation." Here we perceive that the strict line of justice was never departed from; man, unjust, perverse, and cruel, had turned against his fellow man, spreading misery and wretchedness around, and when the God of mercy and love thus saw "the earth filled with violence, it repented Him that He had made man"; nevertheless He for a time withheld His hand from destroying them, so that they might "turn from their evil ways and live." Persisting, however, in their sinful course, the Righteous God finally decreed that the earth should no longer be stained by acts of perfidy and crime; thus the wicked perished, the just and virtuous Noah with his family alone remaining to testify to future generations that, while a just retribution awaits the evil doer, the eyes of the Lord are upon the upright; and that His all-powerful hand is ever ready to shield those who walk with Him in truth and rectitude.

The practice of Justice, when that word is merely regarded in its strictest signification, will carry a man only a short way towards perfection; but when he understands the term in its most comprehensive sense, and exercises it undeviatingly, then indeed will such an individual make a near approach to the most exalted virtue. He will be just to himself—that is, he will cultivate his moral and intellectual faculties, and will strive to be upright, wise, and good; further, he will be just to his fellow-creatures, loving his neighbour as himself; he will be forbearing and charitable, alike in feelings as in act; lastly, he will be just to his God, acknowledging in a thankful and devoted spirit His untiring love and mercy, obeying with a grateful and pious heart His high behests, and reposing in humble trust on His all-protecting arm.

Now, to be just to himself, man must never abuse those faculties with which he has been blessed, but be ever striving to turn them to good account. He is just to himself when he considers time as a loan, and uses it for his moral and intellectual improvement; but he is unjust when he gives reins to his evil passions regardless of ulterior consequences, or heedlessly utters untruthful words. Again, to be just, man must not only do what is right, but must refrain from doing what is wrong; he must mould his actions by God's written law, give to life a high purpose, and strive to make himself ever happier and better by active deeds of kindness and true devotion. When he does all these things he is surely on the high road to virtue; but when he reflects not on an after life, nor seeks to train himself to merit it; when he stores not his mind with useful knowledge, nor warms his heart to good, nor combats things evil;—then is he in every way unjust to himself, and in consequent trials and sufferings will have to pay the penalty of his perverse dereliction from the path of duty and of virtue.

Then, to be just to others is but doing unto others as we would be done by, drawing no line of demarcation between the good of others and our own, but pursuing them conjointly, thus giving our quota to the general fund of happiness, while mitigating or decreasing, to the best of our powers, every case of misery and distress. But he who is a votary of pleasure must inevitably be unjust to others as to himself. Debauch and licentiousness cannot be noxious to one individual only; vice is infectious, excess and dissipation ever drawing others towards the fatal vortex which will surely engulf them body and soul. Again, we are unjust when we judge others by any preconceived notions or standard of our own; when we magnify their foibles, blemishes, and failings, into positive faults; when we turn against any one whom we do not fancy at first sight; and when we hate the sinner and not the sin. Again, we certainly forfeit all claim to the cognomen of just when we are over greedy in the pursuit of gain or pleasure, when we exceed our means and contract debts; but when, on the contrary, we eschew all superfluities, husband our resources by means of moderation and abstinence, and give therefrom to such as need succour, also when we devote time and energies to alleviate distress;—then, indeed, we are just, and nobly walking in the broad pathway of virtue.

Finally, to be just to God is but to acknowledge His ineffable goodness, His fatherly loving-kindness—a truth which "day uttereth unto day"; and then, like dutiful, devoted children, we shall turn towards Him with grateful hearts and walk by the light of His Holy Law. Surely man is unjust to his Maker when he abuses the numerous gifts vouchsafed to him; when he looks not up, but ascribes to luck, or fate, or chance, the incidents which beset his path; and when, instead of enjoying those many blessings which should conduce to his happiness and content, he indulges in vain repinings, covets still more, and murmurs at his lot. But he is just when he submits with pious resignation to the Supreme Will, and even when bowed in sorrow he exclaims, in the words of Job, " the Lord gave and the Lord hath taken away, blessed be the name of the Lord." Again, when he acknowledges in grateful spirit that, while much happiness is open to those who wisely seek it, trials are but blessings in disguise, sent by Him who can have no pleasure in chastising; also when he humbly confesses his own unworthiness, and in gratitude of heart proclaims with pious adoration the all-pervading mercy, love, and justice of the Most High. Thus it is clear that true virtue knows no excess or disproportion, all the moral qualities being well regulated and adjusted, while even the most laudable will be held in proper subjection.

Now the best method of acquiring virtue is to consider it

as our chief good, and thus estimated it will be sought for with all diligence. Of vast magnetic power, every approach made towards it will but insure easier access. Difficult of acquisition as it may appear from afar, each step made in advance will prove it otherwise. Of acknowledged beauty and excellence, nothing but the supposed difficulty of its attainment would cause so many to pass by the object of real worth to pursue its spurious likeness. But let us pray for it, strive for it; the very seeking is the finding, and when attained we possess a treasure which, besides conducing in the highest degree to our happiness and well-being here, will, by securing the approbation of the All Just, receive its high reward in a blessed hereafter.

PRECEPTS.—There is no quality of mind or heart tending to promote virtue which is not enjoined in the Bible,—to which, indeed, the Book of Proverbs alone bears ample testimony; but when we seek to form a summary of the whole duties of man, we find the following verses stand prominently forward. In Proverbs xv, on the question being put, "who shall abide in the Lord's Tabernacle," this answer follows: "He that walketh uprightly and worketh righteousness, and speaketh the truth in his heart; that doeth no evil to his neighbour;" and in Micah we read, what doth God require of thee "but to do *justly*, to love mercy, and to walk with thy God." Then, in Amos, we are told "to hate the evil, love the good, and establish *judgment* in the gate"; again, Malachi, describing the virtuous man, says "the law of truth was in his mouth, and iniquity was not found in his lips; he walked with me in peace and *equity*, and did turn many away from iniquity." Now those who thus act may be truly said to "walk with God", and will assuredly see the fulfilment of the many gracious promises held out in such verses as these: Ps. xcvii, "The light is sown for the righteous, and gladness for the upright in heart"; and Ps. i, "Blessed is the man who delighteth in the law of the Lord; whatsoever he doeth shall prosper"; and in Ezekiel, ch. xviii, when God, in reproving Israel, asks " Is not my way *equal*, are not your ways unequal?" further adds, "Repent ye; turn from your transgressions, make yourselves a new heart; then shall ye not die, but live the life everlasting." Then Prov., ch. x, " Blessings are upon the head of the *just*"; and Prov., ch. iii, " Let not mercy and truth forsake thee, write them upon the tables of thy heart, *so shalt thou find favour in the sight of God and man.*" In Isaiah, ch. iii, " Say to the righteous that it shall be well with him, and they shall eat the fruit of their doings." Now all who have taken these precepts and gracious assurances to heart must have felt, with the Psalmist, that " the Law of God is a lamp unto his feet, and a light unto his path"; and, when discharging the duties it enjoins, have rejoiced in the cheering reflection that " the path of the *just* is as the shining light which shineth more and more unto the perfect day."

Now to cull a few of the numerous EXAMPLES of men who " have done that which is right in the sight of the Lord with a perfect heart." We will mention, firstly, HEZEKIAH, who, as we are told, " Wrought that which was good and right and true before the Lord";* not only " preparing his heart to seek God", but urging his people to put their trust in Him. He prayed to the Lord for pardon on their behalf, and exhorted them to "remove their stiffneckedness". Then in war he strengthened them by the assurance that " with their enemies was but an arm of flesh, while they could put their trust in the Lord of battles." And thus is the character of this excellent monarch summed up : " In every work that he begun in the service of the house of God, in the law and in the commandments, he did it with all his heart"—and prospered. Turning next to SAMUEL, we find him in his old age calling together the people and thus ad-

* II Chron. xxxi, 20.

dressing them: "I have walked before you from my youth unto this day; behold here I am, witness against me before the Lord whose ox or ass have I taken, whom have I defrauded, whom have I oppressed, or of whom have I taken a bribe to blind mine eyes?" Thus did he assert his integrity, while urging the people to be *just* to each other and upright before their Heavenly Father. There is, however, no history which offers a more admirable or useful lesson than that of JOB, "a man that was perfect and upright, one that feared God and eschewed evil." We find him thus declaring his hitherto faithful observance of God's Law: "My foot hath held His steps; His way have I kept and not declined, neither have I gone back from His commandments; I have esteemed the words of His mouth more than my necessary sustenance."* And his determined adherence in extreme affliction to the same virtuous course is thus expressed: "All the while my breath is in me, my lips shall not speak wickedness, nor my tongue utter deceit." "My righteousness I hold fast and will not let it go; my heart shall not reproach me as long as I live."† Then what a beautiful description does he give of his past happy, because virtuous life: "When the ear heard me then it blessed me, when the eye saw me it was favourable unto me; because I delivered the poor that cried, the fatherless and unbefriended. The blessing of him that was ready to perish came upon me, and I caused the widow's heart to sing for joy. I was eyes to the blind, and feet was I to the lame. My glory was fresh in me, and my bow was renewed in my hand. God's candle shined upon my head; by His light I walked through darkness."‡ Then he solemnly declares that he has not allowed sensuality, covetousness, or vanity, to lead him astray, saying: "Did not God see my ways, and correct all my steps? then how could I make gold my confidence, how shut my door to the stranger; how allow my

---

* Job xxiii, 11.   † Job xxvii, 3.   ‡ Job xxix, 11.

heart to walk after mine eyes; how despise the cause of my servants or work wickedness and cover my transgressions."* The few following verses further show how firm was his faith; he says, "Will God plead against me with His great power? No, but he will put strength in me";† and again, "Though He slay me, yet will I trust in Him." Then how pious is his answer to his wife: "What! shall we receive good at the hands of God, and shall we not receive evil?"‡ Truly, the life of Job offers an invaluable lesson to those who would walk the path of truth, of justice, and of virtue.§

---

* Job xxxi, 4.   † Job xiii, 15.   ‡ Job ii, 10.

§ This book has given rise to much speculation. Many persons are of opinion that JOB is only an imaginary character, while others contend that the main facts of his history are true, and that such an individual, pre-eminent for piety and righteousness, did really exist. Now it is beyond a doubt that, though fiction may amuse the mind and even occasionally touch the heart, it rarely leaves any vivid or permanent impressions, and falls far short of the true narrative or biographical sketch in affording practical lessons and sure guidance. Thus, while the question of the authenticity of this admirably instructive book remains unsolved, would it not be well to consider it in the light which will be most productive of good? And, indeed, we venture to suggest the advisability of this course, since probability ranges on the same side. We would ask, is it reasonable to suppose that a work of fiction would be introduced and placed side by side with sacred historical records,— records dating from the remotest antiquity, and carried on to the period when profane history, taking up the thread, directly or indirectly yields its testimony to the veracity of each preceding writer? Without, however, laying too much stress on this consideration, we would revert to two others which will doubtless have great weight with those who, believing in the possibility of such a character as Job, would hold up to themselves this worthy patriarch as an example. First, with regard to the narrative itself, what can be more natural and straightforward when once divested of the allegorical garb wherewith it is clothed in the first two chapters? It is circumstantial, and lacks no fact, even the place of Job's birth being mentioned. There is nought forced, nought improbable; but we have a simple and truthful picture of human vicissitudes, of a noble nature struggling with adversity, and ultimately gaining the victory. Secondly, we will quote the allusion to this patriarch made by the prophet Ezekiel in his Book, "*Saith the Lord God*, though these three men, Noah, Daniel, and *Job*, were in it, they should deliver but their own souls *by their righteousness.*" Now is it to be supposed that the sacred penman would place a mythical character in conjunction with two of God's chosen servants, and represent him as one who might be an intercessor on behalf of a sinning nation? Rather would we believe, till it can be disproved beyond all shadow of doubt, that Job formed one of the band of virtuous men and true servants of God, who shone forth through their superior individual excellence, and taught many a lesson of man's moral capabilities by their practically useful life.

AMBITION.

Gen. xi, 4, "*Let us make us a name.*"

A DESIRE inherent in human nature is here expressed. There are but few individuals in whom this feeling has not pulsated and led to actions more or less commendable; while History proves that this sentiment has been predominant with every nation at marked periods of their existence. A passion, therefore, that has been implanted in the human heart cannot, if kept within due bounds, be either objectionable or detrimental, that is, if the methods adopted for gratifying it lead to no deviation from the paths of virtue and religion. It was however far otherwise in the case of the *Builders of Babel,* as was clearly proved by the final issue of the undertaking. The mere seeking to build a tower that should "reach to heaven" displayed a fearful amount of presumption, and we may further infer there was also much wilfulness and sin in this ambitious project, from the fact that the anger of the All Just was so greatly kindled that He frustrated their devices and brought on them the very evil which they had thereby thought to avert! Their hearts must have been corrupt before God, and He, in His omniscience, seeing that "after this nothing would be restrained which they imagined to do," not only stayed them in their work, but greatly curtailed their future powers of evil doing, for He "confounded their language," and then "scattered them about from thence upon the face of the whole earth." Here, then, we see the fall and dispersion of a great and haughty people, who, forgetful of the mercies displayed by the Almighty towards their forefather Noah, ceased to walk humbly before the Lord, and presumptuously trusted in their own arm of flesh. A just retribution truly; and a lesson for all generations.

To advance is the law of our being, and it behoves us to act in accordance therewith, progressing as life itself progresses. If, however, we allow idleness and indifference to clog all forward movement, life will become a burden, existence a blank. Our faculties and desires were given for a purpose, and we only fulfil a bounden duty when we cultivate our higher powers and stimulate our desires into active usefulness. But while it is a duty not to suffer our abilities to lie dormant, or our energies to remain sluggish and inert, it is not less imperative that they should be wisely directed and subjected to control, excess ever vitiating the noblest purposes and working innumerable ills. Everything declares that to please his God and serve his fellow-creatures is man's high mission here, and that if he gladly and zealously set himself to accomplish this, he will assuredly fulfil the glorious aim of his being, and reap the rich reward of a consciousness of right doing. To that end, then, should he direct his ambition, for there centres all true glory. If, however, he depart therefrom, permitting this lofty and generous motive to narrow into self-interest and self-aggrandisement, then will he find all conspire to thwart his endeavours. Intent on his own ambitious projects, he will be apt to encroach on the just rights of his neighbours, or failing this result, will yet surely find his interests clash with those of other men; and though, at the cost of incessant struggles and but too often at the sacrifice of principle, he may overcome each obstacle and reach the goal of his ambition, how little will he even then find to cheer him in his high estate. The pleasure will be as fleeting as the toil was long, and he will be ready to exclaim in the words of Solomon, "All is vanity."

If, then, ambition is not only justifiable but much to be commended when kept under due restraint and made to subserve general as well as individual good, the greatest possible advantage must accrue from securing some criterion by which it may be accurately judged, some standard whereby we may regulate our acts and desires. Now, assuredly, when we can conscientiously ask God in prayer to prosper our undertakings and crown our desires, we must be walking in the path of duty and honour. Man dare not petition the All Just for selfish and unlawful gratifications which alike debase his own nature and militate against the well-being of his brother man; but he feels he can call upon the Great Searcher of hearts to bless each effort of duty and prosper exertions, which, while put forth for the purpose of self-advancement and worldly success, are rather conducive than detrimental to the interests of his neighbour and fellow-citizens. The inward guide and adviser therefore speaks clearly, bidding man to stay his headlong course in the greed of gain, to subdue insatiable thirst after the world's goods and man's applause, nor pass the limits of a just and honourable ambition.

Now there is a far surer method for man " to make himself a name" and obtain honour and distinction, than the mere accumulation of riches or the attainment of rank and title, which is, to merit the esteem, and with it gain the good will, of his fellow-creatures. And in this he cannot fail, if he strive less after the world's goods than the world's good. Let him recognise and acknowledge to himself that all was made for all, that nothing throughout the Universe is withdrawn without being replaced; let him regulate his daily proceedings in accordance with this wise and beneficial law, then will egotism hide away before philanthropy; ambition will raise up its proud crest and scorn each base unworthy passion. He will not be ever ready to claim the exclusive privilege of all receiving, nought conferring, but, while seeking a fair share of earth's manifold blessings, will cheerfully add his quota to the general store of which he himself is to be a partaker.

It may next be well to remark that nothing could be more suicidal or detrimental to the general good than to offer any discouragement to that noble ambition which is at once the fair offspring of the best and loftiest feelings of our nature, and the parent of high and meritorious deeds. But this sentiment, how exalted soever it may be, will work mischief and produce much individual unhappiness, if it be not tempered by the reflection that, though all may aspire to pre-eminence, few can attain it. There occasionally arise gifted beings, endowed with such vast powers, mental as physical, that, if they only possess the requisite energy and will to direct those powers aright, they must inevitably excel, and, indeed, in soaring high are simply fulfilling a positive duty. These are the recognised pioneers of progress. But with the generality of mankind it would be highly advantageous if some proportion were kept between the desired end and the means at command for its attainment. Let us aspire then, each and all, but let none pay too dearly for *greatness* while the cost of *goodness* is so cheap. It has been justly said, "'Tis moral grandeur makes the mighty man"; thus we should not forfeit peace and happiness in a struggle after wealth and station, nor repine when they are denied, but resolutely pursue the road to goodness, wide open to all, and ever fraught with joy and content. Thus, when engaged in the active pursuits of life, may we be swayed by this grand truth, that every path is the path of glory which leads to virtue and to God.

Although we find no distinct mention in the Bible of the word ambition, there is no lack of PRECEPTS which clearly refer to all its characteristics, and point out how we should regulate and direct our desires. To prove that earthly grandeur should be esteemed far below goodness and virtue, we may quote Prov. xxii, 1, "A good name is rather to be chosen than great riches, and loving favour rather than silver and gold"; then how we may best secure and permanently hold the gifts of earth is shown in Prov. xxii, 4, "By humility and the fear of the Lord are riches and honour"; and Prov. xiii, 22, "A good man leaveth an inheritance (his good name) to his children's children." Next, we are taught how futile is the striving of the wicked, and how certain the final reward of the virtuous; in Job we read, "Who hath hardened himself against God and prospered? the light of the wicked shall be put out; his remembrance shall perish from the earth, *he shall leave no name*"; and in Psalms, "When the wicked dieth he shall carry nothing away, his glory he shall not take with him; but blessed are those who walk uprightly *and whose strength is in the Lord*; they go from strength to strength; God will withhold no good thing, but grant them grace and glory." Then to induce us to curb inordinate desires, numberless verses show forth the vanity of grandeur and riches —thus Eccles. iii, 10, "He that loveth abundance, *and with increase*, shall never be satisfied; nothing of his labour shall he carry away *in his hands;* all are dust, and all turn to dust again." Finally, to prove that worldly possessions are of little worth, and the labour for their attainment but sore trouble and grief, unless we consider virtue as the supreme good, and enjoy every blessing as the gift of God, we have the following verses, with others of like import. Eccles. vi, 4, "Though the years of a man be many, *if his soul is not filled with good*, his life will be but vanity, and his name shall be covered with darkness"; and then, "This is vanity, when a man hath riches, wisdom, and honour, so that he wanteth nothing that his soul desireth, yet God giveth him not power to eat thereof; but good and comely is it to enjoy the good of all his labour, and be glad in his heart for the good gifts of God."

Numerous EXAMPLES, practically illustrating the above precepts, present themselves throughout the Holy Volume. We find HAMAN, the day before his downfall, calling together his friends for the purpose of magnifying himself and parading the golden results of his ambition: he spoke of "the glory of his riches, of the multitude of his children, and how the king had promoted him even above the princes;" yet mark the final consummation—the gallows: while Mordecai, who, on the contrary, only sought the preferment of his much loved niece; himself sitting humbly at the King's gate even when she became queen, rose higher in power than ever did Haman, for "his fame went out through all the provinces, he waxed greater and greater, and was next unto the King." How ignoble the end of the haughty and ambitious Haman; how glorious the career of the humble and truly pious Mordecai.

Three more examples, selected from many others, will also give their quota of evidence that it is not the grasping and ambitious who mostly rise, but they who humbly put their trust in the Lord. First, JOSEPH, who would not do a "great wickedness and sin against God", became ruler over the land of Egypt within two years of the time when he thus meekly addressed Pharaoh's chief butler: "Think on me; and show kindness, I pray thee, unto me when it is well with thee."

Next, DAVID, who, although aware that he would come to the throne on the demise of Saul, not only refused to compass the king's death himself, but even stayed the hand of Abeshai, who was ready to slay him, while, regardless of the monarch's cruel enmity and persecution, he caused to be put to death the Amalekite who had stretched out his hand against the anointed of the Lord, mourning and grieving over that loss which was to be his gain. We can form an idea of the restraint which he exercised over himself by the opening of the 131st Psalm, where he says, "Lord, my heart is not haughty nor mine eyes lofty, for truly I have behaved and quieted myself as a child."

Lastly, there is DANIEL, the poor captive, who when called before Nebuchadnezzar to interpret his dream, instead of seeking to exalt himself in the eyes of that monarch, meekly declared that " this secret is not revealed to me for any wisdom that I have more than any living"; and again, at an after period, before interpreting the handwriting on the wall, he answered the king in these words, " Let thy gifts be to thyself, and give the reward to another." Thus assuredly he did not seek for benefits and power, but they were nevertheless forthcoming, and he rose to the highest posts in the kingdom.

In conclusion, we must remark that the same moral is illustrated in the following verse, which should be well considered and held in remembrance by all who aspire to excellence, " So JOTHAN became mighty *because* he prepared his ways before the Lord."* Here it is clearly demonstrated that he who bounds his ambition by the law of God, not turning aside from the path of virtue to attain his desires, but ever looking up in perfect love and trust to a beneficent Providence, may surely hope to obtain at the hands of unerring wisdom all such gifts as will most conduce to his happiness and well-being, here and hereafter.

* II Chron. xxvii, 60.

FAMILY AFFECTION.

Gen. xiv, 14, "When Abraham heard that his brother was taken captive, he armed and pursued to rescue him."

On looking back to the earlier events which figure in the history of ABRAHAM, we find but little calculated to arouse such generous enthusiasm on the part of this patriarch in favour of his so-called brother, in reality nephew. Left an orphan early in life, Lot had during long years found shelter under Abraham's roof, and, through his protection, been enabled to acquire great wealth and vast flocks. This was surely enough to have inspired the kindliest sentiments towards his benefactor; yet, when it was in his power to show him some slight token of esteem and love, his conduct betrayed nought but selfishness and ingratitude. Quarrels having arisen between their herdsmen, it would have been but a mere matter of duty on the part of Lot to rebuke his servants, and at once stay these contentions; but failing so to do, Abraham was at last fairly obliged to take cognisance of these broils, and then he, who could have commanded as master, only spoke his wishes thus mildly, "Let there be no strife, I pray thee, between me and thee, between my herdsmen and thy herdsmen, we be brethren: is not the whole land before thee? if it be well we should part, select that region which seemeth to thee most desirable, and if thou wilt take the left hand then I will go to the right, or if thou will go to the right then I will go to the left." In this manner Abraham waived the many claims he had to priority of choice; and not only called Lot "brother", but treated him with all the equality which such relationship implies.

Now the selfish and ungrateful Lot, far from responding

to such generosity and self-denial, took immediate advantage thereof, and, "seeing that the plain of Jordan was well watered everywhere even as the garden of the Lord," he without compunction quitted his kind benefactor, and turned his steps eastward to pitch his tent under the walls of Sodom, thus settling in the midst of a luxurious, corrupt, and evil-disposed people. This want of heart and lack of discernment soon bore their bitter fruits, and brought down upon him a host of future trials. When the first of these occurred, he was fortunate enough to find the old protecting hand held out to him. His flocks being taken by the enemy, and himself a prisoner, Lot's case would indeed have been hopeless but for the generous succour afforded him by his warm true-hearted kinsman. It would be impossible not to admire the forgiving disposition and noble devotion here displayed by the great patriarch. Zealous in the path of duty and in obeying the promptings of brotherly love, Abraham looked not back to that past which spoke so plainly of Lot's ingratitude, but, setting all danger at defiance, he marched forward against a victorious army, fearlessly attacked it, and wrested from the conquerors their prisoners and booty. Lot, who well deserved to have forfeited that love and protection which he had enjoyed from his youth upwards, was again free and wealthy, and must have felt during this season of bitter adversity how hallowed was that flame which even his coldness and indifference could not extinguish. Let us, then, take to heart this admirable lesson, and in our homes ever bear in mind how Abraham practically demonstrated his sense of the devotion which should attend on brotherly love; of the obligations and duties which are incumbent on those united by the tender ties of brotherhood; and of the sacrifices which should be made, when necessary, at the shrine of family affection.

Home is the school of the affections; there must they be developed, fostered, and matured. The world and its rough teachings are ill adapted to supply any deficiency in the heart's training, and too often render it both cold and selfish, But, in order that the paternal abode may be truly a home, it devolves on each member of a family to subscribe to that bond or compact to which Nature has affixed her seal, and sedulously to fulfil the duties and obligations it imposes. None may be exempt; each must subserve the common interest, bearing in mind that the good of one is the good of all. If, however, contention, petty jealousy, or rivalry, spring up at the hearth where amity and love alone should reign, then will each one learn by sad experience how inseparably his happiness and interests are bound up with those who, being nearest, should also be dearest to him. The outer world, with its cares and trials, speaks not less forcibly, bidding each unit of the home circle act in accordance with the spirit of the axiom—truly an invaluable family motto—that "in union is strength."

Now, if we would firmly cement the natural ties of brotherhood, it behoves us to keep steadily in mind that affection kindles affection, and kind acts beget kind acts; thus we should learn to bear and forbear, be ever desirous to please, ever ready to oblige. Further, we should endeavour to understand one another; for every mind beholds under a different angle of incident, every heart has emotions and sentiments peculiar to itself; and only in proportion as we become imbued with another's feelings and views can we hope to link our hearts with theirs. This will necessarily demand occasional self-denial, but true love must be prepared to make sacrifices. When the affections are once fairly set in motion, and selfishness is no longer suffered to clog the natural feelings of the heart, then shall we be ever seeking to manifest by acts the kindly sentiments which animate us. Inclination will side with duty, and affection become a practical reality.

Endowed by nature with a yearning for sympathy and love, where can we turn to find truer and better friends than those whom God Himself hath given? The ties of relationship may never be dissevered, strain them as we will by dissension and unkindness; but the affection which sanctifies consanguinity, once departed, can never be recalled. Thus it should be sedulously cherished, and so tenderly guarded, that, on no pretext whatsoever, must we suffer any hasty or unkind word to escape us; nor even permit a sneer or look of incredulity to chill aspirations or check confidences. On the contrary, it behoves us to sun the hopes of those we love, and further give the word of encouragement, so especially acceptable and serviceable to youth; to be "the last to blame, the earliest to commend", while yet faithfully and kindly pointing out blemishes, and affectionately offering wise counsel; to be ever ready to give as to receive with open hand and heart; above all, to unite in charitable acts and useful works, for these rouse mutual esteem and bind heart close to heart. If, however, we fail to secure love, we may rest assured the fault lies with ourselves; for good-will, good temper, and a cheerful alacrity in the performance of kindly offices, will never go long unrewarded; while by disregarding, or obstinately persisting in an adverse course, ties are snapped which can never, never be reunited. Truly, that home is hallowed where love breathes in every tone and actuates every deed, where mutual confidence and trust are felt and freely given; none hiding their wishes, griefs, or joys, but in the sweet interchange of thought, opening wide their hearts in rich sympathy and love. Assuredly, as we would enjoy happiness we must seek to bestow it, our keenest pleasures ever coming to us by rebound. Thus laudably striving, we shall soon gladly acknowledge how fraught with joy is the performing of every trifling office of love, how full of pleasurable emotion is the consciousness of having given the helping hand at some critical juncture; how consoling, how cheering it is to feel we have eased the aching heart or calmed the troubled brain in sorrow or in sickness.

Would we, then, nourish these best affections of our

nature and keep them warm for active exercise, we must never suffer a day to pass without remembering each brother and sister in our prayers; the blessings we invoke for them enrich our own heart, and will inwardly bear goodly fruits. It is a duty to pray for those we love, and we *must* love those for whom we pray. Here, then, is to be found a powerful auxiliary for eradicating all egotism and turning our hearts in sympathy towards one another; also for strengthening us in our duty of love and love of duty. Should we, however, fail to avail ourselves of this happy medium—and, further, if we carelessly or wilfully neglect to perform a brother's part—the pangs of repentance will one day surely overtake us. Dependence on others is our lot here below, and to whom can we more hopefully turn for counsel, support, and loving kindness, in time of sorrow, than to the brother or sister, the associate of our youth, and natural friend of our maturer years? If we have but sown love, we shall assuredly reap its goodly fruits; if we have failed in this our duty, when sickness and sorrow befal us they will surely bring with them the anguish of remorse; —unmerited kindness or neglect serving alike to sting us to the quick.

But it is when misfortune lowers on the whole household that love acquires its supremacy, and practically teaches how strong we are when united, how weak apart. When calumny, ruin, or death, cross the family threshold, then will each member feel how close are the ties of kindred, and how affection tempers affliction. None will undervalue the rich treasures of love when the heart is bowed in anguish; yet surely prosperity and happiness must be far more desirable cements than grief and misery. Thus, while a kind Providence blesses us in Fatherly tenderness, let us learn to dispense happiness around, thereby binding ourselves in fast, enduring love to those whom He, in His unerring Wisdom, has united by the holy tie of consanguinity, the holy bonds of brotherhood.

As love of kin is fully embodied in the PRECEPT, Lev. xix, 34, "thou shalt love thy neighbour as thyself," the Sacred Volume is elsewhere almost silent with regard to this sentiment. There is not one sentence which directly inculcates "brotherly love", and but few which make more than a passing allusion to it, thus allowing full scope to the natural promptings of the heart. But though the injunctions are few, they are ample for every practical purpose, especially when connected with the all-comprehensive commands to "do good" and "to love our neighbour". Let these be duly heeded, and further admonitions on this score become superfluous. The sweet singer of Israel, at the opening verse of Psalm cxxxiii, thus emphatically declares how desirable and blissful is family concord, "Behold how good and pleasant it is for brethren to dwell together in unity," and then proceeds, in an imagery alike impressive and sublime, to liken brotherly love to the "precious oil with which Aaron was anointed, to the dew that descended on the mountains of Zion whence the Lord commanded the blessing of life for evermore." If these glowing symbols and persuasive appeals fail to touch the heart, then must we turn to the reverse picture. Prov. xviii, 19, points to the sad consequences of disunion thus: "A brother offended is harder to be won than a strong city"; also, on turning to Ps. l, wherein the wicked are reproved, we find among the sins enumerated as certain to bring down God's anger that of unkindness or ill-will towards a brother; we read at verse 19, "thou givest thy mouth to evil, thou speakest against thy brother, thou slanderest thine own mother's son. This thou hast done, and I kept silent; but I will reprove thee."

With regard to the natural affections, Scripture teaches mostly by warnings; thus EXAMPLES for imitation are but few. The warm, loving heart needs little prompting, but with the cold and selfish it is far otherwise. To these, then, the Bible offers many useful lessons. Proof to all but the exemplification of their own moral deformity, and the ill-consequences which invariably attend on any dereliction of duty, it is necessary their attention should be called to such practical illustrations as are calculated to awaken a dormant conscience, induce reflection, and lead the heart to acts of self-denial and love. Turning first to the history of Joseph, how favourably does his conduct contrast with that of his brothers. He, so generous, so forgiving; they, rancorous and cruel. How warm must have been that fraternal love which could not only render him oblivious of the injuries they had heaped upon him, but even prompted him to greet them in such words as these, " I am Joseph, your brother, whom ye sold into Egypt; now, therefore, be not grieved nor angry with yourselves that ye sold me hither, for God did send me before you to preserve life."* In his generous breast the spark of love, once kindled, could never be extinguished. All remembrance of their treacherous conduct must have been effaced from his mind; for we find that, after he had shown his deep love for Benjamin, he " moreover kissed all his brothers and wept upon them", and then "his brothers talked with him". Then, turning from the injured to the wrong-doers, what an important lesson and warning is offered us in the words interchanged between them whilst proceeding homewards. "They said one to another, we are verily guilty concerning our brother, that we saw the anguish of his soul when he besought us and we would not hear; therefore is this distress come upon us." Truly their sin rose up spectre-like before them, though thirteen long years had elapsed since their inhuman treatment to the youthful Joseph, nor could they altogether stifle the qualms of conscience, their hearts " failing them" when they found the returned money in their sacks. Gold, for which they had sold their brother into bondage, now came to them as a curse. Hatred had indeed severed the tie of family affection; and it was reserved for Joseph,

* Gen. xlv, 5.

through love and generous forgiveness, not only to unite it again, but even to keep it intact alike before and after the death of their mutually revered parent.

A hardly less remarkable instance of brotherly love and forgiveness than the one just recorded is to be found in the lives of JACOB and ESAU. The former, in his early manhood, had incurred the just resentment of his warm-hearted brother, and this led to their being separated during long years; yet neither unkindness nor absence could extinguish youthful love. The meeting of Jacob with his injured brother is thus touchingly described, "Esau ran to meet him and embraced him and fell upon his neck, and they wept";* then Jacob, when presenting his gift, said "Nay, I pray thee, if I have found grace in thy sight, receive this present at my hands, for I have seen thy face as though I had seen the face of a God-like Being, and thou wast pleased with me!" Thus will love triumph even over just resentment.

This is again exemplified by the conduct of MOSES, when Miriam and Aaron, in a jealous spirit, culpably turned against him, saying "Hath the Lord indeed spoken only by Moses, and has He not spoken by us?" Pride and presumption had evidently taken entire possession of Miriam's heart, else she would never have displayed any such angry feeling towards her meek and unoffending brother. Nevertheless, even this arrogant and unsisterly behaviour was powerless to move Moses to resentment; indeed, feeling deeply grieved on viewing the sad consequences which her conduct evoked, he cried unto the Lord in all the anguish of fraternal love, saying "Heal her now, O Lord, I beseech thee." And when Aaron saw Miriam's deplorable condition, being hardly less culpable himself, he must have bitterly repented having sided with his sister, instead of curbing her rash pride; indeed, his very appeal to the brother he had wronged affords ample evidence of his regret. We read,

* Gen. xxxiii, 4.

"And Aaron said to Moses, Alas! my lord, I beseech thee, lay not the sin upon us wherein we have done foolishly and wherein we have sinned."* It was thus through the loving-kindness of Moses that the breach was healed and amity restored.

But in the next instance we are about to quote we have quite a reverse picture. The selfish and unprincipled conduct of AMMON, one of David's sons, brought in its train much suffering and misery to the entire household. A sadly vile proceeding on his part having engendered hatred and contention between the brothers, we have to mark the disastrous consequences in the murder of the perpetrator of the wrong, the overthrow of David's throne, the usurpation and violent death of Absolom. Thus was the peace and happiness of a whole family for a time destroyed by the misconduct of one of its members.

The opening chapter of the Book of Job presents us with a marked and glowing contrast to this sad scene of domestic broils, and offers an example which cannot be too carefully studied or closely imitated. The God-fearing JOB, who daily prayed for his sons and "sanctified them", must have early instilled into the hearts of his children that mutual love which attained its full practical development in their matured years. Perfect harmony and deep affection evidently subsisted between them; none could have forfeited the rich inheritance of love, for we are told "His sons went and feasted in their houses every one his day, and they called for their three sisters to join them at their festive board."† Thus in constant friendly union did the children of the pious Job cultivate the natural affections, and draw tight the ties of brotherly love. Though no longer dwelling together beneath that roof which had sheltered them in youth, the loving sentiment then inspired continued to animate them, and they continually sought each other's society, finding therein an unceasing source of mutual gratification, an ever-gushing spring of love and happiness.

* Numbers xii, 11. † Job i, 4.

FAITH.

Gen. xv, 6, " *And he believed in the Lord.*"

IN perusing the life of the noble patriarch ABRAHAM, we find that his implicit trust in God never wavered, from the time when, as narrated in Gen. xii, he quitted his father's roof at the command of the Lord, and journeyed with his beloved wife through an unknown land, inhabited by idolators, until he attained a wondrous climax of faith, as manifested in the last sublime act of his old age, the offering up of his much loved and only son at the first expression of God's high Will.

Now assuredly no such glorious consummation could have resulted, had not the youthful Abram, through force of will, triumphed over the adverse circumstances which beset him. Although living and moving in the midst of an idolatrous and benighted people, he nevertheless contrived to cultivate the habit of observation and train his mind to contemplation. As he conned the book of Nature, which lay open before him, and became imbued with the spirit of love which breathes throughout its glowing pages, he readily learnt to ascribe the marvellous and glorious works of creation to an unknown but wise and gracious Author; and no sooner did the feeling of an Overruling Providence ripen into a settled conviction, than faith, love, and gratitude, sprang up spontaneously in his breast, colouring every after action of his life. Pure and excellent must have been that mind which, of its own free-will, earnestly sought, and, through the thick darkness of general unbelief, arrived at a knowledge of the existence of a Great First Cause. Indeed it is evident Abraham must have attained a high degree of moral excellence when under his father's roof, and have so moulded the disposition of his heart as to render its homage acceptable to the Omniscient, since even at the very outset of his career the most gracious promises were vouchsafed him from on High. Now this especial manifestation of favour would assuredly only have been accorded to such superlative merit as every subsequent event of the great patriarch's life proves him to have possessed. Mark his prompt and implicit obedience on receiving the first injunction of the Supreme to go forth into a strange land; and again, when shortly after the Lord "appeared unto him" renewing past promises, what a truly devout and thankful spirit did he display, for he "built an altar unto the Eternal and called on the name of the Lord."

Such acts prove how firm from the very first was his trust in a heavenly Father, and how resolute he was to do that Father's will; while the severe trials he afterwards so heroically encountered give undeniable evidence that his faith must have grown with his growth. Though years passed away and Abraham remained childless, he never repined nor doubted the fulfilment of God's promises; for when the assurance of a numerous progeny was renewed, we are told "Abraham believed in the Lord, and it was counted to him for righteousness."* But the test before which all others pale into insignificance was reserved for his old age, when his faith reached its culminating point. On receiving the command of God, which ran as follows, "Take now thy son, thine only son Isaac, whom thou lovest, and get thee into the land of Moriah, and offer him there for a burnt offering"†—he complied with the heavenly injunction without a murmur or the faintest show of hesitation; for it is related *in the very next verse* that "Abraham rose early in the morning and took Isaac his son, and went three days' journey to the place of which God had told him." To part with the cherished one, the promised boon whose

* Gen. xv, 6. † Gen. xxii, 2.

advent he had awaited during long years, would alone have severely taxed his fortitude; but even more than resignation was demanded of him, for he was called on to sacrifice that beloved one *with his own hand!* Surpassingly severe was the test, for how could he reconcile this command with his reason, his natural affections, and the attributes of the Deity? All events that demonstrate the goodness of God are easy of credence; not so, however, those pains, trials, and griefs, in which we discern nought but evil; these indeed require the most entire resignation and perfect faith, virtues eminently displayed by the God-fearing Abraham, who could attribute nothing but wise and beneficent designs to the Omnipotent, and, whatever the probation, it was enough that the Lord had willed it. Thus, in all submission to the Divine behest, he set forth resolutely, marching onwards for three long days, with the dearest object of his past hopes and aspirations at his side; and, finally, he was about to fulfil the dread decree without a murmur, when his hand was miraculously stayed. He had " obeyed the voice of the Lord." Faith had gained ascendency over the master passion of his soul—love for his only child. God's will was his will. The Lord spoke, and the proved servant was all obedience. Great had been his self-conquest, and great was his reward. A glorious mission was entrusted to him, and the richest blessings promised; but far above all was the renewed gift of his dearly-beloved son and the smile of approving heaven. Thus faith triumphed, for his heart was with his God. Admire we must, imitate we may.

Faith, which has its birth in the soul, yet draws its vitality and receives its development from reason and feeling. Not until it has taken a firm seat in the mind and heart will it become a fixed and permanent principle of action. Religious trust should, therefore, be inculcated from earliest youth, and so made to blend with our very being as to become the mainspring of each thought and deed. It must also be so certain, so entire, that no shadow of doubt can ever obscure its full effulgence. Now, if we will but look around and within us, the smallest degree of discernment must suffice to lead our minds up to the Almighty Framer and Governor of the Universe. God has not hidden Himself from mortal ken, for He is ever present in all His works. His Gracious Hand may be traced, holding the reins and directing whatsoever concerns men's interests; while all creation proclaims its own perfection.

But it will not suffice that we exclaim, "Verily there is a God"; it is an *animating* faith which is demanded of us, we must give ourselves with heart and mind to the study of the laws which regulate the universe and human affairs, marking how they accord with the conception of a just, merciful, and gracious Ruler. This once felt and acknowledged, the next step forward will be to yield a ready obedience to our Heavenly Father, convinced that while nothing can occur without His willing it, all He ordains ministers to the well-being of His creatures; for truly if God is good, all must terminate in good, and thus present evils will redound to future advantage.

Now, Faith mostly concerns the unseen future, and derives its chief strength from the fact. If we have read the historic pages of that past with attention, and not wilfully ignored the love and watchful care of an overruling Providence, if we have sounded the wondrous depths of wisdom and goodness which the teeming creation uniformly displays, and taken to heart the ever-multiplying proofs of Divine Mercy and Justice, then will the unknown future have no terrors for us; we shall learn to entertain just and loving sentiments of God, and while striving to act in conformity with His Supreme Will, place an implicit reliance on His all-protecting and guiding Hand. At each advance in the knowledge of His High Attributes, we shall draw nearer and nearer to Him in religious trust. Faith will urge us on to duty, become our stay in tribulation, turn our hearts in love and gratitude to the great Author of our Being, and thus sanctify our lives and aspirations.

Now, faith in God by no means precludes our having faith in ourselves; indeed, it is every way calculated to awaken and stir up our energies. Has He not declared Himself the friend of those who work in the cause of progress and truth? Has He not gifted us with freewill, and endowed us with reason and strength that we may voluntarily and in a thankful spirit exert ourselves to perform His Holy Will, and in so doing promote our own well-being and the general interests? Assuredly trust in God is the very foundation of character; it is the sun of our souls, ripening all our best resolutions into action, and warming our hearts to the practice of every good and noble deed. Before its cheering rays, diffidence and doubt vanish, while virtuous hope and zeal are roused and made prepotent for good. Moreover, faith has the sovereign virtue of banishing discontent, moderating grief, and checking despondency. Let us strive but to improve the present, while bearing steadily in mind that "the Lord's hand is not shortened," and that nothing can occur without His appointment or permission, then all anxious concern for the future will be dispelled; we shall confide in the tender mercies of a wise and beneficent Protector, and rest secure in His ever watchful care; but let a criminal mistrust once gain supremacy in the mind, and we shall surely bring upon ourselves the very evils we would avoid, and so poison our cup of life. Thus, never let us dare to resign hope when trials come, or be wayward, cast down, and lose faith, if instant relief be not afforded, but trust implicitly in the Wise Disposer of events, feeling Him to be all powerful to save. Do we not read in Exodus "I, the Lord, know thy sorrow", and truly He watches over and guards His faithful loving children the same now as then. To doubt this, is to derogate from His glorious attributes and ungratefully overlook those numerous blessings which are continually being showered down upon us from on High.

Now, had not the future been a sealed book to us, we should have had but little opportunity of exercising or testifying our faith, for which prerogative we cannot, indeed, be too thankful. We may feel assured that God would have permitted us an insight into the hidden and mysterious future were it compatible with our good; and that He has withheld such power is ample proof that it would only prove prejudicial to us. He has, however, vouchsafed us gracious promises if we will only conform our conduct to His written Law, and thus the brightness or gloom of our future greatly depends upon ourselves. But the present likewise calls for the exercise of religious trust, since, though most of the trials and misfortunes which befal us may be traced to our own misconduct or imprudence, yet occasionally this fails to be apparent. It is in moments of grief that it especially behoves us to confide in Him who is Infinite in goodness as in Wisdom, and seek comfort and consolation in prayer. How chequered soever may be our path, or however hard our lot, we should never despair; but reflect that while we take merely a partial view, a wise superintending Providence sees the whole, and that the All Merciful permits only such ills to befal His creatures as will ultimately redound to their good. Once impressed with this grand truth, we shall pursue our course fearlessly, hopefully, and realising our dependence on God, be content to leave the issue of all our endeavours and all our desires with Him who rules above. In Holy truth, loving and obedient, we shall sedulously labour in the cause of truth, of the God of truth, to secure the eternal crown reserved for the virtuous and faithful servants of the Most High.

Though life is subject to many chances and changes, we may well hope to pass through them unscathed, if we but act up to the PRECEPTS of the Bible, which bid us place full reliance in the great Disposer of events, while actively pursuing a course consistent with the expressed will of the

Beneficent Author of our Being. Thus the pithy injunction should be ever present to our minds, "Trust in the Lord and do good", for it sums up nearly the whole of moral ethics. The following quotations are much to the same effect. Proverbs iii, "Trust in the Lord with all Thy heart, and lean not unto thine own understanding; *in all thy ways acknowledge Him and He will direct thy paths*"; Eccles. xii, "Remember now thy Creator in the days of thy youth, and fear God and keep His Commandments"; and Ps. cxv, "Ye that fear the Lord, *trust in the Lord, He is our help and our shield*". Then, by way of contrast, and for the purpose of showing the sad consequences which naturally result from disobeying these injunctions, we quote the following verses from Ps. liii: "The debased hath said in his heart, there is no God. Corrupt are they and no one doeth good: none seek after God, none call on Him"; hence, "they were in great fear where no fear was". Truly, faith alone can banish fear. None are exempt from trials, and even they who have best learnt to repose trust in Omnipotence will be oftentimes subject to doubt and despondency, needing those consoling promises of Scripture, those cheering assurances which necessarily set at rest all disquietude, all misgivings. These indeed abound throughout the Holy Volume. We are told in Ps. xxxiv, "Many are the afflictions of the righteous, but the Lord delivereth them out of them all. He redeemeth the soul of His servants, and none of them that trust in Him shall be desolate"; Ps. xxxiii, "Behold the eye of the Lord is upon them that fear Him, upon them that hope in His mercy"; and Ps. cxii, "The righteous shall be in everlasting remembrance; he shall not be afraid of evil tidings while trusting in the Lord"; and Prov. i, "Whoso hearkens unto me shall dwell safely and shall be quiet from fear of evil." Then II Chro. xvi, "The eyes of the Lord run to and fro throughout the whole earth to show Himself strong in the behalf of them whose heart is perfect towards Him". And Habakkuk ii, "The just shall live by his *faith*". Again in

Psalms, "Our fathers trusted in Thee, they trusted and Thou didst deliver them". Then how comforting and cheering are such verses as these: Isaiah xli, "Fear not, for I am with thee, be not dismayed for I am thy God"; and again Ps. lv, "Cast thy burden on the Lord and He shall sustain thee, He will never suffer the righteous to be moved". Will not, then, every faithful servant of the Most High gladly unite in uttering the pious exclamation of Asaph, Ps. lxxiii, "Whom have I in heaven but Thee? there is none upon earth that I desire besides Thee", and gratefully recognising His all-sustaining, all-protecting Hand, echo the heartfelt expression, at 24th v., "Thou wilt surely guide me with Thy counsel, and afterwards receive me to glory".

The Holy Volume teems with EXAMPLES of men whose lives remain standing proofs of the power of Faith over conduct, and foremost among them is undoubtedly DAVID, as the following brief sketch may serve to exemplify. Though subject through life to the greatest possible vicissitudes of fortune, he never faltered in his religious trust. The whole tenour of his conduct was uniform, alike when in a humble station or when monarch of Israel, when bowed by affliction and adversity or basking in the sunshine of prosperity, for from youth "his heart was fixed *trusting* in the Lord".* Take, in the first instance, his challenge to Goliath, because "he had dared to defy the armies of the living God". Here faith was his breastplate, and, taking only a sling in hand, he fearlessly advanced towards his formidable adversary and thus addressed him, "I come to thee in the name of the Lord of Hosts whom thou hast defied. The battle is the Lord's. He who saveth not with sword or spear will give you into our hands". Thus armed, thus nerved by holy trust, he slew the mighty giant. In the chapter which follows we further read, "And Saul made him captain, and he went and came in before the people; and David behaved himself

* 1 Samuel, xvii, 36.

wisely in all his ways. The Lord was with him and he was beloved by all Israel and Judah". Here we see how sterling was his character, even thus early in life. Next we find him, at a moment of imminent peril to himself, striving with all the deep solicitude of a devoted son to secure the safety of his parents, for which purpose he sought the King of Moab, in whom he placed implicit reliance, and urging him to protect them till "he knew what God would do for him".* Referring next to the taking of Selag, when David's wives were made captive by the Amalekites and his own life was imperilled through the anger of the people, we find him rising superior to what might well seem overwhelming disasters, because he "encouraged himself in the Lord his God".† Boldly pursuing the enemy, he recovered all the spoil together with those so dear to him. Again, his glowing faith manifested by his conduct on the death of his child, the son of Bathsheba; mourning and praying while it still lived, yet resigned when removed from this life, for "it was the will of God". "I shall go to him, but he will not return to me", are words of faith never to be forgotten. And again on David's precipitate flight from Jerusalem, when anguish must have sat heavy upon him, as it did on all his devoted adherents and subjects, he spoke in the fulness of faith to Zadok and the Levites who bore the ark, saying, "carry it back to the city; if I shall find favour in the eyes of the Lord, He will bring me again and show me both it and His habitation, but if He thus says, 'I have no delight in thee,' behold here am I, let Him do to me as seemeth good unto Him".‡ What piety, what submission, what holy trust! Then, passing over numerous additional examples of David's implicit reliance on the Supreme, we arrive at one replete in faith, for when he had to receive a punishment for his sin in numbering the people, and was bid to choose between the three plagues named to him by God, he simply replied, "I am in great straits; let me fall into the hands

* Samuel xxii, 3.   † Samuel xxx, 6.   ‡ II Samuel xv, 25.

of the Lord, for His mercies are great, and let me not fall into the hands of man". His last charge to Solomon and his every act till death, prove how firm was his trust, how animating his faith. His numberless beautiful Psalms afford a like testimony. Take, for example, the 121st, which gives the strongest possible evidence of a mind impressed with a sense of an all presiding Providence; how earnest and inspiring are his words " I will lift up mine eyes unto the hills whence cometh my help, my help cometh from the Lord who made heaven and earth; He will not suffer thy foot to be moved. He that keepeth thee will neither slumber nor sleep. The Lord is thy keeper, He will preserve thee from all evil, He will preserve thy soul". In Psalm 145 he shows how powerfully his soul was imbued with a sense of the majesty and infinite goodness of the Almighty, and proclaims his thankfulness and never failing trust as follows, "I will extol Thee, my God, O King; every day will I bless Thee and will praise Thy name for ever and ever. Great is the Lord and greatly to be praised; His greatness is unsearchable, He is gracious and full of compassion, slow to anger and of great mercy. The Lord is good to all, and his tender mercies are over all His works; He upholdeth all who fall, He fulfilleth the desires of them that fear Him; He will also hear their cry and save them, the Lord is nigh unto all them that call upon him in truth". Virtue and faith, closely united in David's character, were ever promoting and strengthening each other. This 112th Ps. contains promises to the good man of blessings here and hereafter which were peculiarly appropriate to himself and literally fulfilled as far as his worldly life was conceived. Thus speaks this faithful servant of God, " Blessed is the man that feareth the Lord, that delighteth greatly in His commandments. His seed shall be mighty upon earth, life and riches shall be in his house. To the upright there shall arise light in the darkness; he shall surely not be moved for ever. He shall not be afraid of evil tidings, his heart is fixed trusting in the Lord. His horn shall be exalted with honour, and *his name held in everlasting remembrance*". Centuries have rolled away since this psalm was written, yet neither the words, the name, nor the example of King David is lost to us, but remain to exhort to virtue and teach to all generations the power and efficacy of faith.

The Book of Daniel also offers several examples of sublime faith; for instance, when Nebuchadnezzar threatened to commit *Daniel's three companions* to the fiery furnace should they not fall down and worship the golden image he had dedicated at Dura, they resolutely refused to comply with such a command, and when he mockingly asked them "where is God that He shall deliver thee"? they simply replied, "We care not to answer thee in this matter; our God whom we serve is able to deliver us, and He will deliver us from thine hand, O King. (And does not death put an end to all persecution?) But be it known to thee, we will not serve thy God nor worship thy image which thou hast set up".

Then another lesson in faith is taught us by DANIEL himself. Although aware that an edict had gone forth decreeing that "whosoever should ask a petition of any God or man for thirty days save of the King" should be cast into the den of lions, he nevertheless openly prayed, "as he did aforetime", and was found making "supplications before his God", for which he suffered the threatened punishment; afterwards when the King, intent on learning the fate of his faithful servant, himself repaired to the den to interrogate him, mark the answer made by Daniel, "My God hath sent His angel and has shut the lions' mouths, that they have not hurt me, forasmuch as before Him innocence was found in me; and also, before thee, O King, have I done no hurt". In a word, feeling that he had acted uprightly before God and man, he was enabled to banish all fear. The Lord was his

* Ch. vi, 2.

protector, the Lord was his trust, and thus did virtue supply the lamp of faith.

Finally, turning to two important characters, those of Eli and of Jonah, we find that, notwithstanding all their failings, no sooner did trials befal them than they sought Him, under whose wings alone they could find refuge. ELI offered no remonstrance when informed by the youthful Samuel of the fate that awaited his wicked sons. Fully convinced of God's equity, he bent before the mandate in humbleness of spirit, piously exclaiming, "It is the Lord; let Him do what seemeth Him good". And JONAH, who had sacrificed himself for the good of his companions, on being miraculously saved, thus addressed his Maker in prayer: "When my soul fainted within me I remembered the Lord. I will sacrifice unto Thee with the voice of thanksgivings. Truly salvation is of the Lord". Words which, if true to God and to ourselves, we shall, we must, oft echo in perfect love and Holy *Faith*.

BENEVOLENCE.

Gen. xviii, 5, "*Comfort ye your hearts, and after that ye shall pass on.*"

HE who truly loves his God must love his fellow-mortals, and thus it was with the pious ABRAHAM. He no sooner saw travellers than "he ran to meet them", and, without stopping to make any inquiry as to their nation or rank, at once urged them to seek repose within his dwelling and partake of such cheer as he could provide, which, though modestly designated "a morsel of bread", he resolved should be of the best he had to offer. He little conceived who were the strangers he greeted so hospitably; enough for him that they were wayfarers and might need refreshment. With the power to give he had also the will; thus in all courtesy and love he offered them a sincere and hearty welcome.

The benevolence of this revered and noble patriarch is indeed demonstrated throughout his whole career; but in no one instance was it more touchingly exemplified than in his intercession for the inhabitants of the cities of Sodom and Gomorrah. Feeling the keenest sympathy and commiseration for his benighted, sinful, and idolatrous neighbours, he uttered a most fervent appeal on their behalf, and adopted a highly ingenious method to turn aside the just anger of the Lord. Thus, he first simply asked, "Wilt Thou destroy the righteous with the wicked? If there be fifty righteous, wilt Thou destroy and not spare the place for the sake of the fifty righteous? Far be it from Thee to do after this manner, to slay the righteous with the wicked. Shall not the Judge of the whole earth do right"?* And when the Lord acceded to this request, Abraham, fearing

* Gen. xviii, 23.

lest a nation so sunk in ignorance and crime might not possess even fifty righteous men, implored a further boon, and, humbling himself, besought the Lord as follows: "Behold, now I having taken upon myself to speak unto the Lord, who am but dust and ashes, peradventure there shall lack five"? And noncontent to stay his entreaties while he could hope to save his fellow-creatures from their impending fate, he renewed them even at the risk of incurring God's anger, till not fifty but ten righteous men found within the city would have sufficed to save it. Here he stopped. Much, very much, he had done; more he could not do. The forethought, the zeal and generous devotion, which characterised his conduct in this instance are clearly discernible in every transaction of his life. His large, warm heart never ceased to beat for the welfare of others, and he was ever prepared to make any personal sacrifice to promote their interests. Piety was indissolubly united with good works, and religion with charity, in the mind of this noble, generous, model patriarch, and animated all his actions. Sublime indeed was his Faith; eloquent and impressive his Benevolence.

If to appreciate a virtue were to insure its practice, then indeed would the world teem with philanthropists. All who feel their dependence on a Superior Being, and give heed to their own unworthiness, must highly estimate the glorious attribute of Benevolence in the Deity, and most who have suffered either mentally or bodily will have learnt, through human kindness, to appreciate its full value in man. True benevolence is but sympathy translated into action, and is the distinguishing badge of the right-minded. It consists in an ever-ready will to serve our fellow-mortals, in promoting social happiness by acts of kindness and love, in consoling the wretched, administering hope to the abased, relieving the distressed, and zealously striving not only to find a remedy for the miseries and evils which beset the poor and needy, but also in seeing it applied when found. It occasionally requires the open purse, but ever the open heart; for without the latter it degenerates into a cold, frigid charity, nearly powerless for good, whilst when united they are all-potent. In the case of the sinful or benighted, the magnets it employs are sympathy and love, which so well know how to strike the right chord in the human heart and call forth a ready and grateful response. As long as one common humanity unites us, spirit will surely answer to spirit.

Benevolence is also attended by the handmaiden Hope, which with unfailing tact touches that hidden spring of good never altogether absent from the human soul. For is not this soul of divine origin? Thence surely no effort can be fruitless which shall serve to wake it up to a consciousness of its own higher power, and rouse and direct aright those energies which have been perverted or driven by the baser passions to unworthy ends. Verily some bright sparks lurk in the breast of even the vilest men, and true philanthropy is prepared, on the slightest encouragement, to fan them into a flame by the gentle breath of kindness, and heavenly-inspired words of hope.

Benevolence bears a strong affinity to piety, and is greatly strengthened by it, for we truly love God only when we love those made in His image, and are willing to testify such love practically. It is also the true panacea for our own ills, since necessarily withdrawing us from all our engrossing thoughts of self. By taking to heart the misfortunes and trials of others we become less sensitive to our own; by engaging our thoughts and energies in the promotion of general and individual good we cease to be listless on the one hand or worldly ambitious on the other, thereby freeing ourselves from the direst enemies of a healthful mind and tranquil, contented spirit. It is best reared and nurtured in a happy home, whence it will spread and extend till it encircles and grasps within its benign influence the whole animate creation.

Now the practice of Benevolence is both a duty and a

prerogative. Divine bounty is intended to reach all in a greater or less degree through human agency, and none are excluded from becoming the stewards of Him who ever remembers His creatures in their low estate. Side by side we find wealth and poverty, for such is the High Will of Infinite Wisdom; but this decree does not extend to the ultra-extremes, luxury and want. Hence where much has been given, much is demanded, and great responsibility rests with those whose "lots have fallen into pleasant places". Riches are of uncertain tenure, and the prosperity which smiles on us to-day may be gone to-morrow; thus, while we have it in our power to give, let those ample stores, which possibly were granted for no especial merit of our own, be opened wide to all who need our bounty. Charity is, however, but a small part of our duty here, and it behoves us strenuously to endeavour to leave the world better than we found it. Were none to try there could be no improvement, while if each individual, how humble soever he be, will only exert his energies and seek opportunities of benefiting his fellow-creatures, great and glorious must be the result. Thus, if we will but do our duty, and, guided by an active spirit of charity and love, be ever devising means of usefulness, working for the welfare of others, relieving distress with our own hand, and making a generous use of the wealth and abilities bestowed on us, we shall experience the happy consciousness of well-doing, be gladdened by the sight of the happiness we have conferred, and in all confidence and hope await the final issue of each new endeavour, each benevolent intent.

Though inequality amongst men is in accordance with a natural law, for " the poor shall never cease out of the land", yet all are bound to subserve the general good, and they who live in the enjoyment of numerous blessings should not withhold or deny a portion to others. Gratitude for the rich gifts received should continually find expression in acts of kindness and love. Let us, then, be ever ready to kindle another's happiness; it will not extinguish our own, but tend to make it burn with a steadier and brighter flame. We may feel convinced that few things will more surely conduce thereto than the kind and soothing word, which is as easily said as the indifferent or unkind one, and while costing nothing is worth so much.

Now to shun or neglect this duty, which in loving kindness has been intrusted to us, betokens a narrow, ill-regulated, and selfish heart. It surely speaks of a loathness to forego pleasures, though they interfere with the due performance of acts of Benevolence, of an unwillingness to moderate desires for luxuries and gratification, though they tend to abridge the power of responding to the calls of poverty, and finally of a disinclination to cast aside the trammels of idleness and apathy, even when much good might be accomplished by energetic action. It is also occasionally to be traced to the indulgence of ill-will for any petty offence, to some vague feeling of antipathy generating a habit of talebearing and repeating idle scandal. Now He whose tender mercies extend alike over all His creatures will surely visit such conduct with His high displeasure, and would we not stand guilty before Him we must cultivate a good and kindly disposition, train our hearts to compassion and sympathy, and rouse within our breasts those warm and generous sentiments which become the parents of good deeds.

But to be kind and affable to those we love and esteem makes no serious demand on our good nature, which is severely taxed only when we endeavour to stifle resentment and animosity or conquer feelings of antipathy or repugnance. This is self-conquest; it is a glorious victory, an achievement that amply repays the struggle; but if we succumb and allow our heart to turn against any fellow-creature, we may feel assured the sentiment of ill-will will find expression by word or deed, how solicitous soever we may be to hide or smother it. A look, a tone, will escape us, and impart the feeling of aversion harboured in our breast. Love and dislike are too powerful to be at rest, but will ever crop up. Thus, let us exert ourselves to foster the one and eradicate the other, and this will be all the easier if we will only remember firstly that the heart turns in all kindness towards those whom we have once benefited, and next, that the mere suspicion of unfriendly sentiments must surely produce their like, and thus foster animosities.

Now it is highly essential that we should warm our hearts by studying the characters and lives of the benevolent, who eloquently preach to us through their acts, practically demonstrating the powerful influence charity and love exercise in the world as well as on our own inner life and happiness. Once conversant with these instructive biographies, nothing will be left us but to imitate the general tenor of conduct therein portrayed, and thus become deserving of those blessings which mostly attend on a consistent course of right doing. The benevolent man is a noble and trustworthy pioneer in the world's progress, accelerating it by his own untiring energy and well applied abilities. He makes the good cause not the work of days or years, but of his life. He looks upon humanity as upon nature, ever turning his gaze towards its sunny side, and rejoicing in its manifold beauties. His heart is in the right place, and by his urbanity and generous warmth of disposition he becomes the golden link which binds society together. Among his equals his good nature and good will display themselves by kindness in doing kindly offices; by forbearance and considerate attention to their just rights, never allowing selfishness to warp his sense of their deserts; by a generous forethought; by averseness to offend or give pain, and an equal solicitude to impart pleasure. Full of the amenities of life, and impressed with a sense of his own weakness, he is dim-sighted to the foibles of his fellow-mortals, while keenly alive to merit, esteeming men of worth whatsoever their station or religion. On coming in contact with a youth full of noble resolves, far from depressing him in his high aspirations, he gives every possible encouragement and so nerves him to his task. Then, being sincerely and deeply interested in the welfare of his poorer brethren, he is ever seeking to ameliorate their condition and promote their moral and intellectual development. He allows neither theory nor speculation to pass for actual knowledge, but goes among the poor to judge for himself, and learn what best tends to their worldly interests. He thus becomes enabled to suggest expedients for decreasing their expenses and multiplying their comforts, and easily induces them to follow his wise and judicious counsel by winning alike their confidence and respect. Acknowledging that "the earth and the fulness thereof" are for the benefit of all God's creatures and not for individuals only, he wisely uses the portion which has fallen to his lot. Shunning superfluities and husbanding his resources, he is enabled to give with a liberal hand and cheerful spirit, glad of the opportunity of testifying to the great Giver of all good, through some self-abnegation, his sense of gratitude for the share of blessings he is permitted to enjoy. The philanthropist never stops short at the rigid boundary line of duty or justice, but goes in advance of the wants and wishes of those around him; to the best of his powers he stays all contention and strife, is the strenuous advocate of peace and good will among men, and never sanctions, by his presence, acts of violence and wrong. He is ever studying how best to apply a balm to the wounded spirit, soothe the sad, sorrowing heart, and soften the anguish of despair. He endeavours to moderate or dispel prejudices, and is never hasty in condemning or drawing rash inductions, when such would tend to lower one man in the estimation of another. He is ever earnest in the cause of charity and performs his pious mission publicly, not shunning observation as if he were committing a crime, nor courting attention as if doing more than a duty. Assiduous in his vocation, he manifests his zeal openly, so that others seeing may be induced to follow and emulate him in his laudable course.

Such, then, is the true spirit of Benevolence and piety, and he who thus acts will assuredly have a constant source of happiness in the consciousness of duty performed, and a glowing sense of satisfaction in seeing his own smile reflected in the world's mirror. He will feel at his heart's core the full truth of the line of the poet, "To bless is to be blessed", for the remembrance of every good deed done and happiness conferred will endure to cheer his declining years, and give that hope and confidence which, with angel's wings, will waft his spirit up to the realms of everlasting life.

The following PRECEPTS may serve to encourage and stimulate us to acts of benevolence by showing how prolific in rich blessings are the fair heavenly fruits of sympathy, love, and kindness alike to the dispenser and the recipient, how certainly such heartfelt acts will find acceptance at the throne of our gracious and benign Ruler. Thus in Prov. xxii, 9, "He that hath a bountiful eye shall be blessed, for he giveth of his bread to the poor." In ch. xix, 17, "He that hath pity upon the poor lendeth unto the Lord, and that which he hath given will He repay him again." At ch. xiv, 21, "He that despiseth his neighbour sinneth, but he that hath mercy on the poor, happy is he;" and ch. xi, 27, "He that diligently seeketh good procureth favour, but he that seeketh mischief it shall come unto him:" again,"'The liberal soul shall be made fat." Then in Eccles. xi, " Cast thy bread upon the waters, for thou shalt find it after many days." "Give a portion to seven and also to eight." But much more is demanded of us, for we are told at ch. xxv, 21, "If thine enemy be hungry give him bread to eat, and if he be thirsty give him water to drink, and the Lord shall reward thee." We next turn to Deuteronomy xv, which is especially devoted to this subject, and inculcates a universal system of benevolence. The following verses are every way worthy of consideration. "Thou shalt not harden thine heart nor shut thine hand from thy brother, but *open it wide to the poor and to the needy*, giving them sufficient for their wants. Beware that thine eye be not evil against them and thou lendest nothing, so that they cry unto the Lord against thee, and it be a sin unto thee". "Thou shalt surely give and thine heart not be grieved, because that of these things the Lord will bless thee in all thy ways and all thou puttest thine hand unto". But as no man can make any pretence to the virtue of Benevolence whose conduct is not primarily based on strict principles of justice, this high moral duty is repeatedly enjoined throughout the sacred volume. The following quotations on this subject may here suffice. Prov. iii, 27 : " Withhold not good from them to whom it is due, when it is in the power of thine hands to do it. Say not to thy neighbour, go and come again, to-morrow I will give, when thou hast it by thee". "Devise not evil against thy neighbour, seeing he dwelleth securely by thee". In a word, if we would secure for ourselves ever-recurring gratification together with the love and good will of those around us, we have but to act in accordance with the injunction of Isaiah, xxxv : " Strengthen the weak hands and confirm the feeble knees ; say to them that are of a fearful heart: Be strong, fear not, for then shall joy and gladness arise, sorrow and sighing flee away", while in the daily intercourse of life we should bear vividly in remembrance that " Love covereth all sins", and also that " Pleasant words are as an honeycomb, sweet to the soul and health to the bones".

EXAMPLES.—Charity, justice, and love, which form the basis of Benevolence and are the very essence of virtue, stand out in bold relief in the numerous biblical characters which serve as models for imitation, from among which may well be selected NEHEMIAH. This conscientious and self-denying ruler and prophet nobly declined to receive the allowance which had been granted to former governors, so that he might not be burdensome to the people on whom "the bondage was heavy"; yet he contrived to afford a generous hospitality to all, welcoming at his table alike the heathen and the stranger. Nor was his example lost upon the people, for when he urged them to "send portions unto those for whom nothing is prepared", they freely complied, "hushing their grief and making the joy of the Lord their strength".

Again, the disinterested kindness of REBECCA at the well betokens a truly benevolent disposition, and deserves particular attention. We read, "And the servant ran to meet her and said, Let me, I pray thee, drink a little water from thy pitcher";* she hastened to let it down and gave him drink, and then, in the goodness of her heart, said, "I will draw water for thy camels also," which she did, "until they had done drinking". How can we sufficiently admire this strikingly practical proceeding, whereby Rebecca was enabled to show her goodwill and reverence towards the aged and wearied traveller. His being a stranger only made her the more solicitous to oblige, and heartily setting herself to the self-imposed yet arduous task, she ceased not her labour until she had fulfilled that benevolent intent which a less kindly nature would have shrunk from performing.

The few words which passed between BOAZ and his reapers, related in ch. ii of the Book of Ruth, may well serve as a lesson to master and servant, employer and employed. The virtuous Boaz must have been ever considerate to his dependants, for them to have reciprocated his kindly greeting with such evident warmth. A mutual good understanding must assuredly have subsisted between them, redounding to the benefit of both parties. The master's cordial and pious salute of "the Lord be with you" clearly emanated from the purest and most enlightened benevolence, while the ready response of "the Lord bless thee" could be no set form of speech, but a spontaneous outburst of gratitude and respectful love. The generous conduct of Boaz to Ruth on her first visit, before he could possibly have conceived any tender

* Gen. xxiv, 17.

feeling towards her, further demonstrates how benevolent was the disposition of this great and mighty, this worthy ancestor of David. His words were words of gentle courtesy, his acts full of kindness and consideration. That Ruth was a stranger was sufficient inducement for him to offer succour, thus he bid her glean in his field only, and, on being made acquainted with her admirable conduct towards Naomi, he bestowed the heart-warming meed of praise which virtue ever willingly concedes to virtue.

Lastly, ELISHA, with a heart overflowing with sympathy and love for poor and rich, for friend and foe, never failed during the whole period of his mission to manifest those sentiments both by word and deed. Thus, when the King of Israel demanded if he should slay the vanquished bands of Syria, Elisha replied, "'Thou shalt not smite them: wouldst thou smite those whom thou hast taken captive with the sword and the bow? set bread and water before them that they may eat and drink and go to their master".* Again, feeling deeply grateful for the kindness he had received at the hands of the Shunammite, he was not satisfied till he could do her a service, as the following words imply, "Behold, thou hast been careful for us, what can I do for thee? wouldst thou be spoken for to the King or the Captain of the host?"† and when he found she could not be induced to demand anything of him, he asked the advice of his servant as to "what he should do to give her pleasure?" and at once gratified the secret wish of her heart through his powerful intercession with the Supreme. Then again, we find the prophet lending a sympathising ear to the plaint of the poor widow whose sons would be torn from her to become bondsmen unless she was able to pay her debts, and at her appeal Elisha not only gave present relief, but in loving kindness provided her with sufficient for the future wants of herself and sons.

Such worthy teachings should make apt disciples and warm the hearts of all to acts of goodness and benevolence.

* II Kings vi, 22. † II Kings iv, 13.

PARENTAL DUTY.

Gen. xviii, 19, "*For I know him that he will command his children, and they will keep the way of the Lord.*"

THE self-acquired is ever the most prized. That which we have made our own through labour of hand or brain far surpasses in our estimation all adventitious gifts. Now the knowledge of the Supreme possessed by ABRAHAM was attained through no fortuitous circumstance, but by the mere force of will. He had set himself sedulously to cultivate his mental faculties and reasoning powers, thence passing at one bound the deep gulf which separates ignorance from knowledge, a glorious light shed its full radiance on his understanding, and the One Only God, the great Framer of creation, stood revealed to Him in all His Omnipotence. Treasuring this conviction, this fundamental truth, above all else, deep and earnest must have been his solicitude that it should be preserved in its full integrity and transmitted through his beloved son as an imperishable inheritance to future generations. To effect this, he must have earnestly sought to instil into the youthful mind of Isaac those holy and pious sentiments towards the great Father of All which had become so firmly rooted in his own. He will have portrayed in the most glowing colours the glorious attributes of the Supreme, and taken every suitable opportunity of infusing into the heart of his son deep, fervent love towards the wise and gracious Governor of the Universe. Most certainly the moral training and practical example of the worthy patriarch were not lost upon his child, as the few prominent incidents in ISAAC's peaceful life amply demonstrate; indeed, the first and all-important trial to which he was subjected alone suffices to prove this. What but the most ready obedience, founded on filial love on the one hand, and a trusting faith in the Omniscient on the other, would have prompted him to acquiesce in the sacrifice of which he was himself to be the victim. "God will provide Himself with a burnt offering" had been Abraham's response to his son's inquiry when on their way to Mount Abarim, and that was enough for the pious youth. He proceeded onwards, perfectly satisfied with this brief and somewhat evasive answer. When the fatal moment arrived which revealed to him where God's choice had fallen, there could have been no demur. Without a murmur must he have submitted to the terrible fate which appeared to be impending, for we must bear in mind that he was no longer a child, and, with will unfettered, was free to resist the stern decree which doomed him to an early death. But no, the lesser, yet devoted, love he bore his earthly father, the greater, how great a love! that lifted his soul to his heavenly Father conquered every other feeling, and even triumphed over the natural desire of self-preservation. Thus stretched on the altar, he unresistingly awaited the stroke which was to sever him from every tie that youth holds most dear. A brave spirit truly. Faith has had a host of martyrs, and he bid fair to rank foremost among them but for God's interposition.

Thus it is clear Isaac's feelings were in complete unison with those of his father, and, moreover, that he was a willing party to his sacrifice, else he must have considered Abraham's conduct cruel and unnatural, and therefore been inclined rather to hate than regard him with so devoted a love as he evinced throughout his entire life. Thence we may surely conclude that, like his beloved sire, he had devoted his whole soul to do God's bidding, and only reverenced the father the more for the very act which might well have called forth the reverse sentiment in a less religious mind. In Sarah also he must have had a judicious and devoted parent. The training of the heart depends mostly on maternal care, and that his mother was tender and loving is sufficiently proved even by the faint sketch of Isaac's life given in the Bible. On her death how deeply must he have felt the bereavement, for it was not until his marriage with Rebecca, some three years later, that "he was comforted." Now grief that could last so long, clouding the bright sunshine of youth, speaks well for both mother and son; a sweet communion of feeling must have subsisted between them, she must have been his companion as well as guide, for he sought no other loving tie while she was at his side. Then throughout the whole of his married life Isaac proved himself an affectionate and devoted husband, his heart never swerving from its true allegiance, although Rebecca long remained childless. And afterwards, when a change was at hand, we find her seeking to ascertain the cause of her strange, critical position as a mother by "enquiring of the Lord." Truly these facts clearly prove that the righteous Abraham had fully succeeded in drawing the heart of his son, and through him that of his wife, in love and faith towards the Lord. But the benefit accruing from a religious education did not cease with Isaac personally. Faithful to his glorious mission, and rich in the legacy bequeathed him—the knowledge of the true God—he was no less anxious than his parent to transmit it unimpaired to his descendants. Thus did Isaac happily follow his father's example, bidding Jacob seek a wife from the house of "his mother's brother," feeling convinced that a daughter of that race which had some acquaintance with the spiritual religion of Abraham would never draw the heart of his son from the living God as might one of the idolatrous daughters of Canaan, but would be likely to follow her husband in the worship of the Lord as had Rebecca before her. And thus it proved, for while Esau took to wife the daughters of Heth, "which was a grief unto Isaac and Rebecca," who thereby not only saw the labour of years frustrated, but also discerned a perversity of heart auguring evil consequences, their judicious proceeding with regard to Jacob was attended with perfect success. His wife, herself adoring the true God, brought up her children to love and serve Him, and through them the knowledge spread over every region of the habitable globe. Heirs as are all men to that glorious light of truth which first beamed in the mind of Abraham, we must feel how much is due to the judicious parental teachings of the three patriarchs and their wives; indeed, but for their care in propagating the true faith, light would have arisen only to set again, leaving idolatry, with its vile and degrading superstition, to spread incalculable mischief, like a blight, over the land.

Thus each parent should reflect on this practical lesson, and strive to profit by the moral it offers. Let religious principles, founded on love and fear of God, be early inculcated by the pious father, by the tender, devoted mother, and they may then fairly hope to see their children grow up to manhood and womanhood rich in virtues which will do honour to them, and become, in the words of Scripture, "the crown of their old age."

Life of itself is neither a prize nor a blank; but it may be made either one or the other, and it is surely incumbent on parents, who under Providence have given life, also to give it value. When they have sown the seeds of wisdom, virtue, and religion, tended their development and brought them to flourish in full luxuriance, then will they have crowned their work and made the life bestowed both a blessing and a prize. Just in proportion as the father endows his child with these priceless gems will that boon be appreciated and call forth the grateful tribute of filial affection. It would be difficult to over-estimate the good which parents can confer on their offspring by sedulously and conscientiously discharging those moral obligations which love prompts and duty imperatively demands. They hold the key to the heart of their offspring, and woe to them if they enter not that chamber to fill it with rich imperishable treasures and denude it of all that is spurious and noxious. Great and serious is their responsibility, for the soul of the child is in their care. It is a blank sheet on which the parent may inscribe what characters he pleases, and surely to write all that is good and fair therein can be no very arduous task. Only let devoted, heartfelt love be given to the work, and all will be smooth and easy.

Now the richest possible blessing a father can secure for his child when he shall arrive at man's estate is "a sound mind in a sound body," and under Providence this depends on his watchful care, his wise provision for each natural want, and his discernment in staying at once all physical abuse of power; next, on the attention he gives to his son's moral culture; finally, on the interest and solicitude he evinces and the trouble he takes in developing his intellectual capabilities. No scheme for the training of youth could be efficient that should ignore any one of these essentials; but when they receive equal attention, and are brought to work together in perfect harmony, then will education accomplish its desired end, and parents may look forward with reasonable hope to see their children become happy, enlightened, and virtuous men.

A few words, then, as regards each of these points. And to begin with the *physical*. Here the great aim to be kept constantly in view is that there should be no excess in the use of the natural powers; highly desirable as it is to strengthen and develop them, that should be effected only through their steady employment. Irreparable injury is apt to result from violent forcing, and even exercise will only conduce to health and vigour when taken in moderation. A wise discretion, therefore, in this particular, coupled with a mother's natural care and vigilance, a judicious foresight in providing the accessories which help to preserve the vital functions in a sound and healthy state, and, above all, an avoidance of evil courses, as of all excesses, and youth may justly hope to attain a robust, vigorous manhood, and finally secure a happy, cheerful old age.

Next, as to the *moral* culture. If love of God be made the mainspring of life, and love of virtue the ruling desire, little will be wanting to make the character perfect. To this end the parents must address themselves to the heart of their child as well as to its understanding. It behoves them to point out God's infinite goodness, for thus will it be brought to love and serve Him and do His biddings with a cheerful, devout spirit. They must educate its kindly feelings, and continually draw attention to objects suitable to engage and exercise them with benefit to others as to itself. They must gain the entire affection of its heart, so that when the period of adolescence has arrived the youth will never take any serious step in life without their concurrence. They should strictly watch any doubtful or evil propensities, and, above all, use their best endeavours to guard their cherished offspring from temptation. Forewarned is forearmed. A healthy, bracing, moral atmosphere at home, opening the heart, as it must do, to pure and pleasurable emotions, will best serve to check unruly desires, strengthen the sense of shame and dishonour, and stay youth from entering the abodes of infamy, impiety, and vice. Thus let the cultivation of the heart be ever a paramount object; let us draw out every latent virtue, pray *with* our child as well as *for* him, and especially seek to season his mind with devotion, that breastplate and shield which God Himself has given to ward off evil and enable us to resist those unruly inclinations and passions which generally crop up in early youth.

Lastly, respecting the education of the mind. This commences almost in infancy, and devolves especially on the loving mother, the educator of nature's own appointment. Habits early formed take vigorous root, and are always difficult to eradicate; they become a second nature. Thence the importance that they *should be such in the child as we could approve of in the man.* But real education begins with the development of youth, when principles can be understood and inculcated by means of the reasoning powers, when the book of nature can be read and God's beautiful and wondrous works appreciated; also when the will is formed and requires to be governed and controlled. It is then so much depends on the example of the father, as also on the personal interest and trouble he takes in the cultivation of the intellectual faculties of his child. Youth has everything to learn, and if the mind and heart be filled with all that is useful and good we leave no room for what is spurious and deleterious. Thus let the parent teach through nature in the country, at home through well-chosen works, as well as easy and instructive conversation, in the world through lucid and kindly observations on men and manners; in a word, let him cultivate and expand the mind by every devisable means, in accordance with the youth's capacity for receiving knowledge. Intellect is God's distinctive gift to man, therefore should be highly appreciated and used nobly, wisely, for thus only may we in some degree repay the debt we owe to the great and gracious Giver. Now, when the youth has learnt the art of thinking justly and deeply, when he willingly throws his energies into all his studies, freely practices his mental faculties and takes pleasure in culling the treasures of wisdom bequeathed to us by past ages, then will the steps of the young student be rapidly progressive and the task of the parent become light and easy. But it should be borne in mind that a wise economy in the labour of the brain is necessary; if excessive, it cannot be otherwise than injurious; the mental, like the physical, powers are apt to become impaired by being overstrained. Thus it behoves parents to introduce into their home such pleasures and recreations as may serve to relieve the wearied mind and afford healthful occupation. Accomplishments, such as music and painting; games, such as chess and puzzles— which, while they amuse, draw upon the powers of memory and reflection—also problems, historical anecdotes, biographical sketches, and even handiwork, are eminently attractive, and, while serving to divert the mind of youth, will be of essential service when they move in general society later in life. Thus, while the judicious parent will offer every incentive to good and virtuous deeds, he will not neglect to cultivate his child's taste for the fine arts nor fail to give him a relish for literary pursuits. He will train him to habits and inclinations which must promote his happiness, and, being earnestly solicitous that his life should end well, will therefore strive to make it begin well.

One all-essential point, which no father may overlook, is that youth requires encouragement. Few are those who will not be elated by praise or depressed by blame, especially when proceeding from beloved and respected parents; indeed, to the sensitive mind there is no such incentive to good as the former, while the fear of censure tends greatly to arrest the tide of evil passions. It is, however, necessary that the parent should keenly study the disposition of his child, if he would be successful in drawing forth all the good fruits which judicious commendation is calculated to yield; further, he must be able to comprehend and enter into the generous, enthusiastic feelings of his tender charge. A harsh, untimely word has often checked the warmth of youth, and frozen up noble impulses and high aspirations. Nor may the parent look carelessly upon his child's first act of self-denial, or on his first effort to conquer the rising gusts of temper and evil passions, but should express his appreciation and approval, thereby stimulating to like self-combat whenever similar temptations may assail. Youth is rarely callous, but we are apt to make it so, if we deny the merited commendation to good deeds.

Now this mild and discreet treatment is the more imperative that it will surely tend to prevent the necessity for coercive measures, which should only be adopted if all others fail. When once the principles of right and wrong are deeply impressed upon the mind, and the conscience duly attuned to the sense of shame and dishonour, youth may easily be trained up to manhood without corporeal punishment. Blows and unkind words only harden the heart, while love makes all things easy. If there be habits to discard, desires to suppress, or passions to combat, a gentle, hopeful word works wonders; it has a magic power with youth; the young heart 'thrills to it, and yearns to show how fully the good opinion of its elders is appreciated. But encouragement must extend to everything in which the child is concerned. Earnestness of purpose is necessary to make a successful man, and must be carried not only into every pursuit, but into every pleasure. It is an important adjunct to sports as well as to study, and will increase the aptitude for business in after-life. The young should be continually reminded of the axiom, that "What is worth doing at all is worth doing well"; for the endeavour to excel once made a decided habit with the child, it will cling to the man and prosper all his efforts. Thence it behoves the parent to leave something for his son to accomplish; if he take away all motive for self-exertion, he will dry up the very spring whence much happiness should be derived. A wise father will not desire to bequeath to his child more than a sufficiency, after providing him with some career or honourable profession, for which he has been prepared by a fitting education, and which, if followed sedulously, will supply him with any desired luxuries or superfluities in mature years. This will be an ample legacy, if the youth has been brought up to feel that *self*-dependence is the high road to *in*dependence; and, further, that a truly pious life is always a happy and useful one.

It is now well to ascertain why parents so frequently fail in bringing up their children "in the way they should go." The fault rarely arises from want of love, for, whatever may be the failings of mankind in general, this is not one of them. The human heart ever yearns with tender emotion towards its offspring, and would "do it good and not evil." Now the first thing we observe on lifting the domestic curtain is, that the very love, which is so well calculated to effect good when it goes hand in hand with parental duty, but too frequently works in direct opposition to its dictates, causing innumerable evils. Take, in the first instance, the spoilt child, who, through the over-indulgence of its parents, has never been subjected to judicious training. The human mind contains within itself the germs of some evil with a large proportion of good, and, according as the one or the other is developed in youth, so will it preponderate in maturer years. If no restraint has been imposed on the child, but, on the contrary, its every inclination gratified, evil and not good may be apprehended when the age of puberty and manhood is reached. When temptation assails, how feeble will be the resistance of the man whose temper and passions have been left uncurbed in youth. Indeed, he will too surely drug for himself the cup of happiness, and, as he drinks deeper and deeper of the poison of forbidden pleasures, so will he become less and less sensible to the purest and highest delights of his nature. Thus, while inflicting irreparable and lasting injury on himself, he will not fail to embitter the lives of those who, in their blind love, have worked him incalculable mischief. And if over-indulgence be a folly and a wrong when the object of a doating love be an only child, it is positively criminal to select one out of a large family on whom to confer especial favours. It not only injures that one, but sows the seeds of discontent in the hearts of the others, and tends to produce the rank fruits of envy and hatred. Thus it behoves a parent to repress all such feelings as would lead him to show any preference. Partiality is the death of love. The very favourite, who escapes merited punishment or has his requests granted on insufficient grounds, will testify but little, if any, gratitude, self-conceit claiming such indulgences as its due, while what must be the feelings of the less favoured ones?

Children, like men, rebel against injustice; and the parent who is capable of it will certainly fail to secure the respect or love of any one member of his household, and often live to be a repentant witness to the growth of ill-will within his domestic circle, and the innumerable evils which infallibly accrue from family dissensions. Next, the training of parents often proves of little avail, through not being of a practical character. The young must be led as much by example as by exhortation; and, further, they must feel that the precepts enjoined proceed from the heart. Children are peculiarly clear-sighted and impressible. It is only when a father shows, by his acts as well as by his words, that he appreciates knowledge, delights in virtue, and loves the Almighty *with a devout and thankful spirit*, that he may reasonably expect his offspring to participate in his sentiments and emotions. Truly a parent must himself be that which he would wish to make his child, since example exercises a far more powerful influence than precept. Youth requires a standard of imagined perfection, and well is it when that standard is found in the child's natural guardians. Virtue can attain no vigorous growth unless it be matured in a pure, bracing, moral atmosphere; but, if this be amply supplied, the parent will not have to exclaim in the metaphorical language of Isaiah, " I looked that it should bring forth grapes, and lo! it brought forth wild grapes."

The other minor, yet all-important, causes, which prove detrimental to the proper rearing of a family, may be easily enumerated. First, if the parent does not give sufficient heed to the peculiar disposition of his child, nor read its heart aright, he may be led to form a harsh judgment, and possibly use coercive measures when one word of kindness would be more efficient. Next, much mischief may ensue if he fail to give due attention to the individual bent of its mind, seek out its predominant faculties for the purpose of developing them, and watch growing inclinations, checking with a vigorous hand those which are untimely or noxious;

further, if he seek not the confidence of his child, practically evincing his warm sympathy by entering kindly into all its petty cares and testifying his chagrin when having to take cognizance of its faults, and administer reproof; or again, if he stifles at its birth any good resolve either by one cold word or look of incredulity, if he turn aside confidence by the show of stern displeasure or inexorable anger on light occasions, thereby leading to a first deception or falsehood —fatal precedent to a host of others. Finally, if he fail to implant high principles and throws a false light on those follies of the world which surely lead to vice and irreligion. These are all sad, fatal faults on the part of parents, whose paramount duty it is to guard a precious life from the cradle and nurture the soul for heaven. Now, according to the manner in which we have performed these obligations we may expect to reap good or evil fruits; indeed, this life offers few greater pleasures than that of being the parent of dutiful, wise, and religious children, who tenderly love each other, who command respect for their virtues, and steadily rise to wealth and station through their own individual exertions and abilities. It is the triumph of love, the crown justly earned by a "labour of love." Then reverse the picture, and we shall find that neglected paternal duty invariably entails a sad retrospect, more especially to the father who is conscious that the vicious conduct of the youth and the blighted life of the man are but the natural effects of his own culpable weakness and negligence. Had he only reflected that "the child is father to the man," and striven to make the child what the man should be, he would have escaped many an after-pang. The mischief done by his dereliction of duty or by his bad example is irreparable; he cannot even feel himself entitled to respect or love, and certainly does not command either. He will find the past beyond recal, and may deem himself fortunate if he see not penury enter his abode and dishonour cast a lasting stain on his escutcheon.

In strong contrast stands the virtuous and religious parent, who, in the decline of life, finds himself surrounded by devoted loving children, eager to do his will, and minister to his comfort and happiness. Their gratitude will best proclaim that he has performed his duty towards them; their filial veneration will demonstrate that his example has been appreciated, and his moral lessons treasured in their innermost hearts. And when his end draws nigh he will have no anxiety as to their future. He has brought them up to seek strength in mutual love, and to mingle the duties of life with its pleasures, to value virtue and godliness above every earthly possession. Why need he fear for their welfare after having imbued their minds with every high and honourable principle? He bestows his blessing on them, and leaves them in the Hands of the Almighty, to whom he commits his own soul in the fulness of love and faith. All parents who thus teach will assuredly not teach in vain. Their children will not only mourn for them as protectors, but as counsellors and guides, and will consider the memory of their exemplary lives as the greatest treasure they could inherit. It is such parents whom children delight to honour and will hold in perpetual remembrance.

PRECEPTS inculcating parental *affection* find no place in Scripture, they would be superfluous. None but the hardened or grossly selfish could need exhortation on this score, and with such, a mild form of admonition would be altogether inoperative. No rebuke or even command would avail where nature had failed in drawing the heart of the parent in tender love towards his own offspring. But it is otherwise with regard to parental *duty*—which needs both counsel and guidance. Thence precepts referring thereto are readily found in the Holy Volume, together with the important lesson which teaches in what it properly consists. Thus in Deuteronomy vi, 5, we are bid "To love God with all our heart, with all our soul, and with all our might", and to keep his word ever in our heart; a command immediately followed by the words, v. 7, "And thou shalt teach them diligently unto thy children, and shall talk of them when thou sittest in thine house, when thou walkest by the way, when thou liest down, and when thou risest up", evidently implying that to become suitable preceptors of youth, we must show a good example, whilst at the same time making religion the constant subject of sweet communion at the domestic hearth. To the pious parent this must be a continual source of delight; himself impressed with a sense of the Divine attributes, and acknowledging with a thankful spirit God's gracious providence, he will, by the outpouring of his own devout reflections and exalted sentiments strive to awaken an echo in the tender loving heart of his child. To this end the teachings of the Book of Proverbs will essentially contribute, and especially the fourth chapter. Therein Solomon, the wise monarch of Israel, shows what instruction he received from his excellent parent, how he was incited to study the law, to shun evil, to put faith in God, to be good and holy. We read, "I was my father's son, tender and only beloved in the sight of my mother. He said unto me, let thine heart retain my words; keep my commandments and live. *Get wisdom, forsake her not and she shall preserve thee.* Take fast hold of instruction, for she is thy life. *Enter not into the paths of the wicked, and go not in the way of evil men*". And again, v. 20, "My son, incline thine ear unto my sayings, let them not depart, for they are thy life and *health to thy flesh. Keep thy heart with all diligence,* for out of it are the issues of life. *Ponder the path of thy feet,* and let all thy ways be established. Turn not to the right hand nor to the left, remove thy foot from evil". Also, ch. vi, "My son, keep thy father's commandment and forsake not the law of thy mother, when thou goest it shall lead thee, when thou sleepest it shall keep thee, for the commandment is a lamp and the law is light, and reproofs of instruction are the way of life". Next, as to the manner of educating the child, we read, ch. xxix, "Correct thy son and he shall give thee rest, yea, he shall give delight unto thy soul", again, "the rod and reproof give wisdom", showing that punishment, or at least the fear of it, may occasionally be a necessary ingredient in the training of youth. Yet either of these should be availed of only in the smallest possible degree, since proving highly mischievous the moment it is superfluous, while it may frequently be superseded by an appeal either to the understanding or the heart. Then in Prov. xxii we are told to "Train up a child in the way he should go, and when he is old he will not depart from it". The twenty-eighth chapter of Isaiah, v. 10, is also well worthy of the parent's consideration, as showing the best method of giving serious advice and imparting instruction without harrassing or fatiguing the young enquiring mind. It runs thus: "Precept must be upon precept; precept upon precept; line upon line; line upon line; here a little and there a little". Next, we read at the twenty-third chapter of Proverbs, "The father of the righteous shall greatly rejoice", a reward justly earned by the parent who has successfully striven to bring up his children in the path of virtue. Truly, he is a happy and righteous father who can say in the words of Prov. xxiii, 26: "My son, give me thine heart, and *let thine eyes observe my ways, for I walk in the fear of the Lord*".

EXAMPLES which serve as warnings will weigh with many who disregard all such admonitions and wilfully silence the inward monitor when it would speak of duties unfulfilled. Nothing can be better calculated to work a reform in an indifferent parent and induce him to perform his positive obligations than a review of historical facts, wherein the most dire effects are seen to flow as a natural consequence, alike to parent and child, from a dereliction of duty on the part of the former. Thence Scripture speaks principally through this medium, the Book of KINGS especially. Most of the desolating wars in Judea, with their many attendant miseries, are to be attributed to the badly disposed and corrupt monarchs of Israel, who for the most part fell into evil courses from want of good practical training, and also through the vile revolting example of their immediate ancestors.

As a first example, we may take REHOBOAM, who lost his throne through the display of the same cruel rigour and injustice which had characterised the latter years of his father's reign. From the time King SOLOMON, through the influence of his numerous idolatrous wives, allowed his heart to be turned from the living God, he no longer sought the welfare of the nation, except in so far as it ministered to his own ambitious views. His son was tempted to pursue a like course, for thus spake Rehoboam to the people, "Whereas my father did lade you with a heavy yoke, I will add to your yoke; my father chastised you with whips, but I will chastise you with scorpions".* He however found out the gravity of his error when too late, and, although he resorted to force in the hope of retrieving it, the only result was a civil war, which for long years cast a blight over the once happy land. Next, we may mention the wicked King Abijam, who *"walked in all the sins of his father* who had gone before him"; then Ahaziah, who "did evil in the sight of the Lord, walking in the sinful ways of his father, and *according to the evil counsel of his mother*, thereby provoking the Lord's anger. Many others follow, and it is to be observed that while the mother's name is always mentioned, either directly or by inference, she is generally represented as the moving cause of the wickedness of her son.

Among the good kings who present us with a reverse picture is AMAZIAH, who "did that which is right in the sight of the Lord and according to all things as did Joash, his father". And again, the good kings, Jehoshaphat,

* 1 Kings xii, 11.

Azariah, Josiah, who each *"walked in the way that their father had done before them"*.

Many of the misfortunes which befel King DAVID occurred through the ill-behaviour of his sons, especially of Absolom; and the affection he lavished on one so undeserving of his love only too plainly indicates that this beautiful youth was a spoilt child. We even find Joab, his General, presuming thus to speak to the sorrowing monarch, "I perceive that if Absolom had lived and all we had died this day, then it had pleased thee well!" From this and other minor incidents related concerning David, it is reasonable to suppose that the discord and rancorous enmity within his home, as well as the dissensions without, were, in a great measure, the result of the difference injudiciously shown by him towards his children, in this case assuredly a most unjust preference.

The history of ELI offers a further warning, since it is certain he must have ill-discharged the sacred duty of a parent. Had he instructed his children from their youth to know God, it is hardly possible that we should have been told, "Now the sons of Eli were sons of Belial, they knew not the Lord".* Also, that he failed to maintain the authority which it behoves a parent to exercise is clearly indicated by the words "I, the Lord, have told Eli that I will judge his house for ever for the iniquity which he knoweth; because his sons made themselves vile and *he restrained them not.*" It is sad that one who evidently loved his God and put faith in Him, should have acted so reprehensibly as a father. He must have felt this himself when he thus answered the youthful Samuel (who, as a messenger of God, had told him what was to befal his house), "It is the Lord, let Him do what seemeth Him good".

Turning to a character of quite another stamp, we find JOB, as a parent, adopting a proceeding which was eminently successful in binding together each member of his family in

* II Samuel ii, 12.

bonds of affection. He assembled them at the expiration of their days of feasting and *home rejoicings* that he might sanctify them. How greatly this must have warmed their hearts in mutual love! nor was this all, for Job did not feel that he had performed his duty towards his children till he had "offered burnt offerings according to the number of each of them", for, said he, "It may be that my sons have sinned and cursed God in their hearts; this did he continually." Such an admirable example of the fulfilment of parental duty is well worthy of being held in remembrance, and he who thus discharges it may joyfully exclaim in the words of Isaiah, "The living, the living, he shall praise Thee, O Lord, as I do this day; *the father to the children* shall make known Thy truth".

INDIVIDUAL MERIT.

Gen. xviii, 32, "*And the Lord said, I will not destroy it for ten's sake.*"

THERE are certainly no two characters in Scripture which present a stronger contrast than those of ABRAHAM and his nephew LOT, nor, when carefully compared, offer a more instructive lesson. Both had attained a knowledge of the One only God, both were in a position that might have enabled them to disseminate the glorious truth, and through the tenor of their lives prove the loveliness of virtue to the benighted people among whom they moved; yet the former alone, giving full scope to his energies, effectively served the cause of moral progress and conferred on posterity an imperishable boon. The noble-hearted patriarch deemed it a privilege to subserve the general good and work out the will of the Supreme; not so, however, the selfish, narrow-minded, and worldly ambitious Lot, who, being nowise disposed to consult the welfare of others, turned wilfully aside from the glorious career which lay before him, and thereby not only proved himself impotent for good, but even brought down positive evil on his own immediate household.

Various important incidents in the lives of both uncle and nephew throw their respective characters into bold relief, and serve to show how superior was the one, how ignoble the other. Abraham proved himself all-powerful for good, he made himself respected among the surrounding nations, and indeed was held in such high honour that even Abimelech, King of the Philistines, submitted to be reproved by the patriarch, and acted in accordance with his demands, while he also entered into a covenant of peace and goodwill with him at Beersheba, for thus spake this king: " Swear that according to the kindness I have done unto thee thou shalt do unto me, to my son and son's son, and to the land where thou hast sojourned". And again, the monarch, in conjunction with his chief captain, thus addressed Abraham: "We know that God is with thee in all that thou doest"; words which suffice to explain the power he possessed among the heathens, and further show how well he had succeeded in conveying to the king's mind, as also to that of his subjects, a knowledge of the Supreme. His meeting with the King of Sodom, on which occasion he refused in a self-denying spirit to receive aught at his hands, as well as his conference with Melchizedek, High Priest and King of Salem, gives yet additional evidence as to the esteem in which he was held throughout the surrounding countries. Now, while thus respected or feared by the most powerful rulers, he was devotedly loved and revered by his numerous household. Mark the words of his servant to the youthful Rebecca at the well, "Blessed be the Lord God, who hath not left destitute my master of His mercy and His truth; the Lord led me in the way". While thus exhibiting the same trustfulness in God's manifold mercies as did Abraham, he showed how deeply he felt beholden to that master; indeed, his mission was characterised throughout by intense devotion towards him. Then Isaac's dutiful conduct amply demonstrates how well he had been trained, while we find in Sarah the ever-loving and obedient wife. Thus was Abraham's a happy and united household. In no instance, however, was the patriarch more potent for good than in the case of his intercession with the Almighty in favour of Sodom and Gomorrah; indeed, had Lot only fulfilled his duty towards his fellow-creatures, walking in the footsteps of his uncle, those cities would assuredly have been saved.

But as we review the conduct of Lot, it becomes only too evident that here, as in every other instance throughout his entire life, he proved himself utterly impotent for good. Now, be it observed that at the time of Abraham's intercession for Sodom and Gomorrah, Lot had been residing in the vicinity of those towns for some years, and although he must have been an eye-witness to the corrupt practices and disgusting idolatry of the inhabitants, he not only gave no thought to the withdrawal of his family from an atmosphere contaminated by crime and debauch, but even placed its members in direct communication with the depraved population by taking sons-in-law from its midst. Yet Lot had evidently not entirely forsaken the Lord, since, had he turned his heart to idolatry, he would surely not have received the marked favour of Heaven by being rescued from the impending fate, even for his noble uncle's sake. Nevertheless, the ardent zeal and faith of Abraham were totally wanting in Lot. He sought not to impress the members of his household with the abhorrence he must himself have felt at the crimes which polluted the land, nor probably did he admonish them as to their evil courses. He had settled in one of the fertile districts which bordered the towns of Sodom and Gomorrah, with the ardent desire of amassing wealth through the fertility of its soil. All other considerations had become subordinate to this craving, and we cannot doubt that his avarice was for a time gratified, since his accumulated property sufficed to excite the cupidity of the five kings, who laid hands thereon, and would have carried it and despoiled him of it but for the kindly vigilance and determination of his valiant uncle. Yet this temporary reverse of fortune failed to work a change in him. Lot's was indeed a peculiarly defective character, wanting all those higher moral qualities which lend dignity to man and render him serviceable to his fellow-creatures. From the time of his ungrateful conduct to Abraham, when about quitting the roof which had so long sheltered him, till the final close of his brief history, there is a lack of any estimable trait, if we except that hospitality which was seldom wanting among an eastern people. Whatever his virtue, it was of a negative character. The *individual merit* he may have possessed was far too dim to shed a ray of light even within his own household, thus must have been utterly powerless to exercise a beneficial influence over a wider circle. What, then, availed his wealth, position, and superior knowledge? Had he by his example and by exhortation sought to draw his sons-in-law, and through them others of their nation, to a knowledge of the true God and a love of virtue, it may reasonably be supposed he would not have been altogether unsuccessful. Lot surely must have observed some indications of goodness in those to whom he was willing to entrust the happiness of his daughters, and felt some degree of security that such principles of virtue as he had inculcated in their minds would not be lost upon their husbands; but at this point his solicitude must have stopped short, since all goes to prove that when he afterwards saw them following the infamous courses of their nation, outraging every right principle and incurring the displeasure of Heaven, he offered not the faintest remonstrance. From this wilful disregard of duty ensued the most fatal consequences. Abraham's intercession became of no avail, since even ten righteous men were not to be found in the country where Lot and his family had so long resided! Being devoid of religious zeal and faith, he had not used his influence over his sons-in-law or any of the inhabitants to a good purpose, he had not imparted to them a knowledge of the Lord, nor do we find that he seconded the petition put up by Abraham appealing on their behalf to the mercy and loving kindness of the Supreme. Regardless of the welfare of the people among whom he had so long dwelt, he learnt of the catastrophe which was to befal them with the most callous and culpable indifference. His cold heart must have known little of human love; indeed, hardly one spark of right feeling and kindly sympathy could he have brought with him from the hearth where he had been so tenderly nurtured.

Such gross selfishness and utter dereliction of duty could

not fail to entail the heaviest penalty. From the moment Lot had to quit his home and leave behind him a portion of his family, he surely will have become a prey to remorse. He must have felt no little compunction, no little upbraiding of conscience, when, on bidding his sons-in-law follow him, saying, "Up, get you out of this place, for the Lord will destroy the city", he met with no filial response, but seemed unto them "as one that mocketh." He will then, if never before, have acknowledged to himself how signally he had failed in making himself respected, how great had been his omission in not adequately impressing those around him with the love and fear of God. He thus tasted the bitter fruits of his neglect, having now no power to save those whom he should most have cherished. But had he not also to leave behind him that wealth for which he had sacrificed so much? How loath he was thus to depart is shown in the following quotation: "And when the morning arose, then the angels hastened Lot, saying, Arise, take thy wife and thy two daughters who are here, lest they be consumed in the iniquity of the city; and *while he lingered the men laid hold of his hand and brought him forth,* and set him without the city, the Lord being merciful unto him".*
In order to preserve his life he had to relinquish his coveted wealth, a proceeding which evidently cost him no slight pang, since we find that even more than persuasion was necessary to induce its adoption. Moreover, he was to lose his wife, whose disobedience brought a judgment upon her. Thus bereft of fortune, without one friend, or even the pleasing consciousness of duties fulfilled, Lot had finally to retire to a cave, there to end his days, neither missed nor regretted by any fellow-mortal! A blighted life indeed was his, for it had been essentially a selfish one. Had his heart not been wrapped in self, he would so have loved his sons-in-law and some of the inhabitants with whom he associated as to put his soul into the good cause, and have said, I *must*

* Gen. xix, 15.

draw them from their vicious courses. Thus, and thus only, might he have proved himself the good parent and the good citizen.

Now the whole tenor of Lot's life bears evidence that, highly faulty as was his conduct, it proceeded rather from the sin of omission than of commission, yet such, being hardly less culpable in the sight of the Supreme, has nearly an equal penalty attached to it. And this he will have felt in his dreary retreat, his past life and future prospects being alike subjects for sorrowful reflection ; indeed all was gloom around and within. While his miserable condition must have contrasted most painfully with that bright season of his youth, during which he led a pious, happy life at the side of his kind, loving uncle, he will, he must, frequently have glanced back with an upbraiding conscience to the wasteful character of that life, which had brought good neither to himself nor to others. Truly, he had never sought the goal to which wisdom, virtue, and true piety point, as had the righteous Abraham. Thus, he not only missed the happiness which attends on meritorious conduct, but found that certain misery which ever awaits those who neglect their duty to God and their fellow-men.

Assuredly the lives and characters of uncle and nephew afford this one only point in common, that they alike yield profitable lessons to those who will take them to heart. While Abraham has left a name that must endure to all time, the weak-minded, selfish, and covetous Lot would, and might well, be forgotten, except for the warning he holds out to those who shun not the abodes of vice and irreligion, but tamper with evil, instead of overcoming it with good, or who, oblivious of their duty to their fellow-men, only regard their supposed interest, and, by neglecting each paramount obligation, prepare for themselves certain after-misery and regrets.

Character is the sole grand distinction between man and

man. Wealth, station, physical and intellectual powers, are in themselves but appliances and mere passive instruments, which have to be set in motion, and become more or less potent agents for good or for evil as propelled by character. Though men form for themselves social boundary lines, it is the moral character which must, in a measure, define and adjust them. Under Providence, the part it plays in the world is all-important. It has a strength of will that enables it to break through every artificial barrier and triumph over every obstacle, whilst it holds a powerful sway over the works and workings of men. Character is man's insignia; individual merit his badge and true nobility. It is a prerogative denied to none who earnestly labour in the attainment of virtue and excellence. Truly, goodness and merit are equally precious in whatever sphere they may dwell; and they who resolutely pursue the path of duty regardless of all difficulties or opposing interests, place themselves on an eminence to which real desert alone can mount. Now, to reach this height requires force of principle, which, when derived from religion, is the true measure of human greatness. As this is acquired, so the moral standard of the man is exalted, and, if made the mainspring of daily actions, will be fraught with the happiest results to himself and others. In those cases, however, where it is wanting, not only can good find no resting-place, but evil will be sure to harbour, and be perpetually working mischief. The individual who cultivates the highest principles is likely to accomplish much that will redound to his honour and to the benefit of his fellow-creatures; while the unprincipled man, who neglects or disregards all moral teachings, will surely prove himself highly noxious to the circle in which he moves. Indeed, there is no one member of society who is not capable of swelling the aggregate of that which constitutes the general good, or of decreasing it in some measure; nor, indeed, is there anyone so insignificant that he may not, by his acts or by his example, do some harm or render some benefit to those with whom he comes in contact. No one stands alone; he is part of a great whole, and no man has a right to say, "I am of no weight in the scale"; let him but put forth his best energies, and he will assuredly find himself progressing with a progressing world. When an individual shall have brought himself to feel and believe that he is of some weight in the domain of morals and of social advancement, he will hardly fail to give his countenance and support to all that is good and useful. Many is the good deed which waits for a start, and each may fairly ask himself why he should not be the one to give it the first forward impulse. The ardour he infuses into any benevolent or useful scheme must certainly attract and rouse kindred spirits, if none others, to work in unison with him, or emulate his beneficent purposes. By each individual thus making an effort to advance, the whole mass would be carried forward. Much has at all times to be accomplished if the world is to go on progressing. The trammels of superstition, ignorance, and intolerance, have to be unrivetted, religious principles disseminated, arts and sciences promoted, and the tone and moral condition of general society improved. And for these happy results to whom can we look if not to the strong-minded and large-minded, whatsoever may be their station or condition in life? It is they alone who carry with them the weak, the vacillating, and narrow-minded. They are the true pioneers, and the momentum to all human progress is given by them. They delight in action; they concentrate their desires on great objects; give their hearts, with their means, their abilities, and their endeavours, to the good work before them. Being eminently practical, they develope all that is likely to prove serviceable to mankind. Thus subserving the good cause, they not only enjoy the happy consciousness of well-doing, but are entitled to rank among the benefactors of their species; a royal prerogative, and a just tribute to their individual merit.

Now, although all may enter the lists, and honourably distinguish themselves in the good cause, it is but few who will not succumb at times. They who presumptuously believe in their invincibility, and expect their efforts always to be crowned with immediate success, will be the most likely to fail in their laudable endeavours. On becoming disabused—and howsoever lofty and meritorious their purpose, this must occasionally occur—they will get discouraged and proportionably slacken their exertions, if they do not altogether relinquish them. But would every man put forth his utmost abilities, leaving the final result, with fulness of faith, in the Hands of Omniscience, the work of enlightenment would surely prosper. It is impossible not to see and feel that at some times it appears to be stationary, and at others even retrogressive. So is it also in individual life, yet this should be no cause for discouragement. Man may not live to see the full fruits of his labours, but he may reasonably feel assured that they will come to maturity after he has gone to his long home. Thus let him work in the good cause as if all depended on his individual prowess, and he need not doubt the final issue.

But in carrying out any beneficial scheme-there should be no pride, which ever seriously tends to injure and retard it. Too frequently will an individual be led to withdraw his countenance and support therefrom, shrinking away with offended dignity, because, forsooth, that recognition of his deserts which he demands from the world is not forthcoming! The proud man, non-content with the approbation of his own conscience and the approval of Heaven, is apt to overlook or forget that his good acts lie within himself, and not in his reputation for them; thence he will desire and expect general approbation; but all having their own wants and pursuits, few find leisure or possibly have even the inclination to give particular attention to private merit. Pride might also receive its quietus in the reflection that, although man, as a unit, may do much good, yet *that* much is little, till time, carrying it onward, enables it to repeat and multiply itself until it swells into large proportions; and, again, that past achievements are ever being dwarfed and eclipsed by those of the present moment. Thence let us spread the good seed, and ask God's blessing upon it; for thus shall we deserve, even if we obtain not, the acknowledgment of true merit from those who constitute our world.

There are, however, other causes consequent upon individual presumption, which tend to obstruct beneficial schemes, and among them is the desire of the many to hold rank as leaders. All would be Samsons or Solomons; and, if this ambition proceeded solely from zeal or love of the common weal, it could but be pregnant with good; for such sentiments would counterbalance every other feeling, and each individual, clearly recognising that all cannot rank foremost, would rather give up his pretensions, whatever might be his especial claim to priority, than impede the general work of progress. Indeed, in his labour of love, he will be glad to see himself eclipsed by some compeer, and be the first—all honour to him—to acknowledge and crown superior deserts. Not so, however, with the proud and self-sufficient man; he does not lightly forego the high position to which he lays claim. Social benefit is but secondary when weighed in conjunction with those rights to which he deems himself entitled. A few such men will suffice to thwart any useful project. Through them, party spirit, with its fruitless wranglings, will be engendered, time wasted, and opportunities lost, so that general discouragement must finally ensue, and with it all chance of success.

Next, there are others who, though desirous to gain honourable distinction, yet withhold the expenditure of time, means, and abilities, by which alone it is to be justly acquired. Such persons will even occasionally sail under false colours, or seek to shine by borrowed light. This is inglorious, and will surely defeat its own purpose. Individual merit is intrinsic, it is untold gold; to filch it, or place base coin in its stead, is dishonourable; and, although the world may not always take account of true merit, neither will it long allow itself to be imposed upon by a spurious likeness.

Lastly, there are many who will do nothing because they cannot do all! Now it is true that at rare intervals, personal unaided efforts have been so powerful for good as to arouse public attention and compel admiration, yet such pre-eminence can fall solely to the lot of few. And even these, though they be giants, can only perform a part in the work of that great sphere of usefulness to which indeed all may and should contribute their quota, thus effectively helping to complete the whole. Let then each one move onwards and give a stimulus to action rather than be a repellant, for while the best of us cannot do all, the least may do much. It is not, however, enough that we step forward as promoters of any useful scheme, true philanthropy induces us to merge all personal considerations which might retard or impede its accomplishment. Truly, he who is content to follow where he may not lead, never unnecessarily protruding his good office, but seeking to promote harmony and concord, will prove himself a powerful auxiliary of any enterprise, and by thus effectively contributing to its success, will hardly fail to reap due credit. The world ever judges the workman by the work, and will surely, though perhaps tardily, acknowledge merit in whatsoever sphere or station it may be found, proving that while no position can of itself dignify the man, individual worth will ever dignify the position. Let any one, however, withhold his good offices, when any useful enterprise claims his co-operation, and he can expect nothing less than to forfeit the regard of all men, and incur the displeasure of heaven; while he may feel assured that he will in any case offer at most but a temporary impediment. The world has gained so much

I

momentum that it is not to be stayed in its course of improvement and happiness. The All-Wise has decreed that the great work is to be accomplished by individual exertion, and truly, each has his chance of reaching the goal, if he will only seize every golden opportunity, zealously and cheerfully working in the service of God and of humanity.

Now it behoves all God's creatures seriously to take to heart this truth, that there is a certain best course of action for every human being, whatsoever may be his condition, and that it is almost ever in his power to pursue it. The All-Gracious has given man *Freewill* as his birthright, and it is only when, greatly to his own detriment, he would pass certain prescribed limits, that the Omniscient checks or arrests its action. Now to make this prerogative subserve the highest purposes constitutes individual merit. Heir to a written law, which clearly points out the path every one should pursue, both for his own interests and those of his fellow-mortals; possessor also of the internal law of Conscience, which rarely fails to admonish and direct aright, man is left lord of his own course, heaven does not coerce him, he is just what he himself determines, neither more nor less; though poverty stricken, he may be great by reason of moral excellence, or he may be debased though in exalted station. The end assigned him is to work out human happiness, that point to which all God's dispensations appear to converge; yet, withal, each mortal has been left a perfectly free agent. Permitted by the Ruler of the Universe to take an active part in forwarding practical good, only let man work with God as a zealously devoted servant, and his moral force will be almost without limit. Champion for the right he becomes invincible, for the Omnipotent is his "Shield and buckler". But if man labours not for the welfare of his fellow-men as religion demands, and regardless of the voice of God in his heart, wilfully sets himself in antagonism to the great principle which regulates the world for good, he will help to retard, though he may never, never stay the wheels of progress.

Vast is the field of usefulness open before all, and no one individual can have any just plea for not labouring therein. God has ordained that we should serve Him through His creatures, and if we fail to comply with His Divine behest, regret and shame will surely await us in our declining years. Further, if man abuse as well as use the high privilege of freewill, the tenor of his conduct will necessarily clash with the general good, and, as a natural consequence, meet with vigorous opposition and many a rebuff from the bulk of mankind. No mortal may swell the tide of evil or stay the good without injury to his fellow-creatures; how, then, dare he hope to escape unscathed from their just indignation? And if this consideration suffice not to terrify the evil-doer, let him reflect that the Governor of the Universe holds that all who are not for Him are against Him, and that the great Disposer of events watching over the general good, well knows how to stay him, who, by his acts would undermine it, and this without in any way interfering with individual free agency. Thence let the will of the Supreme be our will; let us learn to take such delight in His law that with an entire heart we shall ever seek to follow its teachings, and so truly love the gracious Giver that our greatest pleasure will consist in moulding our inclinations, and with them our daily actions, in accordance with His commands. God controls not that man who wisely controls himself, but his bounds are enlarged in proportion as he seeks to benefit his species. Truly the path of virtue is the path of Freedom, and is the broad, open road which everyone must walk who aspires to individual merit.

Now in this very freedom of choice rests man's personal *responsibility*. With a full and perfect power of selection between those two extremes of moral conduct, right and wrong, being at the same time incited to the practice of the former by God's voice in his heart, he has to march forward, and by his own acts will assuredly stand or fall. That man has been left free to will, but not always to accomplish, often accomplishing that which he does not and would not will, in no way militates against his freedom of action or decreases his responsibility. God reads the heart, and its workings are noted in Heaven's own Book of remembrance. His deeds are his own; there is no coercion, no compulsion; but as God has bestowed on every individual talents or powers of some sort, He will certainly demand an account of how they have been applied. Holding this ever in remembrance, it is further essential we should bear in mind that individual responsibility stands on a much broader basis than the mere negation of wrongdoing. There is the sin of omission as well as of commission. *It suffices not that we do no evil; we must do positive good.* Man has the power to embellish the world by his life, and shower blessings around him by word as well as by deed. He ill performs his duty to God and his fellow-man when he does not accomplish both in a greater or less degree, and thence will surely fail to secure the esteem of the world and the favour of the Supreme. It is barren ground indeed that yields no fruit, nor responds to the fructifying showers of heaven. Let no man's life show such sterility. Each one owes a debt to society, and it behoves all alike to discharge it faithfully. A man's single efforts may seem of little worth in the eyes of mortals, yet if he has done all he can, they will appear far otherwise in the sight of God, who, in His gracious Providence, will watch over and protect the seed of good intent. But the sin of omission is not made so much account of by men as that of commission, because it is less within their ken; nevertheless, the Judge of all the earth takes cognizance of both alike. Acts *committed* are subject to the scrutiny, and with it to the approbation or condemnation of society, besides being answerable to human law when *detrimental to the general welfare;* but duties neglected or *omitted* rarely find any other tribunal here on earth than that of conscience. It is God's voice urging us to succour the needy, console the afflicted, counsel the unenlightened, admonish and guide the wayward and vicious; also to lead, kindle, vivify, and inspire good works, promoting to the best of our powers all that tends to human progress and the public good. If, however, through selfish indifference and apathy, we cast aside all interest in the concerns and well-being of others, then shall we be guilty of the sin of omission in the sight of heaven. The All-Just has spoken to us through the Holy Volume as well as by the voice of conscience, and when we follow their command to the best of our abilities, then our accountability ceases. God recognises no inequality among his creatures except so far as virtue is concerned, for He looks to the heart alone. Thus, would we obtain His favour and ensure our own happiness, we have but to guard our hearts sedulously, and work earnestly in the good cause, ever seeking to do His Supreme Will in an upright spirit and with deep devotional love. This is true greatness in the sight of God, and this then constitutes individual merit.

On the earnest and exact performance of the many important duties incumbent on man depends his merit, and in order that his acts may be in entire conformity with the will of the Supreme, wherein consists his highest virtue, it is especially necessary that he should follow implicity the PRECEPTS which Scripture offers for the guidance of the human race. They are all-comprehensive, pointing to every virtue and accurately defining each right principle of conduct. He who regulates his actions thereby will have raised for himself a high moral standard. Being, however, far too numerous to quote under one heading, we may turn to the pithy summing-up of Micah, who says, "The Lord hath showed thee, O man, what is good. What doth He require of Thee but to do justly, to love mercy, and to walk humbly with thy God?" Thus we may at once proceed to the next point, and show how great may be the influence of every individual in averting evil or promoting good. This is made manifest in Ezekiel, where we read, ch. xxii, v. 30, "And I, the Lord, sought for *a man* among them that should make up the hedge and stand in the gap before me for the land, that I should not destroy it, but I found none; therefore have I poured out my indignation upon them; their own ways have I recompensed upon their heads." Again, in Jer. v, 1, "Run to and fro through the streets of Jerusalem and see now, know and seek if ye can find *a man*, if there be *any* that executeth judgment, that seeketh the truth; and I the Lord will pardon it". Nor indeed are these exceptional cases. Truly the Omniscient is ever watchful, and that He takes cognizance of the ways of each and every individual we find conclusive evidence in various parts of Scripture; thus in II Chron. xvi, 9, "The eyes of the Lord run to and fro throughout the whole earth to show Himself strong in the behalf of them whose heart is perfect towards Him". Again, 1 Kings xix, 18, "Yet I, the Lord, have left me seven thousand in Israel, whose knees have not bowed unto Baal and whose mouth hath not kissed him". And if a doubt could yet exist as to an especial Providence, the following quotations must surely set them at rest: Prov. v, 21, "The ways of man are before the eyes of the Lord, and *He pondereth all his goings*"; Ps. i, 6, "The Lord knoweth the way of the righteous, but the way of the ungodly shall perish"; and Ps. xiv, 2, "The Lord looked down from heaven upon the children of men to see if there were any that did understand and seek Him; they are all gone aside, there is none that doeth good, no, *not one*"; and again, Ps. xi, 4, "The Lord's throne is in the heaven; His eyes behold, His eyelids try the children of men, for He loveth the righteous, His countenance doth behold the upright". The succeeding verses further show the security in which the godly man may trustfully repose: Ps. xxxiv, 7, "The angel of the Lord encampeth round about them that fear Him and delivereth them"; and Ps. xxxvii, 23, "The steps of a good man are ordered by the Lord, and He delighteth in his way; though he fall he shall not be utterly cast down, for the Lord upholdeth him with His hand". Then again, the same thoughts are expressed by the righteous Job, chap. x, 14: "If I sin, then Thou markest me"; and at chap. xxxi, "Doth not God see my ways and count all my steps"; also at chap. xxxiv, "For the work of a man shall the Almighty render unto him, and cause *every man* to find according to his ways". The whole of Ps. cxxxix demonstrates a like conviction on the part of David with regard to himself; take, for example, the opening verses, "Oh Lord, Thou hast searched me and known me, Thou knowest my down-sittings and mine uprisings, Thou understandest my thoughts afar off." Then at v. 7 he says, "Whither should I go from Thy spirit, or whither should I flee from Thy presence? Surely darkness hideth me not from Thee. Even in the uttermost parts will Thy hand lead me and Thy right hand hold me". Then we find it plainly set forth in Ezekiel that every man shall stand or fall by his own good or bad actions; thus in Ezekiel xviii, "All souls are mine, saith the Lord; the soul of the sinner, it shall die; but if a man be just and do that which is right and lawful, he shall surely live"; and in chap. xxiv, "I the Lord have spoken it; according to thy ways and according to thy doings will I judge thee". Then in Jer. xxxii, 19, "Thou, O great and merciful God, Thine eyes are open upon all the ways of man, *to give to every one according to his doings*". We are moreover led to petition heaven that each individual may be responsible for his own acts, by the example of Solomon, who thus prayed at the consecration of the Temple, 2 Chron. vi : "Hear Thou from heaven thy dwelling-place, and forgive, and *render unto each man according unto all his doings*, whose heart Thou knowest, that they may fear Thee and walk in Thy ways." Next, the power for evil possessed by every man is pithily shown in Eccles. ix, thus, "Wisdom is better than weapons of war, but *one sinner* destroyeth much good".

Evil has, however, its prescribed limits, while all that is right and good has no boundary line; each individual may work the largest amount of good in his power, but when He would set the word of God at defiance, there is One stronger than he to say, "Thus far shalt thou go, but no further." Thus our freedom, our individual good, our highest merit, consist in implicitly following God's ordinances, and if we will only resolutely and continuously choose the good and eschew the evil course, then may we reflect with pleasure on the 30th verse of the 2nd chapter of Samuel, where the Lord declares through the mouth of His prophet, "They that despise me shall be lightly esteemed, but *they that honour me, them will I honour*".

It may be taken as a rule that the individual conduct of a monarch will guide his court, and their united influence give moral direction to the nation at large, hence great indeed is the responsibility of those high in rank and authority. Assuredly a people will be virtuous and happy in proportion as the Sovereign who rules over them has the love and fear of God in his heart. From the Book of Kings, so rife with EXAMPLES elucidating this truth, may well be selected that of JOSIAH, who ascended the throne in early youth, and throughout his reign never failed in doing that which was right in the sight of the Lord, declining neither " to the right hand nor to the left". Even at the tender age of sixteen, he began to show the influence he could exercise for good among his people ; as we read, " For in the eighth year of his reign, while yet young, he began to seek the Lord, and in the twelfth year he began to purge Judah from the high places, and the groves and carved images. They broke down the altars *in his presence,* made dust of them and strewed it upon the graves of them that had sacrificed unto them".* This done throughout the land of Israel, he returned to Jerusalem, but when Hilkiah the priest afterwards found the Book of the Law, he took yet more decided steps to draw his people towards their God. He assembled

* II Chron. xxxiv, 3.

the Elders and the priests, the men of Judah, and the inhabitants of Jerusalem "all both great and small", and he read to them all the words of that Book, and he made a "covenant before the Lord to walk after Him, to keep His commandments and His statutes with all his heart", and he caused all that were present to do the same, "*And the inhabitants of Jerusalem did according to the Covenant of God*"; further, Josiah "took away all the abominations of all the countries that pertained to the children of Israel, and *made them serve the Lord their God; and all his days they departed not from following the Lord*".

Then, turning to the Prophets, we find that each, at some one period of his inspired career, stood in the breach, and through his intercession warded off, if only for a time, the just anger of the Lord. Deeply bewailing the sins of the people, they all earnestly exhorted them to reform, though but too frequently in vain. Being addicted to vice, they rather hearkened to and abided by the predictions of those false prophets who chid them not for their degeneracy, as in the instance of HANNANIAH, who "taught them to rebel against the Lord". It is true that for a time he only "broke the yoke of wood",* but afterwards was forced to follow the ordination of the Lord, that "He should make for them yokes of iron". A fearful change, affording ample proof of the mischief which one evil-disposed *individual* may bring upon an entire nation.

Then, among the warriors who proved signally successful in delivering Israel from their enemies is GIDEON. These are his own words when ordered to assume the command of the army and march against Midian, "Oh, my Lord, wherewith shall I save Israel, behold my family is poor in Manasseh, and I am the least in my father's house",† but when assured that God would lend him his countenance, all misgivings vanished, so that he at once built an altar unto the Lord and set about destroying the groves of Baal. Then,

* Jer. xxviii, 13. † Judges vi.

when the idolaters rose up against him for this deed, he thus addressed them: "Will ye plead for him, will ye save him? if he be indeed a God, let him plead for himself". How greatly he distinguished himself and benefited his nation is proved by the fact that the throne was offered to him. But, alas! with his success came a total change in his character, and finally, forgetful of his God, he seduced the people to idolatry, lowered their moral condition, and paved the way to most of their after misfortunes. Thus was he, *individually*, powerful alike for good and for evil.

Descending the social scale, we arrive at those who are content to remain in obscurity till moments of peril, when they step boldly forward, nobly brave every danger to serve and save their fellow-countrymen, and thus prove themselves the true bulwarks of their nation. Such men were CALEB and JOSHUA, whom Moses sent with ten others, heads of their respective tribes, to search the land of Canaan, and give a report thereon to the credulous people who, in a distrustful spirit, had urged this proceeding on their chief. Caleb and Joshua, possessing that courage which confidence in the Lord ever inspires, saw nothing to terrify or appal as did their pusillanimous fellow-travellers. They, indeed, found a well-fortified city, and even saw the Anaks, "who were giants", but what had they to apprehend since assured of the protection of the Most High? While uniting with their companions in extolling the richness of the land to the expectant people, they endeavoured to inspire them with their own undaunted spirit, and urged the malcontents to put trust in the Omnipotent, who had hitherto vouchsafed them His countenance, and led them in safety through every peril. But when they saw that the evil counsel of their timorous companions was about to prevail, both Caleb and Joshua rent their clothes and thus addressed the whole body of the murmurers: "The land which we passed through to search is an exceeding good land, and if the Lord delight in us, then will He bring us unto it; only rebel ye not against the

Lord".* Nevertheless, their efforts to strengthen the hearts of the people were vain, and indeed we find that "all the congregation bade stone them with stones"! They had done much for their own glory and the welfare of the nation, but, though resolute and dauntless, as individuals they found themselves powerless to combat the will of so many perverse and obstinate opponents. Their conduct, however, earned for them a great reward, they alone being spared to enter the promised land, as a token of God's high approbation. The Lord thus announced His Will: "My servants Caleb and Joshua, because they had another spirit in them and have followed me fully, them will I bring into the land whereunto they went". Nor was this all, for when that period arrived they took high rank, Joshua being even appointed by the Lord to succeed Moses as leader. He then proved himself a truly valiant commander, taking eight-and-forty cities, capturing successive kings to the number of thirty-one, and even smiting those very Anaks, whose great strength and huge proportions had terrified his companion chiefs when they went to spy out the land years before! Joshua's trust in the Lord was perfect, but while he ever looked towards heaven, he yet worked for earth. As a Ruler, he greatly conduced to the welfare of the nation, and through the fulness of his faith was all-potent in inspiring others with confidence. Thus, at a moment of great peril, he dispelled the misgivings of his people by addressing the following exhortation to them, "Fear not, nor be dismayed, be strong and of good courage, for thus shall the Lord do to all your enemies against whom you fight"; and afterwards, when they were conquerors, and peace had settled on the land, he, with a heart overflowing with love and gratitude to God, further addressed them thus: "The Lord hath given you cities which ye did not build, and vineyards and oliveyards which ye planted not, now therefore fear the Lord and serve Him with all sincerity and truth. Put away the strange

* Numbers xiv, 7.

Gods which your fathers served and incline your heart unto the Lord God". And greatly must it have cheered their noble and now aged Leader, when the people responded to his appeal as follows: "We will serve the Lord, and His voice will we obey". Truly, had he as the *individual* exercised a marked power for good over an entire people; nor indeed were the glorious results of his wise rule and pious exhortations speedily lost upon them, since we read "And Israel served the Lord all the days of Joshua and the days of the elders that outlived him".*

The next and last example, which we take from the Book of Esther, offers another invaluable lesson. MORDECAI, though at the base of the social column, was at its very apex in point of moral excellence. It would be almost impossible to conceive greater elevation of character combined with an abject position than that portrayed in the 2nd and 3rd chapters, where he is first represented as sitting humbly at the king's gate, and afterwards boldly refusing to rise before Haman and "do him reverence". Then how truly wise were all his proceedings when he learnt the fate that awaited his nation. He first humbled himself in prayer, beseeching the protection of the Lord of Hosts, and when thus fortified he put forth every human effort which he believed might avert the impending evil. Thence his urgent appeal to Queen Esther, who to his mind bid fair to be so potent an instrument for good. But when she demonstrated how utterly futile she believed it would be for her to appear before the king unsummoned, such being an unlawful act punishable with death, he was in no way daunted, nor could he be induced to listen to her remonstrance, feeling that the fate of his nation depended on the prompt and vigorous action of the hour. Therefore he again addressed her, saying, "Think not with thyself that thou shalt escape in the king's house, more than all the Jews, for if thou altogether holdest thy peace at this time, then shall there enlargement

* Joshua xxiv, 31.

and deliverance arise to the Jews from another place, but thou and thy father's house shall be destroyed; and who knoweth whether thou art come to the kingdom for such a time as this?" Herein we may see how firm was the faith of Mordecai, how supreme his resignation. Nor did he falter till he accomplished his end. Afterwards, when placed by the monarch in the highest post, and his fame had spread over all the provinces, his conduct was truly meek and meritorious. Neither flattery nor the homage of a court could warp his warm and noble heart from the path of duty; he ever earnestly sought the welfare of his people, promoting to the utmost of his power all that could tend to their peace and happiness.

Men of this stamp are the real heroes, whatsoever may be their creed or nation. It is through the achievements of such noble natures that the world becomes replenished with good. Hence are they justly entitled to universal esteem, and, while a halo of glory rests upon their names here on earth, they will assuredly have earned for themselves a blessed immortality in heaven.

MORAL COWARDICE.

Gen. xix, 19, "*Oh, not so, my Lord, I* CANNOT *escape to the mountain lest some evil befal me.*"

HAD LOT'S trust in the Lord been firm, these words would certainly never have been uttered by him, but he would unhesitatingly have followed the injunction of that protecting angel who had been sent for the express purpose of rescuing him from the impending catastrophe. Lot's character, however, was full of blemishes; his past conduct had been most faulty, and the concluding scriptural passages in reference to him plainly prove that, although by the favour of the Supreme he was afforded ample opportunity for retrieving his former errors, he in no way availed himself of it. Indeed, his every act on and after quitting Sodom demonstrates his vacillating disposition, his intense selfishness, his want of moral courage and want of faith.

Firstly, we find that although urged by the angel to quit the devoted city with all expedition, he yet lingered, so that it became necessary for the messenger of God to lay hold on his hand to bring him forth, and, when without the city, to bid him "escape for his life and flee to the mountain lest he be consumed". But he again demurred, allowing his judgment, or rather his wishes, to stand in the place of the wise counsel of that guardian angel, whose object, as he should well have known, was not only to rescue him from impending destruction, but also to point out the surest and best place of refuge. Had faith been uppermost in the mind of Lot, he would not, he could not, have entertained any criminal fears or apprehended any danger. But his heart was with the treasures he had been forced to leave behind him, and it is more than probable that he hoped to recover them by abiding near the spot. Such a consideration with so selfish a man would be quite powerful enough to induce him to run counter to the commands of the angel, and account for his seeking permission to fix his residence in the small city that was near by on the plains. Yet even after his unadvised petition was granted he still lingered, and had to be once more urged forward by the angel, who again repeated, "Haste thee, escape thither". But having once arrived at the city which he had been the means of saving from destruction, it was to be supposed he might have settled himself there and given his individual exertions towards promoting the knowledge of the true God among the inhabitants. And assuredly, had he been so disposed, this was an opportune moment. He could have called their attention to That power the magnitude of which had been signally displayed in the overthrow of the neighbouring towns, also have pointed out their own wonderful escape, and thence sought to instil both the love and fear of God in their hearts. Far different, however, was his conduct, for the next and last data we have relative to his movements[*] proves that he shortly after abandoned the city which he had himself chosen for his residence, and retired unbidden to that very spot which had before inspired him with so much alarm, and of which he had spoken to the angel in these words, "I cannot go thither lest I die". Whence this sudden change of views, Scripture fails to enlighten us. Suffice, it evinces a fickle, vacillating disposition, while a high degree of moral cowardice is indicated by the fact of his not quieting all vague fears and implicitly following the injunction of his heavenly adviser to proceed direct from Sodom to the mountains. Surely, his residence in Zoar once sanctioned by the heavenly guide vouchsafed him, Lot should have been content to abide there, though some discomforts, or even trials, might have attended him in his new abode. Sensible that

[*] Gen. xix, 30.

an All-Gracious Being had watched over and saved him in time of danger, he should assuredly have reposed his trust in that same Benign Protector, have dismissed all apprehension, become reconciled to his new life and position, and endeavoured to make it subserve some purpose which might testify his gratitude to his Heavenly Father. But to these considerations he showed not the slightest regard. The boon for which he had so recently and successfully petitioned became valueless in his eyes, since it did not enable him to recover his lost wealth; thence doubtless his change of purpose and wilful departure with his daughters from the city which the angel had appointed for their future residence. How entirely, how sadly, was such conduct at variance with his duty to the Supreme. When he might well have feared resorting to the mountain, since it was no longer at God's bidding, but rather in contravention of it, he had no fear; he was bold when there was ample cause to be timid, while he lacked moral courage and faith when safe in the guidance of an All-Wise Disposing Hand. Now though this gross and almost criminal perversity brought its natural evil consequences, and misfortunes fell thick upon him, they yet failed to move him to serious thought. Had he but asked himself conscientiously why so merciful a Heavenly Father suffered them to befal him, he must surely have discovered how faulty had been the tenor of his life. But he regarded them not as monitors, their teachings served not to change his mind or disposition, thence ensued his last overt act of disobedience, which still further tended to embitter his declining years.

Now, had Lot's past life been useful to his fellow-mortals and pleasing to his God, he might have found some solace even in the lonely cave wherein he afterwards took refuge, but as it was, if ever his mind reverted to bygone years, his reflections must have been attended with compunction of conscience and disquietude. He had been undutiful and ungenerous to his uncle, his benefactor, and now was without even one friend; knowing the Lord, and having received especial mercies from above, yet had he not been "valiant for the truth upon earth," like that instructor of his youth, the virtuous Abraham; he had not influenced his wife and children for good in such a manner as to save them from the punishments consequent on wilful disobedience, nor had he brought even one soul nearer to God, while the much-coveted wealth, for which he had so toiled, incurred so many disappointments, and sacrificed so much, was gone beyond recall. Whatsoever may have been the hopes and aspirations of his youth, none had been realised; the past afforded no pleasurable point on which the mind might dwell, it offered no solace for his old age; the future was a blank, or worse; barren for good had been his life, pitiful and sorrowful was its termination.

Now, it can scarcely be doubted that had Lot, instead of proceeding to the mountain from Zoar, repaired to the abode of his warm, large-hearted uncle, and, humbly penitent, implored pardon for past ingratitude, he would not only have been welcomed, but urged to stay and partake of those rich blessings which the pious patriarch never lacked. Surely, if Lot's heart had been in the right place, if his disposition had been sufficiently noble to appreciate fully the loving and forgiving nature of Abraham, he would have confidently sought that abode which for long years had been his home. His thoughts must have turned thither when weighed down by calamities; and when he sadly reflected on his late family bereavement, he cannot have failed to recall to memory his more than father, his instructor and protector. Yet even his misery, which must have stood out in strong and painful relief when contrasted with the happy home of the virtuous Abraham, sufficed not to touch his heart. The same moral cowardice and almost sinful misgivings which caused him to declare to the angel, "I cannot escape to the mountain," worked on him when he should have gladly appreciated the

K

forgiving spirit and loving-kindness of the great patriarch, and thrown himself into those arms which from his youth upwards had been open to receive him. Surely solicitude for the welfare of his daughters might alone have prompted him to seek that land where the knowledge of the true God was fast superseding idolatry, and that roof where no harm was likely to befal them. But the course Lot pursued was in complete accordance with his senseless and heartless conduct throughout life. Wanting in faith to his God, he drew back from following the spoken injunction of His angel; lacking in love to his fellow-citizens, he strove not to promote the welfare of the people of Zoar, but even departed hastily from their city; oblivious of the noble and generous conduct of his benefactor and guardian, he evinced none of the tender emotions of gratitude, nor felt that filial affection which was due to one who had been to him as the best of fathers. Faith, love, and gratitude were altogether dormant sentiments in his breast, and, never having been exercised, could not be called into vigorous action when they would have proved of infinite benefit to himself. Lot's life was indeed a blank, for it had been totally unproductive of good, and its close a blight, withering not only the parent stem, but even the tender plants that had blossomed at its side! Truly Lot chose an appropriate dwelling-place; he who had never sought a friend, encouraged a neighbour, or shown any marked sympathy for his species, was in old age isolated in a land bare of inhabitants, dwelling within a cave, frigid and narrow as his own heart. Scripture there leaves him, nor offers further comment on his life, and its very silence speaks more emphatically to the reflective mind than any words.

But the full moral to be drawn from Lot's life may be further developed by comparing what he did with what he should have done. It is easy to conceive that the passing events were in every way calculated to impress him with God's Omnipotence and his own weakness; wherefore, it might be supposed, he would rather have listened and acted up to the will of the Supreme, than sought to follow his own wayward inclinations. Had such been his frame of mind, he would have repaired to the mountain in entire trust, and there upraised an altar to the Great God who had so signally and mercifully delivered him. This pious act would certainly have inspired him with that moral courage he so essentially needed; and, further, it would have brought back a vivid recollection of those youthful days, when, at the side of the God-loving Abraham, he must often have bowed down and worshipped. His heart once powerfully moved towards God and his uncle, conscience could no longer have slumbered, but would have prompted him to redeem the past. His very seclusion must have conduced to holy thought, and when from his lofty eminence he looked down upon the desolate and barren spots where the two guilty cities once stood—a fearful proof of the just retribution which had fallen on the sinful inhabitants—he must perforce have been led to contrast that dark scene of human crime and human woe, with the tranquil land, full of bright reminiscences, where dwelt the pious Abraham. Then, also, the hope of improving the friendless position of his daughters; the desire of leading in the future a more useful life than was possible in his barren retreat, with other similarly laudable feelings, would have urged him to action, and confident in the approbation of the most High, he would have proceeded to settle amidst the scenes of his youth, and seek his almost only remaining relative, resolutely intent on regaining the affection which he had done so much to forfeit. By thus pursuing the path of duty, much happiness might yet have cheered his declining years, while his sun would have set with but few clouds instead of in utter darkness.

Now, it is to be observed, that the fact of Scripture halting abruptly in the sketch of a life, has, in most instances, been significant of Divine displeasure, and Lot's case can hardly form an exception to the rule. That no record even of his death or burial-place is left, too surely indicates that his conduct had been such as to render him unworthy of further notice. Miserably sad must have been the closing years of his life, and greatly embittered by the reflection that he had forfeited through his own wilful conduct all further heavenly interposition. Here, indeed, was the culminating point of his misfortune; as here, also, he touched the lowest point of moral degradation.

The whole history of Lot offers ample matter for reflection. We find that the two besetting sins of selfish ambition and moral cowardice warped him from the path of duty, and that an inglorious life was followed by an abject end. Attaching no special importance to the duties he owed God and his fellow men, Lot too often passed them by, saying, "I cannot", and thus frequently became guilty of the sin of omission. Severe was the penalty he paid for this grave and life-long offence, so severe, indeed, that Scripture, after giving but one clue to its extent, draws the curtain upon it.

Thus, while resolutely resisting all sins of commission, let the sad history of Lot induce us to proceed one step further, nor suffer the sin of omission to imperil our future happiness. Then shall we be ever ready to answer duty's call with the words of fair promise: I can—I will.*

---

* Although, at an early period of his life, Lot exposed himself of his own free-will to the contaminating influence of idolatry, yet he is not supposed to have followed its baneful practices to any extent, and, notwithstanding that he was selfish, covetous, and disregardful of the due performance of the higher duties of life, he *may* have occasionally shown himself not altogether devoid of some of those finer qualities which had doubtless been instilled into his youthful mind by his noble preceptor Abraham, and thus in some measure been a fit object for God's especial favour. But, after attentively perusing his entire history, and especially the 29th verse, chap. xix of Gen., where we read "And when God destroyed the cities in which Lot dwelt, *He remembered Abraham*, and sent Lot out of the midst of the overthrow", we

"I cannot" is the language of moral infirmity, and is the ever ready response of the indifferent, the pusillanimous, and the indolent, when called on for exertion in the cause of duty or of honour. Occasionally, however, it is also the language of the true hero; the man of moral courage, who wavers not when temptation assails, but resolutely adheres to the code of morality and religion, exclaiming, as did Joseph, "*I cannot* do this thing, and sin against God". Thus used, what noble words are these! how they exalt the utterer! it were as if he said—I may not, I must not, I *will* not. What fixity of purpose do they betoken, how significant are they of high moral resolve! Like sentinels they stand to watch and warn away all such unwary and seductive thoughts as war upon the moral sense of right, and warp man from the path of rectitude. He who treasures these words within his breast will rarely swerve from the straight line marked out by virtue and piety, for they have within themselves that magic power which holds the upright steadily to his course.

It is far, far otherwise, however, when the words "I cannot" are dropped by the faint-hearted, or by those who have but small regard for moral duty, since they then too surely betray a coward spirit, and prove the man who can, who dare utter them, to be the mere slave of circumstances. Free agency, which is mortals' highest prerogative, will be to him futile for good. Hope, man's greatest strength, and, when embodied into action, the very salt of life, will fail him in his need. Wishes and desires will sport before him, but seldom or never meet their realisation, because unsup-

---

may surely arrive at the conclusion, that the preservation of Lot's life was due in a far greater degree to the virtue of the uncle than to any merit he himself possessed. The moral of his life points in the same direction. He was less criminal than the idolators, and therefore escaped their fearful punishment, but his conduct had been highly culpable, if not criminal, and thus he had to pay the forfeit in a life of gloom, of penance, and remorse.

ported by that personal exertion to which success is mostly due. His existence will be but as a vain show, and his life almost a blank, since devoid of those good and pious works which alone can give it value.

Now when we examine into the *cause* of this desponding and paralysing exclamation, which so frequently stands between life and its moral obligations, we find that it is to be attributed in a great measure to the clashing of duty with inclination, for only when the heart prompts does the hand readily execute. There can be little doubt that it is far more frequently the want of will than the want of power which stays man in the work of progress. He who pursues his duties with the same keen zest with which he follows the chase after the goods of earth may erase from his vocabulary the words "I cannot", for all difficulties will become light to him, all obstacles be but stepping-stones to his success. Another cause is the want of fixed principles, of a just and well-defined sense of what is right or wrong. Now, without the mind is impressed with moral truth, and has arrived at settled convictions through its own ratiocinations, there can be no steadiness of purpose, doubt ever leaving a numbing indecision, which will assuredly impede, if not arrest, any bold or resolute course of action. To secure constancy in our efforts, we must steadily fix our gaze upon some point of duty, some definite object full of good promise, continuously directing our steps thereto. He who thus acts will feel the rapid growth within him of that courage and firmness which are the high prerogatives of the right doer, and in the very consciousness of his strength he will gain full vigour to achieve. Lastly, among the other causes of giant power, which hold men in subjection, and strike at the very root of individual progress as well as moral vigour, are selfish indifference, idleness, diffidence, and vice. Just in proportion as they obtain ascendency, so does man's liberty become curtailed. Dereliction of duty is the sure concomitant of each; they stand as a barrier between man's power for good and its execution. Well would it be if fears and doubts could be aroused in the breast of the indifferent, and be made to alternate with hope; for where there is apathy there can be no advance towards virtue. If the heart warm for others as for self, then all is well. It would not be less serviceable to the idler, who is ever apt to flatter himself that he will gain the end without using the means, and who, by seeking perpetual excuses for doing nothing, numbs those energies which, if developed, might be turned to a good and useful account. Then the diffident or unstable, who have no faith in themselves or others, but are ever wavering, swayed to and fro as fear or hope takes possession of their mind, though acutely feeling they must stand or fall by their own actions, need not have a conscience always quivering if they but do their best and leave the rest to heaven. And, as to the debauchee, seductive passions alone have power to sway his effeminate mind. He " cannot", because he *will* not, resist the allurements of sense, or curb his unruly desires, but allows each fresh indulgence to whet his appetite for further gratifications. The vicious man never thinks of wrestling with the foe or fighting the good fight; devoid of all self-control, he is a very slave to each new temptation. Content to hold communion with sin, he permits himself to be dragged ignobly down without a struggle, and in his course becomes a curse to himself and others.

Once satisfied that these are the chief moving causes of that coward spirit which brings man to exclaim so readily " I cannot"; it next behoves us to seek some panacea for this crying defect of character, and we at once find it in religion. This is, indeed, man's true support; with it how strong is he, without it how weak! Where the heart is fixed, trusting in the Lord, there can be no cowardly fear, virtue will be regarded as the supreme good, and hence followed with an earnestness and intensity of purpose which, while it must prosper our undertakings, will assuredly gain heaven's approval. Resolution, which is the touchstone of success, like an angel will lead us ever onward. Failure will not discourage, for trusting and hoping we shall try again; while each triumph will serve as an earnest for the future. If man would but labour in his true vocation as strenuously as if he were the sole arbiter of his fortune, and at the same time, confidently believing in God's high superintending Providence, rely in implicit faith on that arm of strength, great must be his progress. Of nothing may we be more certain than that though man be weak God is strong, and that the All-Gracious hearkens to our prayers, and will surely help us if we will but help ourselves. Thus let us advance devoutly, hopefully, and in entire confidence in the All-Wise, speeding onwards through life in a course of usefulness and virtue.

Now we may feel assured that it is little less than sinful in any individual to allow those mental and physical powers with which he has been blessed to remain stagnant. It behoves all of us to test them and give them full scope after having arrived at a just estimate of their extent. Whilst they are suffered to slumber they can be of no avail, but judiciously exercised are all potent for good to ourselves and others. It is certain we may ever find something to perform for the glory of God and the general benefit, while we should not only embrace opportunities but even seek to create them, and so kindle a zest for useful action. While we are yet in time, let us be up and doing; there is a future before us when we must rest in the tranquil grave. All moral turpitude will be quickly cast aside when we have brought ourselves to believe in our powers for good; and these will acquire vigour just in proportion as we trust in them. Truly it is faith in our strength which lends us strength.

Due weight should also be attached to the reflection that though we fail, we are never beaten *unless we give up;* determination will almost invariably gain the point it aims at, for hope is no flatterer to the resolute. The virtuous and pious man, ever truly in earnest, invariably finds means to accomplish the task he has assigned himself. With him difficulties are not impossibilities, he overrides them through his indomitable will, and thus in the end must achieve great things. He has learnt to make life's journey thoughtfully but resolutely; religion, ever offering a strong incentive to duty, wins him to his life's task and lends him the vigour necessary to its fulfilment. Truly, the man thus nerved will never suffer to escape him the desponding exclamation " I cannot"; but he will be true to duty, and as firm as true.

The timorous, the slothful, the irresolute who "see a lion in their path" whenever duty calls on them for action, may reflect with advantage on the following PRECEPTS. In Eccles. ix, 10, "Whatsoever thy hand findeth to do, *do it with thy might*, for there is no work, nor device, nor wisdom in the grave, whither thou goest." If they will further couple this with Prov. iii, 5, "Trust in the Lord with all thy heart and in *all thy ways acknowledge Him for He will direct thy path*", and holding this glorious promise in remembrance, ever strenuously seek to derive therefrom that vital support it is so well calculated to afford, then may they hope to throw off all moral turpitude, and make progressive advances towards that goal to which conscience and duty point. At Judges viii, 21, we read, " As the man is, so is his strength"; and truly the virtuous and religious man will have no real apprehension; he will exclaim in the words of the Psalmist, Ps. cxviii, 6, " The Lord is on my side, I will not fear; what can man do unto me?" He will cast from him all doubts and misgivings as he recalls and ponders over the following gracious promises, Isaiah xl, 29, "God giveth power to the faint, and to them that have no might He increaseth strength. *They that wait on the Lord shall renew their strength*". Then in Joshua, "Turn not to the right hand or to the left, observe to do according to the law, *for then shalt thou be strong and very courageous*". Again in

Job xi, 13, "If thou prepare thine heart and stretch out thine hand towards God and *put iniquity far from thee*, then thou shalt be steadfast and *shalt not fear*"; and at ch. xvii, 9, "The righteous shall hold on his way and he that hath clean hands shall be stronger and stronger". Then in Ps. cxii, "The *good man* shall not be moved for ever; he shall not be afraid of evil tidings; his heart is fixed, trusting in the Lord". Truly, we shall ever find verified that which we read in Prov. xxviii, 1, "The righteous are bold as a lion, while the wicked flee when no man pursues". The former never say "I cannot", but seek through prayer for strength at the Fount of all strength; the latter, however, are constantly "in great fear where no fear is", since they dare not solicit God's countenance or His Almighty protection. Now, strange as it may seem, it is nevertheless true that men of this coward spirit will yet confront and follow without dread their bitterest foe, the sinner who would entice them, nor even tremble as they walk the downward path of vice. It is such men who, in the words of Jeremiah, "are not valiant for the truth upon earth, for they proceed from evil to evil and provoke God to anger". But the time will surely come when they shall feel the dire consequences of their sin and folly, or as set forth in Deuteronomy, "The Lord will give them a trembling heart; life shall hang in doubt, and fear shall possess them night and day". Then let the diffident and the vicious alike hearken to and heed the following exhortation of Azariah, given in II Chronicles xv, "Hear ye me, *the Lord is with us while ye be with Him*; and if ye seek Him He will be found of you. Be ye strong therefore, and let not your hands be weak, for your work shall be rewarded". Thus spoke the man on whom fell the spirit of God, and verily they are words well calculated to arouse that moral courage which will enable us successfully to resist temptation, triumph over many difficulties and urge us onward in the true path of piety and virtue.

Scripture presents numerous EXAMPLES of individuals who,

in their daily routine of life, or on especially important occasions have failed in their calling through moral cowardice, bringing misfortunes on themselves and others; while it abounds in characteristic sketches of men whose moral courage, nerved by Holy trust and a strong sense of right-doing, stood proof to every assault from whatever quarter or in whatever guise it came. Among the former we may class the DISOBEDIENT PROPHET (1 Kings), who, being bidden by God Himself not "to go back nor eat bread or drink water", at first refused to hearken to one who urged his hospitality upon him, rejecting the proposal in these words, "I may not return with thee"; and yet, on being further solicited, his resolution gave way, and he acceded to the request. Desire gained ascendency over obedience, and he gave ear to the voice of the tempter! Where then were the words, "I cannot, I may not disregard the expressed will of the Supreme", which would have been so opportune at that juncture! They were wanting, for he was wanting in strength of purpose and that fixedness of resolve which religion and faith alone can give. He transgressed the command of the Lord, and severe was the penalty, for great had been the offence. Passing from this defective character, we turn to one pleasingly dissimilar, the great and good King HEZEKIAH, who ascended the throne at the early age of twenty-five. This excellent monarch, keenly desirous of withdrawing his people from their idolatrous practices and recalling them to a just sense of their religion and its sublime precepts, had had ample cause to be discouraged with the prospect before him. Yet he never faltered, he never tired, or as we read, "And in every work that he begun in the service of the house of God, and in the law and in the commandments to seek his God, he did it *with all his heart* and prospered".[*]
Though he had to contend with a froward and perverse people he nevertheless conquered, and triumphed through fixedness of purpose. Yet this was not all; when about to be

[*] II Chron. xxxi, 21.

attacked by Sennacherib, King of Assyria, "he strengthened himself, and built up all the wall that was broken, raised up another without, and repaired Millo"; in a word, he acted with such vigour and resolution that he saved his country from the ravages of the army of that powerful monarch. He then undertook works calculated greatly to improve his country, and never, even under adverse circumstances, did he relinquish his well-devised schemes and generous purposes. The result was that at the time of his decease the people had become far more powerful and respected; they were also wealthier, happier, and better than in previous reigns. Well, indeed, would it have been had the benefits thus conferred proved lasting, instead of being speedily annulled by the wicked son who succeeded him; nevertheless, he had persistently done *his* duty, had secured the especial favour of heaven, and bore with him to his eternal home the love, respect, and gratitude of his people, for we read, "And Hezekiah slept with his fathers, and they buried him in the chiefest of the sepulchres of the sons of David, and all Judah and the inhabitants of Jerusalem did him honour at his death".* Thus his wise and vigorous conduct redounded to his honour, and met with its just reward.

We next draw attention to Jacob's last prophetic blessing to his children, since it will serve further to elucidate this subject. He had studied and read each of their characters, and from their past life divined their future. This remark more especially applies to REUBEN and JOSEPH, who stand out in bold relief as peculiarly opposed to each other in regard to energy of disposition. To the former Jacob spoke thus, "Thou art my first born; unstable as water, thou wilt not excel." It was this unsteadiness of purpose, a distinguishing trait in his past life, which often caused Reuben to veer from the straight line of duty, and even on one occasion led him to sin grievously against his parent. Jacob, rather in sorrow than in anger, therefore pointed

* 11 Chron. xxxii, 33.

out how he had erred through weak-mindedness; and in all the impressiveness of a dying address, showed him that he might never hope to excel without he should determinately pursue the path of virtue, sedulously avoiding every deviation therefrom. But how different were his words to Joseph, who had stood proof to temptation, who had been ever earnest and resolute for good, loving to his father, serviceable to his adopted country, and faithful to his God. Partly in a retrospective and partly in a prophetic vein, Jacob exclaimed, " The archers have sorely grieved him, and shot at him, and hated him, but his bow abode in strength and his hands were made strong by the Hands of the mighty God; even by the Almighty, who will help and shall bless thee with blessings". How opposite must have been the feelings of the two brothers when they heard the last utterances of their departing parent; the elder must surely have cowed before his gentle reprimand, the younger gloried in having rendered himself deserving of the loving accents which, like heavenly incense, fell from the lips of his deeply-loved and revered sire. Free to choose, let us take example from Joseph, and warning from Reuben; let us be courageous and earnest in good, never drifting into evil through unsteadiness of purpose, but be ever firm as strong, whereby we may secure the approval of our conscience, and attain those blessings which kind Heaven has decreed shall attend on a consistent and virtuous line of conduct.

MEDITATION.

Gen. xxiv, 63, "*And Isaac went out to meditate in the field at the eventide.*"

ISAAC had been trained from his earliest youth by aged parents, and had but few, if any, youthful companions to join him in those pleasures and pastimes which properly belong to the springtime of life. These circumstances alone would doubtless have produced a somewhat thoughtful turn of mind; but, further, the home and the field, his sole schools of instruction, were likewise calculated to induce reflection, and call forth happy thoughts and devotional feelings. The pure calm delights of home, with its tranquil repose and ever-gushing spring of parental love, must have hushed many unquiet passions to rest, melted the heart to good, and often caused it to swell with grateful and pleasurable emotions; while the field, ever presenting a gay and glorious landscape, replete with beauties speaking of the greatness and goodness of God, will have led the observant student to solemn thought, and awakened sentiments calculated to draw him into happy communion with his Beneficent Father in heaven. Nor was this all, for in his youth two highly important events had occurred especially adapted to render Isaac thoughtful and reflective. The miraculous manner in which that life was preserved, which he had voluntarily yielded up at the will of his parent and the command of heaven, as well as the death of his dearly beloved mother, were both events of a nature calculated to make a deep and lasting impression on his sensitive mind. The latter occurring just at that age when the feelings are keenest, struck a chord in his breast which long painfully vibrated. He had ever been at that fond parent's side, listening to the sweet and gentle voice, which spoke of virtue, of happiness, and of God; and his heart was weighed down with the bitterest anguish when that cherished mother was taken from him. Profound, indeed, was his grief, and long his term of mourning. Held in sweet remembrance, her wise counsels must often have formed the nucleus of his meditations, while he must have treasured the soothing reflection, that he had ever been a dutiful and loving son to her who had so cherished him. This consolatory thought would, doubtless, have tended in time to heal the wound inflicted by this first great bereavement.

But on the day on which Isaac is presented to us taking his solitary walk, another important event was at hand, which served to recall his thoughts from the past and fix them on the future. The void which was within his heart was to be filled up. He was awaiting her who was to become his wife. He had chosen the still hour of evening to indulge those solemn reflections which so important a change in life might well induce. How great would be his happiness if that wife should possess those estimable and endearing qualities, that loving disposition, which he had ever learnt to associate with the author of his being. And, remembering that each blessing is a heavenly gift, how devoutly must he have prayed that the fair one to whom he was about to be united would prove every way worthy of his esteem and love. Further, during these hours of meditation, he must assuredly have given some consideration to his own disposition, well aware that very much would depend on himself, and that his own character and conduct would greatly influence his married life, entailing either happiness or misery. Thence he will have resolved ever to do his duty by his wife; and truly we afterwards find him as a fond, good husband, shielding her from trials, calming her fears, and drawing her towards the Supreme Being, whom he had learnt from his revered parents to love and adore. Thus were his meditations fraught with good. They were, indeed, as the ladder that topped on heaven, whence sped down angel thoughts, fructified, and took wing again, soaring with his spirit upwards to the golden region of Supernal bliss.

Reflection is as much a duty as action, and must invariably precede it, would we secure any consistency in conduct. Like every moral duty, it is of the highest moment; and will not only promote our present good, but conduce to our everlasting welfare. It is in solitary communings that the mind learns to distinguish between the true and the false, and discerns much that it concerns us to know. It is in calm moments of reflection, when turning the mental eye inwards, that we read the secrets of our inner selves, and scan the true motives of our actions. It is then, also, that things assume their real shape and colour. He who is ever engaged in the turmoil of business life, and gives no time to meditation, may hardly expect to conduct his various undertakings to a successful issue. It is assuredly a duty we owe to ourselves, as well as to the All Gracious, to mingle religious retreat with our worldly affairs, and if we wilfully neglect this duty, evil consequences will surely follow. Life is full of complexities, each day bringing with it some intricate question to be solved, some difficulty to be overcome; and he who would hope to turn passing events to profitable account must keenly mark his relative position thereto, which can only be done by never permitting a day to pass without giving them calm and thoughtful consideration. But that meditation may be efficient, it is necessary to keep certain objects constantly in view, whereby we may be able to rectify all that is amiss prior to engaging in action.

Now that which is perhaps of the most importance to our well-being, is to acquire a knowledge of our dispositions, and arrive at a just conclusion as to the bent of our inclinations. We must have the moral courage to search into the deepest recesses of our hearts, and impartially view all the good and bad that harbour there. It is a positive duty not to conceal ourselves from ourselves, for only when we have detected the latent evil of the heart may we hope to find a remedy. It behoves us to take a calm, dispassionate view of passing events, and of our thoughts and actions connected therewith; to compare our conduct as it is with what it ought to be; to note what we have done and what left undone, resolving to follow in the future only such objects as are worthy of pursuit. We must closely examine our thoughts, endeavouring to hold them, as well as imagination, under due control, and further learn to methodise them, so that they may be matured to a clear perception. Next it should be our object to ground our principles so fixedly that they may stand us in good stead when time is wanting for calm reflection. We should often take a survey of the field of action in which we have to work, for thus only may we be prepared for aught which can befal. Moreover, we should heed that experience which the past has left us, and endeavour to profit by its teachings. Casting behind us all unavailing regrets, we should make bygone events serve as monitors to advise and guide; for then, and then only, may we hope to perform our part in the world with credit to ourselves and benefit to our fellow-creatures.

Now, once decided what subjects should be uppermost in our thoughts during the calm and precious moments devoted to reflection, we have next to fix upon the best method of making them subserve our every purpose. And here a great difficulty presents itself. Thought has nothing tangible; an essence by nature, it will frequently elude the grasp of such minds as have not acquired the power of concentrating and condensing it at will; indeed, even then it will require much humouring, much care and attention. If, however, these be bestowed, and no effort spared to master thought and reflection, then will they in time become the creatures of our will and the genii of our fortune. Once possessed of the command of thought, of fixed and well developed thought, with the power of controlling and arresting it, of checking it when prone to stray into idle musing or the day dreams of fancy, of stimulating it until it assumes the form of good resolves, of virtuous acts, and we have made an all-important step towards turning to the best use those moments given to meditation. Now, if to the power we add the will, then the task, for such it is at first, will assuredly soon become facile. Yet the will is not to be easily coerced. Reflection must bring in its train much that is pleasing before we learn, as a rule, to devote to it daily both time and mental labour. Only when we can look to its resumption with pleasure may we hope to form it into a habit. Thus it behoves us sedulously to cultivate a feeling of satisfaction in its performance by giving it a lofty aim, and further strive to make it an agreeable pastime, by denuding it of all complexity. To succeed therein, it is well to range our reflections under the three headings of—self-examination;—the world, and its teachings;—Providence, and our spiritual duties—giving to each its due share of attention and thought.

With regard to self-examination, if we entertain a sincere desire to discover our failings in order to correct those errors of conduct which arise therefrom, we must probe the dispositions of our heart, ignoring nothing that we may there find amiss, and set ourselves to regulate them in accordance with the written Word of God. We must study our passions apart from their positive action. Then it will be necessary to take a retrospective glance, endeavouring to understand the past, since every event has its meaning, and works onwards towards good or evil. With experience for our teacher, we should carry forward our investigations, truthfully marking where we have erred, and by the light of the Sacred Volume trace those fundamental principles which are our best bulwarks in the time of action. We must further consider what good seeds we have neglected to sow, what ill weeds to uproot, and lastly, ask ourselves whether we have made any advances, or in what we have retrograded. Next, turning from the past and its experience to the present and that future which lies before us, we should watch each thought, each feeling that shows some doubtful tendency, analyse and trace it to the fount whence it draws its moral taint, and apply the antidote; we should also accustom ourselves to listen attentively to the whispers of conscience, question our hearts concerning our right or wrong doing. These reflections duly solved, we shall seldom be led astray, for it is far oftener the want of any fixed principles than the adoption of bad ones that lead to mischief and dissipation. When once we have formed principles of action that will instantly rise in full vigour at our bidding, we shall obtain a power which will stand us in good stead in the hour of temptation or trial. In a word, we must be true to ourselves and to those principles upon which we have resolved to act in the calm moments of reflection.

Next, it behoves us to give attentive consideration to that which passes around us, for it has been justly observed that "it is not what the eye sees but what the mind reflects on, that supplies us with wisdom". Society and the world at large are ever presenting to us much deserving of careful cogitation, thus let us continually strive to amass their teachings, and take them to heart. With the world pictured before us in the closet, we may, through mature reflection, learn to distinguish between what is shadowy, unreal, or transitory, and what is substantial, true, and fixed. The new objects and thoughts, which are ever arising to baffle and mislead, will not long perplex us when subjected to calm inquiry. We shall not suffer the actions of good men to pass by without reaping some benefit from their example; we shall compare our shortcomings and slackened energies with their well-devised and useful exertions, then strive to imitate and bring forth like results. In a word, we shall give careful consideration to the past, and forethought to the future; thus adopting the wise counsel of the Greek philosopher, which runs as follows: "On leaving thy house think what thou intendest doing, and on returning think what thou hast done".

Lastly, we must draw nigh to God in meditation, and sanctify our hearts to Him, so that He, the All-gracious, may in His infinite love and mercy draw nigh unto us. We must never suffer a day to pass without reflecting on His wise dispensations, nor allow ourselves to remain insensible to His frowns or His smiles. With thankful hearts we should bear in remembrance the continual blessings showered down upon us, and the manifold escapes we owe to His Providential care. Our hearts once touched will permanently improve, we shall become daily more heavenly minded, and our musings be more and more intense and holy. It is not, however, in the closet alone that we should converse with the Great Author of the Universe, there we may think of His infinite love wedded to infinite power, but it is amidst the scenes of nature that we can best observe it. The man who accustoms himself to outdoor reflection will behold God everywhere, and feel that His glorious presence permeates creation. By coupling observation with meditation, he will derive ineffable joy from the works as from the word of God, and his mind, not being altogether absorbed in worldly things, will soar at fitting intervals to the realms above. Truly it is only by thinking of heaven that we can hope to get there, for it may be held as an infallible rule, that he who would surely reach any goal must ever keep it steadily in view, nor allow himself to be diverted from the straight line which leads towards it. This meditation alone can effect for us; thence we should greatly prize those moments we are able to abstract from the world and its pursuits to devote to useful thoughts, serious reflections and pious meditation.

Now that we may fulfil this duty and self-appointed task with alacrity and good-will, we should call in that powerful auxiliary, self-interest, which ever readily co-operates in any work yielding pecuniary advantages, or fruitful in weighty consequences. This is assuredly the case with meditation, and the following are among the rich and important results which may well tempt self-interest to lend its all-potent support. It is through reflection and forethought that we may avert coming evils or be prepared to meet them at their advent. It will induce uniformity and consistency in conduct, quicken good resolves, give us the habit of judging justly and clearly, while it serves to develope thought, which is the life of man, and promotes the due equilibrium of all our faculties. It prepares us to take advantage of every favourable opportunity, and gives us a firm and confident footing in our dealings with the world. Through its medium we shall acquire that foresight which is of talismanic virtue in conducting the affairs of life. It greatly tends to prevent those hasty and ill-considered acts which often leave behind them deep anguish and bitter contrition. It will stimulate the conscience which, though never neutral, occasionally requires a reminder; it will tell us plainly enough what are our powers, and save us from wasting our lives in making fruitless efforts after the unattainable. It will bring experience, reason, and religion to bear upon all our actions, employ and store the mind so as to leave no vacuum for the intrusion of vicious thoughts or vain imgainings. It is a powerful auxiliary to mental and moral excellence; in a word, it is the best guide to greatness and to goodness. Rich, however, as are the worldly advantages of meditation, they are poor indeed when compared to the spiritual benefits it confers. It is pre-eminently useful in setting before us the gracious attributes of God, and giving us an habitual conviction of His wisdom and justice. By frequent intercourse with Supreme perfection, our hearts will become pure, our minds enlarged. Certain it is, the nearer the soul is allowed to approach to God, the easier it will be to keep in the path He has marked out for us, while each pure and holy thought that ascends heavenwards will surely return to us bearing with it a golden ray of happiness.

It is, however, all-important that we should make a distinction between meditation and mere musing, since the former, being all-potent for good, cannot be too frequently resorted to, while the latter cannot be too rigidly abstained from, tending as it does to abstract the mind from what is real and practical. But if musing in general is a noxious habit, being totally incapable of either ministering to good resolves or nurturing them into vigorous action, it is yet more objectionable in relation to sacred subjects, since almost amounting to trifling with them; besides, holding no affinity with strong emotions, it can have little in common with the Book of Nature or the Holy Volume, both of which speak plainly of God and His glorious attributes, often and often making the heart vibrate with rapturous delight. Thus let earnest contemplation and meditation be our frequent companions, for then may we hope to draw down those bright effulgent heavenly beams which melt the soul to love, and waft it to the skies.

The high importance to be attached to meditation is made manifest throughout Scripture. Most of the PRECEPTS which refer thereto serve to impress us with the conviction not only that it is a duty, but that on this duty being properly and rigidly fulfilled must, in a great measure, depend man's temporal and spiritual welfare. In the book of the prophet Haggai, chap. i, 5, we find the following direct command from Heaven: "Thus saith the Lord of Hosts, *consider your ways*", and then, to show us how essential this is to our well-being on earth, it is further added, " Consider that ye have sown much but brought in little, ye have eaten but ye have not been satisfied, ye clothe you but there is none warm, and he that earneth wages earneth wages to put it into a bag with holes." What a forcible admonition, what a mild reproof to those who give no heed to the error of their ways, and, moreover, what a fund of worldly wisdom is here offered. Then thus speaks the prophet Jeremiah in Lamentations, chap. iii, 40: "*Let us search and try our ways and turn again unto the Lord*". And in Samuel we are bid to "prepare our hearts to serve the Lord". In Job xxii, at v. 21, we read, "Acquaint now thyself with God, thereby good shall come unto thee", and again, Elihu, in his eloquent peroration, thus addresses Job, "Stand still, and *consider* the wonderful works of God". From these verses it is clear enough that reflection and meditation will conduce greatly to our advantage and well-being, while the following quotations prove with equal distinctness that its neglect will be productive of evil consequences: Hosea vii, 2, "And they *consider not* in their hearts that I the Lord remember all their wickedness; now their own doings have beset them. Woe and destruction unto them, because they have transgressed against me". The prophet Samuel in his book places before us the paramount duty of reflection in these words, chap. xii, 24: "Fear the Lord and serve Him in truth with all your heart, for *consider* what great things He hath done for thee". Let us also bear in mind that if we will frequently peruse and consult the Holy Volume, and make the glorious truths it unfolds the subject of serious reflection, we shall assuredly derive the greatest possible benefit therefrom. Hearken to the words of Joshua, "This book of the law shall not depart out of thy mouth, *but thou shalt meditate therein day and night*, that thou mayest observe to do according to all that is written therein, for then shalt thou make thy way prosperous, and then thou shalt have good success". And after having taken due time for reflection, how may we better sum up the result of our meditations than in the following words of Ezekiel: "God's ways are equal while man's ways are unequal", confidently believing that man has but to consider his ways, cast from him his transgressions, and make himself a new heart in order to secure the favour of the Most High. But it is especially the Book of Psalms which teems with injunctions on this subject, for the Poet King, throughout the many vicissitudes of his life, learnt fully to appreciate and feel the good which calm reflection and pious meditations can effect.

We may therefore well turn for an EXAMPLE to DAVID. On two occasions only, and those when in the very zenith of his power, do we find him acting without due forethought. In the one case pride led him to number the people, in the other his passion for Bathsheba incited him to the commission of a terrible crime. Now, the deep and sincere repentance he testified for these exceptional transgressions clearly prove that they proceeded from no predetermined course based on a wilful disregard of virtue or a callous indifference to results, but were indeed merely the hasty and inconsiderate acts of the moment. Had it not been thus, we certainly should not read, "And David's heart smote him after he had done this thing". How nearly blameless would have been his entire life, if in those hours of temptation he had devoted some moments to that calm reflection which had so repeatedly saved him from acting in violation of God's laws. Truly with him meditation was well-nigh a necessity, and afforded him positive delight, as the following verses, extracted from his rich treasury of Psalms, conclusively prove: "Of God my meditations shall be sweet, I will be glad in the Lord";* "My soul shall be satisfied when I remember Thee, O God, upon my bed, and meditate on Thee in the night watches";† again, "In the multitude of my thoughts within me Thy comforts delight my soul";‡ "I remember the days of old, I meditate on all Thy works".§ That he experienced inexpressible delight in the close perusal of sacred writings is shown by his pious exclamation, "O how I love Thy law, *it is my meditation all the day*". Now, while David

---

* Psalm civ, 34.   † Psalm clxii.
‡ Psalm xciv.   § Psalm cxix, 97.

urges on us as a holy duty the contemplation of the wondrous works of God, he repeatedly exhorts us, if we would seek spiritual improvement, to meditate on our inner selves; for example, he says, " Stand in awe and sin not, commune with your own heart and be still".* Then, alluding to himself, he declares, "I will meditate in Thy precepts and have respect unto Thy ways"; and again, "*I thought on my ways* and turned my feet unto Thy testimonies". Here, then, is one whom it should be our glory to imitate, and if, like him, we "are wise, and will observe and meditate on the glorious works" around us, then may we hope as he did to "understand the loving kindness of the Lord".

But that we may the better follow the wise example he set us, we should, besides frequently perusing the whole of his numerous collection of beautiful Psalms, give especial attention to the 19th, 103rd, and 104th, which perhaps best define the three subjects which should alike command a prominent place in our thoughts whenever engaged in pious meditation. In the 19th he first proclaims the greatness and power of the Lord thus, " The heavens declare the glory of God, and the firmament showeth his handiwork"; next, he depicts the advantage we shall be sure to derive from the study of the Holy Volume in these words, " The Law of the Lord is perfect, converting the soul; the testimonies of the Lord are sure, *making wise the simple;* the statutes of the Lord are right, *rejoicing the heart;* the commandment of the Lord is pure, *enlightening the eyes;* by them is thy servant warned; *and in keeping of them there is a great reward*". And, thirdly, he calls on us to heed our ways, and ask God's guidance therein, thus, " Who can understand his errors; cleanse Thou me from secret faults. Keep back Thy servant from presumptuous sins; let them not have dominion over me". He then prayerfully concludes this sublime Psalm as follows: " Let the words of my mouth and the meditations of my heart be acceptable in thy sight, O Lord, my Strength and my Redeemer".

* Psalm cxix, 15.

Psalm ciii is to the same purpose, while hardly less explicit. David therein exhorts us, firstly, to hold in remembrance God's Providence and gracious care, thus, "Bless the Lord, and forget not all His benefits; He healeth all thy diseases, He redeemeth thy life from destruction, He crowneth thee with tender mercies", etc.; then he speaks of the attributes and loving kindness of the Supreme in these words, "The Lord is merciful and gracious, slow to anger, and plenteous in mercy"; next, with regard to the justice of God, David declares "He will not always chide, neither will He keep his anger for ever". Afterwards, in alluding to His compassion and our weakness, he says, "Like as a father pitieth his children, so the Lord pitieth them that fear him, for He knoweth our frame, He remembereth that we are but dust"; also acknowledging God's Beneficence, he adds, "But the mercy of the Lord is from everlasting to everlasting upon them that fear Him, to such as remember his commandments to do them"; and then, in concluding this exquisite and truly sublime Psalm, the minstrel King urges all that have breath to "Bless the Lord"; at the same time even appealing to dumb creation to chant praises through the spirit of man; for he would have the inanimate works of the Almighty inspire such sentiments in the breast as must draw forth that tribute of gratitude which finds vent in thanksgivings. Truly all nature proclaims its great and gracious Author, and he who opens his mind and heart to its instructive lessons will find himself translating its eloquent yet mute language into songs of praise, uttering, in the words of David, "Bless the Lord *all His works* in all places of His dominion, Bless the Lord, O my soul".

Psalm civ is also especially beautiful; it is a meditation upon the mighty power and wonderful providence of God, on nature, animate and inanimate. With his heart overflowing at the thoughts he had conjured up, the pious writer rapturously exclaims, "How manifold are Thy works, O Lord; in wisdom hast Thou made them all; the earth is full of Thy riches";* and then concludes with the following words—words which should find a ready response in every heart—" I will sing unto the Lord as long as I live; I will sing praises unto my God while I have my being; *my meditation of Him shall be sweet;* I will be glad in the Lord". Truly David only counselled what he practised; and, regarding the three Psalms quoted above as the best exponents of his teachings, let us take them to heart, for then will they surely stimulate as well as help us to imitate their author, and further enable us to cull from the self-same tree of meditation like sweet and wholesome fruits.

Could we yet doubt the efficacy of meditation, even in a worldly point of view, we should only have to turn for another practical example to II Chron. xxvii, 6, where it is distinctly stated that " JOTHAM became mighty, *because he prepared his ways* before the Lord his God". Here the cause of his prosperity is clearly defined, but he must also have derived great spiritual benefit from his inward communings; for we read at verse 2, " And he did that which was right in the sight of the Lord". Then let it be with us as with him. Forethought and pious meditation are the right methods of " preparing our ways", and as a natural consequence will lead us to good and to God.

* Psalm civ, 24.

PRAYER.

Gen. xxvi, 25, "*Isaac builded an altar there, and called upon the name of the Lord, and pitched his tent there.*"

In all the Sacred Volume there is perhaps no life more concisely or simply depicted than that of the patriarch Isaac; while containing so much, so very much of high moral import. It is beautiful in its very simplicity; a lovely picture of the generally calm, unruffled flow of a good and virtuous man's life, which like the placid lake, reflects heaven's own lights. It plainly enough teaches us that religious sentiments and principles instilled into the heart from earliest youth, and made practical to the mind through the example of tender, loving parents, will infallibly prove a rich, an invaluable inheritance, ministering alike to our temporal and spiritual welfare. Isaac being of a reflective turn of mind and affectionate disposition, his parents could have found little difficulty in implanting the love of God in his heart, and training him in a consistent course of piety. That he undeviatingly pursued this course, gladly following the same righteous path as his father had trodden, the whole tenor of his after-conduct bears ample testimony. Few as were the important incidents of his life, they sufficed to test his fortitude and his faith. On each trial which befel him, he evinced that perfect submission which springs from true piety, ever humbling himself before God in prayer. Indeed, piety appears to have been the very basis of his character, and this love of God so warmed his heart as to give additional vigour to the natural affections. Love radiates with resplendent lustre when emanating from so bright a centre; thus, great was his clinging attachment to his mother, and deep the devoted love he bore his wife. Truly, his affection for Rebecca knew no decrease, no subdivision; she stood alone, and, bound by this *one only tie,* he appears to have been faithful to her memory, even after her death. To his revered father he was a devoted son, up to that last moment when—himself aged threescore and fifteen years—he stood at the side of that loved parent's death-bed. And when, in his turn, himself a parent, what could better speak his praise than the deep, earnest, and lasting love of his sons. Differing as they did in disposition, and the tie of fraternal affection broken, yet one common sentiment animated these twin brothers, the reverential love which knows no decay. When at the advanced age of a hundred and forty years, they met again, after a long separation, for the burial of their venerable parent, they could offer each other the hand of friendship, and, sorely stricken, together weep and pray over the grave of the dear departed.

Such being the fruits of piety, let us now turn to those of prayer. It was the high pleasure of the Supreme to test the faith of Isaac, as he had tested that of his servant Abraham. For long years he remained childless, yet his faith never wavered, he never doubted the fulfilment of God's promise to his father Abraham, and it was only at the solicitation of his beloved wife, *and this after twenty years of married life,** that he besought God to grant him offspring. Thus we read, "And Isaac entreated the Lord for his wife because she was barren".† That the petition he put up was acceptable may be inferred, since he not only met with no reproof, but his prayer was at once granted, or as we read, "And the Lord was

---

* His prayer following in the closest proximity, *even in the very next verse to the one which relates to his marriage,* makes it especially easy to overlook a fact which gives the strongest evidence of Isaac's childlike faith; viz., that "twenty years he *waited* for the Lord"; waiting, anticipating, believing, though with the flight of time came nought but disappointed hopes.

† Gen. xxv, 21.

entreated of him, and Rebecca his wife conceived". Now, this was no solitary instance of faith, no exceptional proceeding on the part of Isaac, as the verse which heads this subject amply demonstrates; indeed, the whole of the 26th chapter of Genesis speaks plainly enough that his life about this period had its full admixture of trials and grief, and that in the midst of many adverse circumstances he was the same pious believer and devout worshipper as in youth, when all smiled around and the bright example of a beloved father cheered him onward in the path of duty. One of Isaac's first troubles began just after he had quitted, or possibly at the very moment of quitting, the land of his birth, from which he was forced to depart owing to the prevalence of a grievous famine. On arriving at Gerar, with the purpose of settling there, he found that he had to apprehend danger on account of his wife, " because she was fair to look upon", and in consequence thereof was led to deny her. When, however, King Abimelek quieted his fears regarding Rebecca, as well as his own personal safety, he set himself to amass wealth, and great indeed must have been his success, since it afterwards afforded the monarch a pretext for thus addressing him, " Go from us, for thou art much mightier than we". That this dismissal was keenly felt is shown at the 27th verse, wherein we are told that when Abimelek and his chief captain sought Isaac in his new place of abode they were at first very coolly received, and certainly not with his natural hospitality, for thus he greeted them, " Wherefore come ye to me, seeing ye hate me and sent me away from you?" Again, it must have been a source of great annoyance to have to contend for those very wells which, having been named by his father, belonged by right to him. Now it is evident that throughout this trying period his conduct met the approval of the Most High, for on Isaac's arrival at Beersheba " the Lord appeared unto him", graciously vouchsafing the same promises of safeguard, protection, and increase as were given to his father. And like that pious father he acted, for he at once " built an altar and called on the name of the Lord, and pitched his tent there", his servants digging a well. Thus on the spot where we find him for the first time settling in a permanent abode, his earliest act was to form a hallowed retreat where he might daily prostrate himself in pious adoration before the Supreme Lord of All. *He* built the altar, and *his servants* dug the well. Both acts were deemed by him vital to the well-being of his household, and thus setting his dependants to the task of providing for their temporal wants, he applied himself to the duty of ministering to their spiritual cravings.

Now, casting back our thoughts to the youth who, at the bidding of his heavenly-instructed father, not only readily carried to the " place which was afar off" the wood for the burnt offering, but when at the appointed spot alone with that father, was willing to lay down his life, a voluntary sacrifice at the command of the Supreme; then collating all the incidents of his after life, and taking the sum total, we have before us an invaluable lesson. Truly did his mature years fulfil the promise of his youth. The worthy son of a worthy parent, he proved himself throughout life, and in its every relation, a highly virtuous and upright man. Of tender heart, he lavished his affections on those to whom they were properly due, and, truly loving, was in turn beloved. Such meritorious traits of character *then* bore with them the rich fruits of love and esteem, *now* they move to admiration—indeed, to the very highest admiration when traced to religion, that prime motive power of all goodness and all greatness. Truly piety was the bright effulgent guiding star of his life, and God's high especial favour his great and glorious reward.

All who have given themselves seriously to reflect on their relation to God must have infallibly arrived at the conclusion that prayer is alike a *duty* and a *privilege*. As to the former, surely no rational being can for a moment deny he owes high allegiance to the King of Kings, the Great Sovereign of the Universe. But how much more is due to the Creator, the Benign Ruler, the Gracious Preserver, the great and only source of every good. Let us ask ourselves if, as weak and erring creatures, we dare withhold confession of our sins, if as dependent and mortal beings we may refrain from supplication before the Infinite and Everlasting One, whether as daily, hourly recipients of Heaven's manifold bounties and mercies, we could possibly fail to offer up thanksgivings in grateful adoration to our Heavenly Father, and then, if all sense of duty be not dead within us, we must infallibly acknowledge it to be a paramount obligation to lift up our souls unto God in prayer, both in public worship and within our own homes. It is indeed a sacred thing to attend the Temple of the Lord, and, conjointly with fellow-worshippers, practically demonstrate how deeply we are moved by a spirit of love and adoration; while we owe it to our children, as to our God, that we should not only pray for but with them in heart and soul. Now, this duty once acknowledged, it behoves us never to suffer aught to intervene to prevent its fulfilment at stated hours—indeed, we shall surely become sedulous and earnest in its performance as soon as we bring ourselves to regard it as a glorious *privilege*, granted in loving mercy by the Benign Ruler who sitteth in the highest heavens. If none are exempted from this duty, so also none have been denied the privilege. It is open alike to every class, to every sect, and no one individual should entertain a doubt that the living, loving God will lend an attentive ear to his supplications if he has endeavoured to render himself in some degree worthy of the gracious prerogative, by cultivating a pious frame of mind and a right disposition of heart. This one condition, however, is imperatively demanded by the Omniscient of His creatures, and on its fulfilment depends the promised reward. Great and gracious as is the boon, it must be sought and earned before it can be adequately appreciated. The mind must become accustomed to turn at times from temporal to spiritual things, to feel its dependence on Omnipotence, and to seek for Divine wisdom to supplement its own. The heart must learn to melt in love and gratitude towards the gracious Donor of the manifold blessings which each new day brings forth, and glow with pious ardour as it contemplates the glorious attributes of the Supreme. Thus animated and inspired, we shall infallibly regard prayer as a high and glorious privilege.

Now it is greatly to be deplored that men are apt to adopt the false notion that it is presumptuous to invoke God's blessing on their daily labours and the noble ambition which leads them to worthy and useful works. This belief is most lamentable and pregnant with evil consequences, being alike detrimental to moral welfare and worldly success. If, however, we would consider that "the Earth is the Lord's and the fulness thereof", and assure ourselves that God not only "taketh pleasure in the works of His Hands", but in His Omniscience also notes the doings of all His creatures, then must we feel that no one human being can be below His ken. In denying this we do not exalt but lower the just appreciation we should entertain of the glorious attributes of the Godhead. We are, indeed, impiously, because presumptuously, setting bounds either to the power or the will of the Almighty to grant the supplications of His servants. It behoves us, therefore, above all things to beware of falling into so gross an error; rather let us cast aside any shadow of misgiving, and, relying on God's infinite goodness, gladly avail ourselves of the high prerogative of prayer. And that we may the more highly value this privilege, let us for a moment conceive it to be altogether withheld, or so greatly restricted that its exercise be only permitted under certain circumstances and in some specified place, some hallowed spot! Assuredly, such a reflection must force on us an acknowledgment of the value of the bond, and afford us ever-present delight in availing ourselves of it. Glorying in the thought that God is near and propitious, we shall sincerely trust and gladly pray.

Far more, however, is necessary than a mere sense of duty, or even the dictates of conscience, would we have prayer fulfil its high purpose. These will, indeed, be but poor and unsteady prompters, if we have not within us a deep devotional feeling, taking its source in a grateful, thankful, and satisfied heart. Considered merely as a duty, prayer would often be found irksome and so avoided, or at best would only be fitfully and hastily repeated, while considered merely as a privilege it would seldom be fully appreciated, and thus become futile for good. All tribute is onerous when the heart goes not with it. If the soul, however, be strongly moved by love and reverence to the great Author of all perfection, and glad earnestness be joined to pious delight, kindling our devotions into a living, lasting flame, then how easy will be deemed the duty, how great the privilege of prayer.

It, therefore, behoves us sedulously to cultivate a just appreciation of God's manifold works and His glorious attributes; the heart welling over with sublime and holy emotions will then seek the Fount of all goodness, and our thoughts thus turned heavenward will be ever carrying winged words along with them. Such true devotion will assuredly bear golden fruits, for we shall then have a will subdued to God's high pleasure, and a heart so imbued with His goodness and mercy that we shall place an implicit reliance, a perfect trust in the wisdom of His decrees. Loving God with an entire heart, we shall love virtue, and to love virtue is to give the first strong impulse towards its practice. We shall feel that under the ever-varying circumstances of our life we may have recourse to the Great Omnipotent, and seeking, find an asylum under His wing during trials and sorrows; or when new blessings crown our earthly lot, we shall delight in the sense of gratitude, and glory in the power vouchsafed, whereby we are enabled to send up to the mercy-seat of God, the spontaneous offerings of a thankful heart.

It may now be well to consider—firstly, when we should pray; secondly, for what we should pray; and lastly, how we may best pray.

As to the first, if we will conscientiously put to ourselves the question *when* we should pray, the answer must infallibly be—pray continually—pray ever. Truly, it behoves us to keep God constantly in our thoughts, to hold perpetual communion with the Great Unseen. At morning's dawn, when a new flood of glorious light gushes forth, awakening us to renewed life and vigour, calling us, as with angel voice, to the fulfilment of duties left unaccomplished, or others yet to be commenced, shall we not give our first thoughts, the thoughts of a *mind not preoccupied* by worldly matters, to Him under the shadow of whose wing we have reposed; shall we not offer up the incense of a grateful heart, and casting ourselves on his mercy and protection, solicit His gracious countenance and Divine favour on the labours and duties of the incoming day. Surely, only when we have made this first step in the right path, may we start forth on the business of life with a well grounded hope that our endeavours will finally be brought to a happy issue. It further behoves us to devote some small portion of time each day to reflection. All we see, all we experience speaks of God, of His power and His goodness. Materials abound which may and should call forth pious meditation. For instance, how can we pass any Temple of worship without giving a thought to that Universal Father and Sovereign Lord in whose honour it was reared? How may we, how dare we, see pass before us the bier, with its slow funereal *cortège* bearing bereaved and sorrowing mourners, without sending one silent supplication to the Great Healer and Consoler of the afflicted and anguish-stricken? And must not a silent prayer ascend on visiting the chamber of sickness and suffering? Again, how can we fail to look up with grateful emotion when some bright, happy, useful thought beams forth, or when about to engage in some good benevolent scheme or action; when walking amidst the glowing scenes of nature, all proclaiming as if with one voice, "God is good"; when enjoying the comforts and delights of home, with happy faces around, when gladdened by some unlooked-for blessing, some new joy. Truly these circumstances and many, many others are ever occurring to call forth words of praise and adoration, but could we possibly be oblivious of these natural feelings then we surely should beseech God in prayer to awaken them in our hearts.

Now it is a fatal error to suppose this prayerful spirit demands any especial degree of sanctity, or that it will interfere with the duties and business of life. Assuredly it is far otherwise; holy thoughts, if not the exception but the rule of life, prove powerful auxiliaries in each emergency and are ever sagacious counsellors in the round of daily duty. This habit of exalting the mind to the Most High has the further advantage of checking or turning the current of any unworthy thought or vain idle fancy, as also of holding temptation at bay or resisting it, come in what guise soever it may and whether covertly or openly. And here it may be well to observe that if we refrain from pious thoughts and words of supplication when they may be easily commanded, the moment will possibly arrive when we shall feel the power withheld, and this but too surely at a crisis when such power would be most needed; say when a blight has fallen on the soul, or when temptation holds dominion over us. Once intent on sin or pursuing vicious courses, we shall feel that we cannot, nay, dare not pray. An impassable barrier ever arises between presiding sin and prayer, the indulgence of unruly passions must withdraw us from God. The voice of conscience, never altogether mute, will tell us that while steeped in iniquity and following a course of self-indulgence in direct opposition to the Divine law, there can be no communion with the Most Holy. Light and darkness dwell not together, one ever chasing away the other. Thence let us diligently seek the former, and gild our daily life with happy holy thoughts.

Evening prayer next calls for consideration, the waning hours being a hardly less propitious time for devotion than the morning. The labour of the day has ceased, its cares, trials, and worldly temptations have partially or totally vanished, and we are left with full leisure to consider if we have, unhappily, been guilty of any dereliction of duty, and how far we have failed in combating evil thoughts and evil passions; or, if in glad distinction thereto, we have resolutely pursued our true vocation and acted in conformity with a strict sense of justice, honour, and integrity. Such a review of our actions, accompanied as it must naturally be by good resolves for the future, will bring with it much peace and happiness, especially if attended by prayer; or should unruly thoughts and passions have arisen and not been quelled, then may we appeal to Him who alone can calm the tempest in our breast. But if, as is only too often the case, we deny ourselves the benefit of evening devotion, then should such reflections precede night prayer. This at least we dare not neglect. It should be impossible for us to close our eyelids in sleep without previously casting a retrospective glance at the events of the day, summing up the peculiar proofs of God's goodness, and noting any signal blessing, asking ourselves what report the day's doings have borne to heaven, and if not such as our conscience can approve, then, with true repentance, imploring God's pardon. This done, we shall seek repose, relying on the Guardianship of an Almighty Protector, and trustful that God in His good pleasure will again unseal our eyes, and awaken us from oblivion to the fresh enjoyment of life. Then, if perchance our slumbers are accidentally broken, or momentarily interrupted, the first waking thought, which of itself is the sense of being, will be of God, and we shall have ready on our lips a word of prayer. When the half dormant brain thus centres its powers without an effort, it may be reasonably inferred that "God is ever in our thoughts". This is to have a prayerful spirit. To cultivate such a pious frame of mind will be our wisdom, and a never-failing source of comfort, strength, and happiness.

The next question, as to what we *may* and *should* petition of heaven, is of vital importance, and, while calling for our best attention and consideration, imperatively demands that we should carry into the inquiry good feeling, good sense, and a firm determination to profit by the conclusions at which we arrive. We must frequently consult our judgment, our conscience, and the teachings of the Sacred Volume, if we would have prayer answer its high intent, and when we can bring the heart into unison with them, then may we feel assured of a happy solution. They all, as of one accord, tell us that, while we crave spiritual mercies, we may also implore temporal blessings; and, indeed, that it behoves us, after carefully sifting and well weighing our desires, to present them all before the Throne of Grace. They bid us reflect that our Benign Ruler may often deny to neglect what he would grant to prayer; and further demands, as an indispensable condition, that while we fit ourselves to receive the benefits He graciously confers, we should never neglect the means we may possess for securing the boons invoked. They will also tell us that He, before whom we place our petition, well knows our wants and the proportion of worldly goods and blessings which will conduce to our well-being and eternal happiness; thence, that we cannot be too meek when supplicating for any accession of temporal gifts, or too quiescent on finding some withheld and some withdrawn. Infinite Wisdom judges and infinite goodness dispenses that which is best for us; and if much that is seemingly good and of fair promise is denied, let us not repine, but gratefully prize those blessings we do possess. That which we covet may, if granted, exert a most baneful influence on our lives; and when we have drained the poisoned chalice, we shall too late regret our rash wishes and blind presumption. Thus, let us cheerfully conform to the Will of God, nor set our hearts too fixedly on things of earth.

But there is much we may petition of heaven, safe that nothing is ever refused which is fruitful of good to ourselves or others. Thus, let us satisfy ourselves as to what should be the especial objects of ambition, and humbly pray for their attainment while working sedulously towards the desired end. Now among the rich boons we may and should be anxious to possess, is an "understanding heart". Even in the very desire there is merit, as is also the case with virtue, goodness, and a thankful, loving spirit, all of which are priceless gems that never dim. Then it behoves us to pray for the welfare of others; to invoke blessings for those we love, and mercies for all who, being in trouble, need our kindly sympathy. How will the heart soften and the soul be exalted as such prayers are breathed forth. We must ever pray that temptation be kept far from us, or that when assailed thereby, we may have the strength of will to triumph over it. We may well implore the Great Physician for health of body as of soul, and beseech the Lord that we may be preserved from evil occurrences; that He will attach us to His precepts; give us the right disposition of mind whereby we may be fitted to receive and profit by the gifts vouchsafed; that He will pardon us in His loving mercy, crown our virtuous resolves, enlighten our darkness and elevate all our powers. Also we may entreat God to make us humble, obedient, grateful, so that, under every possible circumstance of life, we may have on our lips, as the wish nearest our hearts, these pious words, "May Thy will be mine". Such prayers, uttered in truth and faith, will have a talismanic virtue, imparting grace, holiness, and goodness.

And, thirdly, when we carry heart and soul with us to the service of God, then shall we *best* pray. There are few who have not felt that to say prayers, or to pray, is essentially different. How meaningless, how utterly worthless is the form of prayer, if it lack the spirit, the animating principle. Like the soul of man, when pure and holy, it soars heavenward, while the senseless body drops lifeless to the grave. We can only be said truly to pray when we bring into the service in which we are about to engage, reflection, feeling, and faith. Meet and reasonable is it that we should collect our thoughts and give them an upward turn, before we even open a book of prayer, much more so before addressing our Maker or uttering one supplication to Heaven. It is also imperatively necessary to bear in mind this one condition to the acceptance of prayer, that we must not " regard iniquity in our heart". But that we may be prepared to offer up the tribute of a grateful heart, we must give *prior* reflection to the high and glorious attributes of the Supreme; of His Mercy, His goodness, His justice and truth. We must reflect early and late on His works, on the teachings of His Holy Law, on the daily benefits and mercies we experience. When we have further learnt to follow His ordinances, to submit in holy trust to His wise decrees, to lay before Him our cares, our burdens and wishes, feeling assured that no prayer, offered up in sincerity of heart, is ever uttered in vain, there will then be no deficiency of ardour, and but little, if any, wandering of the mind. Loving sentiments, full of earnest faith, will well up spontaneously, and the heart will overflow with pious adoration. Thus should we draw nigh to God, and thus may we best pray.*

* The following suggestions are submitted to those who would sedulously cultivate that fixity of thought which is so essential to all true devotion. Firstly, to retire at such times to some quiet recess, where there can be nothing to distract the attention or engage those inlets of thought, the ear and the eye. When thus completely excluded from the outer world, the mind is left free to look inward and upward, and feel itself alone with conscience and with God. Secondly, we should

Lastly, let us give some consideration to the importance of prayer, enumerating a few of the numberless blessings, both temporal and spiritual, which flow from heartfelt devotion. Now it is clear that prayer was given for our good, and not for that of the Giver; and only when we can trace within ourselves its beneficial effects, may we believe that it is fulfilling its high intent. Ignorant and presumptuous must be that man who can hope to move the immutable will of Omniscience. Certainly not for this was prayer granted, but that it might influence us for good, giving us the right disposition of the heart and proper frame of mind, whereby we may be qualified to receive the rich reward He has promised his faithful and loving servants. Truly, time spent in the service of God and in communion with Divine Perfection must make us better, purer, holier beings. Now, once fully convinced of this, we shall give prayer the first place among life's duties, and watch that it accomplishes the work it was intended to serve. If we find content, happiness, and virtue, taking firm root in our breasts, we shall

diversify our daily prayers; for if the matter presented to the mind be always the same, a certain vacuity of thought is apt to be engendered. It is not words but ideas we need, and we can only hope to call these forth by inducing reflection through change in the form of petition. Further, we should occasionally read aloud, making the ear as well as the eye an avenue to the brain. The sound of one's own voice impresses, and when it breaks suddenly on the ear has a natural tendency to recall roving thoughts. Thirdly, we should enter on prayer with a mind deeply imbued with the solemnity of the act in which we are about to engage, and nought could more surely conduce thereto than first turning our thoughts Heavenwards, and calling to remembrance in whose awful presence we stand. The spirit being thus prepared for communing with the Great Searcher of hearts, we shall regard the book of prayer as we do the Sacred Volume when in the act of attesting our veracity by oath, and press it to our lips with the like intent of making an asseveration of *our truthfulness, of our reverence for God's Holy Word*, as also of our love for the Gracious Ruler of the Universe, and of our heartfelt desire faithfully to perform in His service each moral, each sacred obligation.

have just cause to believe—indeed, we shall have a sure criterion—that our prayers are such as will meet acceptance at the throne of Infinite love; but if these blessings have departed, or are departing, then must we charm them back by earnest, heartfelt devotion. Prayer thus becomes, as it were, a ministering angel, ever showering on us fresh and valuable gifts. And assuredly among these will be vigour of intellect, together with a capacity for close application. The truly pious worshipper has learnt to centre his mental faculties, and direct them at will to one sole object or purpose, and such power once attained will surely prove of inestimable value in every condition and under every circumstance of life.

And here it may be well to observe that we should not be disheartened if occasionally we lack the command of thought, or of that attention which true devotion imperatively demands. Temporary inaptitude of the mind to realise in Whose presence we stand, should only serve to stimulate us to more frequent reflections on our weakness and our entire dependence on Infinite power. It may likewise teach us that we have not only to think of heaven, but also to work for it, and that this may be the right moment for us to turn our full attention to the latter aim, thus making even passing mental infirmity subserve some practical good. To resume, prayer, besides being all-powerful to calm, clear, and elevate the mind, may be made to control all that tends to disturb it, healing the wounded spirit, chasing away alike temptations and sorrows. It will replace vain repinings and gloomy forebodings, the moving causes of much misery, by cheerfulness and hope, for truly, unhappiness will not long find a dwelling-place within the heart which has learnt to feel that Omniscience, with a mighty Hand, is tempering all that befals us. It will further give exercise to our best affections, lend a joy to the heart such as true devotion only can bestow, making us value more highly our being, our health, our faculties, and each gracious gift of Heaven. This drawing nigh to God through prayer and virtuous actions will be an evergushing spring of satisfaction, an ever-present reward; and when death is about to lay its cold hand on us, the mind will take fast hold on prayer, and, as with a passport, fearlessly cross in fulness of faith that boundary line which separates time from Eternity. Thus shall we find in prayer a panacea for every ill; and ever remember that blessings worth having are surely worth asking for. We have, therefore, only to set our hearts aright, and acknowledge this all-important truth, that God's best gifts are consonant with, and in every way adapted to, man's highest interests, to his Eternal welfare, and being such may be ours, if we will but work for them and pray for them. To ask will be to receive.

The Sacred Volume presents us with but few PRECEPTS inculcating the *duty* of prayer, since if the natural instincts of the heart be dumb, the mere reiteration of the call of duty, solemn though it be, must prove altogether ineffectual. Thus, while in the five books of Moses we often find prayer itself, accompanied by a bright picture of the benefit it confers, there are but few instances of its direct enforcement as an obligation. This remark equally applies to every portion of the Holy Volume, wherein there is nought superfluous or redundant. The following extracts, however, show not only that it was deemed incumbent on every individual, but that any breach of this duty called forth admonition, reproof, and oftentimes chastisement. Thus the prophet Hosea, in the 12th chapter of his book, after reproving Ephraim, adds, ver. 6, "Therefore turn thou to thy God, keep mercy and judgment, and *wait on thy God continually*", and in chap. xiv, 2, we read, "Take with you words and turn to the Lord, say unto Him, Take away all iniquity and receive us graciously; so will we pay *that which we have vowed with our lips*". In Job xxii we find, "Thou shalt make thy prayer unto God, He will hear thee; *acquaint therefore thyself with*

Him, and be at peace, for thus shalt thou have thy delight in the Almighty". Jeremiah, in Lamentations iii, after admonishing us to "search and try our ways and turn to the Lord", bids us "lift up our hearts with our hands unto God in the heavens". Then, turning to the Psalms of David, we find most of them especially devoted to work in us that just sense of dependence with which he himself was so deeply impressed, and that prayerful spirit which led him into frequent communion with his God. It is he who bids us reflect that "except the Lord build the house they labour in vain that build it";* from his lips also proceeded the solemn avowal, "I will lift up mine eyes unto the hills, whence cometh my help; my help cometh from the Lord, who made heaven and earth". Then he emphatically declares, "Unto the Hearer of prayer shall all flesh come";† and in Ps. xxxiv thus exhorts the people, "O magnify the Lord with me, and let us exalt His name together". Tracing each blessing to the One high source, he regarded prayer not only as a paramount duty, but as a supreme delight; thus in the exquisitely beautiful 27th Psalm, after bidding all "wait on the Lord", he says of himself, "One thing have I desired of God, and that will I seek after; that I may dwell in the house of the Lord all the days of my life"; and then at the 8th verse continues, "When Thou, O Lord, saidest, Seek ye my face, my heart said unto Thee, Thy Face will I seek". Again, in Ps. v, 3, he declares, "My voice shalt Thou hear in the morning, O Lord, in the morning will I direct my prayer unto Thee, and will look up". He further adds, at the 7th verse, "As for me, I will come into Thy House in the multitude of Thy mercies, and in Thy fear will I worship towards Thy Holy Temple". Then in Ps. lv he says, "*Evening and morning and at noon will I pray,* and cry aloud, and He will hear my voice." But would we prove that prayer is enjoined by Heaven, and therefore an absolute duty, then we must turn to Isaiah xlv,

---

* Psalm cxxi, 1.   † Psalm lxv.

23, where we read, "I, the Lord, have sworn by myself, the word has gone out of my mouth in righteousness, and shall not return, that unto me every knee shall bow, every tongue shall swear"; and at ver. 19, "I have not spoken in secret, in a dark place of the earth, *I said not, Seek ye me, in vain,* but Look unto me and be ye saved all the ends of the earth". There is another especial command at the 8th chapter of Deuteronomy which should have our attentive consideration, since it must dispel all doubt, if any such exist, that we should openly manifest our gratitude to the Great Giver of all good through prayer at mealtime as well as at other appropriate seasons; thus we read at the 10th verse, *When thou hast eaten and art full, then shalt thou bless the Lord thy God for the good things which He hath given thee*".

Next, regarding prayer as a privilege, it may be asked, can there be one of God's creatures, one weak, erring mortal, who feels not his dependence on Omnipotence and his need of pardon? for if such there be, then he, and he alone, may esteem it no blessed privilege to be allowed to approach the throne of heaven in humble supplication and penitent prayer. One so benighted may well consult the 32nd Psalm, take to heart the words of the chosen servant of God, and, before it is too late, cast from him that thick armour of pride and arrogance which will avail him nought in the day of tribulation. Thus speaks the pious monarch, "I acknowledge my sin unto Thee, O Lord; blessed is the man whose transgression is forgiven. Thus shall *every one that is godly pray unto Thee in a time when Thou mayst be found.* Surely in the flood of great waters they shall not come nigh unto Thee". Again, mark the following quotation from Jeremiah xi, which is yet more forcible since the words proceeded direct from God to that prophet: "The inhabitants of Jerusalem obeyed me not nor inclined their ear, but walked every one in the imagination of their evil heart; therefore pray not for these people, neither lift up prayer for them, for *I will not hear them* in the time that they cry unto me for their trouble". And in Ezekiel xx, when the people were again rebellious, God thus addressed them through their prophet, "As I live, saith the Lord, I will not be inquired of by you"; also in Zechariah vii, "They made their hearts as an adamant stone lest they should hear the law and the words of the Lord of Hosts; therefore it is come to pass that as he cried and they would not hear, so *they cried and I would not hear*, saith the Lord". Sad indeed is the condition of those who are brought to exclaim in the words of Jeremiah, chap. iii of Lamentations, "Thou hast covered thyself with a cloud, that our prayer should not pass through."

Now, the following verses will show us how best to secure God's gracious hearing. In Jer. xxix thus spake the Lord, "Ye shall seek and find me when ye shall search for me *with all your heart*, ye shall pray unto me, and I will hearken unto you". At Eccles. v we read, "Be not rash with thy mouth, and *let not thine heart be hasty to utter anything before God*, for God is in heaven and thou upon earth; therefore let thy words be few". Then Isaiah, after urging the people, ch. lviii, "to act charitably, to deal out bread to the hungry, to clothe the wretched, and house the poor, to break the yoke and undo the heavily burdened", promises that "*then* they may call and the Lord will answer, and when thou shalt cry the Lord will say, Here I am". The following verses no less clearly show that would we have the ear of Omniscience open to our supplications, our conduct must be moral, our heart truthful, and our desires carefully restrained within due bonds. Thus we read in Prov. xxviii, 9, "He that turneth away his ear from hearing the law, even his prayer shall be an abomination", and "The Lord is nigh unto them who call upon Him, to all who call upon Him *in truth*". Again, Prov. xv, 29, "The Lord is far from the wicked, but *He heareth the prayer of the righteous*".

Now it behoves us to use great discrimination in considering well what would be beneficial to us, morally as well as physically, before venturing on any petition, else we may too late experience the same sad result as we read of in the Ps. cvi, "God gave them their request, but sent leanness into their souls". Thus let us bound our desires within a narrow compass, and take example by Agar's prayer in Prov. xxx, "Two things have I requested of Thee, O Lord, deny me them not; remove far from me vanity and untruth, give me neither poverty nor riches".

From among the numberless quotations which could be adduced to prove how serviceable and efficacious is prayer when proceeding from a devout and grateful heart, the following may be chosen. In the Book of Job, ch. viii, Bildad thus addresses his suffering friend, "If thou wouldst seek unto God betimes, and make thy supplication to the Almighty, he would awake for thee and make thy habitation prosperous. Though thy beginning was small, yet thy latter end should greatly increase". The other passages selected alike unfold the one grand truth, that the humble, penitent, and devout worshipper has in the Gracious Hearer of Prayer an ever Mighty and Beneficent Protector. Thus speaks David, Ps. lv, "Cast thy burden upon the Lord, and He will sustain thee". And of himself he said, "I humbled myself before God, and *my prayer returned unto mine own bosom*". Ezra, in ch. viii of his Book, declares, "The hand of our God is upon all them for good that seek Him", adding, "So we fasted and besought our God, and He was entreated of us". Samuel no less plainly testifies his belief in the efficacy of prayer when he utters the words, "God forbid that I should sin against the Lord in ceasing to pray for you". David repeatedly declares prayer to be the best refuge under trials or temptations; thus in Ps. xxxiv he says, "This poor man cried, and the Lord heard him and saved him from all his troubles"; and in Ps. lxii he speaks to like effect, thus, "Trust not in oppression or in riches, but trust in God at all times; He will be your refuge *if you pour out your heart before Him*".

We now proceed to the more practical teachings afforded by EXAMPLES, which abound throughout the Holy Volume. At one time it is individual prayer; at another it is an entire nation humbling itself in supplication. The prayer may be one for a safe conduct and a prosperous issue, as in the case of Abraham's servant, who thus addressed his Maker: "O Lord God of my master Abraham, I pray Thee send me good speed this day and show kindness unto my master".* It may be the grateful tribute and thankful spirit after some special deliverance, as in the case of Moses and Miriam, who, after crossing the Red Sea, chaunted the sublime Hymn of Praise, opening thus: "The Lord is my strength and song, He is my God and I will exalt Him. Sing ye to the Lord, for He hath triumphed gloriously. Who is like unto the Lord; glorious in holiness, fearful in praises, doing wonders?" Again it may be offered as an atonement; thus, when the Israelites, brought very low through idolatry and sinking under the yoke of their enemies, gave heed to the voice of God, which reproached them in these words: "Go, cry unto thy Gods which ye have chosen, let them deliver you in the time of your tribulation";† they declared, full of bitter repentance, "We have sinned against Thee, both because we have forsaken our God and also served Baalim". Hannah's vow and prayer of thanksgiving, besides practically teaching us our duty towards God, breathe forth many devout expressions, as, for instance, "My heart rejoiceth in the Lord; He maketh poor and maketh rich, He bringeth low and lifteth up. He is our Rock; by Him, who is a God of knowledge, *are our actions weighed*". Next, we turn to one of the earliest prayers of the pious David, which carries with it an instructive lesson, since betokening not only the absence of ambition, but also indicating a true spirit of humility. When promised through Nathan, the prophet, that his "throne should be established for ever", he thus addressed his Maker, "Who am I, O Lord, and what is my

* Gen. xxiv.   † Judges x.

house that Thou hast brought me hitherto, and hast spoken of Thy servant's house for a great while to come".* But, indeed, David's Psalms are one long prayer, fitted for every hour of man's life, no less than for each event which may befal him from the cradle to the grave. Then we have Solomon's prayer in the Book of Kings iii, wherein this earthly ruler thus supplicates the Lord, "I am but a little child; I know not how to go out or come in, therefore I pray Thee give Thy servant an understanding heart that I may discern between good and evil".† There was another prayer he offered up at the dedication of the Temple, which it would be well, indeed, were each human being to re-echo in all sincerity of heart. Therein a favourable hearing is entreated and the mercy of God thus implored, "Have Thou respect unto the prayer and supplication of Thy servant, O Lord; hearken unto the cry of the servant who prayeth before Thee, hear Thou in heaven Thy dwelling-place, and when Thou hearest forgive".‡ Hardly less deserving of attention is the "confession" of the Levites, from which we extract the following sentences: "Blessed be Thy glorious name, O Lord, which is exalted above all blessing and praise. Thou, even Thou art Lord alone. Thou hast made the heaven of heavens with all their host; the earth and all things that are therein, and preservest them all";§ further adding in acknowledgment of their shortcomings and God's goodness, "Thou, indeed, art just in all that is brought upon us, for Thou hast done right but we have done wickedly, Thou art a God ready to pardon, gracious and merciful, slow to anger and of great kindness".

Finally, we may illustrate the efficacy of prayer by means of the two following characters: firstly, the good King HEZEKIAH. When Sennacherib was about to invade Judea, this monarch, as was his wont, appealed for protection to the Most High, invoking God in these words, "O Lord of Hosts, Who hast made heaven and earth, incline Thine ear to hear and save us",‖ to which he received from above the

* II Samuel vii. † Kings iii, 7. ‡ I Kings viii.
§ Nehemiah ix. ‖ Isaiah xxxvii, 17.

significant answer, "Whereas thou hast prayed to me against the King of Assyria, he shall not come unto the city, but by the way he came, by the same shall he return". Again, when warned of his approaching end by the prophet Isaiah, who bid him "set his house in order and prepare to die", he, in the fulness of faith, turned his face to the wall and thus prayed, "Remember now, O Lord, I beseech Thee, how I have walked before Thee in truth and with a perfect heart and have done that which is right in Thy sight", and immediately his recovery was granted he wrote a psalm of thanksgiving, vouching for his fidelity to God, even "looking upwards till his eyes failed him"; and thus concluded with the exclamation, "The living, the living, he shall praise Thee as I do this day".

Lastly, DANIEL, "the greatly beloved". When a lowly captive or when raised to lordly state, he was the same devout worshipper and humble suppliant. Neither could trials so depress on the one hand, nor grandeur so elate him on the other, as to harden his heart or make him forgetful of the gracious Lord of the Universe. Indeed, prayer was with him a necessity. Living in the city of Babylon where luxury, revelry, and voluptuousness held untiring sway, surrounded by idolaters who, hating him, sought his downfall, needing wisdom and skill in the direction of the affairs of the kingdom, no less than a calm, tranquil spirit, and vast sagacity, whereby he might baffle his enemies, and turn their devices to good, say, where in the midst of such perils, disquiet, and duties could he look for help or seek succour, if not from the One only God? Robed in the panoply of prayer, he resisted all temptations, all the seductions and enervating pleasures of a court, he defied the machinations of his disappointed rivals, and was enabled to perform each duty appertaining to his high office so diligently, wisely, and successfully that even those who sought occasion to injure him in the sight of their King could find no pretext except "concerning the law of his God". Doing his duty towards the Lord and his fellowmen, fearless of all consequences, he allowed the whole course of his conduct to be open to inspection. This is clearly shown in the sixth chapter of his Book, where we read, "Now when Daniel knew that the decree was signed", which prohibited the offering up of any petition for thirty days save to the King, under the penalty of being cast into the den of lions, "he went into his house, and his windows being open in his chamber, he kneeled upon his knees three times a day and prayed and gave thanks before his God, *as he did aforetime*". His piety and faith could not be shaken; confiding in an Almighty Protector, he was not to be intimidated. His traducers had learnt to rely on the unswerving fidelity of his character, if not to appreciate it, for at the eleventh verse we read, "Then these men assembled and found Daniel praying and making supplications before his God". They must, therefore, have exulted in the idea of having accomplished their cruel purpose; but here, as ever, while man proposed, the Great Lord of the Universe disposed, and the terrible doom intended for their hated rival was reserved for the plotters themselves, while Daniel remained unscathed, and gained yet higher distinction and power. Now, although the pious and virtuous Daniel never failed to seek God in prayer, three times daily, yet this sufficed him not, for when he experienced any especial mercy, or at such periods as calamities befel him or his people, he turned prayerfully to his God, and even occasionally gave up the cares of office that he might devote his thoughts exclusively to Him, Who had graciously blessed, or in wisdom afflicted, His servants. Thus, after his night visions, which revealed the secret enfolded in King Nebuchadnezzar's dream, he uttered this pious ejaculation, "I thank Thee, and praise Thee, O Lord, who hast given me wisdom and might; and hast made known unto me the King's matter".* Then, on becoming aware of the long captivity to which his nation would have to submit,

* Chap. ii, 23.

he humbled himself, and after making confession of sins, thus prayed, "O my God, incline thine ear and hear; open thine eyes and behold our desolations, for we do not present our supplications before Thee for our righteousness, but for Thy great mercies". And again, on seeing a vision that spoke only of "hope deferred", he mourned and fasted during three full weeks; or to quote his own words, "I ate no pleasant bread, neither came flesh nor wine into my mouth". Here then we have an example every way worthy of imitation. *Three times a day* or oftener did Daniel hold converse in prayer with the Great Ruler of the Universe, and this each of us may and should do likewise. There can be no adequate excuse for a breach of this sacred duty, and assuredly none is more worthless than the plea of want of time! Let him who dares seek to justify his culpable neglect on so shallow a pretext, reflect on the magnitude of those affairs of office which fell to the lot of Daniel as chief minister and virtual Ruler of a vast Empire, and compare them with his own business engagements. Must he not then acknowledge that it is not want of time, but want of inclination, which prompts him to evade this positive duty? Let us but cultivate the same proper dispositions of the heart towards the Supreme which marked the whole career of the "man greatly beloved of God", and those hours now lost, or, worse than lost, misspent, will be cheerfully dedicated to the service of the Creator as a tribute of gratitude from the creature. In a word, bearing within us a devout, thankful spirit, we shall suffer no long interval to elapse without seeking the great Father of All, and humbly, lovingly, reverently bowing before His heavenly throne in prayer.

DISCRETION.

Gen. xxxii, 20, "*And say ye moreover, Behold, thy servant Jacob is behind us. For he said, I will appease him with the present that goeth before me, and afterward I will see his face; peradventure he will accept of me.*"

It is to be observed that the patriarch JACOB, prior to reaching this point in his history, had passed through two very different schools of instruction, each leaving its distinctive mark upon his character. Reared under the eye of a doting mother, he had during his tender years known little else than ease, comfort, and love; but when just about reaching manhood a sudden change occurred, and a new life, full of care, trial, and distrust, opened before him. He had to quit a peaceful, happy home, and wander forth alone, unbefriended, with scanty means, and, worse than all, with an upbraiding conscience. Great was the trial, and, though at first bitter and depressing, it was fraught with much aftergood, practically teaching him a highly necessary lesson—the peculiar excellence of Discretion. Now Discretion is assuredly no home virtue, but is best fostered and developed in the world where man is constantly rubbing and jostling his fellow-man. Thus it proved with Jacob. This virtue could have been but slightly inculcated during his youth, since it so utterly deserted him at the first critical juncture; indeed, all leads to the conclusion that he was a spoilt child, and had been accustomed to have his own way on every occasion. Esau, being of an easy disposition, must have yielded to his brother in minor matters, as he did in the all-essential point of his birthright, and thus Jacob, being seldom or never thwarted, will easily have brought himself to believe that all would cede before him, and that he had but to desire in order to obtain. This may in a great measure account for his ready acquiescence in the proposal of his misguided, because partial, mother, that he should practise deception on his aged father. But it is also most probable that in perpetrating this one rash, unjustifiable act of early manhood he was carried away by impulse, the great antagonist to discretion. Certainly nothing warrants us in believing that there was premeditation on his part, while all goes far to prove that the deed, if to be carried out in accordance with his mother's bidding, admitted of no delay and little reflection. It had to be done at once or never. Great was the prize to be secured, while the act itself lost much of its heinous dye on account of the several specious reasons to be urged in its defence. Was not the maternal injunction authoritative? was it not pressing? and did not his father's blessing come as the natural appendix to that birthright which was already his? Whether such reflections passed through his mind we may not know; but this is certain, that Discretion being absent at the critical moment, he fatally succumbed, and enacted a part from which each better feeling of his nature must have revolted, when, alas! too late, he found time to review his past conduct. Over-indulged as he had been, there was notwithstanding much, very much, of good in his character. But of how little avail is even goodness of disposition if discretion be not at hand to direct it aright, this episode in Jacob's life furnishes ample proof. Had he only given himself time for reflection, and taken Discretion, with its handmaidens, good sense and right feeling, as his counsellors, he would most certainly never have committed an error so grave as even to border on criminality. Assuredly he made this one hasty plunge into the fearful abyss of sin thoughtlessly, inconsiderately. His was an upright nature; with him there was no wilfulness; his chief fault evidently lay in not pausing to consider the difference that existed between this step and those which had preceded it in the same direction. But there was also much weakness or want of that hardness and force of character which adversity alone imparts. Could he have brought discretion and firmness to his aid, he would have meekly, yet resolutely, refused to comply with the command of his misguided mother, even when she said unto him, "Upon me be the curse, my son, only *obey* my voice," and thus he would have avoided the most serious, the most fatal error of his life, one which entailed much misery alike on himself and on those he dearly loved. But as it was he most unjustifiably perpetrated a fraud upon an aged, blind, and sincerely respected father, gave his twin and only brother Esau ample cause for anger, or even for hatred, and indeed so greatly incensed him that, to escape from his just ire, Jacob had to flee his home and quit the side of the too fondly anxious mother, never again to behold her. To the absence, then, of discretion must we in a great measure attribute conduct which, though attended by some extenuating circumstances, cannot fail to meet with general condemnation.

But this was the turning point in Jacob's life, for in the very next chapter of his early history we find much to incite the reverse sentiment of admiration; indeed, no sooner had he quitted his father's roof, until lately the abode of peace and plenty, wandering forth an exile amidst strangers, and with but scanty fare, than a notable change for the better manifested itself. The estimable traits in his character became more and more marked as many of the defects inherent in the spoilt child disappeared, and then uprose those noble qualities with which frowning fortune repays its tried children. Arrived at Haran, domiciled under the roof of his mother's brother, Laban, and with the prospect of marriage with that uncle's loved daughter, it might be supposed that his lot had happily "fallen into pleasant places", but it proved far otherwise. The unscrupulous Laban, goaded on by the lust of wealth, lost all consideration for his nephew, and imposed on him the most oppressive labour.

For long years did Jacob submit without a murmur, probably feeling that the trial he was undergoing might in a measure atone for the wrong-doing of his youth; at any rate, it is certain that this life of penance effectually served to mature his judgment, improve his heart, and render him wary, prudent, and discreet.

Now, although there can be little doubt that, during the twenty years Jacob passed with Laban, he gave numerous proofs of discretion, yet, as this can only be a matter of opinion, we will leave the speculative for the practical, and at once revert to his proceedings after quitting Haran, intent on safely reaching the land of his birth and the dwelling-place of his brother, with his large family, his flocks and his herds. While well aware that an invincible obstacle lay in his path should he fail to appease the mighty and haughty Esau, whom he had so greatly injured and offended, still right feeling no less than expediency must have prompted him to make the ample atonement which followed. Love and discretion alike told him that it could never be too late to amend, or, if possible, redeem the past, and this course Jacob resolved to follow, whatsoever might be the sacrifice it entailed. His method of proceeding was as judicious as effective. He well knew and greatly appreciated the character of his much wronged brother, but being at the same time fully alive to his proud nature, he felt that by submission alone might he hope to conciliate and secure that brother's forgiveness. He further saw how advisable it would be to give one so impulsive and warm-hearted as Esau, time to reflect and conquer through natural affection any latent wrath still harbouring in his breast. Earnest in repairing to the best of his powers the injury done, he humbly set himself to the task. Taking discretion as his guide, all his measures were characterised by prudence, good sense, and good feeling; and, when every precaution had been adopted which might help to save from peril the loved ones at his side, he sought God in prayer, and thus petitioned his protection against the threatening dangers, "Deliver me, I pray Thee, from the hands of my brother, from the hands of Esau, for I fear him, lest he will come and smite me and the mother with the child". What a lesson is conveyed in these words, when taken in conjunction with Rebecca's parting instructions to her favourite son Jacob, which run as follows: "Now, my son, obey my voice, and flee thee to Laban; tarry with him *a few days* until thy brother's fury turn away from thee and he forget that which thou hast done to him";[*] since they indicate that even the lapse of *twenty years* had not sufficed to obliterate from Jacob's mind the gross wrong perpetrated with regard to that brother, nor quelled the fear such conduct had engendered.

But when we turn to the mighty Esau, and mark the cordial reception given by that chieftain to Jacob, we at once see not only how futile were the fears of the absentee, but that even in entertaining such mistrust (the natural offspring of a guilty conscience) he was still further wronging his warm-hearted brother. The careless youth, who had sold the much coveted birthright, possessed, like Jacob, many sterling qualities, yet in both cases home had equally failed in properly developing the good seed. Naturally hasty and impulsive, Esau could not submit to a personal wrong, and when he found that his rightful blessing had been wrested from him by the "subtlety" of a brother, his anger knew no bounds, and "he hated Jacob because of the blessing wherewith his father blessed him". But such feelings could not long dwell in his generous breast, and the warmth with which he greeted Jacob fully testifies his forgiving and placable nature. Do we not read, "And Esau ran to meet his brother, and embraced him and fell on his neck and wept"? How bitter must have been the thought to Jacob that he had wronged one so noble and so good, and correspondingly great his delight when he had induced

[*] Ch. xxvii, 43.

his brother to be the recipient of his gifts, since this afforded satisfactory evidence that Esau was not only gratified by this show of willing reparation, but that he cordially accepted his atonement. The present given was certainly no bribe, but a peace offering, and from that moment fraternal love and good fellowship subsisted between them. Thus will discretion, when combined with good feeling, repair many a breach, reuniting in bonds of affection those who, through youthful indiscretion or hasty, fitful passion, have rashly or inconsiderately forfeited their just claim to mutual love, respect, and happiness.

Discretion is of a compound nature, and demands alike high moral qualities and well-developed intellectual faculties; indeed, these are its essential characteristics. It will only attain an eminent degree of usefulness when both mind and heart have been enlisted in its service. Feeling, naturally evanescent and varying, needs its companion reason, and even this noble and distinctive attribute will but feebly control our actions, if either callous indifference deadens, or overwrought sensibility and passions unduly inflame the heart. Let discretion have as auxiliaries judgment and prudence on the one hand, good feeling and right dispositions on the other, which being closely united so as to form an entire, a perfect whole, cannot fail to subserve the cause of moral development and moral excellence. Assuredly only when these have all received their due share of attention, and gained strength by culture and exercise, will discretion prove itself a true friend and faithful guardian. Here, then, have we an important task to perform, and one no way difficult, if we have only learnt thoroughly to appreciate the lessons taught by this desirable monitor. Indeed, what does discretion require of us but to map out for ourselves the highest good and follow it undeviatingly? and surely that which in its teachings is so simple will not itself be very complex or difficult of attainment. We have only to follow these easy and effective rules : never to suffer the judgment to be idle, but to train it up from earliest youth to vigorous action; always to consult the cardinal virtue, prudence, and give heed to its counsel; also, to strive after and cultivate right dispositions, ever giving ample play to the best feelings of our nature. Further, we should take experience as our guide, and seek wisdom as our safest preceptor. Valuing reason as God's highest gift, we should lose no opportunity of unfolding and strengthening the noble power with which we have been endowed. We should bestir ourselves in the acquirement of knowledge, and seek to turn it to the best advantage. In proportion to our success in these respects, so far shall we have advanced towards the attainment of discretion.

But here it behoves us to reflect that discretion is, after all, only a worldly light, which, if not kindled by the heavenly beam of piety, will be faint and glimmering. Ever walking amidst the vicissitudes of daily life, and not unfrequently under the dark shadow of trials and misfortunes, surely we would rather march freely onwards, illumined by the noonday sun, than to have to grope our way by twilight. Now Religion is that sun; by its light we may see the boundary line of moral obligation well defined, a line which may not be crossed without fatal consequences to ourselves and others. It further warms the heart to good, invigorating every desire of a pure and holy character, while at the same time checking the growth of evil passions and selfish gratification. In a word, discretion and religion alike mark out the bounds of right and wrong, but it is to the latter alone we may look for that strength which will enable us to control wayward inclinations, and keep us in the path of duty as of honour. And here we may ask, is it not patent that throughout the course of life there is a certain best thing to be done and a certain best manner of doing it? further, is it not beyond all doubt, that the man will not labour in vain who zealously searches for the divine light of truth in the Holy Volume, and diligently consults the dictates of conscience? Assuredly all who seek will acquire that high degree of judgment and discretion, which will enable them to steer safely and steadily through every peril and temptation which beset the path of life.

Now, on taking into consideration the fact that discretion is esteemed a high virtue, and one every way consonant with self-interest, the question naturally occurs why it should be so rare among men? And is not this the true answer?—that it has to contend with many powerful antagonists which are ever seeking to pervert its just decisions and work its downfall. Imperfect culture and want of reflection, though seriously injurious to its development, yet sink into insignificance before those more formidable foes, which, casting aside reason, judgment, and good feeling, stand erect and defiant, ever ready prepared to impede man's progress towards that safe, easy, and direct path, to which discretion and piety point. As these, however, are all slaves of the will, they can be overcome through care and resolution, leaving discretion master of the situation. Foremost among the number are our passions, desires, and appetites, all of which are admirably fitted to subserve the highest purposes; yet, being once suffered to depass due bounds, never stay their course till they have destroyed all moral and exhausted all physical vigour. To direct, to utilise, to moderate and control them, when thus running headlong into sinful excesses, is the true province of discretion. But to enable it to cope with such powerful antagonists, it is imperative that reason, religion, and conscience should lend their aid. They must hold a close watch, and at the very outset of folly and dissipation raise their voice, so as to make it distinctly heard, even above the clamour of passion. When, through their teachings, we have learnt all the happiness which is obtainable from cherishing virtue, and the misery we avoid by keeping within the legitimate path of duty, then will judgment and good feeling regain their supremacy, and discretion come triumphant through the struggle. But it has other enemies no less determined and dangerous; viz., blind impulses, untruth, and ill-temper. In their ungovernable fury and fitful career, these play sad havoc with every right principle, and inevitably wean the heart from good. Now, if it be true that "he who hesitates is lost", how venturesome must that man be who does not even hesitate, but rushes wildly forward regardless of the call of discretion, as of the dangers and sorrows which closely beset an ill-chosen path! Truly, if discretion here fail, piety alone can avail, thus may it be ever at hand to lend its powerful support.

But discretion further has two very dangerous, because insidious foes to disarm and defeat, before it can be in quiet possession of the field. These are prejudice and fatalism. Having once taken hold on the mind, they can only be dislodged by judgment, good feeling, and religion, which must themselves already have been greatly weakened by those remorseless enemies. Now, in order to cope successfully with them, we must make a stand, and, armed with virtue and piety, wage unceasing war against them. They will often call for a severe and hard struggle; yet can we, dare we, hold back from it, when we consider, firstly, how greatly we may wrong our fellow-creatures by allowing prejudice to be engendered; and, secondly, with respect to fatalism, how criminal we become when we derogate from the supreme attributes of the Deity by even admitting chance as an agent in the universe, or imagining that fate can control and fetter man, thereby redeeming him from all responsibility? Truly, we must dismiss all bias of mind and all idea of fate or chance before we can hope to mould our conduct according to the dictates of discretion and piety. But, this done, we shall never prejudge or rashly condemn our fellow mortals; while we shall trustfully strive to achieve permanent good for ourselves and others.

Proceeding next to consider the *teachings* of discretion,

we find them to be simply these; to set the mind and heart on great and laudable objects; also to labour sedulously in our vocation, nor cease therefrom till repaid by complete success. And when we have seriously considered wherein consists the greatest good, learnt to centre our desires therein, and sought for it with all the pertinacity it deserves, then shall we have made considerable advance towards discretion. Now, if goodness and virtue be that highest good, as they surely are, then will discretion bid us persistently and unceasingly aim at their attainment. It will point out to us how consistent they are even with worldly wisdom, and urge us to hold them fast, and draw them into every act, every deed we are called on to perform. Thus prompting, discretion will be a true friend to us in the business of life, a safe guide in our pleasures, and a judicious adviser when joining in social intercourse with our fellow-men. Its aim will be ever lofty, because goodness and virtue are in themselves high and exalted; its instruction will greatly conduce to our well-being, for such is its sure and unvarying tendency. Let us, then, hearken to its teachings, and avail ourselves of its invaluable lessons.

It will tell us, firstly, that in the business of life we must hold integrity, probity, and truth, in the highest estimation, make the love of rectitude our chief care, and cast from us all vain, all sordid desires. Again, that we should strive after things feasible rather than things desirable; make the most of the position accorded us, be it great or humble; gather in all outlying opportunities, and employ all the means at our disposal to accomplish good and worthy ends. It will teach us to regulate our affairs with method, and conduct our train of life agreeably to our circumstances; not to stand thinking when we should be acting, and only to "halt between two opinions" so long as is necessary to arrive at a well-poised and, if possible, just decision. Never to give up our birthright of judgment, but exert all the faculties with which we have been endowed to sift the true from the false; to break through the cobwebs of sophistry, and dispel the mist that will at times obscure the sun of reason. Secondly—With regard to our pleasures, discretion will call upon us to consider both their quality and quantity; for, according to their character and their proportion, so will they prove the elixir or the poison of life; it will bid us esteem happiness higher than pleasure, and urge us to cast aside the latter when a choice must be made between them; further, to abstain from frivolous amusements, and draw nigh to those which are useful, and relax the mind without enervating it; to hold a temperate course between extremes, for "too much of anything is good for nothing"; and, above aught else, sedulously to avoid all wrong doing. It will teach us to regard life as a whole; to consider distant and ultimate good equally with present pleasures, and estimating each according to its real magnitude, set our hearts upon them accordingly. To despise profitless or debasing pleasures, and dread such as undermine health and injure our moral nature. It also bids us value as an inestimable treasure each small gain in the way of virtue. Lastly, as regards our disposition towards our fellow-men, the kindly feeling we should cultivate may be summed up in the command, "Thou shalt love thy neighbour as thyself", and, again, "Thou shalt love the stranger as thyself".*

And here it is well to observe that discretion enforces no curtailment of liberty; it only urges us to set our desires in accordance with duty and the law of God. Pointing to all that is good, right, and just, it bids us make diligent search after the prize of virtue. Our desires thus well directed, we shall never seek to depass the bounds marked out by good sense and good feeling, but be ever ready and glad to conform to the dictates of conscience and piety. Such, indeed, is the only true freedom, and the just reward of a wise discretion.

* Lev. xix, 18, 34.

Finally, it may be serviceable to take note of some of the many *benefits* which Discretion, conjoined with piety, confers, as also of the *evils* that will almost inevitably accrue from its absence. But it behoves us to couple herewith the all-important consideration, whether we would rather profit by the experience of our progenitors, hearken and wisely conform to their practical teachings, or arrive at the same conclusion at the cost of much labour, pain, and sorrow. Surely, with the true and the false, with good and evil besetting the path of life, we should gladly avail ourselves of the experience of ages historically spread out before us, and though much that is new or unexpected will occasionally arise to perplex us, we shall yet find ample light cast by the good, the great, the just and pious, whereby to trace our course safely and with honour and credit to ourselves. Multitudes have spoken, and is it not wiser to listen to their voice, and carefully weigh their words than to push on heedlessly, risking the consequences of our rashness and presumption? Truly the errors and frailties of others should serve to warn us, while the example of the virtuous and pious of all ages may well be our guiding star. Where so many have stranded let not us make shipwreck, but learn through them how to steer the course of life most pleasurably, easily, and usefully. Above all, let us take to heart this important truth, the practical teaching of bygone generations, that without discretion as the foundation stone we can never build up for ourselves a moral structure, wherein shall happily dwell health, content, and peace. Indeed we may read in the pages of the past that where discretion is wanting, there will cloying pleasure usurp the place of happiness, and speedily degenerate into the indulgence of senseless passions and vicious habits, which in their turn will assuredly sap all principle, generate disease, and finally beggar us physically and morally. Now, strange as it may appear, men who give little heed to this truth when it concerns themselves, yet practically acknowledge it in their admonitions as loving parents or guardians. They deem it to be a positive duty to hold sedulous watch over their charges till "years of discretion" be reached, and stay the impetuosity of youth before the first false step be made, which must entail incalculable evils—such indeed as a whole after life, however wisely spent, would possibly not suffice to counteract.

Proceeding to consider the benefits which generally accrue from discretion, let us bear in remembrance that while a wise and beneficent Providence has vouchsafed us numerous rich blessings redounding to our happiness, yet it is only through the early acquirement of this most precious quality that we may securely attain, and moreover retain, such valuable gifts. Indeed, it is mostly owing to folly and presumption that they are so often lost to us. But with Discretion for our faithful friend and monitor, temptation will be eschewed or successfully resisted; indulgence in that careless train of living which is the general cause of ruin to mankind will be checked; in a word, we shall be ever earnest in choosing the better path. Thus may we escape incalculable ills, and even the deep stain of guilt which so frequently attends on vicious courses, while we shall be permitted to rejoice in the glorious thought that each of our good and virtuous acts will infallibly subserve the cause of progress and germinate, yielding fruit after its own kind.

With such an option open to us, shall we invoke the aid of Discretion, with all its estimable benefits, or can we possibly resolve to grope blindly in the maze of difficulties and follies? Of this we may at least feel assured, that our earliest choice will imprint itself on our after character, and in no small degree conduce to make or mar our future happiness. Now, if we will only bear constantly in mind that the fear of the Lord is the beginning of wisdom, also that the love of God is the first step to the "enlightening of the eyes", and strive to follow the dictates of piety and Discretion, then will folly and sin have but a feeble tenure, and we shall be left free to follow those virtuous aspirations, which, while they tend to our worldly interests, will infallibly conduce to our eternal welfare.

PRECEPTS inculcating the virtue of Discretion run, like a golden thread, through the Book of Proverbs. It is there that its doctrines are most clearly set forth, that its inestimable worth is made manifest, and the benefits it will confer on mankind are demonstrated. Therein wisdom is personified, and made eloquently and emphatically to exhort us to cultivate the moral virtues, as also to warn us against their contrary vices; and that we may be more easily led to attend to her admonitions, she opens her instructive lesson with bright and cheering promises to those who will give heed to her voice, adding threats and chidings for those who wilfully violate her laws. Thus we read, ch. viii, "Hearken unto me, O ye children, blessed are they that keep my ways; hear instruction, be wise and refuse it not, for blessed is the man that heareth me, *watching daily at my gates*, waiting at my door. For whoso findeth me findeth life, and shall obtain favour of the Lord. But he that sinneth against me wrongeth his own soul, all they that hate me love death". How all-essential Discretion is to man's well-being the following verses sufficiently testify: ch. vii, 10, "When wisdom entereth into thine heart and knowledge is pleasant unto thy soul, *Discretion shall preserve thee*, understanding shall keep thee"; thou wilt then "walk in the way of good men. It will deliver thee from him that speaketh froward things, that walketh in darkness, that rejoiceth to do evil, and whose ways are crooked". Then Job assures us, ch. xxxiv, 11, "that the work of a man will the Almighty render unto him, and cause every man to find according to his ways". With such glowing promises before us, let us turn to the reverse picture, and satisfy ourselves as to the probable consequences of inattention to the promptings and teachings of Wisdom or Discretion. In Ps. cvii we read, "Fools because of their transgressions and because of their iniquity are afflicted"; again, in Isaiah v, 20: "Woe unto them that call evil good and good evil, that put darkness for light and light for darkness, that put bitter for sweet and sweet for bitter"; and further, we read, Prov. xxii, 3, "While a prudent man foreseeth the evil and hideth himself, the simple pass on and are punished". Now, as reason and foresight are ever undervalued, even if not lost sight of by those who can, who dare, acknowledge such a thing as chance, the following verses tending to correct so gross an error may be of some avail. In Prov. xi we find, "Fools make a mock at sin, the simple believe every word, but *the prudent man looks well to his goings*"; and again (ch. xiv), "There is a way which seemeth right unto a man, but the end thereof are the ways of death". Then Ps. cxii, "A good man will guide his affairs with *discretion*, and surely he shall not be moved for ever". Jeremiah points out to us how men thus erroneously impressed will naturally fall into sin. In ch. ii of his Book we read, "They said not, where is the Lord? but transgressed against me and walked after things that do not profit". Let us now cull such verses as will teach us how best we may acquire wisdom and exercise Discretion in the conduct of life. In Prov. vi we are told, "The commandment is a lamp, and the Law is light, reproofs of instruction are the way of life", and in ch. xxviii, "They that seek the Lord understand all things"; then in ch. xxiii, "Apply thine heart unto instruction and thine ears to the words of knowledge. *Be thou in the fear of the Lord all the day long*". Again, "Ponder the paths of thy feet, and let all thy ways be established". Then, turning to the Book of Job, we find that Elihu, when advocating the cause of wisdom and discretion, says, ch. xxxiv, "Let the ear try words, also let us choose to us judgment, and know among ourselves what is good". Finally, would we learn in what discretion consists, and how it may serve us for good, *without curtailment of liberty*, we may turn to Psalms, where the righteous David speaks in his own person, thus declaring, Psalm ci,

"I will behave myself wisely in a perfect way; I will walk within my house with a perfect heart"; and Ps. cxix, "I will delight myself in thy commandments which I have loved; *I will walk at liberty, for I seek thy precepts*". Then he thus petitions God in prayer, "Cause me to know the way wherein I shall walk, for I lift up my soul unto Thee"; and again, Ps. xc, "So teach us, O Lord, to number our days that we may apply our hearts unto wisdom". Were it necessary, numerous other verses to like effect might be quoted, but here we may stop short, since the foregoing throw ample light on this subject, and clearly indicate the true path of wisdom and discretion.

An interesting episode in the life of ABIGAIL, wife of Nabal, offers an EXAMPLE, which perhaps, of all others throughout the Sacred Volume, most plainly sets forth the high virtue and beneficial effects of Discretion, thence presenting us with the highest incentive to its constant exercise. Abigail had been informed by one of her servants that through the churlish behaviour and imbecility of her besotted husband, a great misfortune was likely to befal her household. He had summarily rejected a mission of peace from David, and refused him that assistance which justice as well as good feeling would have dictated. This ungracious and unfair conduct so roused David's ire that he set forth with an armed escort, determined to avenge the insult and make Nabal pay the penalty in the forfeit of his life and total destruction of his house. But through the wise discretion of Abigail his wrathful project was stayed. No sooner had this noble woman learnt what had occurred than she at once set herself to repair the wrong done, and the whole of her proceedings during this great emergency were eminently practical, and characterised throughout by good sense, good feeling, and prudence. She went forth to meet David, taking with her those gifts which she well knew he had a right to demand; she endeavoured to lessen the offence of her husband by showing that it proceeded in a great measure from sheer folly, while her propitiatory speech at the interview displayed rare powers of discretion, besides great energy and decision of purpose. It is to these high qualities we may attribute so satisfactory an issue, for she not only saved the life of her husband thereby, but also checked David in the commission of a great sin. How grateful he was for this interposition may be judged by his response to her entreaty, for thus he addressed her, "Blessed be thy advice; blessed be thou who hast kept me this day from coming to shed blood and from avenging myself with mine own hand". The life of Abigail up to this period could have been by no means an enviable one. She must have had to humour a besotted husband, attend to the management of those affairs which he neglected, and repair the blunders he committed. Yet it was to this very school of trial and mental discipline that she doubtless owed those qualities which enabled her to turn a seemingly ominous event to good. The death of her husband, however, speedily followed, bringing with it a marked change in her existence, since she was shortly after united to David, who himself possessing like rich qualities of mind and heart, well knew how to appreciate them in another. Thus will Discretion ever repay its followers.

We would now take a passing review of the characters of two men, who in their conduct through life occasionally permitted rash impulse to supersede and usurp the place of Discretion, and consequently falling into grave errors, they became the authors of their own after-trials. The first is the renowned JEPHTHAH, the various incidents of whose life give ample proof that want of discretion was with him rather the exception than the rule, and that he generally displayed great prudence combined with no small degree of judgment. This is especially observable in his embassy to the King of Ammon, where firmness and temper, sound arguments and fair dealings form conspicuous features, as indeed is shown by his words to that king, " Wherefore I have not sinned against thee, but thou doest me wrong to war against me; the Lord, the Judge, be judge this day between the children of Israel and the children of Ammon". His peaceful demeanour, however, not having brought about an amicable arrangement, war was declared, and it was then that, not content with praying to God for success to his arms, he made a vow, as rash as uncalled for, and totally at variance with the dictates of a wise discretion. Whatever may have been the ultimate fate of his daughter—and of this there is some question—it must have been a very sad one, even taking his own words as proof. Returning home elated with conquest, the bright and joyous prospects before him became fatally obscured by the sight of his beloved child, and, rending his clothes, he thus addressed that cherished being, "Alas! my daughter, thou hast brought me very low, and thou art one of them that trouble me, for I have opened my mouth unto the Lord, and I cannot go back", ominous and portentous words drawn from him in the anguish of his heart. Now, while we cannot but pity the man, we must condemn as well as deplore the rashness which led to so painful a catastrophe. God never has demanded nor will demand of his creatures as the price of His gracious protection, any sacrifice except the renunciation of whatsoever is opposed to duty. This being the sole offering that is acceptable to the Deity, we should ever beware of making any rash vow. Incapable of seeing into the future, or even knowing how best to act when that future arrives, we have but this one wise and righteous course to pursue, namely, to place our dependence on the righteous Lord of All, and, in Holy trust, leave events in the Hands of Omniscience.

We now turn to an incident in the life of SAUL which in many points bears a remarkable similarity to the one just considered. This monarch's character underwent a great change for the worse before he had been two years on the throne. Grandeur and power had evidently warped his heart, for not only did his faith in God waver on several occasions, but he also gave a less attentive ear than heretofore to the commandment of the Lord, and even at times acted in direct opposition to His High Will. Samuel's reproof leaves no doubt as to this, for we read, " Samuel said to Saul, thou hast done foolishly, thou hast not kept the commandment of the Lord thy God, therefore thy kingdom shall not continue".[*] Yet even after this we find no reform; on the contrary, he departed further from his God, and, as a natural consequence, his proceedings became less and less characterised by a wise discretion—indeed, his conduct soon became such as to prove highly prejudicial to the nation as well as to himself and those near of kin. Among the many instances wherein we find him ruining the most promising enterprises, and irremediably marring the brightest prospects of his people, the following stands prominently forward. Saul and his army were advancing to attack a powerful enemy, and, being faint, needed sustenance whereby to recruit their waning strength before entering into combat. Yet at this very moment Saul made an unadvised adjuration, placing those of his army who should taste food under a curse! He thus enfeebled the arm he should have nerved. That this injudicious proceeding proved greatly prejudicial may be gathered from Jonathan's words, for when he was told " that Saul had charged his people with an oath, saying, Cursed be the man that eateth any food this day", and that in consequence the " people were faint", he said, " My father has troubled the land; if happily the people had eaten freely to-day of the spoil of the enemies which they found, there had been a much greater slaughter among the Philistines". Thus did Saul frustrate the efforts of his brave son, and impede the victory which he had partially secured at great personal risk. And fortunate was it that the evils arising from Saul's ill-advised oath stopped there, for it well-nigh brought on himself, as well as the nation at large, a serious and irreparable calamity, the untimely end of that son. Jonathan had

[*] Samuel xiii, 13.

shown himself to be a great and valiant commander, and, as his words amply testify, one full of sublime faith, for we read, "Jonathan said to his armour-bearer, Let us go over unto the garrison of these uncircumcised, it may be that the Lord will work for us, for there is no restraint to the Lord to save by many or by few";* and yet, but for the fortunate interposition of the people, this spirited youth would have been condemned to death by his father. Take Jonathan's own words when explaining to Saul what he had done, "I did but taste a little honey with the end of the rod that was in mine hand, and lo! I must die"; and then mark the austere answer, "God do so and more also, for thou shalt surely die, Jonathan". Now, in the case of Jephthah and his daughter we find some compunction on the part of the father, but here there is not even one word of regret expressed, although the penalty of death he is about to enforce on his son is the consequence of his own weakness in making a rash and senseless vow. We may know the feeling of the people by the fact that, although they had said to Saul, "Do what seemeth thee good in this matter", yet, when Jonathan's death was decreed immediately afterwards by his father, they thus remonstrated, "Shall Jonathan die who hath wrought this great salvation in Israel? God forbid, as the Lord liveth there shall not one hair of his head fall to the ground, for he hath wrought with God this day. So the people rescued him that he died not". Thus we see that rebellion was very nearly added to the other evils which this one false step engendered. And what but want of faith in God and want of trust in the righteousness of his cause led Saul to proceedings so repugnant to every principle of right, so totally opposed to good sense and good feeling? He would have made a rash vow or adjuration supercede that necessary discretion and piety of which he was so deficient. Truly his heart was not perfect with God, else would there never have been recorded against him such a verse as the following: "Then came the word of the Eternal unto

* Samuel xiv, 6.

Samuel, saying, I repent that I have declared Saul king, for he is turned back from following me, and hath not performed my commandments". Through his folly and misconduct he had justly incurred the displeasure of the Supreme, and, failing to repent of his errors, he was rejected by the Lord. Thence followed, as natural results, many sad disasters. He met with repeated reverses in the field, constant political disquietudes, and, what was far worse, a morose and gloomy spirit came over him; he allowed himself to be weighed down by superstitious fears, and pined under an uneasy conscience till he met an inglorious death. Truly he darkened his own bright prospects, and forfeited the respect and love both of his subjects and of his son. Such must ever be the fate of those who, like Saul, fearless of consequences, choose the crooked path of their own imaginings and baneful desires, rejecting the teachings of true Piety and Discretion.

CONTENTMENT.

Gen. xxxiii, 11, "*Take, I pray thee, because God hath dealt graciously with me, and because I* HAVE ENOUGH, *and he urged him*" (Esau).

No solitary act should form an index to a life, and would we justly appreciate the character of the patriarch JACOB, it behoves us to bear this vividly in mind. Truly, in his early manhood, he had committed a grave, grave error, yet none other being recorded against him throughout his highly eventful life, we should surely not permit it to cloud from our view his manifold excellent qualities. But even as regards this false step, we have only to survey his whole career attentively, and mark his perfect resignation under trials, his happy content when his lot was most unenviable, in order to conclude that it was not dictated by any base or sordid motive. All indeed would lead us to attribute it to impulse and the wilfulness which ever characterises the spoilt child, but certainly not to covetousness or premeditation. Evidently he erred from want of judgment, not want of heart; since, had there been any admixture of craft or cupidity in this proceeding, such must have cropped up and tinctured the colour of his after-life. We do not, however, find the faintest indication of this, the varied incidents which spread themselves broadcast over the whole of Jacob's career, speaking only of that true nobility of character which knows no disguise, no meanness, no selfish ambition; in a word, he trusted in God and was content. This has only to be proved in order to set the character of the worthy patriarch in its true light.

Now there can assuredly be no safer or surer test of character than that offered by such an adverse change of fortune and condition as befel Jacob without one note of warning. In the household of his father Isaac, there must have reigned plenty even to superfluity, while there could have lacked no comfort or enjoyment which it was in the power of wealth to procure. Reared in such a home, and moreover being the favourite son of an over-indulgent mother, we may suppose that Jacob's wishes seldom remained ungratified. But great was the change from the moment he abandoned the shelter of that roof. The very first scene in which he is presented to us was one of peril and privation. He had to pillow his head on the cold ground, and hunger on scanty meals. Yet withal mark his prayer. Humbling himself before the Throne of mercy, thus much only he implored: "Bread to eat, and garment to put on"; so that he might "return to his father's house in peace"—there was the full scope of his petition; mere bodily sustenance in the present, with the heart's hope in the future. If this simple prayer, made so immediately after his youthful transgression, be a fair exposition of his disposition, then must we acknowledge that his pretensions and views were characterised by moderation; that he was humble-minded, and could never have entertained such ambition as would lead him to set his heart upon supplanting his brother. But further to gauge his natural temper of mind, we must observe his conduct during the twenty years he passed with Laban; and does not his every proceeding during that term of probation practically demonstrate the goodness of his heart, the total absence of overweening desires, of ignoble repinings, of selfish views and passions? From the first, he must have acquiesced cheerfully in the proposal of his avaricious relative, content to serve him during seven years for wages which could no way better his fortune. But even the very payment which was to gratify his heart's desire was surreptitiously withheld, and another seven years of servitude followed. It is further evident, from the perusal of Gen. xxxi, 14-16, that he took his wife *portionless*. Surely, if Jacob had been of a grasping disposition, he would never have submitted to such terms; or if his heart had not been warm and loving, he would not so faithfully and zealously have served one who showed so little kind feeling towards him. Yet, even after the expiration of fourteen years, he was induced, through the persuasion of the hard and covetous Laban, to abide still longer with him; for we read, "Laban said unto him, I pray thee, if I have found favour in thine eyes, tarry; appoint me thy wages and I will give it".* Now what is Jacob's answer? "Thou knowest how I have served thee, that thou hadst little before I came, that *the Lord blessed thee* since my coming, and now when shall I provide for mine own house also?" In all this there is no complaint; he merely states that he had performed his duty to his employer, done to the full all that had been exacted, while he piously attributes that wealth, which his own unceasing exertions had so greatly helped to amass, to the One Great and Beneficent Lord of All. His resolve to comply with his uncle's request must have proceeded far more from a desire to please than from any expectation of profit, for to Laban's question, "what shall I give thee?" Jacob at once answers, "Thou shalt not give me anything" (no fixed salary); only let me "pass through thy flock to-day, removing from thence all the speckled and spotted cattle; and of such shall be my hire. So shall my uprightness answer for me on the day that you finally settle this my hire." Now, strange as may seem the agreement and Jacob's mode of proceeding with regard to it, they clearly demonstrate that *there could have been no craft or imposition on his part*, for then would his conduct have been disapproved of by the Eternal. As it was, when Laban began to manifest his dislike to Jacob, the Lord thus spake unto him, "Return to the land of thy fathers and to thy kindred, and *I will be with thee*". Then mark also these, his own

* Gen. xxx, 29.

words, which are yet more conclusive, " And the angel of God spake unto me in a dream, saying, Lift up thine eyes, and see all the rams are ringstraked and speckled, *for I have seen all that Laban doeth unto thee;* now arise and get thee away". Surely these two quotations testify in his favour more than any arguments which could be advanced. But we have further confirmation of his views in the exposition of facts he places before his wives when about quitting Laban's roof; he says, " I see your father's countenance is unfavourable to me, yet ye know *that with all my power* I have served your father; now has he not deceived me and changed my wages ten times? but God hath not suffered him to hurt me. When Laban said thus, the speckled shall be thy wages, then all the cattle bare speckled; and if he said thus, the ringstraked shall be thy hire, then bare all the cattle ringstraked, *thus God hath taken away the cattle of your father* and given them to me." From this we may not doubt that all unfairness must have been on the part of Laban; and would we have further proof, it is to be found in the following answer made by Leah and Rachel to Jacob, " Is there any portion or inheritance for us in our father's house? are we not counted of him strangers? *for he hath sold us,* and hath quite devoured also our money, for all the riches *which God hath taken from our father,* that is ours and our children's."

Thus, to sum up, the youthful scion of a wealthy house, whose life had hitherto been one of ease and enjoyment, was forced, at one bound, to encounter adverse fortune, to bring his mind to steady perseverance, toilsome duties, and daily privations; to submit to Laban's ungenerous conduct and exactions; and for years to brave alone the numerous dangers which beset his path of life. Note his own words, —words which could only have been wrung from him by Laban's persistently unfriendly treatment and ungenerous conduct—verse 36, " And Jacob was wroth, and chode with Laban, and answered and said, What is my trespass? what is my sin? this twenty years have I been with thee, the rams of thy flock I have not eaten, that which was torn of beasts I brought not unto thee, I bare the loss of it, of my hand didst thou require it whether stolen by day or stolen by night; thus in the day the drought consumed me and the frost by night, and my sleep departed from mine eyes." And again, "I served thee fourteen years for thy two daughters and six years for thy cattle, and thou hast changed my wages ten times; except for the God of Abraham and *the fear of Isaac*,* surely thou hadst sent me away now empty. God hath seen mine affliction and the labour of my hands, and rebuked thee." What trials, and how magnanimously confronted! Totally dependent on Laban for his just wages, he must nevertheless have had frequent misgivings as to their receipt, since such appeared to depend on the interposition of a far distant Protector. Yet withal he never swerved from the path of duty, while ever confiding in the goodness of Omnipotence.

Now, even if these facts did not suffice to prove that Jacob was of a meek and gentle disposition, one in no way given to lust after the world's goods, while yet earnest in "providing for his own house" by labour and a thrifty, prudent economy, we may turn to another chapter in his history, when wealth having taken the place of poverty, he was enabled, without prejudice to his large family, to indulge his generous nature, and make some atonement to a brother whom he had thoughtlessly wronged. For this episode in his career, we must refer to the verse which

---

* It appears as if Jacob had no hope of receiving justice at the hands of Laban except through the interposition of his father Isaac. Act as he might, Laban was ever prepared to take advantage of the easy character of his son-in-law. They who attribute fraud to the ill-used patriarch, and believe that he would circumvent or practise deceit upon a near kinsman—crafty and unjust as that kinsman had proved himself—can have read this chapter of the Sacred Volume to little effect. It is truly to mistake the one sinned against for the sinner.

heads this subject, wherein we find that not only he greeted his brother with gifts, but urged his acceptance of them, and further persuaded him to accede thereto by declaring "I have enough". Now when Jacob despatched the presents he evidently intended them as a peace offering, being greatly in fear of his brother; not so, however, when he afterwards *personally* urged him to take them at his hands, since he had already been graciously greeted by Esau, who "ran to meet him, and embraced him, and fell on his neck and kissed him".* The reiterated entreaty must surely have been prompted by the kindliest fraternal feeling; for does he not say, "Receive, I pray you, my presents at my hands; to have seen thy face is as though I had seen the face of a Godlike being, for *thou wast pleased with me*". Esau, though himself well-to-do, could not refuse such brotherly solicitation, and accordingly accepted the gift.

Throughout the remaining years of Jacob's eventful life, it would be easy to trace the same generous spirit of love, of self-abnegation, of pious resignation, and content, and this, be it again remarked, without even the occurrence of one instance displaying covetousness or selfish ambition. Indeed, the error of his youth was *alone of its kind*, and therefore should not be suffered to dim the lustre of his rare qualities in our estimation or *serve to detract* from his great, his undoubted merit. Truly, his character demands our highest admiration, and is every way worthy imitation, while his words and deeds should receive our especial attention and regard. When they have imprinted themselves on our minds we shall learn to re-echo his words in brotherly love to our fellow-creatures, saying, "Take, I pray thee", adding, with pious gratitude to the Giver of all good, "because God hath dealt graciously with me"; and in a spirit of happy content we shall thankfully and joyously exclaim, "I have enough".

Let, then, the entire verse, so replete with charity, faith,

* Gen. xxxiii, 4.

and love, frequently recur to our minds, and become practically exemplified in our conduct, as it was in that of the long-tried, much-enduring patriarch Jacob, afterwards honoured with the name of Israel, the truly righteous servant of God, of whom it was said, "Thou hast contended with a heavenly messenger and with men, and hast prevailed".* Truly crowning words to his high deserts.

The temper of mind most consonant with every phase of human existence and most conducive to men's well-being amidst the vicissitudes of life, is Contentment. It is a boon which moderation, virtue, and truth alone can confer, and which Piety only can render stable and permanent. It is ever found to abide with light wishes, an easy conscience and a total absence of dissimulation, while it gains its firmest support from a profound and settled conviction that under the governance of a wise and gracious Disposer of Events all must be for the best. It lies not in outer objects, but within ourselves, being the fair offspring of a healthy, pure, devout mind; and just in proportion as the better dispositions of the heart are developed through judicious culture, so will it thrive, mature, and flourish. Now the seeds which will yield the golden fruit of Contentment are happily garnered up in the Law of God, where all may apply and receive. None need go away empty from that rich treasure house. It affords the most ample counsel and guidance. Not only does it materially assist us in acquiring a contented frame of mind, but also points out the infallible method of maintaining a tranquil spirit under every reverse or trial. It further instructs us how to fix our desires aright, teaches us to view objects in their true colour, and to seek those only which confer some lasting good or serve some great and lofty purpose. It also bids us hold virtue and truth far above all worldly possessions. It is then at this fount of celestial wisdom and heavenly truth that we should slake

* Gen. xxxii, 28.

our thirst, strengthen our moral nature, imbibe sentiments, desires, principles, and draw that healthful vigour which will quicken us in the pursuit of all that is good, pure, and noble.

But if we study not the inspired page nor take to heart the instruction and comfort it imparts, vain will be our search for Contentment. It can have no existence but in that breast where goodness and love of God hold sway. These alone sweeten life, add zest to its duties as to its pleasures, give peace to the mind and ease to the heart. Virtue and piety only can maintain the equilibrium of the mind, chase away rising fits of despondency, and vanquish the many enemies of content.

And here it will be well to consider what those foes are, so that we may be prepared to encounter and resist them. Now the most formidable, because the most insidious to our peace, are the passions; they crop up at all times, and but too often urge us on in the chase after pleasure, gains, and vanities, so that we are apt to leave happiness far, far behind. The man who is under their dominion must be restless and dissatisfied, for he will be ever hankering after that " which satisfieth not", and, instead of reasonably husbanding, will prodigally exhaust, those powers and resources which nature and fortune with liberal hand dispense and scatter around. His mind, being in a perpetual whirl of excitement, will have neither time, inclination, nor power to stop short at any fixed point, there to rest to enjoy the blessings at command. Truly that individual must lose all sense of contentment who is thus ever keenly engaged in the search after sensual gratification, for not only will he overlook and thereby miss that portion of happiness which might be his, but he will be following a course which too surely leads to disease of mind and body, often to pain and impoverishment. The value of time will be first disregarded, then squandered or mis-spent, leaving no record but what must be written in dark and sombre colours; means never husbanded or replenished will fail, health and vigour recklessly used and often abused will decline; indeed, all we most prize will depart by degrees. Such are the sad straits to which unbridled passions and a disregard of that word of rare significance—enough—must surely bring us. Further, it behoves us to beware of avarice, vanity, untruth, envy, and selfish ambition, for they all alike gnaw the mind and sap its very life-blood. But should they even secure us a triumph, it must be short-lived, for as desire has already sped on after the unattained, and often unattainable, so with all our gains we shall possibly feel poorer than before. What folly, then, to be as it were gambling for fame, riches, pleasures, staking our all upon the die, and thereby often beggaring ourselves of happiness and content.

Nor is it less weak, while at the same time contemptibly mean, to endeavour to seem other than we are; the mask forced on us by vanity and untruth will surely prove an instrument of torture, racking alike mind and conscience. Now none of these harpies or vultures could find entrance into the mind, much less gain ascendancy over it, if men would seek for esteem rather than for admiration, for excellence rather than to excel; for a light heart in preference to a heavy purse; for happiness bred of virtue rather than doubtful pleasures; and finally, if they would learn to know when they are well off, or, knowing it, be satisfied to leave well alone.

Other foes to contentment of quite a reverse stamp to those of the passions, and hardly less hurtful to the mind, here demand consideration. Indifference and idleness stand foremost; these ever banish content, which abides and holds communion only with duty. They also preclude Hope, the very salt of life, and which, alternating with fear, is the mainspring of human actions. Let us therefore be careful not to hush its soft whispers, nor to extinguish natural desires, which solely require to be moderated and directed to proper objects. Now would the apathetic and the slothful only bear in remembrance that Contentment is not a negative but a positive state of mind, and that it is *true happiness in its simplest form*, the thought might stimulate them to cultivate it, so that before long they would find themselves furthering the cause of moral progress, thereby securing to themselves that heart's joy which the virtuous and industrious alone may know.

It might at first sight appear that trials, poverty, and sickness should have taken precedence of the foregoing, as being elements far more calculated to disturb the mind's equilibrium than any of those already mentioned. Yet is this the case? That we cannot be insensible to them, especially when they entail actual suffering, is certain; nevertheless, they do not gall and shackle the mind in the same degree as the passions. Nor is the problem difficult of solution. With respect to the former evils, hope is never excluded; they may rapidly pass away, and, departing, leave their memory to enhance enjoyment, thus serving at the same time as friendly warnings which we may transplant to bud and ripen into sweet and wholesome fruit. But as regards the passions, what is there of hope? We neither seek nor desire to moderate them, and only too gladly give a loose rein, suffering them to run their course regardless of the goal to which they speed. Further, while the passions generally tend to impoverish us even here on earth, trials, poverty, and sickness, borne in a proper and religious spirit, enrich the soul for eternity. Indeed, a fund of happiness is to be derived from cheerfully submitting to God's all-wise dispensations, and if, with heartfelt homage and love, we learn to bow in humble resignation to His decrees, the mind will become better trained to a feeling of settled, happy content than by any amount of worldly success or prosperity. Let us, then, bear in mind, that although fortune will never arm us against herself, yet she has not denied us the use of powerful weapons wherewith to encounter her, and of these none will serve us so well in contending with trials and sorrows, which have ever a purpose and an aim, as faith, hope, and a grateful, because contented, spirit.

It may be advisable to consider next how much happiness is centred in a humble and contented spirit, and how many benefits it is calculated to confer. That we can hardly over-estimate the boon may be inferred from the fact that the very first sense of its existence in the breast suffices to make us value it, and further, that when, through time and culture, contentment has become a settled habit of the mind, it is prized above all earthly possessions; indeed, it has been justly termed "a continual feast".

And may we, dare we, for one moment suppose that the rich banquet spread by the Hand of Supreme Goodness can be for a favoured few only? Assuredly not; all God's creatures are invited to partake thereof and enjoy the feast of beauty, the pleasures of pure and holy love, the delight procurable from the performance of good deeds and of duty, with numerous other gifts far outweighing in value temporal riches and possessions. Then let all alike learn to appreciate such treasures, and each one give his heart to wisdom and virtue. These once fairly acquired, we shall be enabled to create happiness, and magnify it by dispensing it around. We shall look on the bright side of things, yet without encouraging those sanguine expectations which invariably end in disappointment. The smallness of our earthly possessions will raise no bitter pang of regret, but rather serve as an additional stimulus to exertion. We shall readily stem that under-current of vexations which is not wanting even in the smoothest life, and dissipate anxiety by turning to Heaven for comfort. We shall maintain an equable temper under affliction, nor be violently affected by sufferings or sorrow; indeed, we may be said to have found the philosopher's stone. Proceeding ever in accordance with God's Holy Law —working for heaven as well as for earth—doing our duty manfully, cheerfully, and in a hopeful spirit, finding under defeat a consolation in having acted for the best—thus, and thus only, may we attain that glad and glowing sense of pious content which lends to life a great and lasting charm.

Finally, once convinced that innumerable benefits accrue from the possession of a calm, peaceful, and happily-disposed mind, it behoves us seriously to consider how we may best acquire and then retain this boon throughout the eventualities of life. And here it is well to remember that *Contentment is ever proportioned to the moral character*. It is indicative of piety, morality, and good temper. It derives much of its strength from the conviction of its being a sacred and paramount duty due to the Great Giver of every good, and he who dares deny the obligation, or evades it, will surely court happiness in vain. A cold or ungrateful heart never yet knew true joy or content, nor felt how blissful it is to "enjoy God in all things and all things in God". Thence it behoves us to bring our feelings to harmonise with nature, and to cultivate that warm, thankful spirit which will not only gladly appreciate all blessings vouchsafed, but be ever intent on dispensing and turning them to profitable account. But still more is required would we retain a lasting, calm, and placid temper of mind. We must learn to entertain a perpetual sense of presiding goodness, to repose entire confidence in the great Lord of all, and thence never suffer any dread to oppress us, except it be the fear of His displeasure. Then we must proportion our wishes and imaginings *to our industry and deserts*, that is, we should work more and desire less; we must bring our wants within well-defined bounds and a small compass, seek for quality rather than for quantity in the search after gratifications, be ever earnest in cultivating a growth of small pleasures, and gladly resort to those nearest at hand. Further, we must accustom ourselves to estimate things at their real value, nor hanker after superfluities; lastly, when grief assails us, we must resolutely turn our attention to some new and engrossing objects, some great and worthy purpose, labour zealously in their accomplishment, and thereby chase from the mind all futile, all sorrowful remembrances.

But would we fix the feeling of content in our hearts with yet more enduring strength, we should not overlook, as we are too apt to do, the all-important consideration that there is far more *equality* in the lot of man than most are willing to acknowledge or many are even capable of discerning, and that according as we throw into the scales of human existence virtue on the one side or envy and the worst passions on the other, so will happiness or misery preponderate. Now, when we reflect that every event proceeds from a Divine Hand, that the great Heavenly Father loves alike all those children who willingly serve Him, and that equity and justice are ever before His Throne, we shall easily be induced to believe that there is less dissimilitude in the lot of men than at first sight appears; indeed, if we will but attentively read our own life by the light of others, we must infallibly arrive at this conclusion. But we must bear in mind that we may not judge by any one portion, but should take the *entire* life, with its moments of pure happiness as of grief, of hope and of fear, years of health and days of sickness, nor overlook that trial hour which bears with it untold misery or untold bliss alike to the humble and exalted according to their past good or bad conduct. We have indeed only to take the *mean* happiness of a life—pleasure and pain in the aggregate—and consider how the mind lends its colour to every object, in order to feel assured that on the whole there is no very great inequality in the lot of mankind, and that even this is generally of our own making. This belief may gain additional strength when we reflect on the following facts—that each station in life has its advantages and its peculiar inconveniences, that riches imply trust, and thus that with much wealth there is great responsibility; that none are exempt from trials and physical sufferings, while those bred in the lap of luxury are naturally the most sensitive to them; and further, that the rich have many wants and cares of which their poorer brethren know little or nothing. Next, that habit is a great leveller, familiarity taking off the edge of pleasures and even in some degree of suffering; that while misery may be assuaged by hope, happiness will occasionally be lessened by fear; and that the very clinging to possessions testifies to some vague sense of anxiety. Were additional arguments needed, we should find them in the acknowledged facts that poverty goads less than ambition, and is far less insatiable, a morsel satisfying the one, and accumulated wealth often not contenting the other; that the invalid frequently has more, far more, sunshine of soul than the gay votary of pleasure; that necessity is often at the side of extravagance, that labour gives a keen zest to every enjoyment and makes rest a luxury. Indeed, if there were no such levelling dispensations as sickness, sorrow, and death, yet would the sons of toil not have cause to envy the wealthy and exalted. Simple habits and tastes both sharpen pleasures, and render them easy of acquirement. Let this fact also be borne in mind, that much happiness and pious gratitude often abide where we suppose all to be misery and repining, likewise that anxiety, gloom, and discontent sometimes reign where all *should* be, and is believed to be, gaiety, joy, and thankfulness. Truly the lot of men cannot be considered as very unequal while all alike may be aspirants for heaven, while they may be ever hopefully seeking through their moral conduct to deserve God's favour, and render themselves worthy of those gifts, small or great, which His unerring wisdom has bestowed here below and of those promises which a hereafter will fulfil.

In conclusion, let us bear in mind that in the matter of wealth or station we should ever look *below* us, and thus comparing worldly lots, must hold ourselves as favoured; while ambitioning nothing but fresh accessions of virtue, pious resignation, a glowing love of all that is good and holy, we should look *above* and offer up the incense of praise and adoration, thereby fixing within our heart those blissful and ever renewing emotions which most surely conduce to true happiness and contentment.

PRECEPTS.—The prophet Isaiah in his book has clearly pointed out what will most conduce to serenity of mind, and in consequence to Contentment. At ch. xxxii, 17, we read, "*The work of righteousness shall be peace*, and the effect of righteousness quietness and assurance for ever". At ch. xxvi, 4, he bids us " confide in the Lord Jehovah, who is everlasting strength", and in implicit faith adds, " 'Thou, O God, wilt keep him *in perfect peace* whose mind is stayed on Thee, because he trusteth in Thee". Then in the Book of Job we read, ch. xxxvi, 11, " They who obey and know God shall spend their days in prosperity and their years in pleasures". And again, in Prov. xiv, 14, " A good man shall be satisfied with himself". Similar assurances pervade the Psalms, wherein David declares, " None of them that trust in the Lord will be left destitute", and that " Those who walk uprightly and work righteousness will never be moved". Here, then, we see that trust in God and the performance of good works prove highly favourable to Contentment, while that which is frequently considered so essential to it is in Scripture deemed of little worth, for we read at Prov. xxiii, 5, " Riches make themselves wings and fly away"; thus we should not "set our eyes upon that which is not". And we are admonished at ch. xxi that " He who loveth pleasures shall be a poor man; he that loveth wine and oil shall not be rich". And again, at ch. xiv, " In laughter the heart is sorrowful, and the end of that mirth is heaviness". Thence it is clear that we should never allow the mind to indulge in inordinate desires, but maintain moderate views of human happiness and rationally shun all excesses. Now, to ascertain the benefits contentment confers, we have but to turn to Prov. xvii, 22, where we are told that " a merry heart doeth good like a medicine, but a broken spirit drieth the bones"; and at ch. x, 28, we are reminded that " the hopes of the righteous shall be gladness", or, as David expresses it in one of his Psalms, " *gladness is sown for the upright in heart*". That it is a sacred duty to foster a cheerful and contented frame of mind even Solomon does not deny, although he laboured so zealously to prove that all in life is vanity; indeed, he even inculcates the obligation of temperate enjoyment in Ecclesiastes, for does he not there say, ch. v, 18, " Behold it is good and comely for man to enjoy the good of all his labour which God giveth him, for it is his portion"; and again, he declares, "God hath made everything beautiful", and that "there is no good but for man to enjoy and rejoice therein; also to do good in his life". It is, however, to the Psalms of David we should especially turn, since with him Content was not a mere sentiment, but met with practical illustration during even the most eventful and tempestuous part of his life. Thus in Ps. cxiv he exclaims, "In the multitude of my anxieties Thy comforts delight my soul", and when surrounded by enemies and idolators, who " sought his hurt", far from uttering complaints, he ejaculates, Ps. xvi, " Thou, O Lord, maintainest my lot; my share has fallen in pleasant places; I am *content* with my inheritance". Many Scripture quotations might be selected wherein is shown how much *equality* exists among men. For instance, in Eccles. we read, "The sleep of the labouring man is sweet, whether he eat little or much; but the abundance of the rich will not suffer him to sleep". And in Prov. xxii, "The rich and poor meet together; the Lord is the Maker of them all". Finally, let us ponder over those verses which show us how we may best secure the boon of Contentment. Solomon admonishes us in Prov. x to "*deserve the blessing of the Lord, for it maketh rich, and he addeth no sorrow with it*", whilst David bids us in Ps. xxxiv to " depart from evil and do good; *seek peace and pursue it*". Again, in Ps. xxxvii, " Commit thy ways unto the Lord; trust also in Him, and He will give thee the desires of thine heart". Also he adds, "Rest in the Lord, and *wait patiently for Him*, nor fret because of him that prospereth in his way". And, in conclusion, let us imitate the pious David by thinking often of the goodness of the Lord, and when like trials assail us, may we be led to exclaim with him (Ps. cxvi, 7), "Return unto thy serenity, O my soul, for the Lord hath dealt bountifully with thee". Thus impressed, we shall surely, under every circumstance of life, retain a happy, cheerful, and contented spirit.

For the practical illustration of our subject, we may select the two following EXAMPLES. The brief sketch of the life of the SHUNAMMITE, to be found in the second book of Kings, furnishes us with such particulars as serve to prove, beyond a doubt, that the mind of this excellent woman was imbued with a true sense of contentment. It is true she lacked neither wealth nor station; and if these invariably, or even generally, secured to their possessors a grateful and contented spirit, then might her life, words, and acts, well pass without special notice. But there are few, indeed, whose minds are not stirred by externals, and who are not so dazzled by the glare of outward things, as to be led to ambitionate fresh and ever-recurring accessions of this world's goods. Not so, however, with the Shunammite. Through an act of disinterested kindness to the prophet Elisha, she had secured in him a powerful friend, and one not only willing, but anxious, to serve her, and thereby testify his gratitude; yet, when he proposed to "speak for her to the King or Captain of the Hosts", her only answer was, "I dwell among my own people". Here was the acme of her desires; she coveted no more exalted station, no increase of fortune; she was contented with her lot, and sought none other, howsoever tempting or alluring. Home was to her synonymous with happiness, and what more could the world offer or give? A higher social position might possibly endanger, but could hardly enhance her present happy content.

Several incidents follow, all bearing ample proof that this was with her no casual frame of mind, but that the seeds of self-denial, of home affection, and pious resignation, early sown and carefully tended, had arrived at full maturity. First, then, we find that Elisha, having discovered through his servant Gehazi the secret wishes of her heart, sought to gratify them; and to the pious intervention of the prophet she owed a blessing which must have conduced to increase her home delights. A son was born to her. Years elapsed, and our attention is then called to the sorrowing mother who has suddenly awoke to the agonising reality of the death of her beloved child. Mark now her conduct. Unwilling to distress her aged husband by communicating the sad tidings, she simply asks him for the means to make her way to the Man of God, whose aid she would implore. Firm was her faith in the Lord; if help there could be in this, her hour of dire affliction, it must come from Heaven. Hence her earnest appeal to the prophet of God. But it is evident her calm endurance was spent by the time she reached his abode, else she would hardly have spoken thus, " Did I desire a son of my Lord ? did I not say, Do not deceive me ?" and when Elisha would have commissioned his servant to go to the bedside of the child, the mother could no longer restrain her pent-up anguish, but falling on her knees at his feet addressed him in these words, " As the Lord liveth, and as thy soul liveth, I will not leave thee." The compassionate prophet could not resist this solemn entreaty, and so " rose and followed her". Thus through faith, firmness, and energy, did she regain her much-loved son.

Another episode in the history of this Shunammite proves that when her just rights were concerned she knew how to maintain them. On her return from the land of the Philistines, whether she had resorted seven years before, by the advice of Elisha, on account of the famine, she at once appealed to the king to have her estates and possessions restored to her. From this incident we may learn that an habitual spirit of contentment need never stand in the way of duty, nor interfere with the assertion of our just demands; and further, that they who are at all times studious not to encroach on the rights of others, will best deserve, as most surely obtain, attention, when they have to seek redress and claim their own fair share or privilege.

Thus we have seen that, as the fond mother, this exemplary woman could humble herself to the very ground before the man she had served when needing succour for her child, nor rise until her petition was granted; that, as the despoiled citizen, she pressed boldly forward, demanding justice and equity from the highest tribunal of the land, nor desisted till she had secured the reward of her determination in the renewed possession of her property. Now, though hope could thus prompt and justice thus inspire her to vigorous action, yet was contentment the abiding sentiment of her heart. Appreciating and enjoying the goodly gifts with which God had blessed her, she held her own with a firm and resolute grasp; but she asked no more—she was content.

Now, if it be considered that the foregoing character does not offer a lesson for universal application, we may turn to another; the much-tried and patient JOB, of which this cannot possibly be said. Truly his history affords invaluable instruction to every class; none too high, none too low to be beyond the scope of its teaching, since health and sickness, affluence and poverty, happiness and affliction, may alike be the lot of all. From this example each of us may assuredly derive at once encouragement and moral support.

At the opening of his book, he is represented in the full enjoyment of every valued and valuable gift. He is blessed with a loving family, possessed of high rank and vast wealth; he has numerous friends, and moreover is beloved and respected by both rich and poor. Such was his enviable lot, when the sun of prosperity not only became clouded, but suffered a dark eclipse. The heaviest trials that could befal mortal man came thick upon him. Severe, indeed, were the blows he experienced, yet his past happy condition having in no wise engendered pride or arrogance, he was ready prepared to encounter adversity, and meekly bow before the Will of the Supreme. No sooner was he made acquainted with the loss of his property and of his children, than he fell down and worshipped. Then burst forth those sublime and memorable words, which could not possibly have issued except from the lips of a man of a humble, pious, and contented spirit, " The Lord gave, the Lord hath taken away, blessed be the name of the Lord". Well he knew that nought could befal him which was not decreed by Infinite and Unerring Goodness and Wisdom; thence, though fearful trials followed close on these first calamities, he remained tranquil and resigned. His spirit was undaunted, for his faith was in God. Ample proof of this is furnished in the remarkable words which passed between Job and his wife; for when a loathsome disease was added to his other dire distresses, she became oblivious of her usual trust in the Righteous Lord, and in a frenzy of despair was led thus to address her beloved husband, "Dost thou retain thine integrity? curse God and die". And this was his sublime response, " What! shall we receive good at the hand of God, and shall we not receive evil ?" Thus, his mind not having been softened by prosperity, he met each fresh trial with patient endurance and fortitude.

When, however, after days of mental anguish, bodily suffering, and general exhaustion, he was prevailed upon to enter into conversation and arguments with his wordy and false condolers, he showed he was mortal. Accustomed to the respect and love of all who knew him, the unfair upbraidings of his so-called friends brought his anguish of mind to a climax. It was then he gave way to a sad despondency and uttered bitter complaints. Beset at so trying a crisis by officious and injudicious comforters, how could he be otherwise than querulous? Indeed, these acquaintances must have secretly acknowledged to themselves that such a moment for offering counsel was at best untimely, else Eliphaz would not have begun his answer to Job in these words, "If we assay to commune with thee, wilt thou be *grieved, but* who can withhold himself from speaking?" And that Job keenly felt their unkindness, we may gather from the whole of the sixth chapter of his book; for, after reminding them that "his strength is not the strength of stone, nor his flesh of brass", he further added, "To him that is afflicted *pity* should be shown from his *friend*"; and, after declaring "how forcible are right words", turned to them, saying "I have heard many such things, miserable comforters that ye are. Shall vain words have an end? I also could speak as ye do; if your soul were in my soul's stead, I could heap up words against you, and shake mine head at you; *but* I would strengthen you, and the moving of *my lips should assuage your grief*". Then, after entreating their forbearance, he exclaimed, "My face is wet with weeping, and on my eyelids is the shadow of death. Behold, my record is on High. My friends scorn me, but my witness is in heaven." And again, showing his great misery, he apostrophised them thus, "Have pity upon me, have pity, O ye, my friends, for the hand of God hath touched me".*

But how speedily did he rally from this natural weakness and depression! His pious and contented mind soon regained its equilibrium. Ceasing to upbraid his friends and complain of his truly pitiable state, he turned his mind to high contemplation, entered into sublime meditation on the greatness of Divine Providence, drew down fresh strength from above, and renewed within his breast virtuous and pious resolves. Thus we read, "Till I die I will not remove mine integrity from me; my righteousness I hold fast and will not let it go; my heart shall not reproach me as long as I live."† Finally, at the forty-second chapter, we

* Job xix, 21.   † Job xxvii, 5.

find such resolves crowned with entire success, for, after acknowledging God's power and Omniscience, Job greatly accused himself, and, forgetful of his acute sufferings, turned his reflections solely to Almighty goodness and compassion, so that he was naturally brought to exclaim, in all humbleness of heart, "Wherefore I abhor myself, and repent in dust and ashes".

Truly, here we have the picture of a contented and satisfied mind. Grievous as were the trials Job endured, they were greatly intensified by bringing him almost at one blow from the highest pinnacle of worldly happiness to the lowest depths of misery. Now, that such fortitude and faith as he displayed were pleasing to the Most High, the last chapter of his book bears ample testimony. In his tribulation he had spoken "what was right of God", and those very friends who had so rashly condemned the poor sufferer found that they had themselves lost the favour of heaven, and could only regain it through the intercession of Job! Right conduct and right feeling had come off triumphant; the dark cloud was dispelled, and all was light again. The late trying season of adversity had left behind it only a golden reward; namely, a satisfied feeling that he had not criminally repined or murmured at the Divine dispensation, but that he had practically acknowledged God's ineffable goodness and wisdom, and thence secured the high approval of heaven. Then we find that the Lord not only "accepted Job", but gave him "twice as much as he had before". Many, indeed, were the gracious gifts vouchsafed, while every discomfort was removed far from him; so that, as we read at the twelfth verse, "the Lord blessed the latter end of Job more than his beginning"; and further we find, at the conclusion of the chapter, that he lived long to enjoy the fruits of his goodness, virtue, and practical piety.

Now all may strive to imitate this admirable example, and, by early schooling, advance towards such perfection.

Self-denial, fortitude, and pious resignation, may be cultivated, and just in proportion as we progress in their attainment shall we near that which should be the goal of mortal wishes—a truly pious mind, with a happy, contented, and satisfied heart.

SELF-DISCIPLINE.

Gen. xxxix, 9, "*How can I do this great wickedness and sin against God?*"

WHAT an exquisite epitome of the moral character of JOSEPH is presented to us in this plain and simple sentence, this straightforward, conscientious appeal to his tempter! and when taken in conjunction with his practical fidelity to his employer, his horror of violating a principle of duty to God or man, and consequent utter rejection of an overture involving both, such words acquire, if possible, yet greater significance. To this temptation succeeded others, different in kind and degree, yet in each we may trace the same persistent course of integrity and honour, the same love of the right, and resolute resistance to everything wrong and unholy, either in thought or act. We have, indeed, only to take a brief review of the events of his early life to confirm the truth of this remark; and it will also fully show that to his righteous and unblemished conduct he owed the gradual amelioration of his condition, and his rise from the lowly grade of a slave to a rank and position which finally enabled him to become the benefactor of his generation.

It was Joseph's lot to be the spoilt child of a doting father until the attainment of his seventeenth year, and through that parent's injudicious partiality a marked distinction was made between him and his brothers. This might well have sown the seeds of many an evil passion within his breast; but as the entire history of his tried life discloses none, and only the lightest failings in his character were discernible when under his parents' roof, it is not to be doubted that to a good disposition was conjoined a firm will and steadfast mind, which enabled him, under the most adverse circumstances, to adhere resolutely to its natural dictates. That such disposition and power of self-control were severely tested even in the home of his youth will be easily credited, when it is considered that he had become the especial object of jealousy and hatred to his irascible and vindictive brethren. Frequently must he have been called upon to exercise all the meekness, patience, and endurance of which he was capable, and, being gifted with a sensitive, loving heart, he will have keenly felt the rooted animosity of some of his brothers, and the want of friendliness displayed by others. Their treatment of him at home was, however, but the first bitter drop with which they poisoned his cup of happiness. Their rancour and ill-will increasing daily, the death or banishment of the object of their dislike could alone content these unnatural relatives, and to the latter alternative did they finally resort. No entreaty, no supplication could save him; he was sold by them, and became a slave in Egypt. His young heart must, indeed, have been ready to break in bitterness of anguish when this unlooked for and overwhelming change of fortune befel him. Surely only a well-disciplined mind could possibly have withstood so severe and sudden a shock; the heart remaining ever kind, warm, loving, not even becoming hardened against those brothers by whom he had been so cruelly, so pitilessly treated.

But this was only the beginning of his trials; during thirteen long years, first of servitude, and then as a prisoner, had he to abide the despotic will of others, and humbly submit to the dire exigencies which his degraded position involved. Yet, even as a slave, he obtained, through his sterling qualities, his pious and virtuous conduct, the esteem and goodwill of his masters, and hence also the mitigation of many of the evils and miseries naturally attendant on a state of bondage. For we read: "And Joseph found grace in the sight of his master, and he made him overseer of his house, and all that he had he put into his hands, and the Lord blessed the Egyptian's house for Joseph's sake."* Then, when cast into prison through the false and cruel accusation of that master's wife, we find again that "he obtained favour in the sight of the keeper of the prison"—who "committed into Joseph's hands all the prisoners and looked not to anything, because the Lord was with him". Now, notwithstanding the amelioration of his condition in consequence of the confidence reposed in him by his superiors, his lot must have been very deplorable, for, little as he was given to complain or grieve at aught which befel him, he yet uttered the following words of entreaty to Pharaoh's butler, whose deliverance he had foretold: "Think on me when it shall be well with thee, and show kindness, I pray thee, unto me, and make mention of me unto Pharaoh to bring me out of this house, for indeed I have done nothing that they should put me into the dungeon." What a tale of sorrow is unfolded in this touching sentence, and yet, as "the chief butler remembered not Joseph, but forgat him", full two years more passed away before his position was bettered. But when a change did occur, great indeed was that change, for at one word from the King's lips, the poor prisoner became Viceroy of Egypt.

Now it is to be observed that Joseph expressly declared to Pharaoh, when about to interpret the dream, that, "It is not in me; God will give thee an answer in peace"—thereby disclaiming all credit or title to the King's gratitude; thus pleasurable indeed must have been his feelings on hearing the following expressions from Pharaoh when bestowing that exalted rank upon him, "Forasmuch as God hath shown thee all this, there is none so discreet and wise as thou art; thou shalt be over my house, and according unto thy word shall all my people be ruled: only on the throne will I be greater than thou". How worthy he was

* Gen. xxxix, 4.

of this high distinction is proved by the whole of his after-life, wherein he displayed the same piety, goodness of heart, and integrity of purpose, which had marked his conduct during his long term of adversity. The moral elevation of character which he had acquired through a lengthened course of self-discipline made him superior alike to every vicissitude of fortune and to all the meaner passions; neither affliction nor prosperity had the power to move him from his wise and righteous course; nor could even the remembrance of his brothers' cruelly treacherous conduct stir up feelings of animosity or revenge within his breast. Hence during the latter epoch of his life we find him represented as a wise and thrifty ruler, a grateful steward profiting the very king who had succoured him; finally, as a forgiving and generous relative, who not only sought to allay the natural fears of his brethren and alleviate their remorse, but even strove to quiet their mutual recriminations and animosities by addressing to them these words of comfort, "Do this and live, for I fear God"; and also, "Now, therefore, be not grieved nor angry with yourselves that ye sold me hither, for God did send me before you to preserve life": sentences truly indicative that "God was in all his thoughts". Thus to piety and self-discipline, working on a noble and generous nature, may be traced that goodly assembly of virtues which lend such lustre to the character of Joseph—the injured brother—the poor slave—the preserver of his master's honour—the Ruler of Egypt!

It would be clearly superfluous here to endeavour to enhance the general estimation of Joseph's character, standing, as it does, almost unrivalled in the pages of Sacred History, else would it be easy to compare his conduct with that of his brothers, thereby throwing it into bolder relief; still it may be serviceable to take a brief survey of the deplorable state to which JOSEPH's BRETHREN were brought through their want of moral self-government, and that rectitude which piety conjoined with self-discipline alone can give.

In so doing, that which first excites attention is the marked contrast in which they stood to Joseph. Long years had rolled by since the consummation of their revengeful act, and we then find them as suppliants, crouching abjectly before that brother whom they had sold as a slave and humbled to the very dust. Next, when accused of being spies and in great trepidation lest they should have to suffer an ignominious death, their consciences awoke to the magnitude of their past crime, and seized with remorse they exclaimed, " We are verily guilty concerning our brother, in that we saw the anguish of his soul, when he besought us and we would not hear; therefore is this distress come upon us". Such was the conclusion at which they arrived when in peril of their lives, but no sooner were they in comparative safety than all compunction of conscience ceased, and, though their heart failed them at the very next critical juncture, they could yet ask one of the other, " What is this that God hath done unto us ?" Away from that presence which haunted them as some terrible dream, they would not recognise that just retribution which their eldest brother Reuben had so lately predicted would attend on their misdeeds, declaring in these emphatic words : " Behold, also Joseph's blood is required of us". For thirteen years had their consciences slumbered, and could only be aroused by some pressing emergency; thus when famine had spread over the land, and sustenance for themselves and families depended on that Ruler of Egypt whose very presence inspired them with vague fears, then—and not till then—their " hearts began to be stirred within them", and from that dread moment it was impossible altogether to drown the recollection of the past.

But even these trials worked no sensible improvement; for when Joseph finally discovered himself to his brethren, giving promises of his love and protection, if they had learnt to understand his lofty character and appreciate his virtues, all unjust suspicion must have vanished, and they would have made their minds perfectly easy, assured that they had nought to fear, while much to hope, from their all-powerful, but also all-loving, warm-hearted relative. It was, however, far otherwise; for even the constant solicitude and care displayed by Joseph towards them and their household during the continuance of the famine could not effectively teach them to dismiss their ungenerous doubts. Thus, on the death of their parent, being assailed by fresh fears, they sought from Joseph renewed assurances as to his friendly and peaceful intentions towards them. This fact is clearly elucidated in the following verse: " And when Joseph's brethren saw that their father was dead, they said, Joseph will peradventure hate us, and will certainly requite us all the evil which we did unto him".* Now, with this fear uppermost in their minds, they were but too easily led to resort to a subterfuge, and make a wrongful use of their father's name, for they well knew that, unlike themselves, Jacob had ever put implicit trust in the goodness of his favourite son, and therefore would never have left any command betokening the doubt implied in the words, " So shall ye say unto Joseph, Forgive, I pray thee, now the trespass of thy brethren, and their sin". That this course of action grieved Joseph we may not doubt, for " he wept". But how reassuring was his rejoinder, " Fear not, for am I in the place of God? I will nourish you and your little ones". And further he " comforted them and spake kindly unto them".

With these verses before us the contrast is complete. All was unjust suspicion and cruel wrong on the one side, on the other nought but good-will, generous forbearance, and forgiveness. Truly, Joseph delighted in virtue and, loving, practised it; thence to him be all the honour—to his brethren the shame.

If man would be something more than the mere puppet

* Gen. l, 15.

of every narrow, blind, and selfish impulse, every wayward passion, if he would mould himself to good, and work out the loftier purposes of his nature, he must consider self-discipline as a high moral obligation, and be ever prepared to subject himself to its just control. Man may not evade this moral self-government, a duty which as a free agent he owes to himself and to society, and as a responsible being to his Creator, without proving alike unjust to himself and unfaithful to his God. Gifted with Freewill, endowed with ample powers to exercise it for good or for evil, and further blessed with reason, conscience, and God's Holy Law, to serve as infallible guides to the path of virtue, man greatly wrongs himself when he swerves therefrom, and is only just to his own better nature when he listens to their sacred dictates, and forms for himself a character worthy of God's approbation; a character on which all true greatness and all true happiness depends. Now this consummation can only be attained by an earnest desire for moral improvement, combined with an undaunted and persevering struggle after excellence. Certain it is that, as God has bid us strive to attain exalted virtue, He must have given us all the necessary powers, and, therefore, we only need *the will* in order to succeed. Thus let us apply this capacity of "willing" to the cause of righteousness, and through self-scrutiny, self-discipline, and religion, build up for ourselves a moral structure which will resist the assault of trials and temptations. It can only be reared by studying our inward nature, instructing the mind, and schooling the heart, by ever regulating our actions according to the fundamental principles of God's law, taking a just account of our powers and putting them to the most profitable uses, by keeping imagination under due restraint, by elevating and purifying our conceptions of virtue and goodness. Yet this is not all that should be effected through the medium of self-discipline. There will often be habits to discard, opinions to correct, desires to suppress, errors and prejudices to dismiss or conquer, principles to confirm, and it is only as we near these desirable ends that we become true disciples of the art of being and doing good, for then only shall we be just, truthful, self-denying, forbearing, benevolent, and holy.

Here then is much, very much for self-discipline to achieve; yet withal it should not be supposed that its practice may not become easy. We simply make it difficult by deeming it so. Only let Religion, which should be considered not so much in the light of a duty, as a teacher and strengthener of all duties, enter into and take part in this moral government, and further be admitted, like a good angel, into all our actions, then shall we surely surmount and vanquish every opposing obstacle. Also, be it remembered, that neither religion nor self-discipline demands great sacrifices; they simply call on us to lay down before their high altar sin and baneful pleasures; also slothfulness, apathy, selfishness, and such passions as dwarf the soul and impoverish the heart. When these depart, we escape all thraldom; these expelled, and we become truly free.

Now, once convinced that self-discipline and religion, solely require of us the relinquishment of all that is evil and noxious, and the cultivation of every good disposition; further, that, far from impeding or fettering our movements, they serve, on the contrary, to enlarge our sphere of useful action, and tend to relieve us from the very worst of bondage, then shall we gladly seek the easiest and surest means of bringing them practically to bear upon our daily conduct. Of these, assuredly, none are more effectual than prayer, meditation, love of virtue, abhorrence of vice, and habit.

From prayer, or the heart's worship, we cannot fail to derive a constant source of invigoration; and if we will but turn heavenward when *temptations* assail, and, considering them synonymous with *dangers*, invoke God's Almighty protection through prayer, then may we fairly hope to come off victorious in the strife of passion with duty. Meditation will furnish us with the knowledge of what we are and what we should be, while it will also direct and watch our progress to the desired goal. It will show us that we are often weakest where we think ourselves strongest; it will teach us not to depend on fortune but on conduct, which should be strictly regulated by the eternal principles of justice and reason. Next, the love of virtue and horror of vice will prove powerful auxiliaries to self-discipline, if they stop not short at the mere abstract. Now, in *theory*, most persons are willing to acknowledge that, in order to accomplish the legitimate object of their being they must be upright and resolute in the avoidance of evil, yet withal too many disregard the *practice* on which so greatly depends their welfare. Only when virtue is chosen for its own sake, and when the heart is firmly fixed on all that is pure, great, and perfect, will moral progress have fairly begun ; indeed, it is those alone that aim at perfection who may hope to reach above mediocrity. By ascending high in the moral atmosphere, grovelling desires and vicious inclinations lose their sway, and by thus gaining the mastery over internal passions, we finally become superior to all external influences. Truly to love virtue is to ensure its growth and full development.

Self-discipline, however, like all else, must have a beginning, and herein lies the difficulty. Once begun, habit will soon render it easy. Now, were it necessary to eradicate any natural desire of the mind, then indeed a constant struggle might be required; but surely to temper that which in excess would prove injurious, needs but a little of the perseverance which a brave, stout heart ever brings into its work. Let us once take up the standard of right, give heed to it, act in accordance therewith, and each succeeding step in the same path will become firm and assured. Continued practice in the right insures the right; frequent repetition of kind and generous emotions within the heart will, after a time, from being transient, become permanent.

Let, then, habit, all-potent for good, go hand in hand with self-discipline, and thus secure these goodly fruits.

We now turn to consider on the one hand the benefits we must derive if attentive to moral self-training, and on the other the penalties to which we expose ourselves by its disregard. First, however, we should call to mind that when God gave His Holy Law to His creatures, He demanded of them its rigorous observance; promulgated solely for their good, it surely behoves man to regulate his actions thereby, and conform so entirely to its teachings as to reap that promised good. This is the true province of self-discipline; and among the choice blessings it will assuredly secure to us may be enumerated, that health of the soul which holiness alone can confer, the mental and bodily health which religious rectitude and a virtuous life will best help to preserve, a growing sense of power creditably to accomplish all the duties of life, a self-control which places us on high vantage-ground, enabling us to meet with calm submission all vicissitudes of fortune, all sickness and affliction, as also to subdue or conquer every unruly passion; finally, that inward joy of happy content and sense of freedom which virtue and piety alone can bestow.

These are some of the rewards of goodness, but on reversing the picture the first thought which must strike us is, that while the good have everything to hope, the evil-disposed have everything to fear. With them there will infallibly be much tribulation; they dare not ask or hope to receive God's blessing, but must often, however unwillingly, stand before the high tribunal of conscience, and be brought to feel how greatly they are offending, and how surely Eternal justice will overtake them in their guilt. Man may never hope to elude God's observation, or escape the penalty due to the infringement of His righteous Law, and if unwilling to struggle with vicious habits and evil inclinations, then will sin waste his manhood, and bring on him sorrow and sickness. His appetites will expand with every fresh indulgence, and overgrown passions will corrupt his whole moral nature, thus causing the angel in man to succumb to his more ignoble nature. Such are the sad results of wilfully ignoring or avoiding the duty of self-discipline, and which, if persisted in, will surely be fraught with much after misery and anguish. We shall find that sin, untruth, and all base passions, when left unchecked, breed their like; that evil will crop up from evil, and so strengthen and expand, that even the very hope of amendment must become extinct. Memory, like an accusing angel, will be ever at hand, pointing to the wrong done, and retracing those irreparable acts which have brought *others* to sin and shame. Further, by the sacrifice of our self-respect, which is the very keystone of moral life, we shall bring on ourselves disgrace and obloquy, which alas! must ever rest upon our name.

Now, if we would avoid these culminating evils, with all the gloom and remorse they will infallibly entail, we must early subject ourselves to self-discipline and self-control. We must seize every opportunity to strengthen the principle of good within us, resolutely check in their bud all sinful propensities, all untruth; in a word, uproot all that militates against the Word of God and the law of conscience. Our passions and desires once under due control, our heart with God, and we are safe. Peace and happy content will take up their abode within our heart, and life, God's gift—a sacred charge—will prove itself a glorious blessing.

PRECEPTS inculcating self-discipline will take a strong hold on the mind when we have brought ourselves to believe that we are responsible agents, and become impressed with the conviction that God takes cognizance of our doings. Now, with the Holy Volume in hand, it is easy to establish these important truths, for verses abound therein which incontestably prove both facts. With reference to the former, we find in Jer. xxi, 8: "Thus saith the Lord:

Behold I set before you the way of life, and the way of death"; then at chap. ii, 19: "Thine own wickedness shall correct thee; know, therefore, and see that it is an evil thing and bitter that the fear of God is not in thee". And in Exodus, after setting before the people the law and ordinances for their observance, Moses emphatically bid them "be circumspect"; for on their obedience would depend their prosperity. Then, with regard to the latter fact, we read, Prov. v, 21: "*the ways of man are before the eyes of the Lord,* and He pondereth all his goings"; again, at chap. xii, 2: "A good man obtaineth favour of the Lord; but a man of wicked devices He will condemn". Then Job, chap v, 21, confidently asks: "Doth not God see my ways, and count all my steps?" and in Ps. vii, 11, we read: "God judgeth the righteous, He is angry with the wicked every day; the mischief he hath conceived shall return upon his own head". Next, we should note that numberless benefits and blessings are promised to those who adhere to a course of self-discipline, since such may serve to stimulate and induce its daily practice. Thus we read, Prov. xxi, 21: "He that followeth after righteousness and mercy *findeth life, goodness, and honour*"; and Jer. xvii, 10: "I, the Lord, search the heart—I try the reins, *even to give every man according to his ways,* and according to the fruit of his doings". Identical ideas are found in the Book of Job, ch. xxxiv, conveyed in these words: "For the work of a man will God render unto him, and cause every man to find according to his ways". Again, at ch. xvii, 9: "The righteous will hold on his way, and he that hath clean hands shall be stronger and stronger". Then, in chap. xi: "If iniquity be in thine hand, put it far away, for then shalt thou lift up thy face without spot; yea, thou shalt be steadfast, and shall not fear". Let us next hearken and attend to the language of self-discipline, as it is set before us in various Scripture verses. Thus, in Job xxvii, 6: "My righteousness I hold fast, and will not let it go; my heart shall not reproach me as long as I live; my lips shall not speak wickedness, nor my tongue utter deceit"; and at chap. xxxiv: "That which I see not, teach thou me, O Lord; if I have done iniquity, I will do no more". In Prov. iv: "So teach us to number our days that we may apply our hearts to wisdom"; and, again: "*Keep thy heart with all diligence,* for out of it are the issues of life"; also: "Ponder the paths of thy feet, and let all thy ways be established; turn not to the right hand nor to the left, remove thy foot from evil". Then, in Hosea xii, 6: "Turn thou to thy God, keep mercy and judgment, and wait on thy God continually"; finally, in Micah vi: "God hath shown thee, O man, what is good; and what doth He require of thee but to do justly, to love mercy, to walk humbly before Him?" Next, we should give especial attention to the injunctions and declarations of David which abound in the Book of Psalms. His whole life was a course of self-discipline, and thus, in conformity with his practice, did he exhort us, Ps. xxxiv: "Keep thy tongue from evil, and thy lips from speaking guile, depart from evil, and do good, seek peace and pursue it"; and then in Ps. cxix he puts the query: "Wherewithal shall a young man cleanse his ways?" answering it thus: "By taking heed according to Thy Law". How sedulously he followed out all that he taught, both his statements and acts testify. Firstly, we may quote these, his words, Ps. xvi, 8: "I have placed the Lord always before me; with Him at my right hand I cannot stumble", and Ps. cxix: "Thy word, O Lord, have I hid in my heart that I might not sin against Thee". Then he declares: "Thy word is a lamp unto my feet, and a light unto my path; thy testimonies are also my delight and my counsellors"; again, "I thought on my ways, and turned unto Thy testimonies". Then, on emerging from a series of severe trials, and taking a review of his past conduct, he utters these satisfactory assurances regarding it, Ps. xviii: "I have kept the way of the Lord, and have not wickedly departed from my God". Now, the truthfulness of his words was amply demonstrated by the history of his life, and to this, then, may we turn for one of those

EXAMPLES, so fraught with practical teachings. Throughout his greatly-chequered career, DAVID seldom faltered or erred. That the habit of daily meditation contributed to form his character and direct his conduct in accordance with God's law, has been demonstrated when treating on this subject; yet this was but the first step towards that self-discipline which stood guard upon his actions during the whole course of his eminently practical life. Indeed, from his youth so thoroughly had he schooled himself, that there are but two instances recorded wherein he forsook the right path—committing sins which brought in their train much misery and compunction. Meditation had induced him to make duty his guiding star; but it was self-discipline which enabled him, through the exercise of a proper self-control, to pursue it unflinchingly, steadily, and perseveringly, thereby accomplishing each noble resolve, each lofty dictate of conscience. All the striking events of his life offer ample proof of this, but some few instances will here suffice. The first incident recorded in David's life shows him to have possessed a courageous spirit and pious zeal; for no sooner was he made acquainted with the threats held out by Goliath than he exclaimed, "Who is this uncircumcised Philistine that he should defy the army of the living God?" and he merely awaited his Sovereign's permission to accept the challenge. Thus he spoke when brought before Saul : " Let no man's heart fail because of *him;* thy servant will go and fight with this Philistine". In all this there was neither presumption nor pride; and even when he had slain his powerful antagonist, and thus essentially helped to deliver his country from the enemy, his words and proceedings yet remain marked by extreme humility; for we read : "David went out whithersoever Saul sent him, and *behaved himself wisely.*" Certain it is he might have claimed the reward promised by the King to the successful champion of Israel; but, though this reward comprised great riches, the hand of the Sovereign's daughter in marriage, and also the freedom of his father's house, yet he made no demand, but was content to fill a subordinate office in the royal household! Now, only one capable of great self-denial could have calmly seen his just rights thus remain unrecognised. Truly, his passions and desires must have been under perfect control; for long and patiently did he await those preferments which justice and honour should have prompted the King to confer without delay. But David shortly after experienced far more unjustifiable and even cruel treatment at the hands of his ungrateful and violent-tempered Sovereign; and the meek, pious resignation with which he submitted to the King's relentless persecution, give ample proof that he held his feelings and actions under the most perfect restraint. An instance is presented to us in Ps. lix. Having been informed that Saul had despatched some armed men to murder him in his own house, David thus prayed for succour: "Deliver me from mine enemies, O my God: save me from sanguinary men; for lo! they lie in wait for my soul. The mighty are gathered against me, not for my transgressions, nor for my sin, O Lord". Yet mark the concluding words of his appeal, " Slay them not, these bloody men". And at a later period, when, through bitter persecution, he was forced to quit his home, and wander an exile in a distant land, beset with many dangers, he was yet able to control every rising feeling of rancour and revenge. A proof thereof presents itself when David was in careful hiding within the Cave of Engedi. Being informed by his servants that Saul was near at hand and unprotected, wherefore he "might do to him as it should seem good", he merely cut off the skirt of the king's robe with secrecy; yet, hardly had he executed this simple act, than " his heart smote him", and, turning to his servants, he said, "The Lord forbid that I should do this thing unto my master, the Lord's anointed, to stretch forth mine hand against him". This generous forbearance on the part of one who had been so cruelly persecuted, touched the heart even of Saul, who, after patiently listening to David's mild rebuke, thus addressed him : " Thou art more righteous than I ; for thou hast rewarded me good, whereas I have rewarded thee evil". This feeling, however, lasted only for a time, for being shortly after informed of David's whereabouts, Saul again sallied forth with the object of slaying him ! However, David, whose vigilance had been greatly sharpened by ever-recurring perils, was not to be entrapped, but, on the contrary, the monarch a second time lay powerless before him—sleeping and unarmed. Now, when Abishai, one of David's faithful followers, offered himself as a willing instrument to take Saul's life, in order to put an end to such bitter persecution against his master, David hindered him, saying, "Destroy him not, for who can stretch forth his hand against the Lord's anointed and be guiltless." No, rather than permit such a deed, he would undergo every possible contingency, and submit to whatever trials the tyrannical destroyer of his peace and happiness could inflict ; thus did duty and right again prevail. Finally, being utterly wearied of such a life of hardship and persecutions, he resolved to seek that protection from the hands of his enemies, the Philistines, which was denied him in his own country. Thus did he argue with himself, "I shall now perish one day by the hand of Saul ; there is nothing better for me than that I should speedily escape into the land of the Philistines, and Saul shall despair of me, nor seek me any more ; so shall I escape out of his hands."* He was fortunate enough to take up his residence with Achish, one of the best of their princes, by whom he became greatly esteemed. How he secured the good opinion and favour of

* 1 Sam. xxvii, 1.

Achish may be judged by the following commendation which this prince uttered when regretfully dismissing the poor exile, " Surely thou hast been upright, and thy going out and coming in is good in my sight; for I have not found evil in thee since the day of thy coming unto me unto this day; nevertheless the lords favour thee not". Now, severe as were these numerous ordeals, he had to pass through others of a kind which needed yet more self-command. To meet with reproof and unkindly acts where he deserved, and might have expected, far other treatment, touched his sensitive nature to the quick, and irritated him almost past endurance. A notable instance of this occurred in the case of Nabal, wherein, but for the speedy and judicious interposition of Abigail, it is only too probable his wrath would have gained ascendency over his better feelings, and he would have committed an overt act of violence. This display of temper, however, was the exception, and even in this case great was his self-control, for he was quick to turn from his purpose, the first momentary impulse and vexation of spirit passing away at the voice of reason. Thus he had become truly amenable to self-discipline, and numerous other instances might be adduced to like effect, for as he had not been discouraged in adversity, but had " encouraged himself in the Lord", so when David finally became monarch, he was neither haughty nor elated in his prosperity, but setting himself to the pursuance of a wise and peaceful policy, gained the hearts of his people.

Now, useful as such a biography may be by way of example, it must be yet more so if we give due heed to two of David's remarks with regard to self-discipline. They are of high import, giving a key to the practical knowledge of *easy* self-government, which, though most valuable, is but rarely attained. A better teacher and guide we could not possibly have, and these are his significant words, " I walk at liberty *because* I seek Thy precepts"; and again, " I *delight* myself in Thy commandments which I have loved".

Thence, once resolved to adhere to God's Law, and to take delight in it, our freedom of action is secured, and we truly "walk at liberty". Our natural impulses being in accordance with what is right and what is just, we are left free to pursue them and indulge each well-regulated desire. Thus does self-discipline become light and easy; while the pleasurable consequences of well-doing are placed practically before us by David in the following sentence:* "I have kept the way of the Lord, and He has rewarded me according to my righteousness; according to the cleanness of my hands has he recompensed me".

A man of an entirely different stamp of character is presented to us in the prophet JONAH. He had not, like David, learnt in early life to hold principle and duty paramount to all else; and further, was not accustomed to control his natural wayward and rash disposition through timely forethought and habitual self-government. The first incident, narrated at the opening of his Book, bears ample testimony to this fact. Jonah had received the direct command of God to proceed to Nineveh, and there appeal to its inhabitants, urging them to forsake their evil ways; yet instead of acting in accordance with the Divine injunction, he followed his own devices by taking ship for Tarshish, with intent to "flee from the presence of the Lord"! Now, had he allowed himself time for calm reflection, he could hardly have failed to see both how futile and how culpable was such disobedience, and how certainly he would incur God's just displeasure. But reflection was evidently not the habit of his mind, else, when left tranquilly to himself on board, he could not possibly have dismissed at once all thought of his late proceeding, and calmly retired to rest, seemingly unconscious of having disobeyed the mandate of the Supreme. It is not, however, to the absence of reflection alone that we should ascribe his rash and wayward conduct; for Jonah was of a naturally impulsive tempera-

* II Sam. xxii, 22.

ment, which, being left uncurbed, and seldom made amenable to self-discipline, frequently led him to a course of action, at which his better nature afterwards revolted. A notable instance of this is afforded us in the sequel to the episode before us. We should first, however, observe that the step taken by him could not have been premeditated, or carried out in *wilful* disobedience to the command of the Most High, else assuredly his mission would then, and at once, have been at an end, and he would have forfeited that Divine confidence which had been accorded him. As it was, although trials, the natural consequences of his own misdoings, befel him, the gracious and righteous Lord forsook not his servant, but stood his guardian in the hour of tribulation. Thus much premised, we will now pass in review his conduct during the later events connected with his act of disobedience, since they display his disposition in a favourable light. Firstly, we may note his willingness to make amends to his fellow-passengers, even at the risk, or rather, certain cost, of his life, when he discovered the imminent danger to which he had unwittingly exposed them; then, the speedy acknowledgment of his error and of God's goodness, which give sufficient indication that neither stubborness nor ingratitude formed part of his character; finally, the meek and humble spirit which he displayed in his affliction, and the penitence as well as regret he evinced for errors committed. Sorrowfully, and with a stricken conscience, must he have retraced the past in his mind as he exclaimed: "When my soul fainted within me I remembered the Lord"; and his heart must have overflowed with gratitude to his gracious preserver when he declared: "I will sacrifice unto Thee, O Lord, with the voice of thanksgiving; I will pay that which I have vowed; salvation is of the Lord": But no trials, however severe, could entirely subdue his impetuosity, or quell his wayward disposition. Thus we find him, when entrusted with a second mission, evincing marked ill-temper and a total want of self-government. (But of this, under another heading; see "TEMPER.") Here it suffices to observe that neither a good disposition, nor even circumstances most favourable to moral development, will wholly compensate for the want of self-discipline in youth. Had Jonah early accustomed himself to reflect whether he was doing right or wrong, had he schooled himself in the constant performance of duty, and ever sedulously hearkened to the voice of conscience, he would never have disobeyed the voice of God in so rash a manner, and been thus brought to the very brink of a watery grave.

What a lesson and a warning, then, does this history offer us, and among the thoughts they engender, let these have their full weight: that when Jonah fled from the Lord he was punished, and when he turned to Him he was delivered; that none may or can hide from the Lord; that good and evil can no more dwell together than will light and darkness, the one surely chasing the other; and, finally, that every misdeed will infallibly bring down condign punishment. Thence we must early beware of allowing our judgment and better nature to be warped by passions or blind impulses, and should, by careful self-discipline, so choose and pursue our path of life, that gracious blessings, and not severe retribution, may be finally adjudged us by the All-Beneficent Ruler and Governor of the universe.

FILIAL AFFECTION.

Gen. l, 10, "*And he* (Joseph) *made a mourning for his father seven days.*"

LOVE and reverence for their parents form a distinguishing trait in the character of the patriarchs, and perhaps there is no more prominent instance than that found in Gen. xxxi, 53. Although long years had elapsed since Jacob had seen his venerable sire, yet he neither knew nor could conceive any more sacred or effective oath wherewith to bind himself when making a covenant with Laban, than to "swear by the fear of his father Isaac". Deeply must his youthful mind have been penetrated with filial affection and veneration for these feelings to have remained in their full integrity, and maintained so powerful a sway after a separation of many years' duration.

But, turning to the virtuous and warm-hearted JOSEPH, we can hardly suppose that his heart was animated with less firm or ardent sentiments towards a parent so fond and worthy as Jacob. Richly endowed with every noble and exalted feeling, Joseph's generous nature must have been moved to its very depth by the parental affection lavished on him during his tender years; and, as the whole tenor of his after conduct amply proves, fervently did he love that father who had so loved him. This may be briefly instanced. No sooner had Joseph made himself known to his brethren in Egypt, than he put the all-anxious query, "Doth my father yet live"? Knowing they had been capable of a long course of deceit towards their aged parent, how dare he implicitly trust to their representation and smooth-mouthed assurances that "the old man lived". Hopes and fears alternately welled up in his heart, and, at the bare thought that the divulgence of his secret would bring with it some certain knowledge regarding his aged sire, " he wept aloud", totally overpowered by the acuteness of feelings long, long pent up. This first emotion indulged, he lost no time in ordering the early dispatch of his relatives to their home with the news of his high elevation, at the same time sending such gifts as would conduce to his beloved parent's comfort, together with promises well suited to rejoice his heart. And thus he addressed his brothers : " Haste ye and go up to my father, and say unto him, thus saith thy son Joseph : God hath made me lord of all Egypt, come down unto me, tarry not, and thou shalt dwell in the land of Goshen, and there will I provide for thee. And ye shall tell my father of all my glory, and of all that ye have seen, and shall make haste and bring down my father hither".* After the accomplishment of this first duty, fraternal love obtained the ascendency, and " he fell upon his brother Benjamin's neck, and wept. Moreover, he kissed all his brethren, and wept upon them". The next step taken by Joseph—who could not allow either his high station, or the duties incumbent thereon, to stay him in the filial respect wherewith he delighted to honour his father— was to hasten to Goshen himself, so that he might, at the earliest possible moment, greet that revered sire, from whom he had been parted no less than twenty-two years. And what a meeting it was! The loving son, completely overcome by emotion, "fell on Jacob's neck, and wept thereon a good while". What happiness, what bliss, thus again to embrace one so loving and so beloved! In melting tears alone could the profound sentiment of filial love find adequate expression. But acts were speedily to follow. Pride of office and of rank had never found a resting-place in Joseph's heart ; but great was his filial pride in one so estimable, so good, and so venerable as Jacob, and which he openly testified by presenting him to the King imme-

* Gen. xlv, 9.

diately after his own warm and honourable reception. True, his parent followed an avocation which, in the eyes of the Egyptians, "was an abomination", being but a shepherd; yet what of that? If Joseph had deserved well of the King, it was now he would claim his reward; and well prepared was Pharaoh to accord it, for not only did he receive Jacob most graciously, promising him the "best of the land", but further bowed before him for a blessing! Thus did this loving son delight to honour, and see honoured, his venerable and venerated sire.

Now, aged as was Jacob at this period, yet for no less than seventeen years had Joseph the satisfaction of contributing to the comfort and happiness of his long-lost parent; but the time at length arrived when Jacob was to be gathered to his fathers, and, in the several interesting and pathetic scenes which immediately preceded his demise, Joseph zealously fulfilled every duty which love and reverence could dictate. We find him visiting the sick room of his parent to learn his wishes, and even promising on oath their fulfilment; then shortly afterwards he returned with his children, to obtain for them that benediction which he himself held in such high estimation; finally, in company with his brothers, he drew nigh to the mortal couch to receive a fond parent's parting blessing, and gather strength from his affectionately consoling words and prophetic promises. It was, however, after the decease of Jacob that the apparent struggle between love and duty commenced; for such was the bitterness of his grief that he could not bring himself to quit the couch of death, but in anguish of soul "fell upon his father's face, and wept upon him and kissed him". It was only after this outburst of true filial sorrow that he could command himself, and then love and duty united in dictating the display of every conceivable honour to the remains of the dear departed. Nor was this a difficult task, for so greatly were both son and father loved and respected, that Jacob was not only mourned by the whole nation for three score and ten days, but even the elders of the land and all the servants of the house of Pharaoh followed Joseph when he "went up to bury his father in Canaan", and mourned with him during seven days "with a great and sore lamentation". Thus was all due respect paid to the memory of that excellent patriarch, who, if a shepherd and father of shepherds, was also the father of the wise and virtuous ruler of Egypt. All honour, then, to that devoted, loving son who not only conduced to remove the scorn and dislike which the Egyptians had heretofore entertained towards such persons as pursued an avocation, to their minds, so ignoble, but even brought them to love and esteem the very head of the class, by himself openly testifying on every possible occasion the highest respect and consideration for the illustrious, because worthy, patriarch.

Now had Jacob's other sons been equally solicitous to promote his comfort and happiness, his life would have passed far more pleasurably; but although they certainly loved their excellent father, carried away by their evil passions, they too often acted as if totally indifferent to his wishes, honour, and best interests. Full well must they have known the blow they were about to inflict on their parent when depriving him, by their cruel and merciless act, of his greatly beloved Joseph; yet even this reflection could not deter them from their vile purpose, hatred to their brother prevailing over love to their father. They who would wilfully indulge unbridled passions and gratify jealous resentment at the cost of a crime, would little regard the anguish of a parent, nor would they hesitate in adopting towards him a course of dissimulation and untruth. Their moral nature once warped by an unrighteous deed, they could easily bring themselves to devise crafty tales, and wickedly deceive their sire by laying before him the false tokens of Joseph's death. Yet these sons, on seeing him in the bitterness of despair, "rend his clothes, put sack-cloth on his loins, and mourn, rose up to comfort him". Their hearts were not altogether hardened; and when " he refused to be comforted", saying, "I will go down to the grave unto my son, mourning", they must have felt some regret and no little compunction of conscience for the sorrow they had caused their grey-haired sire. The loving and grieving parent must have stood ever before them as an accusing angel! Nor could this one deplorable consequence of fraternal hatred and malice have been all they had to suffer during the twenty-two years that Joseph remained in unknown banishment. Much mutual distrust and rancour sprang up among these co-partners in crime, and there can be no doubt that they frequently experienced the lashings of guilty reminiscences. Further, a fresh cause of jealousy must have arisen in the person of the youthful Benjamin; for he had become the favourite, as these words of Judah amply prove—" Now, seeing that thy servant, my father's life *is bound up in the lad's life*, it shall come to pass, when he seeth that the lad is not with us, that he will die, and thy servants shall bring down the gray hairs of our father with sorrow to the grave."* There must also have been some distrust and alienation of feeling between them and their parent; for being ever in dread lest the truth should transpire and bring down on their heads a father's curse, they must have had frequent recourse to deceit and dissimulation, which would necessarily have engendered a want of confidence bordering on a sense of estrangement. What they so dreaded did, however, ultimately occur, and let us mark this fact—*from their own lips* proceeded the truth which for twenty long years they had so sedulously concealed! That Jacob was made acquainted with the whole circumstances, and that he deeply felt the deceit which had been practised upon him, his parting words (for blessings they certainly were not) to Simeon† and Levi

* Gen. xliv, 30.

† It may be well to draw attention here to a fact easily overlooked, although it is interesting and full of moral significance. Not only did

amply prove; he exclaimed, "O my soul, come thou not into their secret, unto their assembly, mine honour, be not thou united; for in their anger they slew a man, and in their self-will they digged down a wall". Thus, in spite of Jacob's abhorrence of the crime, he could not bring his lips to utter a malediction on the perpetrators of it—they were his children;—but he expended his ire on the dire passions which dictated their conduct, ejaculating, "Cursed be their *anger*, for it was fierce, and their *wrath*, for it was cruel". Grossly deceived and wronged as he had been in this case, and wilfully disobeyed in others, as, for instance, in that of Hamor, parental love yet prevailed, and, with true nobility of heart, he cursed the sin, but not the sinner. This might well have inspired Joseph's brethren with faith in his fraternal affection, since they had latterly experienced so many proofs that he was actuated by kindred sentiments; but crime, habitual dissimulation, and a constant spirit of distrust had warped their moral nature, and stolen from them the proper standard, whereby to judge of the character of one so infinitely their superior in all that was good, great, and noble. Weak themselves, they could not believe in the strength which piety and virtue give, but based their reliance chiefly on Joseph's forbearance and the certainty of his filial love—a sentiment the force of which they could in a great degree feel and understand. Thence their deceitful

SIMEON fail to receive a blessing from his father Jacob, but though long, long years had elapsed, *no mention was made of his tribe* when Moses gave his parting benediction to Israel! And to what can this exclusion be attributed if not to lack of deserts? The moral condition of that tribe or family had evidently not improved, but it was otherwise with that of Levi, who, individually, like Simeon, received no blessing from his father Jacob, yet the tribe was especially mentioned by Moses; indeed, he even states that they had "observed the word and kept the covenant of God", and therefore should (Deut. xxxi, 10) "teach Jacob God's judgments, and Israel his law". In this latter instance, example had evidently served as a warning, and worked to good, while in the former it had been prolific of evil through many generations.

message to Joseph on the death of their parent and supposed protector. A "command" from Jacob they well knew he would respect, and herein was their trust. And greatly as their unjust misgivings must have grieved his sensitive heart, ever glowing with fraternal love, yet, doubtless, Joseph gladly welcomed even this one sentiment in common, since it might in the future suffice to preclude all further severance.

In conclusion, be it observed that, had Joseph's brothers, like him, regarded filial love not merely as a bond of family union, but had also made it conduce to filial obedience and acts of virtue, then would they have been happily saved from much evil, with its consequent misery; while, further, they would assuredly have received, as he did, that truly golden legacy and ever-present reward—a father's dying blessing.

If love alone can repay love, surely parental love should be met by the warmest filial affection; and again, if gratitude is justly due for benefits conferred, how solemn must be the obligation of the child to the parent, through whom, under God, he has from infancy received every enjoyable blessing. Thus, even if nature did not dictate, and God had not enjoined this sentiment, yet must it have swayed every human heart not dead to right feeling and generous emotions. Truly filial love is a debt we owe, but can never wholly cancel; yet may we be ever discharging it, and herein lies a paramount duty. Now, this is most effectively fulfilled *by repayment in kind*, by fond devotion and loving acts. We should be ever sedulously seeking to ascertain a parent's wishes, and practically demonstrate our earnest will to gratify them to the best of our power. But to what will their every desire tend if not to their children's good? When rearing us with the tenderest care, and training us with the fondest solicitude, seeking to develop in us the germs of virtue and true piety, what was their aim and desire but that we should prove, by our conduct in after life, that their long instruction had not been lavished in vain, and that we should carry down untarnished the good name which they had transmitted unimpaired? What a small compensation demanded for so weighty a debt, yet does it contain the germ of every good, alike to parent and to child. The youth who attends to the admonitions of his fond parents, hearkens respectfully to their advice, and follows it cheerfully, ever striving to walk by the greater light of their experience, and seeking to become deserving of their glowing aspirations, will prove himself a worthy son; and never yet did a worthy son fail in performing his part in life worthily as a man. Earnestly fulfilling every moral duty, he will assuredly secure the respect and love of all good men, and the happiness which smiled upon him first within his home will go forth with him into the world without. And as to the parents, how implicit will be their trust in such a child; how entire their faith that he, the cherished one, ever accomplishing each moral obligation, could not leave unfulfilled the most sacred of all duties, but in their declining years will be at their side, willingly and sedulously administering to their comfort and happiness, never even hesitating at any needful, self-imposed sacrifice. Here, then, we have truly precious fruit; the growth of good seed long since planted. Thus, when the time of their departure draws nigh, they will be enabled to enjoy the glad reflection that they are leaving behind one every way worthy of taking their place, and carrying on those good works which they were powerless to complete; and further, the happy parents may treasure in their thoughts the sweet and consoling belief that their heavenward prayer for their beloved child will find acceptance on high, since God's eternal blessing ever rests on the worthy son and worthy man. This reflection will assuredly give peace to their souls, and lend a bright effulgence to their last hours. Truly, then, filial affection is not alone a duty, but a prerogative; and thrice happy the son who can thus throw so glowing and glorious a halo over the spirit of a dying parent, receiving in return what must spread a hallowed joy over his entire life—that loving parent's parting benediction.

Turning next to the consideration why some children fail in deserving this reward, we shall find that it is mainly owing to the far greater attention paid in their early years to the instruction of the mind than to the direct training of the heart. This surely should not be, for when either is at variance with the right and the true, no goodness of disposition will avail. Even the naturally warm passions and generous impulses of youth, which might be so fruitful in good, will but prove pernicious when deprived of judicious culture. The child needs to be perpetually exercising the keen susceptibilities of his heart in all that is pure, useful, and good, for if they are not thus directed, he will be insensibly, but too surely, betrayed into wrong-doing. Now, where should he more confidently turn for the development of the best and loftiest feelings of his nature than to the cheerful, happy home? There should be kindled the flame of that gratitude and love which will display themselves in a thousand endearing acts. There may fresh springs of pure delight be ever bubbling forth, there holy sentiments and noble aspirations be prompted and encouraged both by precept and example. Truly, when home becomes an abiding place of joy and the centre of tranquil pleasures, when loving greetings from devoted parents and fond relatives are unfailing, then will youth turn thankfully back from the greatest enjoyments which the world can offer to the less exciting but more abiding delights of a happy, peaceful hearth. Home will not then be a mere name, but a sentiment, and one so potent as to be a safeguard against all temptations. The love of his parents will be the youth's true sunshine, their voice his sweetest music.

But there are homes of quite a reverse character, and it is mostly in those that we meet with filial defection. There are some in which the longings of youth are disregarded, where legitimate pleasures are denied, or at least not encouraged, where severity takes precedence of kindness, and where the heart is left to stagnate or rarely roused, and made to pulsate with high and generous emotions. Now, it is but too certain that if during youth the loftier and nobler passions are not exercised in the family circle, the lower will infallibly crop up and seek gratification in the world without. Then will quantity rather than quality of pleasures be considered, and each inebriating draught will harden the heart and turn it more and more from home, its duties and its associations. The world and its allurements then becoming too greatly prized, the peaceful hearth will speedily lose its attractions, while ignoble and slavish passions, stifling the remonstrances of the parent, will infallibly lead to a breach, which neither time nor even a return to duty can always repair. Thus let age kindly consider the requirements of youth, and let youth gladly listen to the voice of experience. Both are duties, and if fulfilled there will be no cause for deception or dissimulation on the one side or for harshness of reproof and exercise of authority on the other. Then will love direct and affection govern each thought, each act, and throw their bright halo round the parental roof.

Now, if children would bear in mind that parents have their welfare constantly in view, and are ever testifying their love by numberless kind acts and often by many sacrifices, they would be less exacting, and when home, from various causes, was not made as entirely happy as their young hearts could desire, would turn to inward resources, and make them contribute to their stock of enjoyments. And further, they would make the most of whatever pleasures were given them, and strive to be content. Thus could they gratify the authors of their being, and withal, by learning not to be too grasping after pleasures, would save themselves much future misery and shame.

But heavy and severe will be the penalty which that youth has to pay, who, regardless of duty and his own self-interest, rashly and wilfully disobeys parental commands. Surely, if every minor dereliction of duty is fraught with evil, sad and painful must be the consequences entailed by filial disobedience. To him who refuses the light of experience, the road to ruin will be as swift as certain. Heart, purse, and health will soon be alike bankrupt. When conscience ceases to struggle for the right, when no chord of sympathy or love is struck by the sight of anguish written in legible characters on that face which it was a son's duty to irradiate with joy, when a father's anger is obdurately defied, and passion is allowed full sway, that goal is nearly reached whence there can be no return. Truly nought but compunction of conscience will be left to him who, besides ruining his own prospects, has disappointed the fond aspirations of loving parents. Nor can his sorrow be otherwise than greatly heightened when he sees death laying its cold hand on that father or mother to whom all reparation has now become impossible. Yet even a severer sting than this will occasionally wound the undutiful child; for if his unfilial conduct has inflicted a blow which in any measure hastened that fatal end, an agony of remorse and self-condemnation will steal upon him; too late will he then remember that parents forgive much, very much; indeed, that the fond mother will pardon nearly all but ingratitude, and that by obstinately persisting in subjecting her to this cruel wrong, he has basely stabbed her to the quick—perhaps broken her heart, and sent her sorrowing to the grave. Let then, the son who would save himself in latter years from the stings of conscience and much bitter grief beware of making his first step in opposition to a parent's counsel. Indeed, it surely behoves him to regard such advice as an inestimable boon, for then will he make a pleasure of obedience, and, wisely profiting by the experience of age and the lessons of love, will become an honour to his family, a pride and a joy to beloved and loving parents.

Although Scripture offers but few PRECEPTS inculcating filial love and duty, since little will avail if the heart has not already prompted this solemn obligation, yet these few are emphatically enjoined, and often enforced by threats of punishment and by promises of reward. Firstly, take Solomon's words, in Prov. vi, 20, "My son, keep thy father's commandments, and forsake not the law of thy mother, bind them continually upon thine heart"; and at ch. xxiii, 22, "Hearken unto thy father that begat thee, and despise not thy mother when she is old". Then at ch. xxviii, 7, "Whoso keepeth the law is a wise son, but he that is a companion of riotous men shameth his father"; and again, ch. xx, 20, "Whoso curseth his father or his mother, his lamp shall be put out in obscure darkness". Then in Deut. xxvii, 16, "Cursed be he that setteth light by his father or his mother". Turning to Leviticus, we find the injunction, "Rise up before the hoary head and honour the face of the old man". Now, if such marks of respects are due even to seniors whom we know not, how may we adequately testify our reverence to parents who have so many claims on our love and veneration? Next, the fact that the All-Merciful Himself ordained that the penalty of death should be inflicted on the rebellious son; and further, that it was at the hands of the people he was to suffer his ignominious fate, is sufficient to convince us that to be undutiful was not only to be criminal in the sight of the Lord, but also that it was essential for the welfare of the community that the entire people should testify, by a public demonstration, their abhorrence of all insubordination to parental authority. Thus only was "evil to be put away".* It is, however, to the Decalogue, replete with laws conducive to man's well-being and moral good that we must more particularly refer. There, at the Fifth Commandment, we read, "Honour thy father and thy mother, that thy days may be long in the land which the Lord thy God hath

* Deut. xxi, 21.

given thee". Thus direct from Omniscience are we instructed as to the duty and reverence we owe our parents; and Infinite Goodness further accompanied the injunction with the most gracious promise of reward for its due performance. Nevertheless, it is not enough to honour and obey our parents; we should gladden their hearts by good and pious conduct, by an ever-ready manifestation of love and gratitude. Without this we fall far short of duty, and may hardly be said to do them proper honour. We read in Prov. xxiii, 24, "The father of the righteous shall greatly rejoice, and he that begetteth a wise son shall have joy of him"; but also to contrast with this we have at ch. xvii, 25, "A foolish son is a grief to his father and bitterness to her that bore him". Thus let youth lay great store on this natural affection, and learn to feel that "The glory of children are their fathers";* for then will they be led to act so that their parents shall gratefully acknowledge, "Children's children are the crown of old men". Truly the good and virtuous son who has proved himself a blessing, a comfort, and an honour, is as a crown of priceless worth to his parents; and assuredly he who has thus acted will have the glowing sense of deserving, as well as possibly the delight of enjoying the like rich inheritance, and thus in his turn receiving the just recompense of virtue, love, and duty.

To RUTH, grandmother of King David, we may turn for an EXAMPLE of filial affection, and, indeed, the Sacred Volume offers no more striking instance of true love and devotion. In Naomi had Ruth and Orpah found a kind and tender mother-in-law, and we may feel assured that they never failed in testifying their gratitude, since these are Naomi's words, when bidding them depart to their former homes, "Go, and the Lord deal kindly with you as ye have dealt with the dead and *with me*". Both had learnt

* Prov. xvii, 6.

to appreciate her estimable qualities, and love her for them; but the affection which her worth and merit had inspired was wholly different in degree. With Orpah it was far more transient, and much less practical in its character, than with Ruth. She evidently did not possess so fond or clinging a nature; and although proposing to accompany Naomi on her journey to Judea, a few words of dissuasion from her kind, indulgent mother-in-law sufficed to induce a change of purpose; for then it was that "Orpah kissed her, but Ruth clave unto her."

Now, there were many considerations which might well serve to deter the daughters from following the poor and afflicted Naomi. They certainly could never expect aught but privations, and possibly would have to encounter many trials which they might hope to escape in their own land. It was against this appalling prospect that the filial affection of Orpah was powerless to contend. With Ruth, however, it was far otherwise; though the dear tie which had united her to Naomi was snapped by death, and gaunt famine had further heightened their sore distress, yet each fibre of her heart vibrated in unison with that of her cherished parent. Indeed, mutual sorrow and suffering apparently served to endear her the more. To convince ourselves of this, we have but to turn to ch. i, 15 of the Book of Ruth, where we read, "And Naomi said, Behold, thy sister-in-law has gone back unto her people, and unto her gods, return thou after her". But though thus urged, Ruth never wavered in her decision; her resolve was unalterable, and she emphatically replied, "Intreat me not to leave thee, or to return from following after thee, for whither thou goest I will go, and where thou lodgest I will lodge; thy people shall be my people, thy God my God. Where thou diest I will die, and there will I be buried; the Lord do so to me and more also if aught but death part thee and me"; and when Naomi saw that she was "steadfastly minded to go with her, then she left speaking unto her". Truly sympathy and

love, bred of esteem and gratitude, glowed within the heart of Ruth; and she was only too happy to be able to testify by acts, her deep and lasting affection for the unfortunate Naomi. It would have been repugnant to her nature to forsake in adversity a relative to whom she had adhered in prosperity. No, rather submit to a life of trial, or even destitution, than be selfishly ingrate to one every way deserving of her good offices and daughterly affection. Being thus prepared to submit to her hard but self-imposed lot, she no sooner reached Bethlehem than she set herself to obtain adequate sustenance by gleaning, and rich were her earnings. She first secured the goodwill of the mighty Boaz, to whom belonged the field she had chosen for her labours, and these were the friendly words which accompanied his promise of protection, " It has been shown to me all that thou hast done unto thy mother-in-law since the death of thy husband, and how thou hast left thy father and thy mother and the land of thy nativity, and art come unto a people which thou knowest not heretofore; the Lord recompense thy work, and a full reward be given thee of the God of Israel, under whose wings thou hast come to trust". Nor did his kindly feeling stop here; for admiration of her conduct soon ripened into a more tender sentiment, and, loving, he woo'd her. Once the wife of the noble-hearted Boaz, affluence took the place of penury, and with her change of fortune changed that of Naomi; for we read, "And the women said unto Naomi, Blessed be the Lord which hath not left thee this day without a kinsman, and he shall be unto thee a restorer of thy life, and a nourisher of thine old age, *for thy daughter-in-law, who loveth thee*".*
Thus through the filial love and generous self-denial of Ruth did Naomi regain her past position. Her plaint uttered when entering Judea was silenced; she could no longer say, " Call me not Naomi, but call me Mara; for the Almighty hath dealt very bitterly with me; I went out full,

* Ruth, iv, 14.

and the Lord hath brought me home again empty: why, then, call me Naomi?" Indeed, all must have been prosperity and gladness; and when, in a truly pious spirit, she contrasted her present happy condition with her past distress and gloom, how must her heart have swelled with gratitude towards that fond, faithful, loving daughter, who had wrought so great and joyful a change! Here, then, was a glorious consummation; and, Ruth thus blessing, was herself most blessed.

An incident in the life of the great law-giver and teacher MOSES is worthy of some consideration, since it presents us with a practical and useful lesson under this heading. And here it may be well to premise that although Jethro stood not in the connection of a blood relation to Moses, yet, never having known any other parent, he had evidently given the natural affections of a son to his father-in-law. Thus in Exodus xviii we have placed before us a meeting little dissimilar to that of Joseph with his father Jacob. It is thus described: "And Moses went out to meet his father-in-law and *did obeisance* and kissed him, and they asked each other of their welfare". Now, it is to be borne in mind that, as in the case of Joseph, a great revolution had taken place in the lot of Moses since he had quitted the roof of his revered relative, then a simple shepherd, now the commissioned deliverer of an entire people; moreover, he had stood face to face with kings, and become the recognised ruler and head of a nation. Yet, great as was his elevation, it could effect no change in his sentiments; thus, not only was the greeting of the kinsmen in the highest degree warm and cordial, but on the side of Moses it was most filial-like and dutiful. The love and respect here shown to Jethro fully testifies to his worth, and indeed the kindly feeling he manifested towards the people of God places his character in the most estimable light. At the 9th verse we read, "And Jethro rejoiced for all the goodness which the Lord had done to Israel and said, Blessed be the Lord who hath delivered the people from under the hand of the Egyptians; now I know the Lord is greater than all gods". But Jethro's deep interest in the welfare of the people was greatly surpassed by his solicitude for the well-being of his son-in-law, as is clearly proved by his proffered suggestions and sagacious counsel. And when we consider that this advice was tendered to one not only greatly advanced in years, but also rich in experience and expedients, we must the more admire its ready acceptance. Indeed, Moses was as willing to be advised as to advise, to listen to words of good counsel and of wisdom as to communicate them, to perform every duty as to urge it on others; in a word, to yield childlike obedience to those he held in reverence, while yet manfully striving to command his wilful people and bring them to submit to their elders as well as to bow in faith before the Holy and Mighty One. But how wise, how pious, how fraught with good to Moses and his people, was the advice of Jethro, high priest of Midian. He first declared to Moses, " The thing thou doest is not good, thou wilt surely wear away, both thou and this people that is with thee; for this thing is too heavy for thee; thou art not able to perform it thyself alone; hearken now to my voice, I will give thee counsel and God will be with thee".* Then, after proffering at some length his opinion as to the best method of instructing and judging the people, and of providing out of all the nation men "such as fear God, men of truth, hating covetousness", that they might be rulers under Moses, he thus concludes: " And let them judge the people at all seasons, and it shall be that every great matter they shall bring unto thee, but every small matter they shall judge, so shall it be easier for thyself, and they shall bear the burden with thee. If thou shalt do this, and God command thee so, then thou shalt be able to endure, and all the people shall go to their place in peace". It was not in the character of the great law-giver to hesitate when love, reason, and duty prompted; therefore we find, " So Moses did all that he had said". Soon after this Jethro departed for

* Exodus xvii, 17.

his home, and Moses was left alone, gladly to fulfil to the end of his course each allotted task in the same willing spirit of devotion with which he had performed his duty to Jethro in his filial relation.

Before proceeding to the last example we shall offer, it may be well to reverse the picture, and look on its darker side. This is found in the life of ABSOLOM, who presents a notable instance of *filial disobedience,* and offers a warning none may disregard. Early in life two dominant and hateful passions, revenge and ambition, had entered his breast, but, far from curbing them, he, with a rare power of dissimulation, cautiously hid them till the occasion offered when he could work out his vile purpose. That he had just cause of enmity towards his brother Amnon may readily be granted, yet he never "spake unto his brother good or bad". Though rage was burning within, yet by his peaceful demeanour he was able to lull all unquiet doubts which may have arisen in the minds of his father and brother, and only at the end of two years, his plans being then matured, did he execute the scheme of revenge he had so long meditated. Amnon was basely assassinated by the orders of the perfidious Absolom. Thus, a fratricide in heart and a destroyer of the peace of his father's household, he, dreading that parent's just resentment, quitted his own country and fled to the court of Talmai, where he remained three years. It was during this self-imposed exile that he conceived the treacherous design of dethroning David, his father, and usurping the government, but while thus scheming and plotting he was recalled to Jerusalem by his over-indulgent parent and reinstated in his high position. Nevertheless, no act of kindness or love could touch his heart or subdue his ambitious spirit. He resolved to make the power thus afforded him conduce to his ultimate designs, and further, he sought by every possible device to rob his father of the affections and loyalty of his subjects. Only too well did he succeed, and when his treacherous projects were ripe, forgetful of every natural tie, he raised the standard of open rebellion, and, numerous partisans flocking to his banner, he took possession of the capital at the head of a rebel army, and David was obliged to flee. Absolom then with an exulting heart declared himself heir to the vacant throne. But his unnatural conduct was not destined to prosper; the bad son could not make a good king, and by slighting the fair promises he had made the people when seeking their support, he provoked a counter revolution, which brought war in its train. Long and fierce was the struggle, but victory finally attended the cause of right. David was reinstated, while the undutiful son met an ignominious death.

In thus reviewing Absolom's downward course, we must observe that he had violated every right principle, made various guilty passions the stepping-stones to his worldly ambition, and so deadened all natural feeling as even to sacrifice his too forgiving father to the attainment of his object. That Absolom expiated his treacherous and criminal conduct by hours of agony and remorse we may not doubt. Suspended by his long, beautiful hair to the thick bough of a great oak, he was left, powerless and friendless, to await a cruel fate at the hands of his enemies! Here, then, do we find that retributive justice which ever awaits the sinner, and indeed it would be hard to conceive a sadder position than the one which he had brought on himself. Present suffering and gloomy prospects will have awakened conscience, and, among many painful reflections which must have flashed across his mind, the most poignant will assuredly have been those of having incurred God's displeasure, of having humbled and cruelly wronged his loving parent, sacrificed his countrymen, and brought much misery on them through a devastating civil war, while his own cherished projects were utterly ruined, even should he be finally spared from a violent death. Now, sad as was his lot, it was but the work of his own hands. As he had sown, so did he reap, and, while his life serves as a lasting memorial of filial ingratitude, it also teaches us that the just and righteous Lord, who commanded us to "honour our parents", will never suffer such breach of love and duty to pass unchastised. Grievously had he sinned, and grievous was his punishment.

We finally turn to an incident in the early life of the prophet ELISHA, which, though briefly and simply related, conveys an admirable lesson as to the duty the adult as well the child owes to his parents. The facts are thus related: "And Elijah passed by Elisha, the son of Shaphat, who was ploughing, and cast his mantle upon him, and Elisha left the oxen and ran after Elijah, and said, Let me, I pray thee, kiss my father and my mother, and then I will follow thee. And he said, Go back again, for what have I done to thee? And he returned back from him".* Arrived at his home, Elisha set himself to feast the people, and then "he arose and went to Elijah, and ministered unto him". Now, we can only justly appreciate this simple act by carefully noting the circumstances under which it was performed. We must first observe that no surprise was expressed by Elisha when thus strangely accosted by Elijah, therefore we may reasonably suppose that he had expected this summons, and was fully prepared to comply with it. Indeed, he must have felt that in following the prophet of the Lord a glorious career awaited him, and eager may he well have been to enter upon it, yet withal, being left perfectly free to act as inclination dictated, he at once sought his parents to ask their benediction and in a long embrace give token of the sincerity and warmth of his affection. This filial, and to his mind paramount, duty being performed, he at once departed his home. How worthily Elisha, as a prophet of God, afterwards accomplished each important mission entrusted to him, his whole career bears ample testimony. He who had been the good, dutiful, and affectionate son could hardly fail to become a faithful messenger, no less than a charitable dispenser of the many rich gifts which the Almighty had vouchsafed him

* 1 Kings xix, 19.

as His virtuous, pious servant and prophet. Indeed, he greatly distinguished himself in all that was good, kind, and humane. Mark his readiness to multiply the poor widow's oil, his benevolent compliance with the Shunammite's request, the tears he shed at the thought of the misfortunes which would surely accrue from the misdeeds of the wicked Hazael, and, most praiseworthy of all, the self-denying, noble spirit he evinced when appealed to by Joram, King of Israel, as to whether he should smite the Syrians, his captives, who had come in a hostile spirit with the express purpose of apprehending Elisha himself! for thus answered the prophet, "Thou shalt not smite them; wouldest thou smite those whom thou hast taken captive with thy sword and with thy bow? Set bread and water before them, that they may eat and drink and go to their master".* And whence this goodness of heart, this kind and humane disposition, if not engendered in the dear home where he had been reared and cherished with a parent's tender care and love? There imbibed and fostered, it afterwards became a settled principle of his nature.

It behoves us, then, while giving our full meed of admiration to the character of this "man of God", and taking to heart the high moral lesson which his unblemished life unfolds, not to forget that which formed its very basis, as perhaps also its most notable trait. Truly to Filial Love and the cultivation of the natural affections did Elisha owe in a great degree his elevation of character and those many estimable moral qualities which distinguished him as a son, as a citizen, and as a prophet of the Lord.

When filial love is thus capable of exerting its kindly influence on character, then, and then only, does it wholly fulfil its high intent and work out the beneficent and gracious design of the Great Father of All.

* II Kings vi, 22.

SABBATH.

Exodus xvi, 26, "*The seventh day, which is the Sabbath.*"

BUT for the frequency with which the observance of the SABBATH was enjoined on the ISRAELITES during their sojourn in the wilderness, and some few practical instances of its violation, it would be hard to believe that a nation of bondsmen, slaves who had long groaned under their burden, should not, on obtaining their freedom, gladly welcome repose, and more especially greet with joy and thanksgivings that day which the Lord had set apart for rest and total cessation from labour. Yet so it was: no admonition, not even the voice that thundered from Mount Sinai, sufficed to eradicate these, their two besetting sins, covetousness, which led them to desecrate the Sabbath, and idolatry, with its deplorable practices, which drew them from the worship of the one only God. Had their hearts been true to the Supreme, sacred would have been the seventh day; but a people who could turn aside from following the commands of Moses, their leader, during an absence of only forty days, and, totally forgetful of their All-potent Deliverer and Protector, make unto themselves a golden calf, and offer sacrifice to it as the god which had brought them up out of the land of Egypt,* would be little apt to regard any ordinance which they believed calculated to interfere with their material interests. And this is observable from the very dawn of their history. The first flagrant instance presented to us is that of the gathering of the manna. Moses had bidden the people collect and bring to their homes on the sixth day two portions of this heaven-sent food, so that they

* Exodus xxxii, 8.

might have ample provisions for the Holy Sabbath, whilst he strictly prohibited their seeking it on that day of rest. But, although this command of their great Leader was accompanied by a miracle—the manna retaining its pristine wholesomeness on that day alone—yet do we find that "there went out some of the people on the seventh day for to gather".* That they found none was a practical reproof, and this was followed up by a verbal one from the Lord through Moses, for thus did he address them, "How long refuse ye to keep my commandments and my laws? See for that the Lord hath given you the Sabbath, therefore he giveth you on the sixth day the bread of two days; abide ye every man in his place, let no man go out of his place on the seventh day." Which injunction was afterwards obeyed, for we read at the next verse, "So the people rested on the Sabbath-day". From this distinct statement, coupled with the fact that no further instance of Sabbath breaking by the body of the people is recorded in the five Books of Moses, it may be inferred that the whole nation had learnt to feel how heinous was that crime, and this supposition is strengthened by the incident related in Numbers xv, 32, where we read: "While the children of Israel were in the wilderness, they found a man that gathered sticks upon the Sabbath-day, and they brought him unto Moses. And they put him in ward, because it was not declared what should be done to him. And the Lord said unto Moses, the man shall surely be put to death, all the congregation shall stone him with stones without the camp. And they did as the Lord commanded". This would tend to prove that there was no early infringement of the Sabbath after the miracle of the manna, though a total disregard of that sacred day, as well as many of the observances commanded by God, must have ensued when the Israelites relapsed into idolatry at a later period. But even if they abstained from violating the holy day of rest, little merit is to be attached thereto,

* Exodus xvi, 27.

since its observance could not have been dictated by a sentiment of gratitude and love to the Supreme. Had, indeed, the Israelites been steadfast to their God, then would their faithful adherence to His ordinances and commands have been fraught with good; as it was, it could only have been a barren, worthless form, since utterly powerless to arrest them when lapsing into idolatrous worship. Now, assuredly, this was not the Sabbath which had been enjoined, the Sabbath which was to make and keep them holy. It could merely have been a day of repose—purposeless, aimless, and in a great measure fruitless. Yet, even in this formal observance, they were not perfectly free agents; they could find no food on that day, therefore little indeed would they have profited by labour. Thus was their cupidity forcibly held in check; thence also the probable cause of their immunity from the sin of Sabbath breaking.

Turning from the time of Moses to that period when Joshua was their leader, a marked change in their conduct becomes discernible. Although, during the rule of Moses, God had in love shown his people Israel ever-renewing mercies; although, in His just anger, He had suffered many trials and reverses to befal them, they resisted each appeal. Not so, however, under Joshua, when a long apprenticeship to freedom began to tell upon the character of the entire people. The errors and tribulations of their fathers had worked to good with the children; the lesson had been severe, but it proved effective. While under the rule of Joshua, the Israelites never once relapsed into idolatry, but served the Lord faithfully, fulfilling His ordinances and doing His High Will. It was, indeed, immediately after the passage of the Jordan that the covenant of Abraham was again observed, the Passover kept, and also assuredly the Sabbath, since it had been yet more emphatically enjoined. In a word, the children of Israel then became true servants of God, and acceptable in His sight, as we read, "The Lord said unto Joshua, This day have I rolled away the reproach of Egypt from off you";* also, "And Israel served the Lord all the days of Joshua and all the days of the elders that outlived Joshua".† A truly happy reform this; and as it may fairly be ascribed to newly-awakened sentiments of love and gratitude to God, it takes its place among the most marked and brightest episodes of their national history.

The strict observance of the Sabbath day is a sacred obligation. To "keep it holy" is a direct command from God, and this at once constitutes it a solemn and imperative duty. None may with impunity overlook or disregard this gracious behest, while all can seek God's favour by making that holy day subserve the high purpose for which it was instituted. With this main object and wise intent, it is especially necessary to keep constantly in view the chief and primary characteristics of the Sabbath; and among these we must recognise the following. Firstly, that it should be a day of rest, of repose for both mind and body; a perfect cessation from care and toil. Now, he who has sedulously fulfilled his duties during the six days which should be devoted to labour, will assuredly need that reinvigoration which a calm and peaceful Sabbath cannot fail to impart. Thence it is imperative on us to regard and conform to the *whole* of the Fourth Commandment; nor forget that, while we are therein bidden to abstain from "all manner of work on the seventh day", we are also distinctly told "*Six days shalt thou labour*". This latter duty duly performed, will surely, although perhaps insensibly, draw us towards the observance of the other solemn obligation. While making a golden use of the intellectual faculties with which we have been blessed, we shall reflect that they rather weaken than expand by over tension, or by an intense and long-sustained application, therefore shall gladly avail ourselves of the day of rest to unbend the mind

* Joshua v, 9. † Joshua xxxiv, 31.

and *give a total change of direction to our thoughts*. This will not only keep the prolific brain unimpaired, but likewise restore to the mind its pristine energy and capabilities each successive week. Also, while giving full development to our physical powers, we shall never exact, either from the vigour of youth or the ripeness of manhood, *unceasing* labour, which must strain the mortal fabric, impair the vital energies, and breed infirmity and disease. The Sabbath will then be hailed with joy as the cessation of daily toil, and wisely made a medium to recruit wasting powers or waning strength.

The next important characteristic of the Sabbath is its sanctity. It is a day to be set apart and kept holy unto the Lord. We should devote no small portion of that sacred day to His service; to grateful worship; to reflection on His glorious and gracious attributes and perfections; to meditation on our spiritual interests. Now he who resolves to act thus piously will seek to free his mind from mundane affairs, even excluding such readings as would draw his attention thereto, and replace them by works calculated to elevate his soul to his Creator. He will make this blessed day subserve a wise and ennobling purpose. His heart will turn to his God; to all that is pure, elevating, and holy. He will hold delightful converse with the Book of books, as with a well-chosen friend; he will read it, study it with the heart, and seek to impress its sublime principles, its beautiful ethical precepts, its high practical teachings, on his mind. He will make it a uniting link between earth and heaven, a medium whereby he may lift his spirit up to God. From that sacred volume he will learn to appreciate the mercy and loving-kindness of the Lord; to understand the wisdom, the power of the Great Ruler of the Universe, and thence to love and revere that Great Being with all the energy of his soul. By its light he will trace his own course on earth, the aim of his existence, and learn to put to profit the glorious truths it unfolds. Now, though he often ponders its inspired pages, he can never weary, as on each succeeding Sabbath he will assuredly find something new to rouse interest and gladden the heart. Considered as God's gracious gift to man, it will be valued and used accordingly. It will be made the subject of repeated meditation, the source of invigoration, the teacher and prompter of his spiritual interests, and eagerly sought as a Sabbath companion as well as a daily guide. Let, therefore, its studied perusal go hand in hand with Divine Worship; let each bear an important part in that day's solemn duty; for assuredly by a heartfelt attention to these conjointly may we best sanctify and hallow the Sabbath-day.

A third important characteristic of the Sabbath is its power for good over mind and heart. It is a day wherein we may and should dismiss the cares, throw down the burdens, and allay the disquietudes which the past week shall have engendered and possibly fostered. It is a day every way calculated to improve our moral nature as also to promote cheerfulness and content. But that it may exercise so beneficial an influence we must justly estimate this heavenly boon, and take delight in making it subserve a useful and healthful purpose. When we cease from all worldly occupations, all earthly solicitude, content to repose entire and holy trust in the great Beneficent Giver and Lord of the Universe, when we make a halt in our march after worldly goods and earthly pleasures, yielding up for a time our ambitious projects, suspending our search after distinction, and giving grateful homage to the Bountiful Bestower of our daily blessings, then shall we penetrate the spirit of its institution and understand as well as acknowledge its wise and gracious intent. Further, when we turn our thoughts from those objects which give zest to our daily business life and ponder holy truths, adjusting our feelings and our minds thereto, when we thus withdraw from the din and turmoil of the world's restless strife, and study to erase unruly passions and desires, quell all spirit of repining, give to the future renewing hopes and manful resolves, then will true content beam forth to illumine the daily routine of our lives. Again, when with minds relaxed from that strain which generally attends earnest efforts after competence, we, on God's holy day, zealously strive to brighten our homes by infusing the sweets of religious joy into the hearts of its inmates, and tighten each natural bond of affection by acts of disinterested kindness and loving devotion, then shall we experience true cheerfulness and happiness. Thus, if on this sacred day we subdue the mind to calm reflection and store it with holy thoughts, if we open the heart to every pure and tender emotion, quickening its pulsation by acts of charity and love, by pious meditation on God's glorious works, then assuredly shall we be fulfilling the gracious design of the Great Father of All. The Sabbath will have brought with it a vast power for good, an ever-renewing strength; truly it will have proved itself our good genius.

Now, it is impossible to review all the important characteristics of the Holy Sabbath without sensibly feeling that the day imposes no duty which should not be in itself pleasurable, and further, that if cheerfully complied with, its every demand, alike the call of nature and of God, will surely conduce to present joy and eternal bliss. Yet, unhappily, the Sabbath is not justly appreciated by all men, nor are its sacred obligations always fulfilled with alacrity and zeal. This consideration should urge us to seek for the prime moving causes of its infringement or frequent neglect, and in so doing we encounter, at the very threshold of our investigation, firstly, *Covetousness*. The man of grasping disposition knows no rest, nor could enjoy it; indeed, with him it is a hardship to abstain from the work of money-getting, not a hardship to undergo it. The calm, peaceful repose of the Sabbath day can have no charm for the busy, scheming, selfish man, who will be ever prone to regard it as a bar to the acquisition of those worldly goods for which he is contending. Could he, however, bring his mind seriously to reflect that "the earth is the Lord's, and the fulness thereof", and that not so much on his powers as on God's goodness depends his worldly prosperity, then might he hesitate in toiling, mind and body, on the Sabbath day, and thereby running counter to the high will of the Great Giver of All. Surely at the close of six days' earnest strivings after all reasonable requirements and those necessities which are essential to the well-being of his dearly-beloved ones, he would gladly cease from labour, and in a pious spirit give up to holy repose the seventh day, relying in the fulness of religious trust on the All-Merciful for each necessary blessing. While, however, wealth is held in higher estimation than worth, and vain longings and insatiable desires are apt to be not only permitted, but encouraged, the Sabbath, if not altogether ignored, must prove totally powerless for good, and only too late will the covetous man be brought by bitter experience to feel that gold may be bought too dear, and have to acknowledge with a sorrowing heart the truth embodied in Prov. xiii, 7, that "there is that maketh himself rich and hath nothing". Thence let him beware of disobeying the fourth and tenth Commandments and incurring God's displeasure while hastening to attain those earthly riches which "make themselves wings and fly away", but rather seek to acquire that heavenly treasure which is beyond all price, a truly pious, devout, and unselfish heart.

Yet more antagonistic to the observance of the Sabbath, to all its obligations, and to its very spirit of morality and piety, is, secondly, *Religious indifference.* He who can be insensible to religion itself will hardly regard any one of its institutions with favour, and certainly not that one which has for especial object to draw us nigh to God in prayer and praise. Truly only they who love God will love the Sabbath and strive to profit by its teachings. To them the sacred day will be especially acceptable, as one on which they can freely stir and warm their hearts in the contemplation of Infinite perfection and the study of God's holy Law, but to the indifferent it will appear a mere form or senseless observance, and be disregarded accordingly. Failing to recognise it as a fitting day for the cultivation of their higher nature—and indeed those who are indifferent to religion will be no less indifferent to that moral nature—it will become neglected, the lower instincts will speedily obtain supremacy, the light of religion will grow dim in the soul, and they will be content to grovel in the mire of licentiousness and all the meaner, baser passions of their nature. Thence assuredly he who would keep his heart pure, warm, and grateful must make the Sabbath his ministering angel, and consider religion as the supreme good; in a word, he must kindle the bright flames of true piety and devotion within his breast, thereby expelling the gloom and darkness which are inseparable from religious indifference and religious insensibility.

Lastly, *thoughtlessness*, besides other minor causes, among which are, the want of those intellectual resources that spring from a well-stored mind; and inattention to the beneficial and kindly influences of a day of rest. All these either militate against the proper observance of the Sabbath, or check the good with which it might otherwise be fraught. As to thoughtlessness, few men are there who will not, when their worldly interests are at stake, give their minds up to the consideration of how those interests may best be served, nor will they ever lose an opportunity of advancing them. But should spiritual matters be less regarded, and the Sabbath, which is part of religion, be dismissed with hardly a passing thought? Surely not; such neglect, such inattention to God's command cannot be otherwise than highly culpable, and will assuredly bear their bitter fruit. Now, if we reflect that we have duties to perform, and that the Sabbath teaches them; resolves to make, and that the day of rest gives time to form them; desires to curb, and that converse with our conscience on the sacred day enables us to subdue and regulate them, then shall we welcome the heavenly-appointed day as a true friend, as a spiritual guide, and hearken diligently to its teachings. Then, again, to the man of few intellectual resources the Sabbath is apt to prove more burdensome than pleasurable. The mind cannot lie fallow, or rest peacefully in listless idleness, and he who finds no delight in sacred readings, in high and ennobling conceptions, and draws no fund of elevating and pious reflections by looking from "nature up to nature's God", will assuredly endeavour to eke out the hallowed day by indulging in trivial pursuits or frivolous amusements, even if not led to desecrate it by business engagements. Thence it is highly essential that we should learn to give vitality to the day; that we should form for ourselves a taste, a relish for subjects which bear upon our spiritual welfare; give the heart and mind to an earnest search after truth, virtue, holiness, and enjoy God in all things, and all things in God. We need not indeed deprive ourselves of such rational recreations as involve no personal weariness, no fatigue to our fellow mortals, no toil to the beast of burden, or which do not tend to draw the mind too exclusively to sublunary objects, but we should likewise reserve no small portion of the day for the acquisition of knowledge, for enlarging and enlightening the understanding. When the mind has been well stored, then will the sacred day, with its pause in all business vocations, be productive of much intellectual enjoyment, and the return of the Sabbath will be looked for with a pure and heartfelt delight.

And this carries us, finally, to the consideration of the other numberless benefits it is calculated to confer; a consideration all-important, since it may induce those who have not *felt* the spiritual, or learnt truly to appreciate the material advantages which surely accrue from the strict observance of the Sabbath of rest, to reflect thereon, and strive after their attainment by a perfect conformity with the Divine injunction and Divine intent. Among the benefits which it should bring in its train may be numbered, bodily and mental refreshment; and for this we must know nothing of idleness, but much of repose. On this day, a day of compensation, lost stamina is to be recovered, power to be restored, energies to be recruited, the weary brain relaxed, and mental quietude engendered by calm, healthy, and trustful reflections. When this result is attained we shall be able to resume with all necessary energy the business engagements of the ensuing week, and efficiently discharge the many obligations and duties which pertain to our position in life. Renewed zest will have been engendered by the temporary suspension of business cares, and the mind, having for a time buried in oblivion thoughts which worried or oppressed it, will have regained its elasticity, its vigor, and with them renewed confidence and trust. The next benefit we may derive from the sacred day of rest is intellectual improvement, for does not the Bible tell us that "they who seek the Lord understand all things"? That mind will be clear and bright to discern the things of earth which has been furnished with heavenly truths, and if these be not taken to heart on the peaceful Sabbath, they will assuredly receive little attention on the working days. Truly, as the week offers unbounded opportunity of action, so does the Sabbath present us with ample subjects for reflection, and if we will only strive to turn them to profitable account, and carry their teachings with us into the active business of life, we may fairly hope for flattering results to our labour. Finally, a benefit which greatly depends thereon, is our moral progress; a truly pious and virtuous character is not to be formed without those reflections which the holy day is every way calculated to suggest. We must thereon learn to *be* and to *do* good; we must turn our thoughts inwards, examine the disposition of our heart, review our past conduct, give heed to errors committed, and fixedly determine the straight line for future guidance. When reflections followed by good resolutions have been made a constant weekly practice, then shall we be well fitted to take an active part in the business and charities of life. We shall have in our moral improvement the surest criterion that we are thoughtfully discharging the moral obligations of the sacred day, and with this guarantee we may work on hopefully, glad in the thought that God sees and approves. Assuredly, such a reflection cannot but be productive of happiness, of holy delight, and true content.

But would we enhance our appreciation of that Sabbath which does so much to promote our worldly interests, and confers on us so many spiritual benefits, we have only for a moment to consider this heavenly boon *withdrawn*, and that we were obliged to toil mind and body without respite. Would not our constitution be undermined, and our health greatly impaired? Would not debility and illness attack our frames, force us from the haunts of men, and injure our worldly prospects? Would not our thoughts gradually centre in the things of earth to the exclusion of our spiritual welfare, and our hearts harden under the never ceasing stimulus of selfish interests? There would indeed be little left to sanctify our lives; we should only at rare intervals, and for short periods, raise our minds to our Maker; study His law, and so frame our conduct thereby. Truly, both our moral and physical well-being would have received a rude shock.

Let us therefore have ever before our eyes its negative as well as its positive advantages, and love the holy Sabbath with its ordinances for its own sake as well as for the good it can and will accomplish. We shall then take for its motto —rest, trust and be thankful,—bearing ever in mind that to disregard the beautiful provisions of Providence is to work against our own well-being, and to violate the Sabbatical appointment is truly a suicidal act. Centering each desire in the one object of improving our moral character, we shall give a willing mind and heart to the search after virtue, holiness, and piety; and when tracing in each succeeding week a sure and steady advance towards them, we may feel assured that the Sabbath has fulfilled, and is fulfilling its true, its high intent.

PRECEPTS.—There is no command so frequently, or so emphatically enjoined in the sacred volume as the observance of the Sabbath, thence we may draw the infallible conclusion that there is none more essential to the well-being of mankind; indeed, the injunctions abounding in Exodus and Leviticus alone, might well suffice to convince us of its superlative importance. Take for example in Exodus xxiii, 12, "*Six days shalt thou do thy work*, and on the seventh day thou shalt rest; that thine ox and thine ass may rest, and the stranger may be refreshed. *In all this be circumspect*". Here we are not only enjoined to rest on the Sabbath but to work on the other six days; also we are not to impose labour even on our beasts of burden, but are to "be circumspect", and see that a calm repose pervades the whole household. Again, we find a like sentence in chap. xxxi, 13, conveying the last injunction from God to Moses when about descending from Mount Sinai; it runs thus, " Speak thou also unto the children of Israel, saying, Verily, my Sabbaths ye shall keep, for it is a sign between me and you throughout your generations, *that ye may know that I am the Lord that doth sanctify you*. Ye shall keep the Sabbath, therefore, for it is *holy unto you*. Whosoever doeth any work therein, that soul shall be cut off from among his people". In the next verse this is again repeated, but with this important addition : " The seventh day is the *Sabbath of rest, holy to the Lord*". Again, we read ch. xxxiv, 21, "Six days thou shalt work, but on the seventh day thou shalt rest, in *earing time and in harvest thou shalt rest*" : a verse of peculiar significance when we consider that with the Israelites agriculture was a vital, an engrossing, a predominant interest. Then in Leviticus xix, which contains a capitulation of sundry comprehensive and sublime laws, we find, verse 30, " Ye shall keep my Sabbath, and *reverence my sanctuary*, I am the Lord," and these identical words are repeated at ch. xxvi, 2. What could more plainly intimate the close connection which exists between Divine worship and the Sabbath, or the like reverence in which they should be held? Further, it is declared, in the same chapter, that if the people will not follow the ordinance of the Lord, but walk contrary to Him, then shall their "cities be made waste, their sanctuary brought into desolation", and they themselves "scattered among the heathens, for thereby shall the land rest, and enjoy her Sabbaths as long as it lieth desolate. This because it did not rest on your Sabbaths when ye dwelt upon it." Turning next to the Books of the Prophets, we find the observance of the Sabbath no less insisted on. There it is again clearly shown to be a paramount duty, and that he who would arrive at the summit of moral greatness and excellence must never fail therein; further, it is demonstrated that the end and aim of the Sabbath, as of religion, are alike goodness and holiness; thus, we read in Isaiah lvi, 1: " Keep ye judgment and do justice; blessed is the man who doeth this, and that keepeth the Sabbath from polluting it, holding his hand from doing any evil." Now while righteousness and the keeping of the Sabbath are here coupled, it is also shown in Ezekiel that sin and impiety are the natural faults of its desecration; thus, chap. xx, 16: "They despised my judgments, and walked not in my statutes; they polluted my Sabbaths, and their heart went after their idols." Further, at verse 20, we are distinctly told that a blessing will attend its observance: "Hallow my Sabbaths, and they shall be a sign between me and you, that ye may know that I am the Lord your God", and this promise is made yet more clearly in Isaiah, where we read, ch. lviii, 13, "If thou turn away thy foot from doing thy pleasure on my holy day, and call the Sabbath a delight, the holy of the Lord, honourable, then shalt thou delight thyself in the

Lord, and I will cause thee to ride upon the high places of the earth; the mouth of the Lord hath spoken it." Here, then, is our duty, and rich indeed is the promised recompense.

But precepts thought to be addressed to one peculiar people, or supposed to be intended for only a defined and limited period, will fail in a great measure to impress their sublime truths on the mind; thence, if there were no other quotations than the above (all-comprehensive though they be), it *might* be possible to take exception to them, since they certainly were given to a distinctive people, and that at a marked period of their history. Therefore, we proceed to give others of especial value, since they must put an end to all doubt on this score. With Gen. ii, 3 before us, it would be utterly impossible for even the most sceptical to assert that the observance of the Sabbath is not a fundamental principle, coeval with creation, and intended by the Supreme to subsist in its full integrity throughout all ages. We read, "And God *blessed* the seventh day, and sanctified it, because that in it He had rested from all His work which God created and made". The Almighty One sanctified that day; and may, then, His creatures desecrate it? Again, all who hold sacred the Decalogue may not, *cannot*, infringe the Fourth Commandment. It is part of a whole code of laws given for the good of all mankind, and to be rigidly observed, under the penalty of God's high displeasure. Turning to Isaiah, we find that he always enjoined on others, equally with the Israelites, the strict observance of the Sabbath; for we read, ch. lvi, 6, "Also the sons of the *stranger* that join themselves to the Lord to be His servants; *every one* that keepeth the Sabbath from polluting it will I bring to my holy mountain and make them joyful in mine house, which shall be called a house of prayer *for all people*". Other verses might be quoted to like effect, but these are enough to show that the day of rest is incumbent on "all people", and that they who would be righteous in the sight of the Lord must keep that day holy.

Nor does Scripture stop short at mere exhortations, but with nearly every injunction to observe the Sabbath we are instructed how it may be best and most serviceably employed, and how made "holy to the Lord". Thus we are bidden to hold the seventh day as " an holy convocation; *a Sabbath of the Lord in our dwellings*"; " to sanctify it", " to hallow it". Then we are told in Psalms that " it is good to give thanks unto the Lord, and to sing a Psalm or Hymn on the Sabbath Day "unto the Most High"; and are bid to reflect that " God is our refuge and strength, a very present help in trouble"; also we are exhorted to " delight ourselves in the Lord". Finally, Jeremiah, who in his Book so earnestly seeks to impress us with the sanctity of the Sabbath, likewise places before us the most fitting subjects for contemplation thereon; thoughts whereby we may consecrate the day—thoughts in which " we may glory". These are of the utmost importance, since coming from the Lord Himself; they run thus, ch. ix, 23, " Let not the wise man glory in his wisdom, neither let the mighty man glory in his might, let not the rich man glory in his riches, but let him that glorieth glory in this, that *he understandeth and knoweth Me,* that I am the Lord which exercise lovingkindness, judgment, and righteousness in the earth, for in these things I delight, saith the Lord". By studiously entertaining reflections like these, we shall assuredly shed a halo of peace and joy within our hearts and our homes; by such pious meditations we may spiritualise our natures, and show our love and gratitude to the Great Father of Mercies, hallowing that day which He, the Lord and Creator of the Universe, has declared "holy."

We now pass on to the few EXAMPLES which present themselves in the History of the ISRAELITES during the *rule of their judges and kings.* It has been shown that, while Joshua and the elders that outlived him, " they who had known all the works of the Lord that He had done for

Israel",* held sway, the heart of the nation turned towards the Lord and His ordinances; but when we proceed to consider that period wherein the judges were rulers, we find that the feeling of the people frequently veered round to idolatry and its baleful practices. Love of God, with its natural consequence, delight in the observance of His statutes, became fitful, and mere transitory gleams of sunshine were apparent in the benumbing, chill, and darkening moral atmosphere which was enveloping the new generation. Then must the institution of the Sabbath have lost much of its significance, and indeed altogether ceased to be observed under many of the judges. But, about the time of Saul's elevation to the monarchy, an improvement became observable, and made further progress during the reign of David and the early part of that of Solomon. The better feeling which set in was, however, no way due to Saul, but received its impulse from the good and righteous Samuel, who succeeded Eli in the office of high priest. His pious exhortations and the devout worship he so zealously enforced, coupled with admonitions and remonstrances to the people whenever they were departing from the path of righteousness, or smarting under some signal defeat, speedily brought them to acknowledge their errors and amend their doings. He even for a time succeeded in bringing to repentance their back-sliding King, for Saul was led to declare, "I have sinned; for I have transgressed the commandment of the Lord *and thy words*".†

That the Sabbath and all God's ordinances were piously kept during the reign of David we may not doubt, since some of his beautiful and devout Psalms are especially adapted to that day, while he also repeatedly refers therein to the observance of the laws of Moses. Nor did he omit to urge it on the attention of his son, as we may judge by his last charge to Solomon, which runs thus, "I go the way

---

* Joshua xxiv, 24. † 1 Sam. xv, 24.

of all the earth, be thou strong therefore, and show thyself a man; keep the charge of the Lord thy God, to walk in His ways, to keep His statutes, and His commandments, and His judgments, and His testimonies, *as it is written in the Law of Moses*".* And for a time both King and people served the Lord in all sincerity of heart. A truly religious spirit appears to have been imbibed during the rule of the God-fearing David, which eminently displayed itself also in the early part of his son's reign, not only in the erection of a surpassingly magnificent temple dedicated to the Supreme, but likewise by the zealous observance of rites and ordinances conformable to the injunctions of the Pentateuch, and by that mode of worship which was most pleasing to the One only God. Yet herein there was no stability; a sad, sad reaction speedily set in. The Israelites had touched the culminating point alike of their spiritual glory and their earthly grandeur, and rapid was the descent that followed. With the fall of Solomon into idolatry fell nearly the entire nation; and in the future it was only during the reign of some of their best and most pious kings that the Laws of Moses were observed. We have an example of this in the words of the good King Hezekiah to the Levites, II Chron. xxix, 6, where he declares that "Our fathers have transgressed; they have turned away their faces from the habitation of the Lord. They have turned their backs thereon, and shut up the door of the porch, put out the lamps, and have not burned incense, nor offered burnt offerings in the Holy Sanctuary. Hear me, therefore, ye Levites, sanctify now yourselves, and sanctify the House of the Lord God of your fathers, and carry forth every abomination therefrom". And further, when we refer to the records connected with the rule of that excellent monarch, Josiah, we find that during several of the preceding reigns the Sanctuary had been closed, and that even the very books of the law had been lost sight of. But it is especially to the writings of

---

* I Kings ii, 2.

the prophets we must turn, would we surely ascertain particulars as to the observance of the Sabbath by the Israelites during the latter period of their monarchy; and from their perusal there is but this one conclusion to be drawn, that it was rarely held in due reverence, and thus in no way subserved its holy purpose. Indeed, it is fully shown that its pious obligations were not only frequently disregarded, but that the day itself was often desecrated or altogether neglected and forgotten. Thus, in Isaiah i, the prophet, after reproving his hearers for "having gone away backwards, and provoked the Holy One", bids them, in the name of the Lord, " bring no more vain oblations; incense is an abomination unto me, the new moons and *Sabbaths* I cannot abide; *it is iniquity;* they are a trouble unto me, I am weary to bear them". Then, in Jer. xvii, we find the people resisting the command not "to carry forth burdens from their homes on the Sabbath day; neither to do any work"; for we read at the twenty-third verse, "But they obeyed not, neither inclined their ear, but made their necks stiff". And again, we read in Ezek. xxiii, 38, "Moreover, this they have done unto me, they have defiled my sanctuary, and have profaned my Sabbaths; and at ch. xxii, after showing the general corruption which existed, and how the people and even the princes had "set light by father and mother, had oppressed the stranger, vexed the orphans and widows", he continues, "thou hast despised mine holy things, and hast profaned *my Sabbaths*"; and at the twenty-sixth verse further adds, "Her priests have violated my law; they have put no difference between the holy and the profane, and have hid their eyes from *my Sabbaths*, and I am profaned among them".

Now, it is well to note that among the several causes which conduce to such profanation of the Sabbath and to proceedings so totally at variance with the Divine pleasure, must be ranked covetousness. This is clearly shown in Amos viii, where the prophet puts into the mouth of the people the following significant words, "When will the new moon be gone, that we may sell corn, and the Sabbath, that we may set forth wheat?" and again, in Ezekiel, where that prophet, after declaring that the people had profaned the Sabbath, adds, "They have taken gifts to shed blood, they have taken usury and increase, have greedily gained of their neighbour by extortion, and have forgotten me, saith the Lord God". There is one other important point from which all doubt is removed by the prophets in their writings, viz., that the cause of the decline and fall of the Kingdom was in a great measure owing to the non-observance of the Sabbath by the people, for does not Jeremiah declare at ch. xvii, 27, "But if ye will not hearken unto me to hallow the Sabbath day and not to bear a burden, even entering into the gates, then will I kindle a fire, and it shall devour the palaces of Jerusalem, and it shall not be quenched"? And Ezekiel, to show the entire nation how certain would be their downfall should they continue to desecrate the Sabbath, brings forward an example of what befel their forefathers in these inspired words, "Moreover, I gave them my Sabbaths *to be a sign between me and them*, that they might know that I am the Lord that sanctify them, but they rebelled against me in the wilderness, they walked not in my statutes, and my Sabbaths they greatly polluted; then I said I would pour out my fury upon them to consume them".*

But happily there are examples which stand out in contrast with this dark picture, and, though few, they are well worthy of remark. They severally beam forth from the surrounding gloom, speaking of God's past displeasure and the repentance of his chosen people. Thus in the Book of Nehemiah we find that on the return of the captives from Babylon they willingly entered into a covenant, among the many high moral obligations of which are the following: "That they would cleave to their brethren, their nobles; that they would enter into an oath to walk in God's law, and to observe all

---

* Ezekiel xx, 12.

the commandments of the Lord; *and if the people of the land bring ware or any victuals on the Sabbath day to sell*, that they would not buy of them on the Sabbath or on the holy day".* Spiritual interests had thus triumphed over the temporal. Then Jeremiah, in his Lamentations, speaks much to the same effect, telling us in metaphorical language at chap. i that " Jerualem remembered in the day of her affliction and of her persecutions all the pleasant things she had in the days of old; the enemies saw her and did mock at her Sabbaths"; next, making that capital speak for the people, he adds, " Is it nothing to you, all ye that pass by, behold and see if there be any pain like unto my pain which is inflicted upon me, wherewith the Eternal hath grieved me in the day of the kindling of his wrath. Zion spreadeth forth her hands and there is none to comfort her"; but after this sad complaint, the sorrowing city brings herself to confession and to acknowledge the justice of God's judgments, thus declaring, " The Lord is righteous, for *I have rebelled against his commandments*". Thus did trials and troubles here again bring repentance in their train, and with true repentance and amendment came a bright and happy change. The words of promise made by Jeremiah were in every point verified. Referring to the last chapter of II Chron. we read, " Zion had enjoyed her Sabbath three score and ten years, and as long as she lay desolate she kept Sabbath". After that, the All-Gracious stirred up Cyrus to build His House in Jerusalem, and for this purpose the mighty King of Persia not only released the Jews from captivity, but even urged them to proceed to their own land, saying, II Chron. xxxvi, 23, " Who is there among you of all his people? the Lord his God be with him and let him go up".† Thus out of evil sprung forth good, for we find that in the seventh month after their departure the foundation of the Temple was laid amidst " shouts of joy and singing of praises and thanksgiving unto the Lord because He is good, because His mercy

---

* Nehemiah x, 29. † Also Ezra i, 3.

endureth for ever towards Israel". And when the building was finally reared, and the altar set up, much to the delight of the people, the true worship of God was established, and His holy fast and Sabbath solemnly kept. Now, though this happy consummation promised more than it fulfilled, yet it must be reckoned among one of the bright pages in Israel's history, while it is also well calculated to work to present good, since affording instruction, hope, and trust to all who will turn to the past as a guide for the future, and further, as a pleasurable Sabbath duty, seek by the light of Scripture the true and shining path of piety, of virtue and of godliness.

RELIGIOUS ZEAL.

Exodus xxxv, 21, "*They came every one whose heart stirred him up.*"

THE history of the early ISRAELITES is the history of an entire people just liberated from the shackles of slavery, and this reflection should be uppermost whenever we are about to consider any subject matter wherein their failings and misconduct take too prominent a place. It is hardly to be supposed that bondsmen, crouching during long years beneath the yoke of a merciless tyrant, and writhing under the lash of cruel task-masters, should not suffer alike in their mental and moral as in their physical condition, and even lose most of the finer susceptibilities of their nature. Certain it is that we have but to turn to the second Book of Moses, so admirably descriptive of the great and miraculous deliverance of the chosen people from bondage, and of their wanderings in the wilderness, to assure ourselves that such was the case with the great body of the down-trodden Israelites. Only by a long apprenticeship to freedom were their hearts to be softened, refined, and made fully susceptible to those high influences of which they had nearly lost all cognisance. Thus it was that the early Israelites, as a nation, rarely displayed any great fervour of devotion or religious enthusiasm. While they could not fail to acknowledge God's superintending Providence, they yet *felt* not His presence, and though they were awakened from their moral torpor at moments of imminent peril, and on their escape therefrom roused themselves to demonstrate their sense of gratitude, they nevertheless speedily relapsed into their former apathy and indifference. This fact is even discernible at that momentous crisis of their fate, their Exodus from Egypt. The entire people had crossed the Red Sea, the boundary line between slavery and freedom. Hope, which in the past had been alternating with fear, met its realisation; the ruthless monarch and his armed host had been submerged; the cruel taskmaster left far, far behind, to be seen no more; the promised land lay before them; Moses, the faithful of the Lord and champion of their rights, was in their van; the cloud by day and the pillar of fire by night rested above them in token of God's watchful care and fatherly interest; such had been their marvellous release, such their hopeful change, when from the whole body of the Israelites burst forth that exquisite song of Moses, so sublime in its very simplicity. Witnesses of the miracles which the Lord had wrought in their behalf, a flood of gratitude welled up within their hearts, and the entire nation raised their voice with one accord to glorify Him and proclaim His power and goodness. But unhappily this demonstration of feeling vanished in the empty utterance of words. The thrilling sounds of praise and thanksgiving had hardly subsided than the echoing tones of discontent were distinguishable; words of adoration had but just ceased, when broke forth " murmurings against the Lord". Their signal deliverance had indeed made but a faint, thus temporary impression, and altogether failed in kindling that true religious zeal which ever displays itself more by deeds than words.

It was otherwise, however, in the next instance. The lapse of time had ripened the fair fruits of freedom, and a decided moral improvement was clearly perceptible in the national character. The entire people had at length become capable of much which was good and noble. Ever-renewing proofs of God's mercy and goodness had softened their hearts, had taught them to love their All-Gracious Ruler and be sincerely grateful. Their gratitude was not now to be, as in the past, a mere barren and evanescent sentiment; truly, it had become an animating principle, and was to find

U

practical expression. Thus, when Moses spake unto all the congregation of the children of Israel, bidding them bring rich offerings for the service of the Tabernacle, and aid in its construction, the whole people, both men and women, at once responded to the call with a "willing heart".* Articles of luxury of every kind, as also valuables, such as "jewels of gold, bracelets, and rings, and precious stones", were brought as free gifts in such profusion as to make it necessary for Moses to restrain the donors in their laudable zeal. But material wealth was not all the people bestowed; they likewise gave the labour of their hands, and further evinced the true love they bore their religion and its rites by strictly conforming to the words of the Lord during the progress of the work. Exodus xxxix, 43, besides confirming this, also shows that their efforts were crowned by the Divine favour. We read, "According to all that the Lord commanded Moses so the children of Israel made all the work, and Moses did look upon the work, and behold they had done it as the Lord had commanded, even so had they done it; and Moses blessed them". Truly, a happy consummation this, a just and fitting reward for religious zeal.

That such a display of enthusiasm on the part of the *entire* body of the Israelites during their sojourn in the wilderness was of exceedingly rare occurrence is certain; indeed, they were but too apt to depart from the true worship, and fall into the iniquitous practices of the idolatrous people by whom they were surrounded. It was at such sad moments of their history that uprose numerous faithful servants of the Most High, who, deploring the national depravity and back-sliding propensity of their more ignorant brethren, strove boldly and resolutely to stay them in the downward course. Though the multitude would continually swerve from their true allegiance, there never lacked *individuals* who, glowing with religious zeal, eagerly sought to do God's bidding whenever the occasion called for a prac-

* Exodus xxxv, 21.

tical expression of their love and willing obedience. PHI-
NEAS, for instance, stood pre-eminently forward as the champion of right and holiness, the avenger of crime and gross idolatry. By his prompt and vigorous action at a moment of extreme peril for the nation, he gave the first check to sin and turned away God's wrath, so that the plague which had broken out among the children of Israel was stayed. A large body of the people, following after the gods of the Moabites, had become utterly corrupt; they violated every moral law, and even openly indulged the bent of their licentious passions. Indeed, to such a point of immorality had they arrived, and so widely had the contagion of sin and debauch spread, that only a very decisive measure could stay the torrent of crime, which threatened to engulf the entire nation. At this juncture the individual Phineas, grandson of Aaron, came prominently forward, and before the whole camp, javelin in hand and with dauntless front, slew Zimri,* a vile and debased prince in Israel, together with a Midianitish woman, thus acting in accordance with the injunction of Moses to the Judges, to "slay ye every one his men that were united unto Baal-peor". That such an effective display of zeal was pleasing in the sight of the Lord we may feel assured since the Most High spoke thus unto Moses, "Phineas hath turned my wrath away from the children of Israel that I consumed them not, wherefore say, Behold I give unto him my covenant of peace, even the covenant of the everlasting priesthood, *because he was zealous for his God*".†

But prior to this period the Levites had distinguished themselves in like manner, saving the people from much after misery. An instance of their devotion in the cause of religion is to be found at Ex. xxxii. The Israelites had prostrated themselves before the golden calf, and were practising the grossest and most shameless rites of idolatry, when Moses presented himself before them and at once appealed to his would-be followers in these words, " Who is on

* Numbers xxv, 7.   † Numbers xxv, 11.

the Lord's side let him come unto me", and then, in accordance with his injunction, they put to the sword all those who "had sinned a great sin", and through their vile conduct incensed the Lord, bringing on the whole nation that sorest of afflictions, the plague. None, however, after their leader, Moses, worked more zealously in the cause of religion and of the people's good than did JOSHUA and CALEB; they were the very heart and soul of moral progress, while ever the bravest and staunchest opponents of all that retarded alike the temporal and spiritual interests of their brethren. As, however, the characters of these pious and faithful servants of the Lord have formed the subject of remark under the heading of "Individual Merit", nothing more need here be said than that their true religious zeal brought as a natural consequence its golden reward—God's especial favour.

If before concluding we briefly allude to the guilty KORAH and his associates, it is solely for the purpose of showing how selfish ambition may assume the garb of religious zeal, and in that guise work incalculable evil. It is difficult to conceive how one of the tribe of Levi, vested by God with priestly duties and standing high in authority, could be induced through lust of power to foment rebellion and seek to overthrow that religion of which he was one of the head ministers. Yet so it was, nor did his example lack ready imitators. Two hundred and fifty princes of the congregation seconded him in his ambitious and treasonable projects, when, being joined by all the evil-disposed, a formidable body stood up proudly and defiantly before their leader, Moses, and heaped on him the most unmerited reproaches. They even tauntingly upbraided him for a pride, a presumtion which dwelt only in their own evil hearts. Nor could the extreme meekness and forbearance of their leader subdue their obduracy. Their arrogance naturally angered the Supreme; indeed, they who for their own worldly purposes set at defiance the Divine law, and turned against God's chosen servant, might, when the occasion offered, work on the entire people to evil and sap the very fount of all morality and order. To check such insubordination, to warn others from indulging in a like proceeding, and further, to justify his righteous servant in the eyes of the people, God decreed the severest retribution on the offenders; "the earth opened her mouth and swallowed them all, so that they perished from among the congregation". Thus did these hypocrites, these simulators of religious zeal, meet an early, sudden, and fearful death, while most of those who served the Lord in singleness of heart lived to enter the promised land, or, as we have it in the words of Moses, "Of all the men that followed Baal-peor the Lord thy God hath destroyed them from among you, but ye that did cleave unto the Lord your God are alive every one of you this day".

A contrast and a lesson well worthy of remembrance.

An earnest, heart-inspiring performance of all that religion inculcates constitutes religious zeal. Owing its birth and vital principles to the two exalting sentiments of gratitude to God and love to man, it will, if pure, loyal, and genuine in character, manifest itself in an eager desire to do God's bidding and fulfil His commandments, in an ever-ready will to forward each good, each holy work, subserving the cause of true philanthropy. If, however, it diverge therefrom or seek other channels, if it be not God's word, but man's devices, which give it form and colour, then assuredly it is spurious, and will be fraught with much evil. Now, if we will only cultivate sedulously that religious and benevolent spirit which has but one aim, the true, but one impetus, the right—if we will make the two ennobling sentiments of grateful love to the Supreme and kindly sympathy towards our fellow-men abiding principles, and take them as the basis of our conduct—then will our pious zeal turn to good account, and we shall frequently find ourselves in active co-operation with the Divine purpose. Now surely,

* Deut. iv, 3.

when we feel how great, how glorious, is this prerogative, we shall need no further stimulus or incentive to induce us to rouse these motive powers into vigorous action on every suitable occasion. Besides, do not all the best feelings of our nature prompt and loudly call for their exhibition? Thus let us duly reflect on God's manifold mercies, for then must gratitude infallibly become a predominant sentiment in our minds, and our zeal in His service will know no hindrance, no bounds. Loving the Lord " with all our heart and with all our might", we shall delight in glorifying His name in prayer and praise, we shall testify our reverence by a willing and implicit obedience to His law and ordinances, we shall sanctify our love to Him in trampling under foot each lower interest which interferes with our solemn duty, and earnestly strive to make our every act and deed pleasing in His sight.

Now, how can we more effectually accomplish this latter purpose than by loving and *materially* serving His creatures? The Great Framer and Ruler of the Universe cannot be satisfied with a mere tribute of grateful praise and adoration, but further demands of us that fervent zeal which takes for its object the promotion of human happiness and the general welfare, since therein consists the most exalted virtue. The adequate fulfilment of this high obligation, this solemn duty, necessitates on our parts the frequent exercise of self-denial, much perseverance and great good-feeling. We shall only make an important advance in the good work when in the true spirit of benevolence we forego our own advantage for the sake of others, when we sacrifice our ease and comfort to benefit our fellow-mortals, and when we contribute our means to the needy, our sympathy to the afflicted. Aware that happiness only abides where religion and virtue dwell, we shall earnestly seek to kindle the one and promote the other, while being sensible that misery is greatly lessened in the world when poverty is relieved and the stricken heart cheered, we shall be ever ready as God's almoners to serve the cause of charity, and as his truly pious servants shall in kindliness of heart minister to the comfort, happiness, and consolation of the sorrowing and infirm. These, then, and other laudable efforts to ameliorate the condition and promote the happiness of the human race are the true end and aim of religious zeal, which must thus commend itself to all, except indeed to the cold-hearted, the selfish, and the indifferent, who know little of and appreciate less these outpourings of a pious and beneficent spirit.

Now, when we find that the mere mention of religious zeal only too frequently excites a sentiment of antagonism, engenders distrust in its exponents, and is rather shunned than courted by mankind in general, we are naturally led to question why that which should be fraught with so much good to the human species can raise up such untoward, such depreciatory feelings, and why, instead of being regarded as a virtue, it should be placed under a ban, as if indeed it were a moral deformity. Assuredly the reason is this: human infirmity on the one hand, and human presumption on the other, disfigure and distort it by means of the garb wherewith they clothe it. Thus is it rarely to be seen radiant in its own native beauty; but dark, forbidding, and austere, it stands forth repellant to our feelings and offensive to our moral perceptions. Do not, then, the causes which dim, though they may not totally extinguish the refulgent light of religious zeal, and which tend to dry up this vivifying source of human happiness, demand serious attention? Surely we may not suffer them to blight the fair fruits that a heartfelt zeal should bear, nor permit them unchecked to taint the parent stem and poison all that comes within their baneful influence, as does the upas tree. Hence, it behoves us to heed them well and observe their numerous ramifications, each working more or less evil. Now, among those attendant on human weakness is Bigotry, which is nothing else than a senseless and ignoble zeal, often degenerating into the gloomiest and grossest superstition. The light of reason and religion shines but feebly on the mind wherein it harbours, which will thence become more and more contracted and sombre as age advances. Totally opposed to all true enlightenment, bigotry is quite a thing apart from true religious zeal, yet often assuming its name to mask its own deformity. We have next to deal with impulsive zeal, a flickering light easily extinguished by the fear of ridicule, moral lassitude, or selfishness. It is the mere prompting of feeling, or sometimes indeed of conscience, but it usually passes away with the momentary cause which has excited it, and too often sinks into indifference. Its aim, if not altogether purposeless, is generally fanciful and utopian, scheming for remote and improbable good, while blind to that which may be effected at our very doors. It kindles its temporary flame from passion and imagination rather than from reason; it is never either uniform or consistent; it may for a time dazzle by its brilliant show, but it will assuredly pale before the steady light of holy zeal.

Nor do the effects of human weakness stop here, since to the moral infirmity of man we owe that human presumption which plays such havoc with all that is most sacred, and works such incalculable ills in the assumed garb of religious zeal. Pride in religion is indeed itself a crime, and ever productive of a thousand crimes. False to its would-be sanctity when it throws off the garment of humility and robes itself in intolerance, it darkens that which should be most fair, and finally receives its due desert in the opprobrium of mankind. Moreover, it has frequently to pay a yet more severe penalty. Scripture tells us that "none may ascend the holy hill or receive blessings from the Lord but they who have clean hands and a pure and humble heart". Intolerance is indeed of monster birth, and writes its character in blood. It is ever ready to sound the tocsin of oppression, forgetful of the Supreme injunction in Lev. xix, 18, "Thou shalt love thy neighbour as thyself". But human pride or presumption does further injury to the good cause by setting itself in constant antagonism to virtues which are every way calculated to temper our zeal and make it rational. To take an example, we shall find it opposed to the virtue of discretion. The injunction, " Be not righteous overmuch", would assuredly be far less frequently disregarded could we hush the "voice of the charmer" self-conceit, to which we in a great measure owe extravagance of zeal or fanaticism, the spirit of bigotry, the arrogance which lays claim to uncommon sanctity, religious animosity, and cant, with its affected strictness and austerity of manner. What is it but pride and self-sufficiency, in direct opposition to practical good sense and self-knowledge, which causes us to over-estimate our religious lore while undervaluing that of others, which leads us to believe that we exclusively hold the key to the truths as to the mysteries of religion ; what, indeed, but presumption permits us even for a moment to conceive that we honour God when we heap opprobrium and injury on his creatures, that induces us to believe in our own infallibility, and then, so impressed, emboldens us to use the " Divine fire" to spread desolation here on earth ? But spiritual pride, so frequently working untold evils without, has also power to ruin the inner man by deadening or chasing away each virtue, and when comes its certain downfall, then will it too readily hurl its victim into the opposite extreme of indifference or even scepticism.

Now, it would be hard to say whether spiritual pride or callous indifference most wrongs the soul or makes the deadliest thrust at truth, and all that man should most revere. Thence let us beware of falling into either extreme. We may, and should, show fervour in religion, nothing being more abhorrent to our nature than coldness of heart; but then, our devotion must be free from all excess of enthusiasm. While never neglecting aught which religion inculcates, we should render it easy and pleasurable by avoiding the institution of unnecessary forms, for assuredly we cannot overload the conscience without incurring the certain risk of rendering it sluggish and inert in matters of vital importance to our moral nature. Finally, while firm in our own religious convictions, we should yet agree to differ with our fellow men of other creeds, and expound our religion by its practice, by morality, by charity in its most extended sense; in a word, by our strict adherence to God's Holy Law. And in conclusion, let it be remarked that to religious zeal is especially applicable the aphorism "the tree is known by its fruit", and only when we can trace therefrom an inheritance of rich blessings to ourselves and others may we believe it to be genuine.

Among the numerous advantages and benefits which we may expect to flow from or accompany devotional fervour, is a cheerful and contented spirit, for such is the boon true piety ever confers; a mind well attuned to the beauty of nature and a pleasing sense of gratitude to its Beneficent Author; also a heartfelt satisfaction attending each act of philanthropy, and that happiness which is caught by rebound. Further, a fervent desire to secure the approbation of heaven will incite us to control or suppress all tumultuous passions, give us a yearning after excellence and goodness, and make us emulate what we love. Religious zeal, however, should not be a mere inward feeling, but rather a bright and glowing light that will warm and vivify the heart of others. And to effect this purpose we must exemplify by our daily practice the good sentiments we have stored up in our breasts; we must eloquently and openly manifest the benevolent spirit which animates us, and no way seek to hide any worthy or charitable deed, as if, forsooth, it were deserving of condemnation. We must meekly, lovingly endeavour to stir up others to the good work, and unite in hearty fellowship with all who, in a true spirit of philanthropy, strive to promote and perpetuate the happiness of their species.

Such, then, is the object of religious zeal, and here also are some of its fair and promising fruits; but would we have a yet further inducement to persevere zealously in our labour of love, let us ever bear vividly in remembrance that the good performed works onwards and onwards, ever renewing, ever extending, and, while thus prospering here on earth, will carry with it an eternal blessing.

PRECEPTS.—The following Scripture verses amply elucidate in what religious zeal consists. David, in his beautiful Psalm xxxv, bids us "magnify the Lord"; and then declares "my tongue shall speak of Thy righteousness and of Thy praise all the day long". The same pious feeling manifests itself in Psalm lxxi, where he says, "May my mouth be filled with Thy praise and with Thy honour all the day; it shall show forth Thy righteousness, and I will praise Thee more and more"; and again, in Psalm ix, "I will praise Thee, O Lord, *with my whole heart;* I will show forth all Thy marvellous works. I will be glad and rejoice in Thee, O Thou Most High". Then, in Psalm cvii, after enthusiastically exclaiming, "Oh, that men would praise the Lord for His goodness, and for His wonderful works to the children of men", he calls on them to "sacrifice the sacrifice of thanksgivings, and *declare His works with rejoicing*". Turning to Psalm c, which may be said to be a brief epitome of the sublime Psalm ciii, we are exhorted, as the creatures of God's bounty and Fatherly tenderness, to "be thankful and bless His name"; and to "serve the Lord with gladness, for He is good". But David stops not here; he bids us not only "give thanks unto the Lord, and sing praises to Him *with understanding*", but also to "*make known His deeds among the people*, and declare His glory among the heathens" (the ignorant and benighted), testifying his own pious zeal in this respect in the following words, O how I love thy Law; it is my meditation all the day". Also the prophet Isaiah thus proclaims in what religious zeal consists, ch. lxi, "To preach good tidings unto the meek, to bind up the broken heart, to comfort the afflicted, to give the oil of joy for mourning, and the garment of praise for the spirit of heaviness"; and then further declares, "I will greatly rejoice in the Lord, my soul shall be joyful in the Lord". Malachi thus describes the pious man; one full of pure and holy zeal, "God's covenant of love and peace was with him, because of the fear wherewith he feared the Lord. The law of truth was in his mouth; he *did turn many away from iniquity*".* Indeed, genuine religious zeal might almost be summed up in the words of Jeremiah, "To be valiant for the truth on the earth", this being its distinctive feature. The heart that is true to truth, and warm as true, will assuredly never lack the bright heavenly flame of holy zeal. Scripture, while thus instructing us in what it consists, also bids us use therein a wise discretion. In Eccles. we are told, "be not over righteous"; all excess of zeal only prejudicing the cause we desire to promote; our own powers will become weakened and impaired by immoderate exercise, while at the same time we rather deter than attract others by any undue or intemperate display of zeal. Overstrained, it becomes spurious, and thence is undervalued by many who stop not to distinguish between the false and the true. It is possibly to this cause we may attribute the fact that, if perchance religion becomes the subject of conversation, many take alarm, yet are we bid, Psalm cv, 2, "To talk of all God's wondrous works"; and in Malachi we are told, ch. iii, "They that feared the Lord *spake often one to another*, and the Lord hearkened and heard it". Assuredly, if God is "in all our thoughts", we cannot, we may not deny, the temperate expression of our religious feelings on suitable occasions. That which we have near at heart will always find a voice. It is *excess* of fervour against which we must guard. Also we should beware of that pride or presumption which by word, or look, or deed, leads man to declare to his fellow-man, in the words of Is. lxv, "Stand by thyself; come not near me, for I am holier than thou"; and further, it

---

* Isaiah ii, 6.

behoves us not to set our hearts so fixedly on the goods of this world that religious zeal becomes a dead letter to us, and spiritual interest as an unopened book; but take heed to the following exhortation of Haggai i, "Consider your ways, ye have sown much and bring in little; ye eat, but ye have not enough; and he that earneth wages, earneth wages but to put it into a bag with holes". Now, while these words of the prophet clearly enough show us the futility of worldly gifts if we are destitute of the spiritual element, the following verses point out in favourable contrast incalculable benefits which flow from this latter. Nehemiah thus speaks to us, "The joy of the Lord is your strength". David's words, in Psalm xvi, are to like effect; he says, "I have set the Lord always before me, because He is ever at my right hand; I shall not be moved". Also, in Psalm lxxxix, he declares, "Blessed is the people that know the joyful song of praise; they shall walk, O Lord, in the light of Thy countenance. *In Thy name they shall rejoice all the day,* and in Thy righteousness they shall be exalted". Then, in Psalm iv, he calls on us to " know that the Lord hath set apart him that is godly to Himself"; and, in Psalm xcvii, he tells us, " Light is sown for the righteous, and gladness for the upright in heart". But the pious David, who was also eminently practical, assuredly arrived at this conclusion—that a holy zeal is not only compatible with our worldly interests, but is most conducive thereto. We might hardly doubt this, even if we had no other quotation to offer in confirmation than that following, taken from his Psalm xxxvii, "Delight thyself in the Lord, *and He will give thee the desires of thine heart*"; such desires, indeed, as a merciful God can grant in love to His creatures. King David further repeatedly urges us to apply our hearts to the study of the Holy Law; for thereby we may justly learn to distinguish between the lasting commandments of God and the superstitions of men; as also to perform faithfully and zealously the former, since then shall we undoubtedly find "its ways are ways of pleasantness, and all its paths are peace".

Let us, then, never weary in well-doing, but seek through our daily practice to fulfil His Law, and ever subserve the good cause; for then may we feel, with the good King Hezekiah, that "With us is the Lord our God to help us and to fight our battles".* Truly, in the service of God are to be found both joy and strength.

EXAMPLES.—It has been shown that in the time of Moses, national displays of religious zeal were with the ISRAELITES but of rare occurrence, and then in most instances proved mere temporary impulses, seldom surviving the emergency or joyous deliverance which had called them forth. Nor, unhappily, was it otherwise during the whole period that they were under the sway and guidance of their *judges, kings, and prophets*. Indeed, if we consider that their later history extended over more than one thousand years, the instances of spontaneous religious enthusiasm were remarkably few. Two, however, are worthy of all attention. The first refers to the building of the Temple by Solomon, and its dedication. David had made every possible preparation for its construction by his son, being himself denied that privilege, owing to his having "shed blood abundantly, and made great wars". He amassed "gold, silver, brass, and iron without number", so that the "House built for the Lord be exceeding magnifical; of fame and of glory throughout all countries".† He bid his son be "up and doing", and also urged upon the Princes of Israel to help him, and "*set their heart and soul to seek the Lord*", so that the work might prosper. With true liberality did they and the entire people respond to the call. They brought very much gold and silver; indeed none of their richest possessions were withheld, so that we read, "they with whom precious stones were found gave them to the treasurer of the

------
* II Chron. xxxii, 8.   † I Chron. xxii, 5.

House of the Lord"; and that " the people rejoiced, for that they offered willingly, and with a perfect heart to the Lord". Then, on the completion of that magnificent Temple, came the dedication, when songs of praise and adoration broke forth from the multitude, and swelled into one Hallelujah. Further, their devotion was accompanied by a practical display of true charity and holy zeal, in the shape of enormous sacrificial offerings. They brought freely of the best of their flocks, herds, and agricultural produce, such as flour, oil, and wine, in which consisted the bulk of their wealth, and laid it down as a freewill gift to be disposed of for the benefit of the Levites, and for the sustenance of the poor and the stranger. Their religious zeal had found an appropriate channel in labour and gifts, while through the sacrifices they were enabled to testify a liberal and self-denying spirit, with a heartfelt sympathy for the cause of genuine charity.

The Book of Ezra furnishes us with the second instance alluded to, which is similar to the foregoing in most particulars. It has reference to the laying the foundation of the second temple—" *The whole congregation gave* according to their abilities unto the treasure which was to be appropriated to its building; they offered burnt offerings continually, both morning and night",* and bestowed freely sustenance and money alike upon those who were to be employed in the holy work. And when the Levites had made all the necessary preparations, and the foundation was about to be laid, then did the entire people unite and " sang together by course, praising and giving thanks unto the Lord, because He is good, and all the people in the joy of their heart shouted with a great shout".† In both these instances the entire nation appears to have been moved by one common impulse of heartfelt devotion and pious zeal; for although it was David in the one case, and Ezra in the other, who touched the springs, the general enthusiasm may

* Ezra ii, 64. † Ezra iii, 11.

yet be deemed genuine national outbursts, and certainly more spontaneous than any to which we have now briefly to refer. In each of the following examples the individual takes especial prominence, prompting and directing the people, and conducting the good work to a successful issue. Well, indeed, was it for the nation that in their midst ever existed God-loving and God-fearing men; men faithful in the service of the Lord, and actively zealous in the righteous cause. Truly, it was a bright spot in the history of the Israelites that on each recurring emergency up rose brave and noble spirits, who reanimated the desponding, incited the indifferent and backsliding to turn again to their God, and offered a bold front to the powerful enemies of their country. In the Book of Judges, to which we shall first turn, this characteristic is brought prominently before us, and we read, first of license and anarchy, in the words, "every man did that which was right in his own eyes"; and afterwards of repentance and reform. During the whole period of the Judges, which extends over three centuries, did light and shade alternate. Repeatedly did the people decline from the true worship, and as certainly were they again brought back through the instrumentality of the individual. Often led captive by the surrounding idolatrous nations, they ever regained their freedom through the exertions of the brave champions of Israel. Thus *Othniel*, endowed with the spirit of the Lord, as was his uncle Caleb, with true religious zeal, fought the enemies of his country, and was triumphant. He was then raised to the honourable post of Judge, and, during the forty years he held sway, the "land had rest"; peace and order prevailed, for he had brought the people to do that "which was right in the eyes of the Lord". This high office not being hereditary, was often vacant, and only from time to time do we find any one pre-eminent for piety, for courage, or for worth, filling this post. At such periods, however, peace settled on the land; Baal's altar lay shattered, and the people, following the lead of their chief, sought the Lord, and were zealous in His service. This is especially observable under the rule of the prophetess Deborah, of Gideon, and Jephtha, each of whom wrought much good for the Israelites. Before leaving this portion of their history, it may be well to revert to one of its later incidents; the violent outrage committed in the country of the Benjamites, and the general indignation it excited throughout the other cities of Judea. God's holy law had been violated; " a folly had been wrought in Israel", which called for summary punishment, and the entire people with one accord resolved it should be inflicted on the perpetrators of the crime. Therefore, assembling, and " knit together as one man", they " gathered against the city" to demand of the Benjamites the delivery of the criminals—"these children of Baal"—but, being refused, a war, breathing the most ardent spirit of zeal against moral evil, was declared by the united eleven tribes; nor did it cease till nearly the whole body of the Benjamites was exterminated. It had been resolved by the Israelites that none should return to his home till just reparation for the wickedness committed had been made, and they held to that resolve. But the atrocity once avenged, a revulsion of feeling instantly set in. Their former sentiments of brotherly affection revived; they wept in sore compassion at the injuries they had thought it necessary to inflict; and further, full of eager zeal on behalf of those that remained, they sought the House of God, and, after sacrificing unto the Lord, they thus prayed, " O Lord God of Israel, why is this come to pass in Israel that there should be to-day one tribe lacking?" All, indeed, was forgiven; all was forgotten, except the forlorn state of the remnant of that tribe to whom every possible reparation was made. The cause of justice and of religion thus vindicated, the zeal of the nation took a most praiseworthy direction; they offered up peace-offerings before the Lord, befriending those who had been so recently their foes, and thus was love and harmony restored to the entire camp of Israel.

The period of the Kings was no less marked by light and shade than had been that of the Judges. Occasionally, through the piety of the ruling monarch, or the religious zeal of the prophets, the entire people were stimulated to true devotional enthusiasm. Such was the case when Asa held the sceptre, for we read, "And Asa did that which was good and right in the sight of the Lord, and when he heard the words of Obed, the prophet, he took courage and put away the abominable idols out of all the land of Judah and Benjamin, and renewed the altar of the Lord. And when Israel saw that the Lord was with him, they gathered themselves together at Jerusalem, and offered unto the Lord abundantly; they entered into a covenant to seek the Lord God of their fathers with all their heart, and with all their soul. They sware unto the Lord with a loud voice, and with shouting, and with trumpets, and all Judah rejoiced at the oath, for they had sworn with all their heart, *and sought Him with their whole desire*, and He was found of them, and the Lord gave them rest round about."* Again, Jehoash in the first years of this reign, when, under the guidance of Jehoiada, the high priest, did that "which was right in the sight of the Lord, as did also the entire people, who, zealous in the service of the Lord, went into the House of Baal, and brake it down, and slew the priests of Baal before the altars"; at the same time giving money liberally for the repair of the temple. Then, when the good King Hezekiah began his reign, the House of God, which had long been closed, was re-opened and cleansed. The whole people consecrated themselves to the Lord, brought abundant sacrifices and thank offerings, rejoiced with their King before God. Indeed, so great was the rejoicing that "since the time of Solomon there was not the like in Jerusalem." Finally, during the reign of Josiah, the people testified the greatest possible zeal in the cause of their religion. "They levelled

---

* II Chron. xiv, 2; xv, 8, 11, 15.

to the ground the altars of Baalem; they cut down, brake in pieces, and made dust of their molten images, strewing it on the graves of them that had sacrificed unto their idols"; they gave liberally for the service of the Temple, fulfilling every ordinance, and joyfully observing the Passover.

But even these excellent Kings would possibly have been unsuccessful in bringing the heart of the nation to its God, but for the earnest co-operation of the prophets. Bewailing the wickedness of the times, they upbraided and exhorted, threatened and encouraged in turns, and this in the sublimest strains of eloquence. Indeed, these God-loving men were "valiant for the truth". Zealous in the cause of Him to whom they had sanctified their lives, they walked fearlessly forward in the path of duty, never losing sight of the right and the holy. But it was more especially at periods when the throne was filled by sinful princes, and the nation was hopelessly sinking into the grossest idolatry, that they stepped resolutely forward, fronting the corrupt and hardened monarch on his throne, and braving the obdurate and depraved people in the very midst of their wrong-doings, nor desisting in their pious efforts till they had effected a reform. One instance may here suffice, and we select ELIJAH, not only because he stands foremost among the faithful and zealous servants of the Lord, but also because the events about to be narrated effectively illustrate that which has been advanced. Thus, at the opening of his history, he is presented to us as standing before King Ahab, who " did evil in the sight of the Lord above all that were before him", and at the hazard of his life, upbraiding that vile monarch for his great wickedness, while prophesying a protracted drought and famine as the consequence thereof. He then fled the country, but returned again to face the irascible monarch when the predicted calamities had long prevailed in the land. That such a proceeding

* 1 Kings xvi, 30.

was attended with the utmost risk is manifest from the words which passed between the prophet Elijah and Obediah, the God-fearing and faithful servant of the Lord, when they met perchance on the way. Fully persuaded that not even one so resolute as Elijah would have the courage to face the incensed monarch, Obediah shows himself most disinclined to go back as bidden and announce to Ahab the prophet's return. He even thus remonstrates, "What have I sinned that thou wouldst deliver thy servant—who feared the Lord from his youth—into the hands of Ahab to slay me"? As the Lord liveth there is no nation or kingdom where my Lord hath not sent to seek thee, and now thou sayest, Go tell thy Lord, Behold, Elijah is here".* However, upon the prophet repeating the assurance in these forcible words, "As the Lord of Hosts liveth before whom I stand, I will surely show myself unto him to-day"; Obediah departs at once to give the message to the King. Truly, the God-loving Elijah was not to be intimidated or moved from his purpose by any such representations. Relying on the goodness of his cause he prepared himself to encounter his Sovereign, and on their meeting it certainly was not the lone prophet who was most awed. Ahab could only find words to put this simple interrogatory, "Art thou he that troubleth Israel?" while Elijah thus fearlessly answered him, "I have not troubled Israel; but thou and thy father's house, in that ye have forsaken the commandments of the Lord, and thou hast followed Baalim".† But Elijah stopped not here, he felt his vantage ground, and added, "Now, therefore, send and gather to me all Israel unto Mount Carmel, and the prophets of Baal"; nor did Ahab hesitate, but at once conceded all that the dauntless prophet demanded. And now a scene is presented to us unrivalled in the records of history. Elijah, standing alone, resolutely defiant, before some four hundred and fifty priests of Baal, and with undaunted front boldly addressing the monarch

* 1 Kings xviii, 9.   † 1 Kings xviii, 18.

himself, and the whole concourse of his subjects, in these stirring and vigorous words, "How long halt ye between two opinions? If the Lord be God, follow Him, but if Baal, then follow Him". Indeed, so irresistible was his appeal that "the people could not answer him one word". Then followed a mocking rebuke to these worshippers of Baalim, and after proving to them how impotent was their idol god, he called the people to witness a sign, a Divine miracle which they no sooner saw than "they fell on their faces, and said the Lord He is God, the Lord He is God". Further, acting in accordance with the command of Elijah, they took these prophets of Baal, and "letting not one escape, slew them all." But the prophet had also to deal with the cruel and wicked Jezebel, and judging that his life was in imminent peril through her vile machinations, so long as he abode in the country, he had to pass over into Beersheba, and even seek refuge in the wilderness. It was at this period when, exhausted and wearied by the trials and fatigues he had undergone, that being interrogated by the Lord as to his doings, he set forth the criminal conduct of this unhappy people under their vile rulers, his own earnest zeal in contending with their infatuation and obduracy, as also his perilous position, and these are his words, "I have been very jealous for the Lord God of Hosts, for the children of Israel have forsaken thy covenant, thrown down thine altars, and slain thy prophets with the sword, and I, even I only, am left; and they seek my life, to take it away". Truly, was his life one act of devotion; he "walked with God". He was faithful in the service of the Lord, and of untiring zeal in each good, each holy cause. Here, then, is one of the true lights of Israel, an ever-shining light—the example and the *man* alike immortal.

* 1 Kings xix, 4.

RESIGNATION.

Leviticus x, 3, "*And Aaron held his peace.*"

LIFE is mostly what we make it. Trials there must ever be, but their intensity and their number will greatly depend on past conduct and on character. The individual History of AARON fully exemplifies this truth, and thus affords a useful lesson to those who will review the incidents of his life, and trace his every act in relation thereto. The first mention of Aaron's name is to be found in Exodus iv. He is there presented to us as "glad in heart" at the prospect of greeting Moses, his brother, from whom he had been separated during long and trying years; also, as being fully prepared to undertake a mission—second only in importance to that confided to Moses—which the Lord had intrusted to him. Now, when we read of the kindly salutation which passed between the brothers on their meeting in the wilderness, when we find their names coupled together as boldly facing Pharaoh in his wrath, and working out the deliverance of Israel, we may not doubt either the fraternal affection of Aaron or his resolution and courage; indeed, we are naturally led to entertain a high opinion of the worth of one chosen by the Supreme as a fitting instrument for His great purpose. But all is comparative; and when we come to test his character at other periods of his career, we find that he fell immeasurably short of the moral excellence of Moses.

Certain it is that no one ought to have comprehended better the powers of the Most High than he who had been instrumental in performing the miracles God graciously wrought for Israel, and thence it might well be supposed that, inspired by pious reverence, awe and faith, he would have moulded his conduct by the will of the Almighty under every conceivable circumstance. Unhappily, however, Aaron possessed but little strength of mind; a sad and fatal infirmity of purpose marred his natural goodness and nobleness of disposition; indeed, he was only too easily led to the commission of acts which militated greatly to his discredit, and brought the severest after-consequences in their train. The first instance of this occurred within a brief period of the departure of the Israelites from Egypt, and faint, indeed, must have been the impress of the glowing past in the feeble mind of Aaron for him so soon, so easily, to forget what was due to the Majesty of the Supreme. Assuredly he displayed a fearful weakness of character when he yielded, on the very first appeal, to the wilful yearnings of the people after idol worship; but how much more culpable must that weakness appear to us when we reflect that, instead of sternly rebuking them, he himself undertook the task of accomplishing their evil intent. We find no remonstrance whatsoever on his part; he neither urged them to abandon their sinful purpose, nor did he place any obstacle in the way of its attainment, and, by thus retarding its execution, give time for the return of their resolute leader. Now, although second only in power to Moses, he sought not to turn his authority to account, but weakly bent before the wish of the people—indulging, instead of curbing, their idolatrous propensities. Truly he lacked the faith, with the strength of character, which would have led him to dare the anger of the people rather than incur the displeasure of Heaven. But he had not even the plea of fear to offer as an extenuation of his highly culpable conduct, the people not having shown any intention of resorting to violence; and as proof of this, let us note the words Moses addressed to Aaron on his return, together with the feeble and somewhat meaningless response they elicited. To the query, "What did this people unto thee that thou hast brought so great a sin upon them?" Aaron simply replied, while evidently cowering under the rebuke, "Thou knowest the people that they are set on mischief", as if this fact, forsooth, was an adequate excuse for his conduct. Nor do we find that he endeavoured to make any reparation for his wrong-doing. Although he had, through great moral pusillanimity, been instrumental in bringing sad calamities on the entire nation, he nevertheless sought not to make atonement for their iniquity, and stay the anger of the Lord through prayer and self-sacrifice. A weakness, amounting to cowardice, stole over him at this moment of a national crisis, and seemed to rob him of any pretence to moral excellence. And this becomes yet more observable when we compare the conduct of the two brothers; for, while Aaron is content to remain perfectly quiescent, Moses proceeds with his characteristic energy, coupled with an unparalleled sublimity of self-abnegation, to serve the cause of his erring countrymen, as we read, "And Moses said unto the people, Ye have sinned a great sin, and now I will go up unto the Lord, peradventure I shall make an atonement for your sin".* Then follows his supplication to the Lord, " Oh, this people have sinned a great sin, and have made them gods of gold, yet now, if Thou wilt forgive their sin; and if not blot me, I pray Thee, out of Thy book which Thou hast written". Thus sought this noble spirit to stay the deplorable evils which resulted from the people's gross and shameless depravity, and Aaron's senseless and culpable conduct. Nor could Aaron himself have escaped the penalty of his wrong-doing but for the intercession of Moses, as we read, "And the Lord was very angry with Aaron to have destroyed him, and I prayed for Aaron also the same time".† Be it observed, however, that although God's anger was thus appeased, yet from this time forth Aaron's name is rarely coupled with that of Moses. Nor can it be a matter of surprise that, having minds so dissimilar, no

---

* Ch. xxii, 40. † Deut. ix, 20.

long or close union of feeling and consequent action could subsist between them; indeed, the next incident that occurred but too clearly points to a momentary estrangement on the part of Aaron, originating in his own culpable weakness. Assuredly to moral cowardice must be attributed his siding with his sister Miriam, when, in a spirit of petty jealousy, she " spoke against Moses, because of the Ethiopian woman whom he had married", since there was not even a shadow of pretence for such conduct. But more than mere weakness—indeed, the base passion of envy—is clearly discernible, when, in a spirit of sedition, Aaron haughtily exclaimed, " Hath the Lord, indeed, spoken only by Moses; hath He not also spoken by us?" Thus permitting jealousy and pride to rankle in his heart, he forgot how greatly he was beholden to the merit of Moses for his high position, with its accompanying advantages, and ignobly turned against that excellent brother. But such reprehensible conduct was not suffered to go unreproved or unpunished. The Lord, after vindicating his faithful servant, thus called both Aaron and Miriam to account, " Wherefore, then, were ye not afraid to speak against my servant, Moses?" a reprimand instantly followed by mention of the severe penalty they had brought on themselves, as we read, " The anger of the Lord was kindled against them, and He departed from them". Truly culpable must Aaron then have felt himself; indeed, the words he immediately after addressed to Moses afford ample evidence that he had overcome all feeling of envy, and become humbly penitent. They at once prove a willingness to acknowledge not only the spiritual superiority of his meek, forbearing brother, but also his higher, far higher, claim to the regard of heaven, as we read, verse 11, " And Aaron said to Moses, Alas! my Lord, I beseech Thee lay not the sin upon us, *wherein we have done foolishly, and wherein we have sinned"*. Now, the All-gracious only designed to produce self-reproach on the part of Aaron, but with Miriam it was otherwise; her chastisement must be so marked as to be discernible to the entire congregation, since she it was who had instigated the spirit of insubordination; and, indeed, but for the lovingkindness of her much-wronged brother, she would have had to suffer a yet more severe punishment. Again, for the third time, Aaron kindled the anger of the Lord; but on this occasion it was in conjunction with Moses. This leader of a rebellious people, greatly provoked by their murmurings, disobeyed the word of the Supreme, in a moment of temper, and smote the rock, when he had been charged to speak to it. Now Aaron had received the like injunction to "sanctify the Lord in the eyes of the children of Israel",* and again he showed himself devoid of that moral courage which would have enabled him to face the people, assert his authority, and check their momentary exasperation, or, if powerless to effect this, would at least have inspirited him to stay the hand of his brother, so to withhold him from committing a deed which was to render them alike culpable in the eye of Heaven. Truly herein each had greatly, grievously erred; therefore was it decreed that both alike should suffer the penalty, and neither brother was spared to see the promised land. Now, to be deprived of that sight after which their hearts had so long yearned must have been a severe trial to them both; but surely Aaron must have experienced the bitterest pang of regret, since he had to reproach his own coward heart for not arresting the hand of the worthy relative to whom he owed a deep debt of love and gratitude, thereby standing his true friend at a moment when, for once, his intervening might have proved so serviceable.

Finally, turning to the heading or subject matter especially under consideration, we must in some measure ascribe the impious conduct of Aaron's sons to the same inherent weakness of character, which restrained him from duly exercising his parental authority. Before, however, lending our atten-

* Ch. xx, 12.

tion to this most painful incident in the life of Aaron, let us carefully note the one circumstance which naturally tended to produce such faint-heartedness, for then shall we be more apt to pity than condemn him. Aaron was more than eighty years of age when he quitted the land of bondage, and though he could for a time rise to vigour of purpose and vigour of action through the interposition of the Deity, his spirit was so cowed by long, long years of slavery, that he had become weak and nerveless. Aaron, together with the entire people, had to serve an apprenticeship to freedom, which alone could teach them that they were responsible agents, as well as other lessons not to be learnt during a cruel servitude. Weak and faulty, then, as Aaron proved himself on various occasions, we have this extenuating circumstance to bear in mind when considering the high position to which he rose. Certain it is, that had there not been much good in his character, the High Priesthood would never have been conferred on him, even for the sake of his brother, whose own sons, be it observed, were not exalted to any high dignity. The Great Searcher of hearts will have seen in His servant qualities fitting him for the sacerdotal office, and indeed during the forty years he ministered before the altar, he never once faltered in the performance of his ministerial duties. Alas! that he had not duly counselled his sons, disciplined their minds, drawn their hearts into the service of God, and so impressed them with the solemnity and sacredness of the functions they had to discharge, as to have rendered it almost impossible that they should have wilfully disobeyed the Divine injunction in the sight of the entire people assembled, as we read, "And Nadab and Abihu, the sons of Aaron, took each his censer and put fire therein, with incense thereon, and offered strange fire before the Lord, *which he commanded them not*". Is it not also probable that even prior to this period Aaron had seen indications of unfitness on the part of these two

* Lev. x, 1.

sons for the proper discharge of their important duties, yet lacked the moral courage to dismiss them from a post they were unworthy to fill? Be this, however, as it may, no such flagrant breach of duty could be suffered to pass unpunished. They had, in utter disregard of the sacredness of their office and the high trust reposed in them, not only failed to "sanctify the Lord in the eyes of the people", but had even outraged every sense of propriety and acted in direct opposition to the command of the Supreme. Though they had bound themselves to inculcate the principles of truth to the people, whose idolatrous propensities called for careful supervision, they nevertheless were the first openly to violate God's ordinances and turn from the path of duty! Death alone could atone for such sinfulness, and as their crime had been publicly committed, so was it publicly expiated, thus, "There went out a fire from the Lord, which devoured them, and they died before the Lord". Now, how did the poor bereaved parent bear this awful shock, this fearful trial? Truly, it was borne with a fortitude and *resignation* which could leave no doubt as to the marked and beneficial change that had at length been wrought in his character. The enfeebled mind recovered its tone under affliction and trouble, and on Moses considerately exhorting him to seek consolation by not regarding his sorrow as a parent, but solely in relation to the Supreme will, we find that "Aaron held his peace". No murmur, no word of dissent even, was heard; his perturbed spirit was evidently calmed by the following mild yet forcible words of Moses, "The Lord hath said, I will be sanctified in them that come nigh me, and before all the people I will be glorified",* and the solemn admonition they conveyed striking him to the soul, at once subdued all idle, all impious repinings. His silence was indeed a tacit acknowledgment of the truth breathed forth in his brother's gentle reminder, and a heartfelt recognition of the equity of the Supreme. More than any form of speech it eloquently said, My sons

* Lev. x, 3.

have grievously sinned, whether they presumed wantonly to transgress the law, or whether, with minds darkened through inebriation, they lost sight of the reverence due to their sacred office, their crime could not but be equally offensive to the Majesty of heaven, and demanded the forfeiture of their lives, whereby even-handed justice might be satisfied; I therefore bow and humbly submit to God's all-wise decree. A sense of his own past parental weakness must have struck a painful chord in his heart, and much self-reproach will have mingled with the thought of his son's crime to increase his mental anguish. Now, it must not for one moment be supposed that Aaron's silence was caused by either apathy or indifference; he deeply, keenly felt the death of his sons, as his words and conduct alike testify. To his mind, "after such things had befallen him", it would have been a desecration to partake of the sacrifice; his heart, weighed down with grief, lacked the proper spirit wherewith all offerings should be made, and therefore such could not be acceptable in the sight of the Lord. It was assuredly this sentiment which prompted the following rejoinder on the part of Aaron when Moses angrily demanded the cause of his deviation from the usual and authorised practice: "Behold, this day have they offered their burnt offering before the Lord, and such things have befallen me, and if I had eaten the sin offering to-day should it have been accepted in the sight of the Lord?" The parental love, the grief, the sublime spirit of faith, which breathe in these words were fully appreciated by the Divine Legislator, since with this answer "Moses was content". The feeling of the father was held sacred, and religion, which never asks any unnecessary or harsh sacrifice, claimed none here. A true spirit of *resignation* had marked Aaron's conduct throughout this trying season of adversity, and assuredly obtained the approval of heaven, since he was permitted to retain the sacred office of High Priest to the very close of his long life, to watch, in gladness of heart, his remaining sons sedulously discharging their high functions, and, above all, to know through the Divine assurance that on them and their posterity would devolve the everlasting Priesthood.

And here, before closing this sketch, it may be serviceable to remark that throughout the whole of Aaron's long after-career (for he passed away from earth at the venerable age of 123)* no further instance of weakness is recorded, while all betokens that he faithfully, earnestly, and resolutely fulfilled his heavenly-appointed mission. Recurring trials had gradually imparted to his character a stability and firmness which, ever after holding sway, kept him consistently, rigidly in the right path. Thus fulfilling the duties of his office, he will have forgotten the past, that past beyond recall, and working for the moral good of his people, secured their respect and love (proved by their mourning his loss for thirty days),† as also a name here on earth and a rich inheritance in the realms above.

Life would be but mere existence had it not its hopes and its failures, its expectations and its disappointments, its joys and sorrows. It is these waves of fortune, the constant ebb and flow of aspirations and desires, the incessant pulsation and agitation of pleasure, with occasional throes of pain and anguish, which keep it from stagnation. All these test, as they also serve to develop, the moral character, and give to life its form, colour, and motion. Now, amongst these many springs of action adversity and trials hold a prominent place. Like life itself, they have a high purpose, and, while they best gauge man's moral condition, they are also every way calculated to strengthen and improve it. But for them many an exalted virtue would be nearly dormant, and the power, the energies, the higher faculties of the soul would never be roused from their slumber—indeed, we should know little of faith, fortitude, or resignation.

However, before proceeding to consider the many benefits

---

* Numbers xx, 28. † Numbers xx, 29.

which trials are calculated to confer, it behoves us to distinguish between those which are of our own making and the afflictions which enter into and are part of the plan of the Great and Wise Ordainer. At first sight this might seem to require a large amount of discernment, and yet assuredly such is not the case. The character of each, with but few exceptions, is well defined, and we have only to search conscientiously for the truth, discarding pride, which infallibly obscures the mental vision, in order to arrive at a well-grounded and approximate, if not certain, conclusion. An impartial investigation must result in this conviction, unpalatable as it may be, that we are almost invariably the authors of our own sufferings. They are mostly attributable to misconduct or improvidence, to want of forethought or rashness, to wilful excesses, imprudence, resistance to duty, or impatience. Subtract these, and the larger proportion of evils, as also the minor vexations of life, would altogether vanish. We have only to cast from us all inopportune desires, all vain and restless longings, in order to dissipate many an imaginary as well as many a real trial. It is simply because we leave folly unchecked, and do not earnestly seek to profit by experience, that recurring trials and sufferings befall us. And if indeed serious defects of character are the principal causes, not to say the very origin of trials, so trials in their turn promise the surest and most speedy cure for defects of character. Nor do their beneficial effects stop here, for, besides promoting virtue, they also tend greatly to check physical ills. This once proved, we shall assuredly no longer be inclined to bemoan trials, but rather seek to trace them to their source, and learn to profit by them. Now, for instance, we must acknowledge that sickness or bodily infirmity is generally the result of some imprudence or excess, and that suffering, its natural attendant, often kindly steps in to warn, admonish, and check us in our perilous and venturesome course. Indeed, pain is nothing more than nature calling for relief, and woe to them who neglect its call, and allow to pass unheeded the useful lesson it would teach. Truly it is well for us we have so stern a monitor to second the voice of reason and stay us in any rash or headlong course, before, too late, we discover that our vital strength is sapped and the fatal seeds of premature decay are sown, never to be uprooted. Now if pain, so seemingly detrimental, is yet, in the vast majority of cases, ultimately beneficial, we may not doubt that all other misfortunes which God suffers to befal us will also work to good if taken well to heart. Trials, sorrows, failures, make the man, the martyr, the hero; they lend to the soul pity, love, sympathy, and other kindred emotions, while they afford scope for good offices. Adversity brings reflection in its train, displaying to us our weakness and dependence on God; it recalls unatoned errors and sins, it shows happiness and misery in their true light; it also enhances through contrast the joys which succeed to grief, while it further incites hope, whets our sagacity, and stirs us to vigorous action. Supreme satisfaction is likewise sure to result when, after bravely combating with calamity, we have overcome those trials which seemed invincible and won the great prize of virtue which is in its keeping. Then, as to the more marked heavenly dispensations, and especially those of bereavement and death, which certainly are not a consequence of personal demerit, since they befall alike the virtuous and the sinful; reason and religion tell us that, being universal, they cannot be evils, but rather blessings in disguise; indeed, we must be the more convinced of this when we consider death as the especial messenger of a Wise and Beneficent Father. Thus regarded, it will assuredly not present itself as a dark and dreaded phantom, but be recognised as an angel of light—of light eternal. Such a view of death can hardly fail to lighten the trials of life, while the glowing prospect of a promised heavenly diadem, shining ever brighter and brighter, will cheer and gladden man's lot here on earth.

Before next proceeding to consider why trials and adversity but too frequently fail in producing such happy results, it behoves us seriously to reflect that these are never negative in their effects; if they do not soften the heart, they will surely harden it; if they do not urge us to seek God in prayer, they will certainly tend to draw us from Him. Now, since trials will assuredly overtake us at some period of our lives, we should be prepared for their encounter, and ever ready in true piety and faith to cope with or repress their too common adjuncts, sinful repinings, and disbelief, black despair, or discontent. Resist or disarm these enemies to our peace and happiness, and we may feel assured that from trials good fruits alone will spring; neglect or suffer them to have a place even as impulses, and nought but evil can ensue. Therefore, it becomes a bounden duty to combat these antagonists to right feeling and moral principle at their first approach; or should they, unhappily, have found a resting-place in the heart, to uproot and cast them from us. And surely, if we will only consider how sinful is the indulgence of discontent, we should have little difficulty in curbing it. *Truly it is an oblique reflection on the goodness of the Deity;* nothing but wanton folly will cause us to cavil at the wise dispensations of Providence. We must, indeed, rise to the level of Divinity before we can dare to judge the Great Judge of All; we must see every concurrent event, and, in fact, have those attributes which can alone appertain to the Supreme, before we can reasonably complain of any one occurrence which is suffered to befall us. Let us, then, look on affliction as the medicine of life; and seeing that happiness, and not misery, is the normal condition, let us not be unmindful of the many blessings which are within our reach, but, freeing ourselves from pride and presumption when reflecting on our deserts, learn to moderate hopes, and be content with a fair quota of happiness. The mind will thus become inspired with the surpassing mercy and goodness of God, and we shall assuredly feel that gratitude for the numberless benefits received which is due to

Him, who is at once a gracious Ruler and an even-handed Judge.

One additional consideration remains, and that is, how we should act when trials and afflictions overtake us. This is of vital importance, and demands our best attention; for according as we allow ourselves to be affected by them, so assuredly will be the close of our life. And here let it be observed that trials are divided into two very distinct classes, necessitating a totally different course of action. There are misfortunes which we can remedy, and those which we cannot. Hence it behoves us to endeavour to distinguish between them, so that in the former case, casting from us all unnecessary repinings or cavillings, we may set ourselves to check or repair the evil, while in the latter, stilling useless and unavailing regrets, we may submit with a perfect acquiescence to God's all-wise decrees, and *be resigned*. Now, with reference to such trials and misfortunes as are capable of being remedied, and which, if bereavement and death be excluded, will be found to form the larger proportion of them, only a passing observation is needed, for it must be clear to all those who reflect, that their cure must chiefly depend on the rejection of those errors and weaknesses to which they owe their existence, as also to the vigorous prosecution of a wiser course in the future. Then, if we will only listen to, and profit by, the experience of the past, we shall have little cause to apprehend a return of disappointments, anxieties, and sorrows, while we may reap those many rich gifts which the future ever offers to the hopeful, the industrious, and the virtuous. But when we come to regard those afflictions and sorrows over which we have absolutely no control, we can hardly fail to perceive that for them there is but one certain panacea, and that is *resignation*. Palliatives there are, which should be called into requisition, and the foremost, to which alone we can here allude, is the exercise of sympathy. The heart that can feel for others' woes, and be interested in the well-being of fellow-creatures, will not long smart under its own wounds. They who make it their province to soothe the stricken and the sorrowing, who minister to the wants of the poor and suffering, in a word, they who serve the cause of charity and brotherly love, will find their own burdens sensibly lightened; and further cull their full share of the happiness they impart, for in blessing will they be most blessed. Thus, while we should seek for palliatives, it behoves us never to lose sight of that heavenly spirit of resignation which is the only true cure for the severer trials and sorrows of life. Now this, like every other virtue and duty, necessarily requires culture; it must be made a fixed principle of the mind before it can be really serviceable and domiciled as a home sentiment in the heart whereby it may be ever ready at command.

Let us then consider how such a frame of mind and disposition is to be advanced, bearing in remembrance at the same time that resignation is not insensibility, and indeed that there must exist strong feelings to be curbed before it can even have birth. Now, assuredly, to secure its vigorous growth we must call to our aid the powerful auxiliaries reason, religion, and faith. These must bring with them a spirit of resignation, since they not only induce us to reflect piously, but further cause us to recognise the important truths, that God's dispensations are all adorable, how dark soever they may seem; that good greatly predominates over evil; that events seemingly most unfavourable are often calculated to contribute to prospective, if not to present, happiness; that we are apt greatly to err by overrating existing evil, and undervaluing present good; finally, that Omniscience having permitted sorrow to be distributed in so happy, so bright a world, is proof positive of certain advantage accruing therefrom to his creatures. But true resignation demands much self-abnegation. Each willing sacrifice will bear its own proof that resignation is not mere indifference, but deference to the high will of God.

Now, surely if we sincerely love the Great Giver, we shall be ever ready to yield up those treasures which He so graciously bestowed, remembering with humble gratitude that although we may have lost much, many blessings yet remain to us.

In conclusion, let it be observed, that it behoves us to await the issue of events without that overweening anxiety which is the poison of life; indeed, we should ever strive to look on the bright side, for thereby do we honour the Supreme, and further, we should seek for consolation at the only true fount, remembering that although God is sometimes invisible, He is never, never absent. But most important is it that we should not dwarf ourselves to the lowest possible standard by doubting God's Providence or God's justice. Doubt anything rather than this, whatsoever may betide. Mourn we may, we must, but let us not permit the eye to be continually dimmed with tears, that it be unable to see God in the universe. Let us seek to fulfil each duty, leaving nothing undone whereby we may merit the favour of heaven; let us kindle the holy flame of faith with pious zeal, so that we may learn to trace nought but goodness in God's all-wise dispensations, for then, assuredly, we shall walk the path of life manfully, meeting each danger and difficulty, each trial and affliction bravely, fearlessly, and in a perfect spirit of resignation.

PRECEPTS.—We may well turn to the writings of the Sacred penmen for their views on the sorrows and trials of life, since nearly all of them were tried children of the Most High, and thence could be as essentially practical on this vital question as they were in their other teachings. Now, undoubtedly, they all arrived at the one important conclusion, that trials have a purpose, and serve to work out moral good to reasoning man. David thus speaks of the effects of sorrow on himself, Ps. xxx, 6, "I said in my prosperity I shall never be moved, but as soon as Thou, O Lord, withdrawest Thy countenance I was troubled; then I cried unto Thee, O Lord, and unto the Lord I made supplication". It had thus fostered a prayerful spirit, and further led him to recognise and gratefully acknowledge God's loving kindness, for he adds, " Sing unto the Lord, O ye saints of His, *for his anger endureth but a moment*, in His favour is life". In Ps. cxxvi, we again read, "They that sow in tears shall reap in joy", and truly the softened heart melts easily into gladness. Also "the preacher", who could see so little " profit under the sun", and said of "laughter, it is mad", expresses a like sentiment when he tell us, Eccles. vii, 3, " Sorrow is better than laughter, for by the sadness of the countenance the heart is made better". Then Isaiah, in his beautifully figurative language, ch. lxi, shows that sorrow leads to the glorifying of God, and that the righteous will give "the garment of praise for the spirit of heaviness". Turning next to Deuteronomy, chap. xxxi, we are there distinctly told that sin cannot be suffered to go unpunished, and that the trials consequent thereon should serve to draw the offender from his course, and lead him to his God. Thus, "the Lord spake unto Moses, My anger shall be kindled against them, and I will hide my face from them, and many evils and troubles shall befall them, so that they will say in that day, Are not these evils come upon us, because our God is not among us?" And Asaph, in Ps. lxxviii, recapitulating the history of the Israelites, pointedly remarks on the effects which trials exercised on this rebellious people, by saying, verse 34, " When God slew them, then they sought Him; and they returned and inquired early after God". Jeremiah exhorted a later generation to like effect in these words, chap. ii, 16, " Thine own wickedness shall correct thee, and thy backslidings shall reprove thee : *know therefore and see* that it is an evil thing, and bitter, that thou fearest not the Lord thy God, but hast forsaken Him". Truly, trials cannot but prove beneficial to each of God's erring creatures, and happy is it for us when we can conscientiously aver with the pious and much tried David, "It has been good that I have been afflicted". Now, to encourage this view, and thereby dissipate all vain repinings, all sinful discontent, we should well consider and take to heart the following quotations, Ps. xxxiv, 19, "Many are the afflictions of the righteous, but the Lord delivereth him out of them all". And again, Prov. iii, 11, "Despise not the chastening of the Lord, neither be weary of His correction, *for whom the Lord loveth He correcteth*, even as a father the son in whom he delighteth". Further, while we should bear in mind that "God's hand is not shortened that He cannot save, nor His ear heavy that He cannot hear"; we should also reflect that if we cease our endeavours to deserve His favour, He may deprive us of the power of enjoyment, or, as we read in Eccles. vi, 2, "A man to whom God hath given riches, wealth, and honour, so that he wanteth for nothing, yet God giveth him not power to eat thereof". But here it must be observed that merely to attain a belief in the efficacy of trials and affliction does not suffice; such belief should be made serviceable, and to be so, it must, on the one hand, be made to influence our conduct for good, and on the other, should warm our hearts in humble trust to the Great and Wise Disposer, for then, in the first case, we shall avert many a sorrow, or, in the next, if trials come, as come they will, we shall be enabled to support them with true fortitude and pious resignation. Sacred writers seek to impress each of these considerations upon us under the most divergent points of view; thus, as to the first, we are told in Ps. cxix, "Great peace have they who love thy law, and nothing shall offend them". Grief, indeed, seldom overwhelms any but the wrong-doer; a sad and heavy spirit being ever the ultimate penalty paid for the infringement of God's holy law. But if such belief be duly taken to heart, then will it prove a sovereign balm, as it did to the pious David, who thus speaks of its efficacy, verse 92, "Unless the law had been my delight, I should have perished in my affliction". Jeremiah's words are much to the same effect when thus addressing the backsliding Israelites, chap. ii, 17, "Hast thou not procured this calamity unto thyself in that thou hast forsaken the Lord thy God, yet thou saidst I will not transgress". And in the second instance, the sacred penmen also afford much consolation by showing us that God ever befriends and strengthens his tried and suffering children. Thus we read, Ps. cxlv, 14, "The Lord upholdeth all that fall, and raiseth up all those that be bowed down"; and in Psalm cxlvii, 3, "God healeth the broken in heart, and bindeth up their wounds"; and again, Ps. xxxiv, 18, "The Lord is nigh unto them that are of a broken heart, and saveth such as be of a contrite spirit"; then in Nahum, chap. i, 7, "The Lord is good; a strong hold in the day of trouble, and He knoweth them that trust in Him"; and in Isaiah, chap. lvii, 15, "I, the Lord, whose name is holy, dwell with him that is of a contrite and humble spirit, to revive the heart of the contrite ones, for I will not contend for ever"; then in Prov. iii, 26, "Let the Lord be thy confidence, He will keep thy foot from being taken"; and in Job xi, 13, "If thou prepare thy heart, and stretch out thine hand towards Him, then thou shalt forget thy misery, and remember it only as waters that have passed away"; and again, in Lamentations, iii, 32, "Though God cause grief, yet will He have compassion according to the multitude of His mercies, for *He doth not afflict willingly*, nor grieve the children of men"; then Habakkuk in his own person bids us not to be cast down if *poverty* assails us, for, says he, chap. iii, 17, "Although the fig tree shall not blossom, neither fruit be on the vines, nor the field yield meat, and there be no herd in the stalls, yet I will rejoice in the Lord who *is my strength*"; nor if *sickness* come upon us should we forget to appeal in faith to the Great Healer as did King Asa, of whom we read in II Chron. xvi, that "when he became greatly diseased he sought not to the

Lord, *but* to the physicians"; finally, David, in the beautiful Ps. lv, thus exhorts us, "Cast thy burden upon the Lord, and He shall sustain thee, He will never suffer the righteous to be moved"; and in Ps. lvii he thus speaks of himself, "My soul trusteth in Thee, O Lord, yea, in the shadow of Thy wings will I make my refuge, *until these calamities be overpast*". Truly, under the wings of an All-Wise and All-Gracious Protector do reason and religion alike bid us ever seek for strength, for strength of will to resist temptations in the time of prosperity, and for fortitude to endure adversity in a meek, tranquil, and resigned spirit.

Scripture records no more marked EXAMPLE of endurance coupled with fortitude, of mental and bodily suffering, tempered with *resignation*, than the one presented to us in the life and character of JEREMIAH. Of all the prophets he had the heaviest trials to combat; of all the champions of their faith, he suffered most. Indeed, the mission confided to him was of a peculiarly disheartening character. It could only be brought to a successful issue through the sincere repentance of a king and people who had become hardened by a long course of sinful indulgence, and had fallen to the lowest depths of degradation. But as a true and loving servant of the Lord, utterly regardless of the gloomy prospect and dangers which lay before him, he set himself to his heaven-appointed task with undaunted courage, and carried it through with unswerving fidelity. Now, the energy with which he laboured, the resolution he manifested, the sacrifices he made from a sincere love for his countrymen, the perils he braved, in the hopes of rescuing them from an impending crisis, with the utter failure of his noble purpose, will be disclosed in the following brief epitome.

The culminating crimes of an entire people necessitated the mission of the noble-hearted, self-sacrificing Jeremiah, and in no instance throughout his Book is this more clearly demonstrated than in the following verses. On God thus speaking to his prophet, "Run to and fro through the streets of Jerusalem, and see now, and know, and seek if ye can find a man, if there be any that executeth judgment, that seeketh the truth, and I will pardon it",* Jeremiah dejectedly answers, "O Lord, are not indeed thine eyes upon the truth? thou hast stricken them, but they have not grieved; *they have refused to receive correction*, they have made their faces harder than a rock, they have refused to return". To the same effect we read in chap. viii, "I, the Lord, hearkened, but the people of Jerusalem spoke not aright, no man repenteth him of his wickedness, saying, What have I done? they called out, Peace, peace, where there is no peace"; and again, in chap. ix, the prophet thus reprobates their conduct, "They deceived every one his neighbour, and will not speak the truth; they weary themselves to commit iniquity". How bitterly the tender-hearted prophet bewailed their sinful propensities, and the certain misery they were entailing on themselves is shown in his exclamation, "O that my head were waters, and mine eyes a fountain of tears, that I might weep day and night for the slain of the daughter of my people";† and how onerous he felt the task before him the following verse discloses: "Oh that I might leave my people and go from them, for they be an assembly of treacherous men". Yet he quickly rallied from this discouragement, and, passing to the next chapter, we find him praying for the people, proclaiming God's covenant unto them, and finally exciting their ire against himself by rebuking them for their disobedience and by prophesying future evils should they continue to offer incense unto Baal! Indeed, a conspiracy was formed to take his life, and, according to his own words, he would have been "like a lamb or ox that is brought to the slaughter and cut off from the land of the living" had not God averted the impending danger. No

* Chap. v, i. † Chap. iv, 1.

change, however, being wrought in the conduct of the Israelites through the wise counsel of Jeremiah, they had to bemoan the fulfilment of his prophecy in the shape of a grievous famine overspreading the land. Vividly does the sorrowing prophet pourtray the dearth in chap. xiv, where he tells us that the nobles of Jerusalem " sent their little ones to the waters, yet found none, and returned with their vessels empty, that the people were ashamed and confounded because the ground was chapt, for there was no rain in the earth"; and then, viewing the " great breach", with the sickness and deaths thereby occasioned, he exclaims, "Let mine eyes run down with tears, let them not cease, for my people are broken with a very grievous blow". Yet even these calamities failed to bring about any radical, any permanent reform; thus was Jeremiah once more bid to exhort and threaten, but again without avail, as may be judged by the answer he received, "There is no hope, but we will every one walk after our own devices and do the imaginings of his evil heart". His perseverance in the good cause indeed only drew on him general contumely, and even Pashur, governor of the House of the Lord, who "had prophesied lies", hating God's true prophet, vented his illwill by first smiting him, then causing him to be " put in the stocks which were in the high gate". Such treatment roused a momentary ebullition of angry feelings in Jeremiah's breast, and complaining that the word of the Lord should be " made a reproach unto him and a derision daily", he hastily declared, "I will not make mention of Him nor speak any more in His name, for every one mocketh me"; he further " curseth his birth, and lamenteth that his days should be consumed in shame". Nevertheless, on the subsidence of this momentary gust of irritability, he resumed his task, for, as he declared, "God's word was in his heart as a burning fire, he would weary with forbearing". And truly he greatly needed such zeal and determination, since from this time forth he had to contend with trials which, in point of severity, made all preceding ones pale into insignificance. As the insensate, reckless king, his corrupt nobles, and the false prophets with whom he had to deal became more and more conscious of the approach of the calamities foretold by Jeremiah, so they hardened their hearts more and more, and, instead of seeking to avert them through timely repentance, they merely vented their cruel wrath on the prophet who had dared first to exhort them, then threaten them into submission.

An instance of this is afforded us in the reign of Jehoiakim, for after openly denouncing God's threats, and thus addressing the entire people, "Therefore now amend your ways and your doings, obey the voice of the Lord your God, and He will repent Him of the evil that He hath pronounced against you",* Jeremiah adds, "As for me, behold I am in your hands, do with me as seemeth good and meet unto you", words testifying his sublime courage, since he was then addressing an incensed people who not only "had gathered against him in the House of the Lord", but by whom he had already been sentenced to death! God, however, was with him, and his submissive language had the desired effect, so far at least as his life was concerned, for thus argued the nobles among themselves, "If we put him to death might we not procure great evils against our souls?"

It was, however, especially under the rule of Zedekiah that Jeremiah had to endure many an indignity and much cruelty. That monarch, though indebted for his throne to Nebuchadnezzar, showed himself neither grateful nor submissive. He followed in the footsteps of Jehoiakim, "filling Jerusalem with innocent blood", and finally rebelled against the mighty King of Babylon, who thereon marched with a formidable force to the gates of Jerusalem, alarming Zedekiah to such a degree that he sought Jeremiah to ascertain the probable issue of this warlike demonstration. The an-

* Chap. xxvi, 13. † Chap. xxvi, 19.

swer was such as greatly to displease the king, showing that since he would not return to his God or conform to the will of Nebuchadnezzar, "the city would be delivered into the hands of his enemies" and he himself made captive; indeed, so great was his anger that he ordered the daring utterer of this dreaded threat to be at once imprisoned. But when the siege was prolonged, and famine began to desolate the land, whereby opposition became less and less practicable, the King, remembering how prophetic were the words of Jeremiah, showed him kindness and liberated him. The nobles of the land, however, who dreaded his threats, while yet unwilling to hearken to his exhortations, continued their persecutions; they first smote, then placed him in close confinement, and assuredly he would have perished of hunger had not the king, at his entreaties, "commanded that the keeper of the prison should give him daily a piece of bread until all in the country was spent". Now, deplorable as his plight must then have been, his trials had nevertheless not reached their climax, since the princes of the land, growing yet more hardened at the sight of the ravages caused by the famine, and more and more irritable as they became sensible of the utter fruitlessness of resistance to the besieging foe, sought to vent their rage on the prophet, who, in accordance with the word of the Lord, once again urged them to submission. Nothing less than his death warrant did they demand of the king, who, willing to conciliate these powerful nobles, yielded to their wishes, and gave Jeremiah into their hands, whereon they "cast him into the dungeon that was in the court of the prison, a dungeon wherein there was no water, but mire, so Jeremiah sunk into the mire"!* And well was it that under such desperate circumstances, further heightened by the too certain prospect of starvation, he found one individual to succour him, else must he have surely succumbed. To the compassion of Ebed-melech, the Ethiopian, did the long-tried prophet owe his rescue, which was ef-

* Chap. xxxviii, 6.

fected only in time for him to bear sorrowful witness to the total overthrow of the army, the spoiling of the city with the conflagration and total destruction of the Temple! Furthermore, he had to learn of the capture of the king, of his being cruelly deprived of his sight, as also of the massacre of the princes, his sons, and all the nobles of Judea. Now, long as these dire calamities had been foreseen by Jeremiah, the consummation of his prophecies touched his sensitive heart to the quick; not even the maltreatment he had received at the hands of his countrymen could dull his sympathies, and greatly he grieved over their exile, while bitterly deploring the destruction of God's House and the desolation of the city. As proof of this, we have only to turn to that exquisite Book of "Lamentations", wherein he bewails the wretched condition of Zion, and vents his overwrought feelings in the most sorrowful and plaintive expression of compassion for the people of God. What a spirit of patriotism, what generous sympathy, what resignation and holy trust, pervade this eloquent and beautiful composition. Only one who had beheld Jerusalem in the flush of its prosperity, had exulted in the sight of the Temple in its full glory, and had afterwards witnessed the city in its sad, fallen state, with God's House levelled to the ground, could have bemoaned the change in such pathetic language, such touching accents of uncontrollable anguish, as the following: "How doth the city sit solitary that was full of people! how is she become as a widow! she that was great among the nations; she weepeth sore in the night, and hath none to comfort her. Jerusalem remembered in the days of her affliction and of her miseries all her pleasant things that she had in days of old. All her people sigh; they seek bread".* Then in chap. ii, "What thing shall I liken to thee, O daughter of Jerusalem; what shall I equal to thee, that I may comfort thee, for thy breach is great, like the sea, who can heal thee? All that pass by clap their hands at thee, they hiss,

* Lam. i, 1.

and say, Is this the city that men call the perfection of beauty, the joy of the whole earth?" Again, in chap. iv, "How is the gold become dim; the stones of the sanctuary are poured out in the top of every street. The Lord hath accomplished His fury; he hath poured out His fierce anger, and hath kindled a fire in Zion, and it hath devoured the foundations thereof. The kings of the earth, and all the inhabitants of the world, would not have believed that the enemy should have entered into the gates of Jerusalem; and again, chap. v, "We have drunken our water for money, our wood is sold to us. The joy of our heart is ceased, our dance is turned into mourning, the crown is fallen from our head; woe unto us that we have sinned". Then what depth of sympathy for his suffering brethren do the following sorrowful words betoken, " Mine eye runneth down like rivulets of water for the destruction of the daughter of my people. Mine eye trickleth down without any intermission".* Further, with what earnestness does he implore them to seek God in prayer, saying, " Arise, cry out in the night, pour out thine heart like water before the face of the Lord; lift up thy hands towards Him for the life of thy young children that faint for hunger in the top of every street".† "Let us search and try our ways, and turn again to the Lord. Let us lift up our heart with our hands unto God in the heavens". He also seeks to console them, while counselling amendment, thus, "God doth not afflict willingly, nor grieve the children of men. The Lord is good unto them that wait for Him; to the soul that seeketh Him. Though He cause grief, yet will He have compassion according to the multitude of His mercies; He will not cut off for ever."‡ And assuredly Jeremiah himself needed all the consolation and strength which a perfect trust in God alone can give in time of trouble. On the taking of Jerusalem by Nebuchadnezzar, his own private trials might have ceased, since that monarch, appreciating the

* Ch. iii, 48. † Ch. ii, 18. ‡ Chap. iii, 33.

high character of the prophet, gave charge to the chief in command to grant him perfect freedom of action, in pursuance of which order the captain of the guard thus spake unto him, " Behold, if it seemeth good unto thee to come with me into Babylon, come, and I will look kindly upon thee; but if it seem ill unto thee, forbear; behold all the land is before thee, whither it seemeth good and convenient for thee to go thither go".* Thus was Jeremiah left at liberty to quit the desolate, famine and panic-stricken city, nevertheless he departed not, but stood resolutely to his post. While one duty remained to be fulfilled, one task to be accomplished, he could not be turned therefrom either by personal suffering or by the surrounding scenes of misery, which must have afflicted the tender-hearted prophet yet more deeply. To this noble-spirited man, his own private hopes and sorrows were as nothing when taken in conjunction with the distress and hopeful regeneration of the nation. With a heart solely beating for the general welfare, he cast off all thought of self, and merged his own griefs in those of his countrymen. He was content to abide in their midst; sharing alike their privations, trials, and dangers. Truly he discharged to the last his arduous mission with ardent zeal and pious fortitude, as is clearly demonstrated in chapters xl to xliv of his book, wherein we find a short sketch of those events that followed the taking of Jerusalem, to which we will now briefly refer. Jeremiah, on being permitted to proceed wheresoever it "seemeth convenient", went to Jedaliah, the newly-appointed Governor of Judea, and "dwelt with him among the people that were left in the land"† But, unhappily, neither he nor the nation was destined to know aught of peace and tranquillity, for, after only a brief rule, the Governor was murdered by Ishmael, "one of the seed royal", who aspired to regal honours, and he, in his turn, had shortly after to vacate the throne and fly the country, being chased therefrom by

* Chap. xl, 4. † Chap. xl, 6.

Johanan, a powerful chieftain and friend of the late Governor. The first step taken by this mighty captain gave promise of a respite from the ever-recurring troubles which beset this people, for we find him with "the captains of the forces and all the people, even from the lowest unto the greatest",* drawing nigh unto Jeremiah, and supplicating his intercession with the Lord, so that they might be shown the way wherein they should walk, and the thing they should do. Jeremiah at once expressed his willingness to comply with their request, promising "to keep nothing back of the words which the Lord shall speak unto him". This readiness to fulfil the desires of the people elicited a show of gratitude, and they even called on God, as witness that they would act in accordance with what the Lord had commanded through him, saying, "This we will do, so that it may be well with us when we obey His voice". Now could Jeremiah have put faith in these words of good omen, he would have been greatly cheered, but he too well knew his countrymen, and his answer certainly evinced no sanguine expectation as to the fulfilment of their fair and specious assurances. Gladly, however, if not hopefully, he carried out their wishes; but when they afterwards refused to comply with their promise, he remonstrated with them in the most emphatic and pathetic language, pointing out how sinful would be their conduct if, in direct opposition to the known will of the Supreme, they should persist in quitting their native soil with the object of settling in Egypt, the land of idolatry. With all the eloquence of the earnest man, he exhorted and expostulated; he also threatened and promised alternately. On the one hand, he foreshadowed for them a bright and prosperous future if they would only abide in their own home, and adhere to the true worship; while, on the other, he foretold their fall into idolatry, with intensified calamities, should they wilfully quit their native soil. Thus he declared unto them, "Now if ye say, we

* Chap. xlii, 1.

will not dwell in this land, neither obey the voice of the Lord, but we will go into the land of Egypt to sojourn there, then it shall come to pass that the sword which ye feared shall overtake you there, and the famine, whereof ye were afraid, shall follow close after you, and there ye shall die".* He then added, "Thus saith the Lord of Hosts, As mine anger hath been poured forth upon the inhabitants of Jerusalem, so shall My fury be poured forth upon you when ye shall enter into Egypt; and ye shall be au execration, and an astonishment, and a reproach. Therefore, O ye remnant of Judah, go ye not into Egypt; know certainly that I have admonished you this day". He then reverted to their past hypocritical conduct in the following words, "Ye dissembled in your hearts when ye sent me unto the Lord, saying, pray for us, and according unto all that the Lord our God shall say, so we will do; for ye have not obeyed His voice, nor done anything, for the which He hath sent me unto you". But neither Jeremiah's words of counsel and reproof, nor his threats of God's displeasure, could subdue their stubborn will, or stay their projected exodus, for we read, " And when Jeremiah had made an end of speaking unto all the people the words of the Lord, then answered Azariah and all the proud men, saying, Thou speakest falsely, the Lord hath not sent thee to say, Go not into Egypt to sojourn there",† &c. " So Johanan, and all the captains of the forces, and all the people, obeyed not the voice of the Lord, but departed, and took with them Jeremiah the prophet. So *they came* into the land of Egypt". Here we see that Jeremiah himself was carried away to Egypt, where he again wrote and prophesied, and finally witnessed the fulfilment of some of his most gloomy predictions. Great, indeed, must have been his anguish of spirit when he saw how utterly futile were his struggles against such perversity—such obduracy. One consolation, however, was left him in his later years. As he had pre-

* Chap. xlii, 13.   † Chap. xliii.

dicted the decline and fall of the nation, so also had the Lord bid him prophesy for it a bright and glorious future in these words, "But fear not, O my servant, be not dismayed, O Israel; for behold, I will save thee from afar off, and thy seed from the land of their captivity; Jacob shall return, and be in rest and at ease, and none shall make him afraid. Fear thou not, saith the Lord, for I am with thee; for I will make a full end of all the nations whither I have driven thee, *but I will not make a full end of thee*". With so glowing an assurance of the ultimate welfare of his people before him, Jeremiah could view present trials with some composure; and though destined to close his days in the land of idolatry, far from the home he so much loved, and for which he had made many, very many, sacrifices, he humbly bowed before the Supreme will, and was *resigned*. We find no selfish repining even in his "Lamentations;" for though he declared in chap. iii of that exquisitely-beautiful Book, "I am the man that hath seen affliction; I am filled with bitterness; my soul has been far removed from peace; I forgat prosperity", with other similar passages, he adds, "Remembering mine affliction and my misery, my soul is humbled within me. This I recall, and therefore *have I hope*. It is of the Lord's mercies that we are not consumed, because His compassions fail not; *they are new every morning*; great is God's faithfulness". Truly, Jeremiah's was a tried life, claiming our pitying sympathy, while demanding yet more our unbounded admiration. Such a tribute is due at once to the tender-hearted man, who though painfully afflicted at being the bearer of evil tidings to his people, yet resolutely performed his sorrowful mission; to the noble-spirited patriot, who bent the full vigour of his soul to his country's good, never relaxing his efforts, though dangers threatened, and injustice, cruelty, and oppression were heaped upon him; finally, to the champion of truth, to him who stood defiantly forward,

* Chap. xlvi, 27.

manfully, zealously contending with the degenerate spirit of his age.

All honour, then, to this spiritual hero, who, though worsted at each fresh encounter, worked bravely on till death released him from his arduous, self-sacrificing, and devoted labours. All honour to the fearless prophet—the true and faithful servant of the Lord.

A few allusions to the marked *resignation* displayed by the most tried of men, the pious JOB, will here suffice, since his character has already had our attention. But, firstly, we must observe that the trials which befell him were certainly not consequences of former misconduct, else we should not read, "*There is none like him in the earth,* a perfect and an upright man, one that feareth God and escheweth evil*", while, further, we have his own solemn protestations of past integrity in the several duties of life, at the very moment when his afflictions had reached their climax, and he is brought pathetically to exclaim, "Terrors are turned upon me, they pursue my soul as the wind, and my welfare passeth away as a cloud, I am become like dust and ashes". We may be equally certain, however, his trials were not without a purpose, and well they served to test his faith and prove how entire, how all-potent it was. Did ever words more demonstrative of perfect resignation pass the lips of man than the following words, uttered when unspeakable calamities had just befallen him, "The Lord gave, the Lord hath taken away; blessed be the name of the Lord". Nor was this a momentary ebullition of piety; indeed, Job rather appeared to gather strength and endurance as ills accumulated and bodily ailments were added to the sad catalogue of suffering. We could have no surer proof of this than is to be found in the pious words wherewith he addressed his desponding wife, "What! shall we receive good at the hand of God, and shall we not receive evil?" And although time passed on without bringing him any

* Chap. i, 8. † Chap. xxx, 15.

alleviation, we yet find no change of sentiment; there is the same holy trust and belief in God's providence. To instance this, we have only to turn to chap. xxiii, wherein this patient man vouchsafes an answer to his troublesome and meddlesome reprovers; for, after declaring, "My stroke is heavier than my groaning, though to-day is my complaint bitter", he adds, "But God will not plead against me with His great power; no, He would put strength in me". He then proceeds to express his belief in an especial providence as follows: "God knoweth the way that I take", and further shows his thorough conviction that good will accrue from his afflictions in these words, "When he hath tried me I shall come forth as gold". Next, he clearly pronounces his sorrows to be dispensations of God, saying, "The Lord performeth the thing that is appointed for me". Thence we find that his trials, instead of inducing a spirit of repining, only prompted him to persevere in a course of virtue, for, after declaring that "the Almighty hath vexed my soul", he adds, "But while I breathe my lips shall not speak wickedness, nor my tongue utter deceit. My righteousness I hold fast, and will not let it go, my heart shall not reproach me as long as I live; till I die I will not remove mine integrity from me".* And then follows this humble confession, full of true piety and faith, "Behold, I am vile, what shall I answer thee, O Lord; I will lay mine hand upon my mouth, nor proceed to answer thee further. I know that thou canst do everything, and that no thought can be withholden from thee, wherefore I abhor myself and repent in dust and ashes". Yet, virtuous as Job had ever been, he nevertheless declared, on the passing away of his trials, that they had been productive of good, bringing him nearer to his God, for thus he spoke, "I have heard of Thee, O Lord, by the hearing of the ear, *but now* mine eye seeth Thee". From Job, then, let us learn to receive heaven-sent trials with true fortitude and *resignation*, and earnestly,

* Chap. xxvii.   † Chap. xl, 4.

resolutely, make them subserve to that highest good, our moral well-being.

Before concluding, another character calls for recognition under this heading, namely, that of the worthy Queen ESTHER. Raised from a lowly sphere to become the beloved consort of Ahasuerus, a mighty sovereign, ruler over one hundred and twenty-seven provinces, her future, seemingly all bright and smiling, was speedily to be obscured by a storm-cloud that threatened to burst and overwhelm her, together with all her race. The fortitude, the noble self-devotion, the pious *resignation* she displayed at this critical juncture, gives colour to a life which, as far as we may judge by the book bearing her name, was otherwise barren of incident. To this one point in her history, then, will we especially direct the following brief remarks. The extermination of the whole body of Jews dwelling within the vast dominions of King Ahasuerus was decreed through the machinations of the wicked and wrathful Haman, a favoured noble who " sat above all other princes". As we read, "And Haman caused to be sent letters, sealed with the King's seal, unto all the provinces to destroy, to kill, and to cause to perish all Jews, both young and old, little children and women, in one day, and to take the spoil of them for a prey".*
On the promulgation of this dread fiat, which, according to the laws of the Medes and Persians, could not be revoked, the poor devoted and doomed people bewailed their lot with "a loud and bitter cry". Doubtless there were many of this persecuted race who, trusting in God's gracious providence, could not altogether abandon themselves to despair, but strove to avert the threatened danger, and foremost amongst these stood the virtuous and God-fearing Mordecai, uncle to the Queen. A brave, dauntless, and pious spirit had kept him from yielding undue homage to the base and proud Haman, and it now nerved him to repair an evil of which he had indeed been the innocent cause. With this

* Chap. iii, 31.

object he sought the queen, hoping through her instrumentality to gain the royal ear. But when he first urged her to supplicate the king, she hesitated, not indeed from want of love or respect towards her uncle, whose commands she continued to obey as "when she was brought up with him", nor because she did not feel deeply for her people, nor yet from the belief that her exalted rank would shield her in the hour of danger, but because while incurring a known peril in appearing unbid before the king, she apprehended certain failure through so rash a proceeding. Nevertheless, on a second representation from her much-loved uncle, she at once acquiesced, doubtless feeling that there was truth in these his words, "Who knoweth whether thou art come to the kingdom for such a time as this?"* Yes, we may well believe that the self-imposed terrible ordeal of this high-minded queen was principally dictated by a sense of duty, while the request she made to her people through Mordocai, and the concluding words of her reply to him, were the natural offspring of true devotional feeling and pious resignation. They run thus: "Go gather together all the Jews and fast ye for me; I also and my maidens will fast likewise, and so will I go in unto the king, which is not according to the law, and if I perish, I perish".† Thus having sought God's gracious protection, she was prepared for aught that might befall. With the memorable words on her lips, "If I perish, I perish", words indicative of dauntless courage and the most sublime resignation, she stood forth as the champion of the right and achieved a glorious triumph. Through her bold daring, a daring not of the mere heroine, but rather that of the pious child of God—she rescued her people from a violent and untimely end, saved a worthy monarch from committing a heinous wrong, and brought about the downfall of the ruthless persecutor of her race, the vile Haman, while she also indirectly secured for her much-revered uncle the most exalted rank in the empire, and withal gained for her-

* Chap. iv, 14. † Chap. iv, 16.

self a yet greater hold on the king's affections. This latter fact is proved by the promise Ahasuerus made at the second banquet with the granting Queen Esther's suit " even to the half of the kingdom"! while as to the benefits she secured for her uncle and people, they are plainly set forth in chap. viii, where we read : " And Mordecai went out from the presence of the king in royal apparel and with a great crown of gold, and the city of Shushan rejoiced and was glad". Furthermore, " the Jews had light, and joy and honour, and many of the people of the land became Jews, for the fear of the Jews fell upon them".

Let, then, this truly glorious consummation yield its practical lesson, teaching us that even the darkest cloud is not without its silver lining, and, further, that it behoves us ever to do our duty resolutely, fearlessly, abiding, like the pious and noble Queen, the all-wise, all-gracious dispensations of the Lord with perfect trust, and in a humble, devout, and *resigned* spirit.

OBDURACY.

Numbers xiv, 41, "*And Moses said, Wherefore now do ye transgress the commandment of the Lord? but it shall not prosper.*"

THERE is perhaps no more marked feature in the national character of the early ISRAELITES than stubbornness of disposition. A state of bondage had left this blighting heirloom; and years elapsed before the people, who during their long apprenticeship to slavery had been amenable to brute force alone, could be brought to yield to the milder sway of reason and reproof. Yet had a cruel servitude rather debased than altogether corrupted their moral nature. Its finer susceptibilities had, indeed, been deadened by the iron rule to which they were so long subjected; nevertheless they could occasionally be roused to a sense of virtue, as was shown under the heading of "Religious Zeal," where the brighter side of the national character was depicted. But here its darker pencillings must necessarily be most visible, since we have to trace the doings of a people not only sadly prone to evil, but who too frequently persisted obdurately in their sinful course in utter disregard of the remonstrances and warnings of their leader. Self-willed and perverse, they rarely sought to quell their unruly passions, and turn from their evil ways till they had kindled God's just displeasure, and brought on themselves the chastisement of Heaven.

This dark outline we have now to fill up with incidents prominently figuring in the Books of Moses, and the first which presents itself is the murmuring of the people at the waters of Marah, which spirit of discontent was the more culpable, as they had been but recent witnesses of God's miraculous interposition in their favour, as we read, " And

Israel saw that great work which the Lord did upon the Egyptians, and the people feared the Lord, and believed the Lord and his servant Moses".* Again, a fresh cry of discontent broke from them in the wilderness of Zin, and also at Meribah, notwithstanding God had just satisfied their cravings by sending them "Angels' food". The Divine succour they thus repeatedly received no way served to remove their mistrust. Though Moses expostulated with them in these words, " your murmurings are not against us, but against the Lord", they nevertheless obdurately persisted in upbraiding him, and further tempted God, saying, "Is the Lord among us or not?" Now, assuredly, while they could question God's continual presence, and harden their hearts against proofs of His superintending providence, past lessons must have been singularly barren of good; indeed, discontent surged up at each new trial, and revilings were continually heard in the camp. Well indeed would it have been had the evil stopped there, but the next incident recorded is of a yet more painful character. The evident want of faith in God, and trust in their leader, which the people had manifested at repeated intervals, took a more tangible shape at the first opportune moment. They no longer confined themselves to murmuring against the All-Wise, but " turned quickly aside out of the way which God commanded them". Although prior to the departure of Moses for the ascent of Mount Sinai, they promised to " do all that the Lord had said, and be obedient"; although they witnessed "the glory of the Lord, like a devouring fire, on the top of the Mount", yet, after the lapse of only a few weeks, they again turned aside from the path of duty. Impatience at the absence of their chief conquered all sense of fear, and in a body the people went to Aaron, and thus spake unto him, " Up; make us gods which shall go before us"; and having made a molten calf, " they worshipped it and sacrificed thereunto, and said, These be the gods which

* Chap. xiv, 31.

have brought us out of the land of Egypt". Thus it was that when Moses, after an absence of only forty days, again approached the camp, he found them dancing and shouting before their graven image, and enacting the vilest idolatrous practices. Now, mark his prayer thereon, "O Lord, remember Thy servants, Abraham, Isaac, and Jacob; look not unto the stubbornness of this people, nor to their wickedness, nor to their sin".* Truly, they were stiff-necked and obdurate, when they neglected the counsel of their great deliverer and preserver; when they forsook the living God, whose benefits and mercies they had so long experienced, and yet more so when they wrought gods after their own imaginings, and bowed before them in sterile and senseless worship. Greatly indeed did such a people need such an intercessor.

In the incident which followed shortly after the one just referred to, the self-will and perverseness of the Israelites is especially marked. The land of promise was before them— the land which "God had given them to possess it". They had only to advance, as commanded by Moses, yet they hesitated. Seized by sudden doubts and misgivings, they besought him to send forth spies to search the land, and "bring word regarding it". Devoid of faith and holy trust in their All-Merciful Guardian, little was needed to dismay them, and the evil report brought back by the more timorous of these searchers threw the people into a state of consternation. Nothing that could be advanced by the brave and undaunted men, Caleb and Joshua, both of whom accompanied the expedition, nor the assurance given to them by Moses that "the Lord, who goeth before you, He shall fight for you", wrought any change of feeling. "The whole congregation murmured against Moses, and against Aaron, and said unto them, Would God that we had died in the land of Egypt, or in this wilderness".† Nor did their insubordination stop here, for "they said, one to another, Let us make a

* Deut. ix, 27. † Numbers xiv, 2.

captain, and let us return into Egypt". But their wilfulness and obduracy became yet more apparent, since the interposition of the Lord alone prevented them from stoning the faithful Joshua because he thus mildly rebuked them, " Rebel not ye against the Lord, neither fear ye the people of the land, for they are bread for us; their defence is departed from them, and the Lord is with us; fear them not". Such perverseness, however, met its condign punishment. They who brought the evil report from Canaan died of the plague, while, notwithstanding the intercession of Moses, all who had murmured were excluded from entering the promised land. Thus spoke the Lord in His just anger, " Because all those men which have seen My glory and My miracles, which I did in Egypt, and have tempted Me now these *ten times*, and have not hearkened to My voice, surely they shall not see the land which I swore unto their fathers. To-morrow turn ye, and get ye into the wilderness. Forty years shall ye bear your iniquities. I, the Lord, have said it; I will surely do it unto all this evil congregation that are gathered together against Me; in this wilderness they shall be consumed, and there they shall die".*

Now, had not this people been obdurate beyond all belief, they surely would have sought, by conforming to the will of the Supreme, to merit His ever-renewing mercies, and thereby possibly avert the sad fate consequent on their past misconduct. On the contrary, however, they grew yet more perverse. As formerly they had been timorous when they might well have felt themselves safe under the protection of the wing of Omnipotence, they now believed themselves secure when, indeed, they had many causes for apprehension. Far from turning back at the distinct command of the Lord of Hosts, they determined on acting in direct violation of His will by advancing to attack their formidable enemy. Little regard did they pay to their leader, who thus addressed them in God's name, " Go not up, for the

* Chap. xiv, 22 35.

Lord is not among you, that ye be not smitten before your enemies; *wherefore now do ye transgress the commandment of the Lord, but it shall not prosper*".* With rebellion at their hearts, they were not to be deterred; but "they went up presumptuously against the Amorites, who chased them as bees", defeating them with great slaughter. Now, during the forty years longer they were thus doomed to abide in the wilderness, they too frequently disobeyed the word of the Lord by uniting themselves with surrounding nations and bowing down before their gods in idol worship. Fresh trials followed, but their stubborn spirit remained unsubdued, and indeed no radical reform in their character could have been effected even at the close of their long wanderings, else Moses would not have addressed them thus, " Hear, O Israel, not for thy righteousness, or for the uprightness of thine heart, dost thou go to possess this land, but for the wickedness of these nations the Lord thy God doth drive them out from before thee, and that He may perform the word which the Lord sware unto thy fathers, Abraham, Isaac, and Jacob".†

This is truly a dark picture to draw, but how can it be otherwise when obduracy and stiff-neckedness have to be held up to view? Had the early Israelites only shown the same dogged determination to adhere to the right path as they had manifested in the pursuance of evil courses, such decision and stability of character would have proved truly valuable qualities, deserving the highest commendation. Desirable, however, as this would have been, yet was it to be expected of them? Assuredly not. A hard, unbending spirit, born of and long fostered by a cruel bondage, was little likely to lend itself to good, more especially as several concurrent circumstances worked in an adverse direction. Such, for example, was even the very boon' of freedom. An ignorant people, burning with ardent desires, thirsting after the pleasures of sense, could but regard their

* Chap. xiv, 42.   † Deut. ix, 5.

sudden liberation from thraldom as a fitting opportunity for those gratifications which had been so long denied them; the rebound was indeed all the more violent from the low and prostrate condition into which they had fallen. They did not even seek to control their hopes, nor could they calmly brook any impediment which stayed them in the way to the promised land, "flowing with milk and honey". Any occurrence retarding the fulfilment of their sanguine expectations, roused at once a strong spirit of discontent. They reflected not, or at least gave no heed to the reflection, that their All-Gracious Deliverer and Protector well knew what would most conduce to their welfare; they wilfully ignored the penance they were to undergo by God's all-just decree, and thence chafed at each new trial, each privation, nor could they be brought to bow before His wise dispensations in a resigned and tranquil spirit. Now, had they regarded their moral rather than physical progress, and followed the path of virtue to the desired goal, then assuredly they would never have rebelled, nor seen the frustration of their sanguine hopes. The circumstance, however, which worked them most evil was the proximity of idolatrous nations, who sought by every possible device to inveigle and seduce them from the worship of the One only God. Every intoxicating temptation which could rouse their worst passions was held up before them, and they but too soon learnt to prefer those orgies which formed part of the rites of idol worship to the pure, calm delights which their own religion was calculated to afford. In the paroxysms of their mad passions all holy and spiritual feelings lost their attractions, while the licentious and material reigned supreme. Becoming thus a prey to their lower instincts, they rushed wildly on, abandoning themselves to every sensual indulgence.

 Now withal, and this is a bright spot in the history of the Israelites, they were reclaimable. Not wholly lost to a sense of the right, like the idolators who ensnared them, they could be brought to hearken to reproof. Obdurate and stiff-necked as they were, they yet made spasmodic efforts after self-restraint, and occasionally with some success. Indeed, had they not the All-Merciful for their help and guide? He never failed to school the children of His love, and although He had again and again to reprove them through His servant Moses, because of their obstinacy, He never forsook them, nor shut his ear to their cry. Faulty as were His chosen people, He, in His wisdom, must not only have seen in them many redeeming qualities, but also have deemed them fitted to fulfil His gracious purpose. Indeed, the words of Moses, in one of his last addresses to the Israelites, lead infallibly to this conclusion. After exhorting to obedience, and bidding them " utterly destroy the idolatrous nations which were to be delivered into their hands, to burn their graven images, and make no intermarriages", he adds, " For thou art an holy people unto the Lord thy God; He hath chosen thee to be a special people unto Himself. He did not set His love upon you because ye were more in number than any people, for ye were the fewest of all people, but *because the Lord loved you*, and because He would keep His oath which He had sworn to your fathers".* Wholly corrupt or iniquitous they could not possibly have been, thus to have gained God's all-gracious love. But yet more was required of them; they were to be a holy people, thence the moral training, the rude discipline to which they were subjected during their long sojourn in the wilderness. Nor did this schooling fail to accomplish its purpose; indeed, the very hardness and inflexibility which characterised the Israelitish nation became alike a virtue and a shield in succeeding generations, forming an everlasting bulwark to their imperishable faith.

Were it not that the distinguishing traits of obduracy are as repugnant as they are marked, there could be no possible difficulty in detecting them both in ourselves and others,

* Deut. vii, 7.

but if the natural aversion they inspire does not always suffice to make them shunned, it will at all events induce their withdrawal into the darkest recesses of the heart till they can issue forth to the light of day, either so garbed as to escape observation, or so disguised as to pass for virtues! Now, the knowledge that the hateful and repulsive features which characterise obduracy can be thus masked, might well suffice to induce a vigorous inward search, and so whet our sagacity as to enable us to trace to its fount each questionable passion—each sentiment of the mind. But for this purpose it is essential we should learn to know in what obduracy consists; and may we doubt that it consists in a resolute persistence in wrong-doing, or in its mildest form, in a laxity of principle frequently growing into a confirmed habit, or temper of mind? And again, it is characterized by a wilful shutting of the mental eye to the blessings and mercies which are "new every morning", and by lending a too ready ear, on the one hand, to the voice of sensuality, which, making us the slaves of our selfish passions, draws us from our God, and on the other, to the promptings of pride, which tempt us to rebel against the Majesty of Heaven, and set at defiance God's holy law, our reason, and the admonitions of conscience. Indeed, obduracy takes its firmest root in the depraved and unfeeling heart, which, hearkening only to its own vile imaginings, its evil inclinations, and selfish desires, will, without scruple or compunction, seduce others to wrong, thereby darkening their future with sorrow and shame; while it also flourishes in the fertile soil of the stunted and uneducated mind which seeks not, but rather shuns, the light of truth, and resists the force of argument, the teachings of virtue and religion. Now, once impressed with the conviction that obduracy is a wilful deflection of the mind from the paths of justice and righteousness, also a hardening of the heart to moral principles and right feelings, we shall surely never be likely to mistake it for firmness, which is the true friend and stay of every virtue, and therefore itself a virtue. This indeed is a most valuable quality, and the indispensable foundation of all great and good deeds. Born of right principles, it will lead its possessor steadily and tenaciously to resist any deviation therefrom; it will keep him from trimming between God's will and his own inclinations; it will cause him resolutely and courageously to overcome every unruly impulse and temptation, while it will enable him in a noble, lofty, and generous spirit to throw his whole strength of volition into those duties which devolve on him in relation to his fellow man and his Creator.

On proceeding next to consider the cause of obduracy, we find yet further evidence of the dissimilarity and antagonism which exists between it and firmness, or resolution, for which it but too frequently passes current; nay, more, since firmness consists in a resolute resistance to evil, while obduracy is a wilful persistence in sin, it is self-evident that the latter could have no existence if the mind and heart had remained unsullied through the sway of the former. Indeed, we have sown the first seeds of obduracy in our breast when we permit one guilty passion to gain supremacy over principle and duty. It is, therefore, to infirmity of purpose, or want of a resolute will to cope with sin, itself so peculiarly hardening, that we must infallibly trace the primary cause of this signal defect. Nor do its baneful effects stop here, for it engenders a spirit of procrastination which seriously impedes all reform. Though conscience may tell us we are gravitating to ill, and that sin is becoming habitual, we, nevertheless, through its agency, find ourselves ever resolving on amendment, yet never accomplishing it, while becoming more and more callous under this system of self-deceit. Another cause is an insufficient or defective training of the youthful heart. When the loftier impulses are not cultivated, baser passions will assuredly attain luxuriant growth; the greed of gain and abuse of this world's pleasures will warp it from the right, the true, the holy. If lively gratitude to God be not made the predominant sentiment of the mind, softening, refining, and exalting it, unruly desires will enter, and usher in with them temptations; selfish indulgence will quickly follow, the sense of virtue and religion be speedily effaced or banished, and the heart necessarily hardening will finally petrify into obduracy.

How to prevent, check, or cure, so deadly a malady of the soul forms another important matter for consideration. If we will but early implant virtuous principles in the mind, and give to it a fixedness of purpose based on a love of rectitude and a love of God, we shall surely have accomplished our aim; moral firmness in youth utterly precluding obduracy in manhood. But if perchance the foundation of virtue has been shaken, and we have not been altogether proof to the seductions of sense, then must we set ourselves sedulously to the task of uprooting the evil propensities, and checking the distempers thus engendered. And here we must bear in mind that there should be no delay, no deferring to a future day; no one becomes entirely profligate at once. We deviate step by step from the path of virtue, and only by resolutely staying our downward course at an early stage, and directing our thoughts upwards, may we hope to escape from the perilous position in which we have placed ourselves. If, however, unhappily through procrastination or stubbornness we have persisted in wrong doing, to the prejudice of our moral health, and drank freely from the poisoned cup of intoxicating pleasures, let us remember while there be yet time that through God's infinite mercy we may find an antidote in penitence, a cure through contrition and amendment. And truly, what will not sincere repentance effect for us? On each approach to the throne of God in prayer the heart will sensibly soften, so that obduracy will be finally subdued, and we shall turn again with delight to the path marked out in that holy law which He gave for the guidance and the good of His creatures. Heed-ing the soft voice of conscience rather than the logic of vice, which declares—I have done it once with impunity, so I may do it again—we shall resolutely abstain in the future from violating its dictates, though hitherto no ill results may have followed therefrom; indeed, having once strayed from the straight line of virtue, duty and religion, we shall the more sedulously keep in view that heavenly bliss to which they point, and placing our dependence on God, pursue the path of right manfully, hopefully. And here it is essential to remark that there can be no permanent reform without such dependence, coupled as it must ever be with a keen perception of God's glorious attributes. The obduracy which pride and ingratitude engender is indeed only to be subdued and conquered by a sense of our weak and erring nature, by a thorough belief in God's goodness, His Omniscience, His never-failing justice. Let us but see and acknowledge our own weakness, and then shall we feel how great has been God's forbearance; the heart will soften into love at the thought of His goodness, His fostering care, His solicitude for our well-being, and we shall be led to submit cheerfully to that restraint of our passions which He, in his wisdom imposes for the general welfare. Besides, the consciousness that His all-seeing eye is watching over us with fatherly tenderness must further tend to curb all rash presumption, and check us in the commission of evil. But should the thoughts of our own unworthiness, or of God's benign attributes, be powerless to subdue our obduracy and kindle love, then may He in His mercy work on our hearts through the sense of fear. He will possibly force on our minds the conviction that none may wilfully disobey His holy law, or obdurately resist His all-wise decrees without incurring a fearful penalty. Indeed, though slow to anger He yet holds the scales of justice with an equal Hand, and will not suffer the sinner to escape the chastisement due to his misdeeds.

With the object of promoting this salutary conviction, we shall pass in review some few of the numerous ills, mental as well as physical, which are inseparable from a course of vice. Foremost, and possibly not the least distressing to the mind, is the sense of self-abasement; indeed so powerful is this feeling in the yet unhardened heart, that if it be not made to subserve the cause of virtue and reform, it will assuredly enlist on the side of evil, and hurry its ready victim, with ever-increasing celerity, to the brink of moral perdition. Then as sin gains upon us, and headstrong passions obtain ascendancy, we shall find our physical powers and mental faculties impaired; conscience, which cannot always slumber, will at times make its warning voice heard, and rob us even of those fleeting pleasures for which we have toiled and sacrificed so much. Each fresh day, however, given to dissipation will make the appeals of the inward monitor less audible, and bowing under the yoke of sin, the heart will harden, and be drawn further and further from its God. Now, how deplorable is the condition of him who, running counter to the will of the Supreme, has ever to dread the show of His displeasure? Can, indeed, that man know aught of happiness or peace who sets himself in opposition to the will of his Creator? Must he not feel how abortive will be all his plans; how vain and fruitless his desires; how certainly disappointment and misery will attend on his senseless folly and disobedience? Must not the conviction often flash across his mind that any evil committed recoils on the wrong-doer, and that sure retribution awaits him who, taking advantage of the liberty God has given, rebels against His rule, perversely wronging his own nature, and injuring his fellow-mortals.

Let, then, those who make pleasure the business of life—who tamper with vice, and permit the coil of sin to encircle the heart—stop short before "their cup of iniquity is full", and, through a moral reform, a heartfelt repentance, stay the wrath of the Infinitely-Merciful Lord, and avert the dire consequences incidental to the violation of His Laws. Let them set themselves to the stern duty of self-correction before their misconduct and misdeeds call down upon them correction from above. This hopeful step once taken, a happy consummation will assuredly not be far distant. Learning to heed their spiritual interests, and remembering that God has offered heaven as a reward for virtue and piety, they will resolutely reject all such seductive pleasures as render the heart callous and obdurate, while they will gratefully seek and keep steadily in view these guardians of all true honour and peace of mind ; these assured friends to happiness here ; these faithful pioneers to the blessed realms above.

Before considering the PRECEPTS which bear on this subject, we may cull a few Scripture verses which pourtray its chief characteristics, and show in what it consists. Thus does David, in Psalm lxiv, 5, speak of wicked and *obdurate* men, "they encourage themselves in an evil matter ; they commune of laying snares privily ; they say, Who shall see them ; they search out iniquities ; they shoot suddenly at the perfect, and fear not": and again, to like effect, Psalm xxxvi, 4, " the wicked deviseth mischief on his bed, he setteth himself in a way that is not good, he abhorreth not evil, he flattereth himself, and there is no fear of God before his eyes"; and in Psalm x, 4, " The wicked through pride will not seek after God ; he boasteth of his heart's desire, and blesseth the covetous, whom the Lord abhorreth ; his ways are always grievous ; he sayeth in his heart, I shall not be moved, for I shall never be in adversity". Jeremiah is not less forcible in his description of the impenitent and obdurate. Thus he says, in ch. viii, 6, " They spake not aright; no man repented him of his wickedness, saying, What have I done? Every one turned to his course, as the horse rusheth into the battle. They receive not correction ; truth is perished, and is cut off from their mouth". And again, ch. xviii, 12, " They say, There is no hope, and we will walk after our own devices ; we will every one do the imaginings of his evil heart". Isaiah, in ch. xlvii, 10 of his Book, speaks thus of the bold defiance of the obdurate man, " Thou hast trusted in thy wickedness ; thou hast said, None seeth me". Zephaniah also, in figurative language, thus draws attention to the ways of the hardened sinner (chap. iii, 2), " She obeyed not the voice; she received not correction; she trusted not in the Lord; she drew not near to her God". Then Samuel tells us it is " like unto iniquity and idolatry". Solomon makes the obdurate man speak of himself in these terms (Prov. v, 12), " How have I hated instruction, and my heart despiseth reproof; I have not obeyed the voice of my teachers, nor inclined mine ear to them that instructed me; I was almost in all evil". And further, in Job, the obduracy of man is thrown into a clear light in the question put by the Lord (ch. xl, 8), " Wilt thou also disannul My judgment? Wilt thou condemn me that thou mayest be righteous?" Surely this is significant enough; for if God is right, then man, when acting in opposition to His High Will, must be in the wrong, and it is a persistance therein which constitutes obduracy. Proceeding to consider the causes of it, we find them briefly reverted to in the Book of Ezekiel, ch. xvi, where we read, " How *weak is thine heart*, saith the Lord God, seeing thou doest all these things, *and are contrary*". Again, ch. xxxiii, " The people hear Thy words, but they will not do them; for with their mouth they show much love, but *their heart goeth after their covetousness*". And further, with an utter want of reflection and an intense pride, they declare " the way of the Lord is not equal"! Jeremiah thus also elucidates the causes of this dire defect (ch. vi), " Because their ear is contrary they will not hearken; *the word of the Lord is unto them a reproach;* they have no delight in it". Then in the following quotation he traces it to the *habitual* indulgence of sinful pleasures (ch. xiii), " Can the Ethiopian change his skin, or the leopard his spots? then may ye also do good that are accustomed to do evil". One of the causes assigned by Solomon is also worthy of our most attentive consideration (Eccles. viii), *Because sentence against an evil work is not executed speedily*, therefore the heart of the sons of men is fully set in them to do evil". Now, in order to prevent, check, or cure all spirit of obduracy, let us give well-timed reflection to such thoughts as the following verses must necessarily stir up within us (Prov. xvi), "By the fear of the Lord men depart from evil; by mercy and truth iniquity is purged". In Jeremiah, xxiii, " Can any hide himself in secret places that I shall not see him ? Do not I fill heaven and earth ? saith the Lord". And after thus calling to our remembrance God's Omnipresence, he seeks, in Lamentations, to impress us with a sense of His gracious attribute of mercy, thereby inducing a reform in conduct either through the fear or the love of God. Thus we read, chap. iii, " God doth not afflict willingly, nor grieve the children of men; He will have compassion according to the multitude of His mercies". Again in Ezekiel xxxiii, the Lord God hath no pleasure in the death of the wicked, but that the wicked turn from his evil way and live". A consideration of the following verses can hardly be less serviceable. We find in Job xxxiii, "Why dost thou strive against God, for He giveth not account of any of His matters"; and in chap. xxxi, " Doth not God see my ways, and count all my steps". Also in the Book of Proverbs, xv, *" The eyes of the Lord are in every place, beholding the evil and the good"*. Then again in Psalm xxxiv, "The Lord is nigh unto them that are of a broken heart, and *saveth such as be of a contrite spirit"*. Now, surely such reflections as these might well induce the obdurate man to throw off his load of sin by seeking God in prayer, and in a spirit of deep humility declare, in the words of the good King David, Psalm xix, "Keep back thy servant from presumptuous sins, let them not have dominion over me, then shall I be upright, and shall be innocent from the great transgression". Further, he will resolutely shun all evil companionship, and utter the words of that pious monarch, Psalm cxix, 115, " Depart from me, ye evil-doers, for I will keep the commandments of my God"; and in the like sentiments ejaculate with him, Psalm xxxviii, " I will declare mine iniquity ; I will be sorry for my sin". This will enable the penitent man implicitly to follow the injunctions of Samuel to " fear the Lord, and serve Him in truth, obey His voice, and rebel not against the commandment of the Lord". But if this teaching be not heeded, then will most surely follow the sad consequences of which Scripture so emphatically forewarns us, as we read in Isaiah lvii, " The wicked are like the troubled sea, when it cannot rest, whose waters cast up mire and dirt. There is no peace, saith the Lord, to the wicked". And in Proverbs v, " His own iniquities shall take the wicked himself, and he shall be holden with the cords of his sins". Then in Psalm xxxiv, " The face of the Lord is against them that do evil, to cut off the remembrance of them from the earth". Also Isaiah declares, chap. iii, " Woe unto him that striveth with his Maker ! Woe unto the wicked, it shall be ill with him ; the show of their countenance doth witness against them ; woe unto their soul, for they have rewarded evil unto themselves". And this is corroborated in Psalm cvii, " They sit in darkness and in the shadow of death, bound in affliction, because they rebelled against the word of God, and contemned the counsel of the Most High". And again, " Fools because of their transgressions, and because of their iniquities are afflicted". Then in Job iv, " Thus I have seen, they that sow iniquity reap the same". He further tells us, chap. ix, " If I be wicked, why then labour I *in vain*". Again in Proverbs we read, chap. xxviii, " He that covereth his sins shall not prosper", corroborated by the words of Zechariah, Chron. xxiv, " Why transgress ye the commandments of the Lord *that ye cannot prosper?* because ye have forsaken the Lord He hath also forsaken you". Such considerations might well suffice to induce a reform, but further severe penalties are attached to obduracy or persistency in wrong-doing; for do we not read in Prov. xxix, "He that being often reproved hardeneth his neck, shall suddenly be destroyed, and that without remedy". Again, chap. xi, "As righteousness tendeth to life, so *he that pursueth evil pursueth it to his own death*". And finally, to the same effect, we read in Ezekiel xviii, "The soul that sinneth it shall die; but if a man do that which is lawful and right, walketh in God's statutes, and keepeth His judgments to deal truly, he is just, he shall surely live (the life everlasting), saith the Lord God".

EXAMPLES.—The later portion of the history of the ISRAELITES now to be considered, and which commences with Joshua and the Judges, offers many a strong contrast with that which preceded it, yet none is more striking than their improved moral condition. Their wanderings, extending over a lengthened period and accompanied with much suffering and many privations, had been prolific of good, as trials proceeding from All Mighty Goodness should ever be. Not only had the national character gradually improved under reproof and chastisement, but, further, the rising generation had wisely profited by the errors and misconduct of their fathers, and taken salutary warning from the examples afforded by the backsliding propensities of their benighted parents. For undoubted evidence of this we have only to turn to the Book of Joshua. Throughout its pages no single instance of idolatrous worship is recounted, nor one trait of that obduracy which in the past had been so prominent a feature in the conduct of the entire people; indeed, rebellion and contumacy had become most hateful to them, and was made punishable with death. In its place, however, happily figured its counterpart, firmness of will ever displaying itself in a staunch adherence to the right. Thus schooled, thus tempered, this defect of character had not only become a powerful auxiliary to virtue, but had actually grown into a virtue itself. Here, then, we have a people whom God deemed fitted to enter into, inherit, and enjoy the good land of promise, the land for which they did not labour, cities to dwell in which they did not build, vineyards and oliveyards from which they might eat but planted not. They could appreciate the rich blessings vouchsafed by the Lord in a grateful spirit, and partake of his bounty without in any way abusing it. Not to them, as to their stiff-necked fathers, could apply the words of Moses, "Jeshurun waxed fat and kicked".* They repaid not God's benefits with rebellion, but with gratitude, and during "all the days of Joshua and all the days of the elders that outlived Joshua, they served the Lord".

In the next book, that of Judges, the history of Israel again enters into one of its darker phases. With the new generation a great change for the worse occurred. Their fathers, though serving the Lord with all their hearts, had overlooked or disregarded one important part of the commandment given by God through his servant Moses. Although they had themselves kept "the statutes and judgments of the Lord", they did not "teach them diligently unto their children and to their sons' sons".† For proof of this we have only to refer to the Book of Judges itself, where we read, "When Joshua and all that generation were gathered unto their fathers there arose another generation after them *which knew not the Lord* nor yet the work which He had done in Israel"!. Now, had the children been imbued with the spirit of their sublime religion as were their fathers, they would doubtless have kept firm to their God, and thus resisted the attractions and temptations which were paraded before them by the idolatrous nations in their vicinity. They would have especially avoided all intermarriages as contaminating, and shunned the profane rites and licentious practices of their pagan neighbours as utterly re-

* Deut. xxxii, 15.   † Deut. vi, 7.   ‡ Judges ii, 10.

pugnant to all sense of the pure and holy. Sad and fatal
error indeed on the part of the parents was this omission of
duty! Their neglect of one of the fundamental principles
of the Mosaic code was indeed rife with evil consequences to
their progeny, and to it must we in a great measure attribute their early fall into idolatry, with the subsequent re-
lapses of each new generation throughout the whole rule of
the Judges, lasting some three hundred years, as also their
successive conflicts with surrounding nations, their many
calamities and trials. And assuredly it would hardly be
possible that a people who had never been taught either to
love or fear God, who had never been led to feel how closely
blended were mercy and justice in His All-Wise Dispensations, could altogether resist the contaminating influence
and example of idolatrous neighbours. But though they
succumbed before the temptations held out to them, and forsook God and the right path, they were brought speedily
back to the Lord and His Holy Worship on being subjected
to chastisement or even reproof. Indeed, those generations,
criminal though they were at times, never displayed the in-
veterate obduracy which had characterised their progenitors;
and when we consider that they had not, like them, been
witnesses of God's miraculous workings, or been made sensible of his immediate presence through ocular demonstration,
we must clearly see that a decided improvement in the national character had taken place. Knowing much less of
the All-Merciful, they were nevertheless far more easily
brought to bow down humbly before Him and conform to
His gracious will. Instances of this, as of the heartfelt repentance of the people, were rife under the rule of those
noble patriots and national deliverers who figured in their
history as judges. One only of the numerous examples can
be here adduced, and this is found in chap. x of the Book of
Judges. The Israelites had subjected themselves to the displeasure of the Lord, who "sold them into the hands of the
Philistines", and in their sore distress they called unto the

Lord, saying, verse 18, " We have sinned against Thee, both because we have forsaken our God and also served Baalim". The Lord, however, hearkened not unto them at this first sign of repentance, but spake thus, " Go cry unto the gods which ye have chosen; let them deliver you in the time of your tribulation". This answer from on High made them yet more sensible of their past blindness and wilfulness of conduct, thence in all humility they thus again besought the Lord, verse 13, " We have sinned; do Thou unto us whatsoever seemeth Thee good; deliver us only, we pray Thee, this day. And they put away the strange gods from among them and served the Lord". What followed ? No sooner did they thus give practical proof of their sincere repentance than " God was grieved for the misery of Israel", and gave them a deliverer in the person of Jephthah. Though in this manner they frequently offended, nevertheless they were again and again saved through repentance and through God's infinite mercy and goodness.

We may now, however, turn not only to a brighter, but even a bright era in the history of the Israelites. The alternations which lasted throughout the whole period of the Judges had not been profitless; indeed, during their long rule the higher and nobler qualities of the entire people were in course of development, and when it drew to its close the national character was altogether less faulty, even giving promise of future moral excellence. Of this we have ample proof in the last of the judgeships, that of Samuel. Only once while he held sway did the Israelites lapse into idolatry, and then a single remonstrance from that exemplary ruler sufficed to bring them back repentant to their God. They had indeed become less prone to indulge in idolatrous worship, and, further, had lost much of that obduracy which had hitherto characterised their proceedings. Nevertheless, the national failing had not unhappily become entirely extinct, as the following incident but too clearly proves. Through the misrule of Samuel's sons, " who walked not after his ways, but turned aside after lucre, took bribes and perverted judgment", the Israelites had become weary of their judges, and thence sought occasion to urge him to institute a monarchical form of government. This demand for a king gave that good old judge great displeasure, yet as the elders who appealed to him showed no disposition to yield to his views, he sought counsel of the Lord, and was thus answered, " Hearken unto the voice of the people in all they say unto you, for they have not rejected thee, but they have rejected me, that I should not reign over them, howbeit, yet protest solemnly unto them and show them the manner of the king that shall reign over them". Surely such words, coming from the Supreme Ruler of heaven and earth, might well have stayed them in their rash importunities; but neither this consideration nor the gloomy predictions of their able seer could deter them from following the bent of their inclinations. What cared they in their stubbornness and self-will for the prophecy, "Ye shall cry out on that day because of your king which ye shall have chosen, and the Lord will not hear you in that day". Heedless of after consequences, they refused to obey the voice of the Lord, and said, " Nay, but we will have a king over us, that we also may be like the other nations".

Now, wilful as was such conduct, it formed a solitary exception; indeed, throughout the reign of Saul, whom Samuel presented to them for their King, as also during that of David, who succeeded him on the throne, and likewise in the early part of the reign of his son Solomon, not even one instance of obduracy or defection stands recorded. Truly, these were palmy days for the Israelites, and this the brightest era in their history. The national character had gradually attained a high standard of moral excellence, the entire people had learnt to love their Heavenly Father, and yield glad obedience to His Supreme Will. To extol His name in the sublime psalms of David, to chant His praises,

* 1 Samuel viii, 7.

and sedulously observe His holy precepts, became with them a sacred and pure delight. Faithfully did they adhere to the true worship, and even abstained from all communication with their idolatrous neighbours till the dire moment when, alas! Solomon, their King, impiously disregarding the injunction of the Lord, sought out strange wives from among the heathens, and "clung to them in love", so that he inclined his ear to their evil promptings. Then fell that fatal blight upon the Israelites of which they had been forewarned by Samuel, and though during the reign of some of their good kings its evil influence was sensibly lessened, it was never entirely dissipated, but finally gained such intensity as at times to deaden the heart of the nation, and depress their moral condition to nearly as low an ebb as that of their depraved and sinful neighbours. Indeed, their subsequent history is again of the darkest hue, and the incalculable evils foretold by the venerable Seer came thick upon them. They suffered intolerable burdens under many ruthless kings, and in no case was the condition of the people more pitiable than just before and after the accession of Solomon's vile son, Rehoboam. The words of the king himself amply testify to this, for when his oppressed subjects, desirous to obtain some alleviation of their "grievous yoke", remonstrated with him, he answered them thus, "My father made your yoke heavy, and I will add to your yoke; my father also chastised you with whips, but I will chastise you with scorpions"!* Previously accustomed to the mild sway of Saul and David, such tyranny and oppression could not be long endured, thence arose rebellion, speedily followed by the partition of the kingdom, ten tribes revolting and nominating a second king in the person of Jeroboam. This monarch having no temple in his new capital, and therefore fearing his subjects would forsake him, and "return to the house of David", so that they might again "sacrifice to the Lord in Jerusalem", set up two calves of

* 1 Kings xii, 14.

gold, and bade his people bow down and burn incense unto them. Thus, through the evil counsel of their king, idolatry once more polluted the land, and this time for a long continuance, while from this cause we may also trace the permanent severance of the nation. The only holy tie sundered, dissension, with civil war, quickly followed, and, exhausting alike both parties, rendered them an easy prey to their many powerful neighbours now that the Lord of Hosts was no longer in their midst. But even defeats and other calamities did not always bring them to repentance, and though on the accession of their few good kings they showed some compunction and a desire to reform, no sooner did a wicked monarch take possession of the throne than the whole people returned to their evil courses. Idolatry had, indeed, hardened their hearts, and rendered them as obdurate as they were criminal. Numerable proofs of this are manifested throughout the writings of the prophets which furnish us with the last portion of the history of the Israelites, a period no less sad than eventful. The All-gracious, though greatly angered by the obstinate persistence of His chosen servants in rejecting Him, the King of kings, for an earthly monarch and idol worship, still befriended them, and with the object of checking His people in their wilful practices, sent His prophets to them with promises of a bright and happy future would they reform their ways, whilst holding out threats and denunciations should they stubbornly persist in their evil doings. Unhappily all the efforts of these brave spirits proved of no avail; though with undaunted courage they exhorted and admonished, though they upbraided the people for their shameless impenitence, and boldly lifted up their voices and testified against that vice and corruption which had found an abode even within the walls of the palace, they were baffled by the obduracy and wickedness of the reigning monarchs, who held absolute sway over their subjects, and seduced them from the paths of virtue. Thus, though many a "physician in Gilead" dispensed balsams of wondrous efficacy, the moral leprosy still remained unhealed; although the prophets were gifted with all the eloquence of truth, though fired by the keenest solicitude for the well-being of the nation, their words were powerless to work any permanent change in the hearts of corrupt kings and a hardened people; obduracy ever stood as an impassable barrier between them. Yet how sedulously these prophets of the Lord sought to impress the entire nation with a sense of God's goodness and justice, how earnestly they strove to bring the people to repentance and reformation may best be judged by some few extracts from their several writings.

To these books, then, in conclusion, let us turn. Firstly. Isaiah distinctly told them that "The Lord's hand is not shortened that it cannot save, neither his ear heavy that it cannot hear, but *your iniquities have separated you and your God*, and your sins have hid His face from you".* He pointed out to them their wrong-doings in the following words, "The earth is defiled because *thou hast transgressed the law, and broken the everlasting covenant*"; and further added, in the name of the Lord, "put away the evil of your doings from before mine eyes, cease to do evil, learn to do well, be willing and obedient". Secondly, The Lord spoke thus through the mouth of Jeremiah, "Turn, O backsliding children, and I will give you pastors according to mine heart, which shall feed you with knowledge and understanding; O Jerusalem, wash thine heart from wickedness that thou mayest be saved. How long shall thy vain thoughts lodge within thee."† He also alludes thus to their stiff-neckedness, "This people hath a *revolting and a rebellious heart*, neither say they in their heart, let us now fear the Lord our God".‡ "They spake not aright, no man repented him of his wickedness, saying, What have I done? They have rejected the word of the Lord, and what wisdom is in them?"§ Even "the priests said not, Where is the Lord?

* Isaiah lix, 1. † Ch. iii, 15; Ch. viii, 6.
‡ Jer. v, 23. § Ch. viii, 6.

the pastors also transgressed, the prophets prophesied by Baal, and walked after things that do not profit". He then forewarns them, in these terms, "Thine own wickedness shall correct thee, and thy backslidings shall reprove thee; know therefore, and see that it is an evil thing and bitter, that thou hast forsaken the Lord".* Thirdly, God's goodness is shown in the commission He thus gave the prophet Ezekiel, " I, the Lord, do send thee unto them, and whether they will hear, or whether they will forbear (for they are a rebellious house) yet shall they know that there hath been a prophet among them".† But the Omniscient was fully aware of their perverseness, for we read, " But the house of Israel will not hearken unto thee, for they will not hearken unto me; they are impudent and hard-hearted".‡ The righteous Lord then admonishes and remonstrates with them thus, "Ye say the way of the Lord is not equal. Hear, now, O house of Israel, is not my way equal? are not your ways unequal? Therefore, I will judge you, every one according to his ways. Repent and turn from all your transgressions, so iniquity shall not be your ruin".§ Fourthly, Hosea makes manifest the sinfulness of the people, and exhorted them to repentance in the following verses, " Hear the word of the Lord, ye children of Israel, for the Lord hath a controversy with the inhabitants of the land, because there is no truth, nor mercy, nor knowledge of God in the land. O Israel, return unto the Lord thy God, for thou hast fallen by thine iniquity; take with you words, and turn to the Lord".∥ He then reproves them in the name of the Supreme, "They consider not in their hearts that I remember all their wickedness, now their own doings have beset them about. Woe unto them, for they have fled from me, destruction unto them because they have transgressed against me. They have not cried unto me with their hearts, though I have strengthened their arms, yet do they imagine

---

* Ch. ii, 19.   † Ch. ii, 4.   ‡ Ch. iii, 7.
§ Ch. xviii, 25.   ∥ Ch. iv, 1; xiv, 1.

mischief against me; they have sown the wind, and shall reap the whirlwind".* Fifthly, Zephaniah thus figuratively shows the Israelites how grievously they had sinned, " Woe to her that is polluted, she obeyed not the voice, she received not correction, she trusted not in the Lord, she drew not near to her God, her prophets are light and treacherous, her priests have polluted the sanctuary, they have done violence to the law; the just Lord is in the midst thereof; every morning doth He bring His judgments to light, He faileth not. Though He punished them they rose early and corrupted all their doings".† He then exhorts them to repentance, saying, Seek ye the Lord before the decree goeth forth; seek righteousness, seek meekness, it may be ye shall be hid in the day of the Lord's anger". Sixthly, Zechariah, addressing the people after the captivity, urges them in the name of the Lord to reform, and shows their past stiff-neckedness with its final result thus, "I, the Lord of Hosts, say unto thee, Execute true judgment, show mercy and compassion, oppress not the widow, nor the stranger, nor the poor, and let none of you imagine evil against his brother. But they refused to attend, yea, they made their hearts like an adamant stone, lest they should hear the law, therefore came a great wrath from the Lord of Hosts. Thus it is come to pass that as he (the prophet) cried, and they would not hear, so they cried, I, the Lord, would not hear, but scattered them with a whirlwind among all the nations whom they know not, and the land was desolate after them".‡ Now, the captivity here alluded to occurred in the reign of Zedekiah (who was the last of a line of kings which had extended over a period of about four centuries and a half), and this sad episode in Israel's history is yet more fully enlarged on in the last chapter of the Book of Chronicles. Therein God's loving mercy, the king's obduracy, and the people's stiff-neckedness, is clearly demonstrated as follows, "And Zedekiah did that which was evil

* Chap. vii, 2.   † Chap. iii, 1.   ‡ Chap. vii, 9.

in the sight of the Lord, and humbled not himself before Jeremiah, the prophet, speaking from the mouth of the Lord, and he also rebelled against King Nebuchadnezzar *who had made him swear by God*, but he hardened his heart from turning to the Lord God of Israel. Moreover, all the chiefs of the priests, and the people, transgressed very much after all the abominations of the heathen, and polluted the house of the Eternal which he had hallowed in Jerusalem. And the God of their fathers sent to them because He had compassion on His people, but they mocked the messengers of God and despised His words, and ill-treated his prophets, until the wrath of the Lord arose against His people, and *there was no remedy*". Then came their great calamity, their signal chastisement. Nebuchadnezzar besieged the famine-stricken city of Jerusalem till it was destroyed; the king was made prisoner, and afterwards cruelly tortured; the nobles and the people, old and young, were put to the sword or taken captive, the treasures of the house of the Lord, and of all the kingdom, were appropriated; finally, the temple and palaces were burnt, and the walls of the city broken down.

Thus did God's attributes of long-enduring mercy and fatherly tenderness finally yield before His no less fixed and certain attribute of strict justice. For three-score and ten years had the Israelites to drink from the cup of God's wrath, and in a long, sorrowful, and ignominious captivity expiate their past criminality, their perverseness, and *obduracy*.

TEMPER.

Numbers xx, 10, "*Must we fetch you water out of this rock.*"

DID not Scripture inform us parenthetically that MOSES was the "meekest of men", we yet could not possibly fail to arrive at this conclusion after an attentive perusal of his history. Truly, his was no ordinary career, and when we note the varied trying incidents which rapidly succeeded each other during the last forty years of his life, the untoward circumstances against which, almost single-handed, he had to contend, the hardships and perils by which he was beset, the constant pressure from a rebellious people, and even unjustifiable provocation from members of his own immediate family, we must rather marvel at his equanimity, his evenness of disposition, his mild and generous forbearance, than wonder at his having been betrayed on three separate occasions, and this at distant intervals, into a display of animosity and ill-temper. Indeed, if we further consider that he had been brought up in a school altogether unfavourable to the culture of the gentler and more amiable qualities of the heart, it is impossible not to feel greatly surprised that mildness should have formed so marked a trait in his character during the latter years of his life. Now, if knowing how cruelly his countrymen were afflicted, his heart had yet remained soft and impassive, proving that the luxurious, not to say voluptuous, life he led in youth within the precincts of a palace, had subdued rather than inflamed his passions, then would this mildness of disposition appear in a far less estimable light; but an incident which occurred at this precise period proves it to have been just the reverse, and that feeling and passion were strong within him, needing only the occasion to call them into vigorous action.

Moses was forty years of age when he "slew the Egyptian" whom he found "smiting an Hebrew, one of his brethren". Now, although this highly reprehensible deed was evidently perpetrated on the impulse of the moment, yet assuredly it would never have been committed had not the sufferings of his oppressed brethren long excited his keenest sympathy. Often must his heart have bled at the thought of their cruel treatment and of his utter inability, even partially, to alleviate their pitiful condition. Yearning to succour and relieve those who were smarting under the lash, a feeling, firstly of ill-will and then of rancour, must have been engendered towards the relentless Egyptian taskmasters. And these angry emotions once generated in the breast, how fatal their spell! When, indeed, do unfriendly or hostile thoughts fail to translate themselves into action on the slightest provocation, and work incalculable evil to him who entertains them? Assuredly never; and though the act of avenging an injured brother was unpremeditated, though it was a passing impulse, dictated by an almost irresistible burst of natural indignation on the part of Moses, he had raised his hand against a fellow-mortal, and was justly doomed to pay the penalty of a long, trying exile, for violence and wrong-doing. Thus we read, "Now when Pharaoh heard this thing, he sought to slay Moses, but Moses fled and dwelt in the land of Midian".* Here was indeed a change. He who had hitherto basked in the sunshine of a palace, knowing naught but ease and luxury, had to submit to privations and endure those toils and hardships which were inseparable from a shepherd's life. Yet, apparently sad as was this change, it was nevertheless fraught with the happiest results, and indeed but for the many trials and sufferings Moses experienced during his forty years' residence in the desert land of Midian, his numberless ex-

* Exodus ii, 15.

cellent qualities and virtues would probably never have attained their full expansion. He made that long term of probation subserve to a course of self-discipline and that moral training which is so essential to the formation of an exalted and *model* character. We have to contend before we can conquer, and Moses, while nobly contending with the hardships and braving the perils of the outer world, thereby acquiring that fortitude, that sagacity, that foresight, that indomitable persistence which afterwards so greatly distinguished him, must also have nobly triumphed over the fiery spirit within. Indeed, his wonderful aptitude in marshalling the invaluable qualities of his mind and heart at critical junctures was only surpassed by his marvellous power of self-control, an auxiliary which pre-eminently qualified him for the important mission which he was afterwards called on to discharge. It assuredly was this command of temper, this almost perfect moral self-government, which made him equal to every emergency, as it was doubtless this also that inspired both a mighty potentate and a rebellious people with mingled feeling of respect and fear. Now, when we consider that Moses had to humble the proud and hardened King of Egypt step by step, and that he had to avoid any rashness or precipitancy, lest such might defeat his purpose, we shall feel that no small degree of self-control must have been needed. The ever-renewing obduracy of Pharaoh, in spite of the miracles wrought and the successive appeals made to him in the name of the Most High, might well have irritated Moses; nevertheless he retained perfect command over himself, and simply exhorted the monarch in these terms, "Let not Pharaoh deal deceitfully any more in not letting the people go to sacrifice to the Lord".* Nor do we find any exhibition of temper when, on a like occasion, he was driven ignominiously from the palace. He again and again returned to the charge, and only desisted when Pharaoh, becoming desperate, addressed

* Exodus viii, 29.

him thus : "Get thee from me, take heed to thyself, see my face no more, for in that day thou seest my face thou shalt die".* This decided Moses, who felt such to be the final answer to his past fruitless appeals, and therefore responded, " Thou hast spoken well, I will see thy face again no more".

It was not, however, till after the deliverance of the Israelites from Egypt that the temper of their Leader was most sorely tried. He then had to contend single-handed with the wilfulness and obduracy of a whole community, and to strive with a slavish and benighted people who " were discontented because of the way". Rebellion followed on rebellion, and yet in almost every instance he succeeded in disarming and quieting the most seditious of his followers, thus restoring peace within the camp. On one occasion the people were well " nigh to stone him"; on another, they prepared to choose a captain who should conduct them back to Egypt; nor was this all, pestilence, famine, destroying fire, war, and other disasters, came thick upon them, and Moses had to abide their angry murmurings ; but, after meekly bearing their reproaches, he each time calmly but resolutely recalled them to a sense of God's presence and their own duty. Justly to estimate the force of this great Leader's character and his wonderful power of self-mastery, we should review the several rebellions, and mark how he was generally singled out for vituperation and overt acts of hatred. It will, however, here suffice to cite one instance from many bearing the same imprint and tending to the same conclusion. Korah and his associates, in their pride of heart, "rose up before Moses", and in a rebel spirit thus upbraided him and Aaron, " Ye take too much upon ye, seeing all the congregation are holy and the Lord is among them, wherefore lift ye up yourselves above us ?"† Such an unjust accusation might well have excited the ire of their chief, and induced him to take the law into his own hands; instead

---

* Chap. x, 28. † Numbers xvi, 3.

of which, with characteristic meekness, he simply appealed to the entire body of the people as to his past conduct, and in order to curb their presumption and check the disaffected spirit which, should it spread, must undermine all temporal and spiritual authority, he sought the Lord, and thus entreated Him, "Respect thou not their offerings". This, then, was all the punishment he invoked on the highly culpable offenders; and possibly his generous forbearance might have prompted him to be yet more lenient, but that he felt they had proved themselves utterly unworthy of fulfilling the sacred office of ministering unto the Lord. The severity of the chastisement which the Omniscient afterwards decreed and inflicted with His All-Merciful Hand proves still more forcibly the forgiving spirit of this meek-tempered, angel-like man.

We have now, however, to cite two instances wherein Moses openly gave vent to ebullitions of wrath, yet even here, trying as were the circumstances which provoked such exhibitions of temper, his hot anger speedily passed away, leaving not one trace behind. The first occasion was when he threw down the two tables of stone, so that they broke at the foot of Mount Sinai. Nearing the camp, after only forty days' absence, greatly to his horror and dismay, he beheld his people following the vile and criminal practices of their idolatrous neighbours. At the sight of this utter dereliction of his spiritual teachings, involving as it did a total forgetfulness of what was due to their All-Gracious Protector, the natural impetuosity of his nature manifested itself. Wrath and indignation momentarily gained entire supremacy, and in a fit of uncontrollable passion, he cast from his hands the tables which had been entrusted to him from on High. However, no unkindly sentiment towards his followers could long dwell within his breast, and his just ire once passed, he generously sought to avert the evils consequent on their crime, and further endeavoured to lead them to repentance. This incident occurred at quite an early period of their wanderings; but the second, to which we would now briefly refer, took place when they were approaching the final stage of their journeyings. Notwithstanding the ever-renewing proofs of God's gracious Protection, the Israelites remained stiff-necked, and the frustration of their hopes or sensual desires ever produced much discontent in the camp, and too frequently roused a spirit of insubordination against their noble Leader. Thus it was at the waters of Merabah, for we read, "The people chode with Moses".* Again and again had their chief been obliged to rebuke them for seditious murmurings, and yet, in this instance as in every other, he sought the alleviation of their physical sufferings, as well as his own distress of mind, by humbling himself in supplication before the throne of Mercy. But alas! on this occasion his prayer failed to accomplish both purposes. Though it enabled him to relieve the physical wants of his people, it sufficed not to calm his own perturbed spirit. Their unceasing revolts had evidently irritated him beyond endurance, and provoked by the menacing attitude of the people, he angrily exclaimed (in the words of the text), "Hear now, ye rebels, must we fetch you water out of this rock"—and then, losing all self-control, struck the rock *twice,* instead of merely speaking to it, as the Lord had commanded. Here, then, at the close of a long and trying career, did the faithful servant of the Most High act for the first time in direct violation of the Divine Will! Sad as is this exceptional instance of temper triumphing over principle, we must glory in the thought that on many hardly less trying occasions Moses had been able to restrain the rising gusts of passion, and labour calmly on in the oft rugged path of duty, fulfilling in a humble and meek spirit the honourable, though onerous, post assigned him by Providence. Truly the Great Teacher offers us a lesson in self-control, alike in his one failure and his many triumphs.

* Numbers xx, 3.

It may be well next to consider how it was that Moses, who had been so impetuous and hot-tempered in youth, should have become under apparently adverse circumstances so mild in authority, so meek and generously forbearing under provocation, since such a review cannot fail to furnish much useful instruction. Now, if we reflect how surely selfish ambition and pride of heart conduce to ill-temper, how piety and philanthropy stand directly opposed to it, a brief review of the latter incidents in the career of this champion of Israel will enable us to find the clue we need. As regards ambition, the acts of Moses throughout the whole of his long and chequered life betrayed not the faintest indication thereof, except indeed when it would surely redound to the general welfare, while many instances occurred wherein he resolutely rejected honours and advantages, and on more than one occasion did he, of his own freewill, share with others those to which he alone was justly entitled. This complete absence of all selfish ambition meets with the clearest demonstration at the very outset of his mission, for when God, angered by the stiffneckedness of the Israelites, thus addressed Moses, "Let me alone, that I may destroy them and blot out their name from under heaven, *and I will make of thee a nation mightier and greater than they*",[*] he not only declined the promised honour, but, hoping to save the sinful people from the consequences of their crimes, he fasted for many days and humbly supplicated the Lord to take them once more into favour. Again, on the mere suggestion of his father-in-law, he ceded a portion of his authority to the seventy elders, whilst we also find him entreating the Lord to " make Aaron the leader" instead of himself, and his disinterestedness is hardly less discernible in his total disregard of ties of kindred when such might interfere with the general good. He sought no preferment for his immediate family, neither did he strive to prolong his dynasty through his sons. But if he had no selfish ambition, so also no trace

---

[*] Deut. ix, 19.

of self-glory was discernible; indeed, his answer to Joshua, who in his youthful zeal entreated Moses to forbid Eldad to prophesy, clearly demonstrates the total absence of all pride or selfish considerations. Here are his noble and philanthropic words, "Enviest thou for my sake ? O, would God that all my people were prophets and that the Lord would put his spirit upon them!"* He would have had all the people wise; he would have had them understand God's holy Law, and thence attain a true knowledge of the Supreme. Next, as to prayer, we need only peruse his many exquisite productions to be convinced that it was his ever present refuge and delight. What humility, what heartfelt earnestness, pervades the whole of his beautiful 90th Psalm; what grateful adoration tunes his sublime song of deliverance, and in what exalted strains does he ascribe greatness unto God, and hymn forth his love of human kind in that last song which welled up spontaneously from the deep recesses of his heart prior to his departure for Mount Nabo, his final resting place!† Then how exquisitely simple and touching is the supplication for his erring sister, "Heal her now, O God, I beseech thee";‡ and would we have proofs of his humble and entire dependence on God, then we may find them in such a prayer as this, "If thy presence go not with me, carry us not up hence".§ Finally, philanthropy runs like a golden thread through all his acts. It shows itself in his numerous supplications to God for his erring people, culminating in an unexampled act of self-abnegation, since he even entreated the Lord, "Blot me, I pray thee, out of thy Book which thou hast written".‖ Thus being devoid of all selfish ambition, his interests never clashed with that of others, but generally became identical through the love and goodwill he bore his fellow men. Nought, therefore, remained to excite his mind or sour his temper but that spirit of discontent and repining which ever hovered over the camp, and this con-

---

* Numbers xi, 29. † Deut. xxxii. ‡ Numbers xii, 13.
§ Exodus xxxiii, 15. ‖ Exodus xxxii, 32.

taminating influence he successfully baffled through prayer. Now, well would it have been had his piety also enabled him to curb the impetuosity of his nature at the Waters of Meribah, but here human infirmity triumphed, and in one moment of rash impulse he brought on himself the mild displeasure of the Supreme, and wrecked his earthly hopes.

Following the thread of this sad incident, another practical lesson, sublime in its teaching, may be adduced from the calm submission, the holy spirit of resignation, with which the inspired prophet bowed before the decree of the Most High. Moses well knew he had greatly erred, and was content to pay the penalty of his misdeed. Thus without the faintest murmur did he relinquish the wishes nearest his heart, because such was the will of Infinite Goodness. He prayed for remission of the sentence, but on such being denied, he prepared at once with the most perfect equanimity to quit the scene of his labours. To the exalted piety and supreme faith he displayed in each succeeding act we do not here allude, since they will receive our attention when treating on the next subject. Thus much only we have to add, that on the subsidence of this rash and impulsive fit of momentary passion, the same holy temper of mind, which during nearly forty long and trying years had but this once failed to influence his conduct, again displayed itself, and held, if possible, yet more firmly its wonted ascendancy. The spiritual in his nature had indeed gained complete supremacy, and this *meek* "man of God", in a frame of mind moulded by the sublimest faith, cast aside all worldly hopes, and calmly, resignedly, and in perfect trust departed for the home where awaited him an eternal rest, a blessed immortality.

Temper is the practical expression of the inward disposition of the heart, and ever takes its bent from emotions and passions working therein. Thus considered simply as an effect, in contradistinction to innate temperament, our first object will naturally be to discover each latent cause, and, further, ascertain the character, the influence, and the relative strength of each prime moving power. But for this purpose we must regard it in two very distinct lights, and as these open before us, we shall hardly fail to observe that good temper is the embodiment of lofty and kindly emotions, while ill temper arises from the indulgence of ignoble and slavish passions. To these two extremes, then, will we now direct our attention, commencing, however, with the latter, since the former is necessarily excluded from the breast where this holds sway. Indeed, such is their antagonism that we must entirely eradicate the one, all dark and forbidding, before a single bright and cheering ray of the other can find admittance.

Now, among the desires and passions which will most surely breed ill-temper, and strike at the very root of all that is amiable and kindly in the disposition, we may class, firstly, covetousness; and dark indeed is the shadow it will throw over the mind. Truly, insatiate desires and selfish longings ever carry in their train anxious care and disappointments, while the lust of wealth and power will as surely engender an envious and discontented spirit. Now, there is not one of these defects but will goad the mind beyond endurance, and help to produce an irritability and acerbity of temper. Mundane objects viewed through such distorted mediums lose their due proportions and are over-prized; thence we become greedy in their attainment, and another's success, or our own failure therein, will consequently suffice to rouse the most vindictive feelings. We shall smart and brood under a sense of injury or imaginary wrongs till the heart hardens, and all kindly sympathy for our fellow-creatures is extinguished. Nor will the gratification of this restless craving restore a proper temper of mind. Avarice has no bounds; it knows no defined limits, and all encroachment on the coveted path of fortune will most certainly rouse wrathful feelings. Truly inordinate desires are totally incompatible with kindliness of disposition, or a sweet and gentle temper.

Secondly, we have to consider pride, which is assuredly a great fomenter of ill-temper; indeed, the proud, vain man is ever opening for himself new sources of disquietude—new springs of jealousy and hatred. He stands upon his dignity, and all are deemed offenders who overlook his humour, or disregard his slightest wishes. His heart being elated with a presumptuous self-love and self-sufficiency, any opposition necessarily stings him to the quick. The most trifling provocation rouses a tempest of angry passions. He is ever prone to look with an evil eye on all who differ with him, while his vanity frequently leads him to repel advances and kindly sympathy. But pride not only sours the temper of him who is unhappily under its influence, it also generally arouses bitterness of feeling in those who are forced to crouch humbly before it. Pride indeed engenders pride; and few can with perfect equanimity see their own shining light overpowered or extinguished by the superior lustre of another. Truly pride seldom fails to foster ill-humour and spleen alike in its shallow-minded victim, and in those who move within his orbit. Now, among the several causes of ill-temper we might further note idleness, jealousy, and religious indifference, but we pass to their opposites, since they will not only tranquillise the mind even under the most unfavourable circumstances, but oftentimes chase away ill-temper, and allay irate and vindictive feelings. Only a few words, however, are here necessary as regards industry and benevolence, since these subjects have been treated on previously. Suffice it to say, a useful activity of brain and heart for the benefit both of ourselves and others will ever be found productive of cheerfulness and good temper. The mind that is profitably engaged will have no leisure to brood over cares or indulge in vain repinings; the heart that beats with love and sympathy for others will neither harbour ungenerous resentment, nor long hold in remembrance past injuries. These, then, are marvellous safeguards against ill-humour, peevishness, and rash anger; but one far more powerful is piety, which throws a perpetual sunshine over the mind, and, though this may sometimes be dimmed through infirmity of temper, it will never be totally obscured. Occasionally the storm-cloud of passion may sweep past, but assuredly it will not long dwell in the breast of the truly religious man; and though bodily sufferings and physical ailments tax his equanimity, faith in God will yet enable him to check all repinings. Piety is indeed twin-sister to gentleness and cheerfulness. They who truly love their God will love His creatures; they who delight in serving Him will be ever endeavouring to impart happiness to others, and thereby culling it for themselves. Friendly then as it is to good temper, it is if possible still more serviceable in repressing ill-temper, standing as it does in direct antagonism to vice and those selfish passions whence such irascibility almost invariably springs. Thus, would we be proof to infirmity of temper, we must never pursue those vicious courses which weaken the mind and corrupt the heart, but seek through piety that peace, content, and healthful disposition which are the sure concomitants of virtue.

We next propose to consider the effects of good and ill-temper as regards ourselves and others. It requires no argument to enforce the belief that good temper is beneficial alike to its possessor and to those who may come within its charmed circle. Powerful indeed is the magnetic attraction of mildness, cheerfulness, and benevolence. They form a centre round which all will gladly revolve. He who has a kind word ever ready, a genial smile of encouragement for those who seek it—a fund of good humour, and a warmth of good feeling towards his fellow-creatures—never fails to win his way to every heart, while the happiness he would impart returns with a natural rebound into his own breast. Good temper, like a good conscience, is indeed a constant feast; it basks in the sunshine of God's beautiful creation; it revels in the cheerful and sunny scenes of its own creating. Drawing its source from piety and gratitude, it runs but little hazard of being ruffled from without. The friendly smile it casts on the world will be reflected back as from a mirror. And when we come next to consider the effects of ill-temper upon ourselves, a like illustration is applicable, for we shall certainly meet from society the frown or dark looks we cast on it. Truly bad temper is a kind of distemper, and wont to be infectious. The quarrelsome and the peevish are justly shunned. They who are prone to speak an unkind word and give a quick retort, will surely estrange many a friend; and then, when the day of sorrow comes, where may we hope to find a sympathiser or comforter? Or if death should suddenly summon one with whom we are at enmity, how great will be our after regret; how shall we grieve at the thought that the hasty and unkind word, uttered possibly in a moment of passion, can never be recalled, and that the smile of forgiveness and reconciliation, speaking of renewed amity and goodwill, can never, never again greet us! Truly we use a double-edged sword when in anger we wound another's feelings, for assuredly this may not be done without sorely lacerating our own in the encounter. But the indulgence of anger and discontent is prejudicial in many other ways. The former must embitter our existence by the severe bondage it imposes; for we are indeed slaves when it shall have dethroned reason and usurped the supremacy. It will derange the health, and prove a traitor alike to our sense of justice and our peace of mind. And again, discontent cannot fail to darken the mind, rendering us incapable of performing aright our part in life, as also it will surely harden the heart and deaden it to all sense of gratitude and love towards God.

Now, if each individual could only bring himself to acknowledge that the world is large enough for all; if he would help to brighten it with a portion of good humour and good will, while resolutely resisting all feelings of rancour, hatred, and envy, how greatly would the social community be benefited. It has been justly observed that " God made one world, but man has made another through infirmity of temper"; and indeed many of the evils which disfigure God's beautiful earth are solely due to this cause. Truly, in the slight affront or ungenerous remark wherewith the susceptibilities of our fellow-men are wounded, as in the passionate rejoinder and angry blow which stir up revengeful feeling and convert a friend into a foe, we may frequently discern the source of private sorrow and public calamities. In them we may trace the storm-cloud which has darkened many a home—the thunderbolt which has desolated many a city. Now would all men consider from what small beginnings discord often arises, as well as to what a fearful height it may grow, and thence be led to watch over their thoughts and subdue the first angry emotions, much misery would be avoided; if, further, each one would seek to diffuse happiness around, and strive to quell the violence of discussion, and spread wide the seeds of mutual goodwill, then would the world be such as God— through man's free will—would have it. There would then be a presiding good feeling, melting differences into harmony; men would not be for ever wrangling, but, remembering that while there is many a case in which both sides cannot be right, yet both may be wrong, they would stay all words of anger, which only embitter controversy, and, ceasing to dogmatise on matters of conscience, would, in the true spirit of good will, "agree to differ". Good humour would then be a constant guest in social circles, of which indeed it is the very soul; nor would the domestic hearth ever lack its true, its genial, its best friend—good temper.

From the foregoing it is evident how much, how very much, happiness or misery depends upon the government of temper, and the disposition of the heart, and thence we are naturally led to the final considerations, of how *we may conquer ill-temper*; how *best acquire good temper?* Now, it has been observed that bad temper is simply an effect, and therefore as a matter of course will proportionably lose its hold as the causes which gave birth to it are removed. Thus it behoves us seriously to grapple with, firstly, discontent, which is nothing less than ingratitude to God! What indeed is mental fretting but an oblique reflection on the goodness of the Deity, and therefore closely allied to criminality. Now, to this consideration, which might well suffice to nerve us in all encounters with so dire an enemy to our peace, let us superadd that, while discontent is totally incapable of altering events, it is every way calculated to give additional poignancy to the trials and troubles of life. Thus on the score of religion, as well as of self-interest, we should endeavour to cast aside all vain hopes—all longing desires, which but too surely end in disappointment and vexation of spirit. No less resolutely should we contend with overweening pride, with envy, vanity, and petty jealousies, from which spring many an angry passion, and most of the dissensions, factions, and contentions, which are rife in the world. Thus purposed, we shall take cognisance of our own defects, and, ceasing to form too high a notion of our deserts, shall be less prompt to resent the indifference, the neglect, or even the acumen of others with regard to ourselves, while more inclined to be indulgent to the faults and failings of our fellow-creatures. We shall seek to view objects of luxury and pleasure in their true colours, and make their acquisition subordinate to a sense of justice and right. By casting from us all vanity, and attaining a knowledge of our own defects of character, we shall become more forbearing and less ready to take offence at empty words; finally, we shall guard the heart against all ungenerous sentiments, and utterly discard petty and ignoble rivalries, thereby setting at rest all unkind, vindictive feelings.

Our next consideration is, how to acquire good temper, and

here early discipline will prove a powerful auxiliary. Let the heart of youth—naturally so soft, so warm—only receive due culture, and there will be little to apprehend as regards the temper of the man. We have only to turn the generous enthusiasm of youth into proper channels, to develop the germs of good, and all the gentle emotions which are mingled with fierce passions in every man's nature, and just in proportion as the former gain the ascendency so will amiability and good temper become the distinguishing characteristics of the adult. For this purpose, then, we must rouse humane and kindly feelings in the child, while checking aught which betokens a departure therefrom. Benevolent impulses should be encouraged, and any exhibition calculated to excite fiery emotions be altogether prohibited. The flames of passion once thoroughly lighted in the breast will certainly not be extinguished without much difficulty, while kind deeds become easy and yet more easy on each repetition. Should home, however, not have taught good temper to the child, the world, with its cares and the jarring of self-interest, will be little apt to remedy the evil. The neglect of proper training during youth can only be compensated by much good sense and good feeling in the man, and hard must be the struggle which shall curb passions which are the growth of years. Now, as considerations of religion or principle, of expediency or self-interest, may serve to facilitate the task, the former by improving the heart, the latter by attracting it, some few of these shall here be briefly alluded to. Religion would tell us that kindly feelings, forbearance, and generous self-denial are due to our fellow-men, and would bid us sympathise with the distressed of our own species and compassionate the suffering brute, that we should think of others as we would ourselves be judged, and that we should wish well to all men and act in a like spirit, such being our positive duty and assuredly the temper of mind which God approves. Further, that if we have harboured unkind thoughts, and in an ebullition of temper affronted or injured another, we are bound to atone and repair the evil done to the very best of our power; also, that it is our bounden duty resolutely to contend with all rising gusts of passion, all fits of resentment, and refrain from giving expression to our feelings till a silent prayer has winged its way to heaven and changed the current of our thoughts and sentiments. Then, as to expediency, would it not speak to us thus? Why withhold the kind word; is it not just as easily said as the unkind one? Why harbour unfriendly thoughts which infallibly lead to ungenerous acts? In each case only one result can accrue: we shall turn the hearts of others against us, and lose all claim to the three most precious boons granted to mortals—sympathy, love, and friendship. It would also tell us that ill-temper has made many an enemy, good temper many a friend. It would remind us that the suppression of word or sentence provocative of strife has saved many from humiliation and self-reproach, many even from crime. It would draw our attention to the important fact that good humour and good temper are among the best passports into society, and that they are peculiarly conducive to health. Nor would expediency fail to urge us to avoid all acrimonious disputations, which only engender acerbity of temper, to accommodate our minds to dispositions differing from our own, to respect opinions though they may not accord with our preconceived ideas, and to show our superiority by the forgiveness of injury or the resolute avoidance of all animosity. But indeed religion and self-interest ever point in the same direction, and are as inseparable as good sense and good nature. Both alike teach us to pursue virtue as the supreme good, as the source of cheerfulness, serenity, and happiness, to make God our friend, and tune the heart through prayer to all that is bright around, to seek pure joy through rebound, through loving words and kindly acts.

Before concluding, it may be well to remark that we must not mistake easiness of disposition for good temper, nor be content with the former, which in truth is rather a defect than a virtue. Not being grounded on religion as is good temper, it has a tendency to lead us astray, and therefore needs careful watching. Thence it is important to note some few of their distinguishing traits. Now, we shall find that good temper knows no servility, it never dissembles, never yields up principles to the desire of pleasing, nor seeks to gratify at the cost of truth; though never calmly submitting to wrong, it knows well how to hold indignation within due bounds, whereas easiness of disposition is only too frequently the reverse of all this. The phlegmatic man is apt to acquiesce tamely in much to which reason and conscience give a negative. He holds principle and duty with a feeble grasp, and will depart therefrom on the slightest provocation. He will be compliant rather from a disinclination to resist than from firmness of will. Though he may give or grant favours, his pliancy will be no sign of amiability, since dictated rather by the fear of offending than by love or the desire of gratifying. He will often say yes through cowardice, simply because he has not the moral courage to say no. Assuredly, the only affinity which easy good nature can claim with good temper is that while the latter is a positive, the former is at best but a negative virtue. Let us, then, ever strive to merge one in the other, which can only be accomplished by constantly warming the heart in the sunshine of piety. The man who "walks with God" will enjoy a fund of inward happiness, and be ever seeking to diffuse it through sympathising words and kind deeds. These are indeed the true index of kindliness of temper, the golden links which unite heart to heart, the practical expression of piety and of the angel spirit in man.

PRECEPTS.—Many are the Scripture verses which serve to enlighten us as to the prime moving *causes* of ill-temper and contention, and among them several point to the presumptuous man as being prone to indulge in feelings of indignation and hatred, and thus only too apt to rouse like passions in the breast of others. We are told in Prov. xxi, 25, "The *proud* and haughty scorner dealeth in presumptuous wrath". Also, ch. xxviii, 25, "He that is of a *proud* heart stirreth up strife"; and again, chap. xxix, 8, "Scornful men bring a city into a snare". Then *Covetousness* greatly taxes the temper, as the following verses indicate, Prov. xv, 27, "*He that is greedy of gain troubleth his own house*". The preacher also tells us in Eccles. iv, 8, "There is one that hath neither child nor brother, yet is his eye not satisfied with riches, neither saith he, for whom do I labour, and *bereave my soul of good*". That hardness of heart or the want of charitable feelings towards our neighbours, is incompatible with good temper, while frequently the associate of that ill-temper which displays itself in ungenerous and unkindly acts, is clearly shown in the following verses, Prov. xxvi, 20, "Where no wood is, there the fire goeth out; so where there is no *tale-bearer*, the *strife* ceaseth". Again, "As coals are to burning coals, and wood to fire, so is a *contentious* man to kindle strife". We are also told to beware of all officiousness, ch. xxv, 17, "Withdraw thy foot from thy neighbour's house, lest he be weary of thee, and *so hate thee*". And again, ch. xxvi, 17, "He that passeth by and meddleth with strife that belongeth not to him, is like one that taketh a dog by the ears". Indeed, many a contest, many a scene of violence, would never occur, or occurring, not be prolonged, but for the spur given by the presence of spectators. Then we are warned to beware of bribery, because it "induceth strong wrath". Also, "not to answer a fool according to his folly". Finally, that vice and ill-temper, sin and discontent are ever coupled, the following verses clearly indicate, ch. xvii, 19, "He loveth transgression that loveth strife"; again, "The foolishness of man perverteth his way, and his heart fretteth against the Lord". The effect of extremes in temper next demands our consideration, and many are the verses that may be quoted, showing the benefits which good temper confers. Thus we read, Psalm xxxvii, 11, " The meek shall inherit the earth, and shall delight themselves in the abundance of peace". Then in Prov. xii, 25, " A good word maketh the heart glad"; and ch. xv, 1, " A soft answer turneth away wrath". Again, ch. xxi, 23, " Whoso keepeth his mouth and his tongue, keepeth his soul from trouble". Still more numerous are the texts proving the injurious effects of bad temper, from which we may select the following, Hosea viii, 7, " They who sow the wind shall reap the whirlwind"; and Prov. xix, 19, " A man of great wrath shall suffer punishment". Then in Psalm xxxvii, 14, " The wicked have drawn out the sword to slay such as be of upright conversation"; but the ill results will not affect the virtuous alone, for we further read, "Their sword shall enter into their own heart". Also the sad consequences which may ensue from wrathful and unkind words are yet more forcibly delineated in the following verses, Prov. xviii, 21, " Death and life are in the power of the tongue; they that love it will taste its fruit". And at ch. xvi, 28, " A froward man soweth strife, and a whisperer separateth chief friends"; also, " a violent man enticeth his neighbour, and leadeth him into the way that is not good. By the moving of his lips he bringeth evil to pass". Again, ch. xxvi, 24, " He that hateth, dissembleth with his lips and layeth up deceit within him". Then we are told, ch. xxix, " There is more hope of a fool than of him that is hasty in his words"; and chap. xxix, 22, " a furious man aboundeth in transgression". Also, ch. xvii, 13, " Whoso rewardeth evil for good, evil shall not depart from his house". The moral weakness of the man who holds no control over his temper is thus figuratively shown, Prov. xxv, 28, " He that hath no rule over his own spirit is like a city without ramparts". Then how surely happiness will depart from that home where even one of its inmates is disputative and ill-tempered, we may gather from the following, ch. xxv, 24, " It is better to reside in a garret than to dwell with a quarrelsome woman even in a large house". Lastly, we will quote several verses which are peculiarly applicable to our purpose, since throwing into juxtaposition the effects of good and ill temper. Thus we read, Prov. x, 12, "Hatred stirreth up strife, but love covereth all sins"; and ch. xiv, 29, "*He that is slow to wrath is of great understanding,* but he that is hasty of spirit displayeth folly". Again, ch. xii, 10, "A righteous man regardeth the life of his beast, but the tender mercies of the wicked are cruel". Before proceeding to the next and final object of ascertaining how we may acquire good temper and a spirit of benevolence, how best conquer ill temper, and uproot each malignant passion, it may be well to set forth some few texts for reflection, which should serve to nerve us to a vigorous prosecution of our task, and among the many which might be selected we cull the following, Psalm xi, 5, "The wicked and him that loveth violence, God holdeth in abhorrence". Again, "he who loveth cursing, it shall come unto him; *he who delighteth not in blessing, it shall be far from him*". Then in Proverbs xx, 3, "It is an honour for a man to cease from strife, but every fool will be meddling". Also ch. xvi, 32, "He that is slow to anger is better than the mighty, and he that ruleth his spirit than he that taketh a city". Next we are told in Eccles. ch. vii, 9, "Be not hasty in thy spirit to be angry, *for anger resteth in the bosom of fools*". Also, "The patient in spirit is better than the proud in spirit". Zephaniah leads us to infer that meekness is next best to righteousness when he says, chap. ii, 3, "seek righteousness, seek meekness, it may be ye shall be hid in the day of the Lord's anger". Then Isaiah emphatically declares, ch. lii, 7, "Beautiful are the steps of that messenger who proclaimeth good tidings, that speaketh of peace and happiness". Truly, "a word in due season, how good is it!" Now, if we will only take these considerations to heart, and also seek to comply with the following injunctions, which inculcate discretion, benevolence, and piety, we can hardly fail to attain an even, peaceful frame of mind, a happily-disposed and cheerful spirit, a benign and tender regard for the feelings of others, which is the invariable companion of a good and healthful temper. Thus, Psalm xxxvii, 8, "Cease from anger and forsake wrath, fret not thyself in any wise to do evil". Again, Prov. xix, 11, "The *discretion* of a man deferreth his anger, and *it is his glory to pass over a transgression*". We are likewise told not to search for grievances in Eccles. vii, 21, "*Heed not all words that are spoken*, lest thou hear thy servant speak ill of thee". Also we are urged not to communicate with the scorner, for then "contention shall go out, yea, strife and reproach shall cease". Next, Benevolence thus speaks to our hearts, Prov. xxv, 21, "If thine enemy be hungry, give him bread to eat; if he be thirsty, give him water to drink"; "Rejoice not when he falleth, and let not thine heart be glad when he stumbleth". Again, verse 28, "Be not a witness against thy neighbour without cause, and deceive not with thy lips; say not, I will do so to him as he hath done to me". Also, "*strengthen with kind words, and with the moving of the lips assuage grief*", as did the kindly disposed and righteous Job. But Benevolence makes itself also heard in the five books of Moses, especially in Leviticus, where we are commanded (ch. xix) to "honour the old man and rise up before the hoary head", and forbidden to "go up and down as a talebearer; *to avenge or bear any grudge*". Again, we read, "Thou shalt not hate thy brother in thy heart; thou shalt not humble thy neighbour nor vex the stranger", but "*thou shalt love thy neighbour as thyself*". It also clearly speaks to us in the sixth, ninth, and tenth commandments, bidding us not to stretch forth our hands to injure others; not to permit our tongues to calumniate a fellow-creature, not to covet anything that is our neighbour's. Finally, piety thus dictates (Job xxii, 22), "Receive the Law and lay up God's word in thine heart; acquaint thyself with Him, *for then shalt thy spirit be peaceful*". To like effect we read (Prov.

xx, 22), "Say not I will recompense evil, but wait on the Lord, He will save thee". Truly God will prove our safeguard when angry emotions strive for mastery and darken the mind, if we "wait on the Lord" in prayer, and like David, entreat His gracious aid in curbing our rash and hasty spirit. These are the words of his supplication (Ps. cxli), "Lord, I cry unto thee, give ear unto my voice, let my prayer come up before thee. *Set a watch, O Lord, before my mouth, keep the door of my lips*". Thus watching, thus striving, thus praying, we may assuredly hope to restrain ill-temper, and even secure for ourselves that prize of great worth, good temper.

EXAMPLES.—When we would ascertain the temper or disposition of a man, and yet are unable to make ourselves acquainted with his every-day acts, which furnish the best criterion thereto, we naturally turn our attention to his life as a whole, and impartially weigh each important deed that figures therein, since this outward manifestation is the next surest index to the subtle working of the heart within. And it is this latter course we are compelled to follow when reading Scripture characters through the long vista of time. Though the Holy Volume in its numerous biblical sketches seldom supplies us with minor particulars, it never fails to give important details and such landmarks as may enable us to arrive at just conclusions with regard to the character and disposition of the individual. Now, if it be agreed that acts speak and deeds proclaim the temper of man, we shall hardly hesitate in classing most biblical characters under the two headings of the good and ill-tempered. Only those who distinguished themselves by their virtues, and therefore are admirable examples for imitation, or such as obtained an unenviable notoriety through their evil passions, thereby acting as warnings, could secure a prominent place in the pages of Sacred History, and thence a permanent niche in the temple of time. Simply a name, and not a character, have we before us, if no facts are portrayed whereby the temper of a man can be ascertained. The Holy Volume, however, deals not with names only, and many of the earlier patriarchs, whose lives were most calm and, like the tranquil lake, reflected heaven's own image, shine forth with immortal lustre. These, then, would undoubtedly have been selected for illustration when treating on good temper had they not already found a place in this work under the headings of Benevolence, Virtue, Individual Merit, and other like subjects. All, therefore, that here remains for us is to note such men as by their acts displayed ill-temper and ungovernable passions.

Before proceeding to sketch two characters by which we intend to exemplify the former, we shall briefly review some few which should warn us against the indulgence of the latter. Equally clearly and explicitly do they speak to us; this caste of character permits not our misunderstanding or mistaking it—indeed, we cannot fail in discerning the causes and effects of actions which have received their impetus from the rude gales of angry passions. Misinterpret if we will the character of the man whose life has been inwardly peaceful, and whose acts have been fanned by the warm, balmy zephyrs of good temper, we yet must read aright the character of men of violence and strife. To instance this, though the whole incidents of CAIN's life are summed up in a very few verses, we may nevertheless trace his fratricidal act to *envy*. He was "very wrath, and his countenance fell" when Abel's sacrifice was accepted and his own rejected. Indeed, so completely had anger gained the ascendency, hushing every better feeling, that he could not even be brought to hearken to the Lord, and take to heart those words of fair promise, "If thou doest well shalt thou not be accepted, and if thou doest not well sin lieth at thy door",[*] but in a fit of jealous rage he vented the full measure of his fury on his unoffending brother. SIMEON and LEVI also

---

[*] Gen. iv, 7.

would have been fratricides but for their eldest brother Judah, and here likewise was it not a spirit of jealousy which made them overlook the ties of kindred and prompted their criminal proceedings towards the youthful Joseph? Mark the solemn words of the aged patriarch Jacob in reference to their conduct, " In their anger they slew a man and in their self-will they digged down a well. Cursed be their *anger*, for it was fierce, and their *wrath*, for it was cruel". NABAL's churlishness was evidently the result of *intemperance*, and how ungovernable must have been the temper, how sad the moral condition of this man is clearly portrayed alike by his dependents and his wife in the following sentences : "Know that evil is determined against him, for he is such a son of Belial that a man cannot speak to him. As his name is so is he ; Nabal is his name, and folly is with him".* And to what violent man will not this verse more or less apply? Intoxication and passion equally sap and destroy reason, nor will they lose their hold till they have engulfed their victim in the abyss of crime or dragged him to the gates of death, as in the case of Nabal. Again, NAAMAN's rejection " *in wrath*" of Elisha's counsel when he bade him "go wash and be clean", must be ascribed to *pride*. Although a leper, he was a renowned champion, and scoffed at the notion of being cured by so simple and easy a process. Gladly would he have obeyed the voice of the prophet had some daring enterprise, some dangerous exploit, been proposed to him, for such would not have lowered his self-esteem ; but how could he, the great deliverer of Syria, demean himself by conforming to an every-day proceeding, one involving no hazard, imparting no glory? Also HAZAEL's course of almost unexampled tyranny and crime was greatly due to pride. Ambition first made him a regicide, and having secured the throne, when once in the full tide of prosperity and kingly power he hesitated not in perpetrating deeds at the very thought of which he had revolted whilst

* 1 Sam. xxv, 17.

in a humble, dependent state. Worldly success, riches, and grandeur too often debilitate and certainly never strengthen the mind, while they are apt to engender a haughty spirit and harden the heart. Thus it was with this wicked Syrian monarch. By crime, the offspring of ambition and pride, he obtained possession of the crown, and maintained his hold of it, practically answering his own query, "Am I a dog?" for lower indeed than the brute did he fall in the scale of creation when standing on the highest pedestal of earthly grandeur and power. SAUL had been humble-minded in his youth, but, once seated on the throne, all trace of humility was lost, and in its place we find inflated pride with its ever sure attendant, irritability of temper. It was not enough that he possessed power and vast dominions, he yet viewed with a jealous eye any compeer, and brooked not the faintest opposition to his wishes. Thence his never-dying animosity to the God-fearing David. When this youth was merely a dependent, Saul sought to smite him to death with his javelin. Again, when at a later period David became his son-in-law, he nevertheless continued to persecute him, and even when this persecution finally made him a voluntary fugitive, the king never relaxed in his cruel and murderous intent. Pride and jealousy numbed each generous emotion, and so hardened his heart as to make him unjust to man, unfaithful to his God. A few words uttered by the wicked AHAB suffice to demonstrate how *vice and self-indulgence* foster the worst passions of our nature and engender a cruel and vindictive spirit. It was impossible that this vile King of Israel should appreciate the noble character of the prophet Micaiah, who stood bravely forward to thwart the evil-disposed monarch, and prophesied ill and "not good" concerning him. Now, though he was forced to acknowledge that the Lord was only to be "inquired of" through Micaiah, and therefore only through him might the truth be ascertained, nevertheless he could not bring himself to appeal to this messenger of God. Pride and rancour here proved his dire enemies, for one word from the prophet would have been his safeguard. As it was, the ruthless king heeded only the passion which raged within his breast, and declaring "I hate him",* departed for the field of battle. However, before proceeding thereto, he sought to demonstrate his inimical feeling by acts, and thus commanded his servants regarding the prophet, "Put this fellow in the prison and feed him with bread of affliction and water of affliction until I come in peace".† The words "I hate", uttered in reference to the good, the virtuous man, God's chosen messenger, form the title-page to the volume of his sinful life. Before concluding our faint sketch of the characters of men notorious for their ungovernable temper, one more must here be pencilled, since we ought not to omit the wicked HAMAN. The *pride* he manifested in requiring obeisance from his fellow-men, the hatred he evinced towards the humble individual Mordecai, who "bowed not down nor did him reverence", the cruel animosity he displayed in working the downfall of the entire race of the offender, with his own sudden fall and ignominious death, should not be altogether passed over in silence, furnishing as they do a most useful lesson. The whole narrative, indeed, speaks of wounded pride, of a heart smarting under supposed wrongs, and hardening into implacable hatred and resentment. It also affords practical proof that the man whose heart is most impressible to personal affronts, and whose sensibility and self-dignity are easily wounded, is the very one who will be most callous to the sufferings of others. The softness of such a nature is purely egotistical, and thus it was with the haughty Haman. He who writhed when merely his dignity and self-esteem were hurt, could yet decree the wholesale massacre of an unoffending people without a single pang! Passion, born of pride, exercised its fatal influence and called for satisfaction. It ejaculated those burning words which scorch the heart of the man who utters them, "Vengeance is mine", words which should be-

* 1 Kings xxii, 8.   † 1 Kings xxii, 27.

long to Omnipotence alone, and which in this instance were put into execution on the proud defier of God's people, who speedily fell a victim to his own crafty, wicked devices, his senseless and cruel hatred.

Infirmity of temper claims our especial attention, and therefore we purpose considering at somewhat greater length the characters of BALAAM and JONAH, who, though differing essentially in point of moral worth, alike fell into error and sin through this common blemish. Both allowed temper to govern their movements, both disobeyed the Lord, and therefore were equally culpable. Nevertheless, we have only to mark the causes which swayed their actions in order to feel inspired with some sympathy for the one, even if we cannot entirely exonerate him from blame, whilst we should be led unhesitatingly to condemn the other. We must clearly perceive that Jonah was of a naturally hasty and impulsive temperament, and that his ill-considered acts were not the fruits of badness of heart, but were the almost certain consequences of an undisciplined mind; not so, however, with the avaricious, crafty, and calculating Balaam. Covetousness was the prime moving cause of his every act, and assuredly his irritability of temper, his cruelty and dissimulation were due to corruptness of heart. Jonah's worst defect was over-sensitiveness, which, in other words, is a mild form of vanity; Balaam was hard-hearted and rapacious, he worshipped Mammon, and sacrificed principle at its altar. Interesting episodes in their respective lives amply exemplify this.

To begin with Balaam, one who, though a heathen, had yet attained a knowledge of the Lord, and possessed occasionally a clear insight into His ways. It was, doubtless, this superior knowledge of the Will of the Supreme which had insured him the high renown he enjoyed, and induced the King of the Moabites to appeal to him under the following adverse circumstances. The people of Israel had "pitched in the plains of Moab, and the Moabites were sore afraid, and said, This company shall lick up all that are round about us, as the ox licketh up the grass of the field".* Now, Balak, who "was King at the time", sought in his distress to avail himself of the influence of Balaam, whose presence he well knew would calm the fears of his people, and greatly encourage them to resist the enemy at their gates. Therefore he sent messengers to him, and the words wherewith he charged them clearly show the King's high appreciation of the service which this prophet could render to his cause. They are as follows, "Come, I pray thee, curse me this people, for they are too mighty for me; peradventure I shall prevail, that we may smite and drive them out of the land, for I wot that he whom thou blessest is blessed, and he whom thou cursest is cursed".† Balaam, however, doubtful how to proceed, awaited the Divine command, and God spake unto him thus, "Thou shalt not go with them, thou shalt not curse this people, for they are blessed". Whereon he refused to comply with the desire of the King, and the messengers departed without him. Thus did he this once act in obedience to the will of the Most High, but on receiving a second and more pressing summons from the King, accompanied with tempting offers, and promises of great honours, he made duty subordinate to inclination, and started for the capital! Now, let us for one moment grant that selfish ambition did not prompt his conduct, and that he deceived himself into a belief that the Lord had changed from His original purpose. Surely, in such a case, the first check he received on his journey would have roused within his mind a question as to the correctness of his proceedings, brought to his remembrance the immutability of the Supreme, and recognizing the finger of God, as well as a reproof therein, he would have immediately retraced his steps. We may not, however, doubt that he was aware he was acting in contravention to the will of the Lord; indeed, we have proof positive that this

* Numbers xxii, 4. † Numbers xxii, 6.

was the fact, since we are told, "And God's anger was kindled because he went".* He had allowed himself to be seduced by the wily king's tempting bait; he saw at his journey's end all that his heart lusted after, and with the golden vision before him, quieting all conscientious scruples, he wilfully determined to prosecute his plans, nor permitted aught to balk him therein. Thence his cruel conduct towards the poor animal which had served him so long and so faithfully. Now, had he not been blinded by self-interest, he might have seen in the unprecedented resistance of his ass more than mere chance, especially when each fresh effort he made to overcome its apparent obstinacy proved unavailing. But he had hushed both reason and conscience, allowing covetousness and passion to direct his conduct. He lost sight of humanity in his struggle to attain his avaricious desires, and his wrath waxed greater and greater as his hope of securing the promised reward became fainter and fainter. Indeed, so completely had anger gained possession of his breast, that, not content with belabouring the patient beast, he would willingly have killed it. Well did he deserve the following rebuke of the angel of the Lord, "Thy way is perverse before me", for had he not done that which was wrong while full well knowing what was right? And what but utter failure could attend such conduct? Although allowed to proceed on his journey, he was obliged implicitly to obey the mandate of the Lord, and thereby incurred the disfavour of the King. No rich prize could be his, and gladly must he have turned homeward, though, alas! not humble and repentant. He had been forced to bless the people of Israel and prophesy their greatness, but he hated them in his heart. They had stood in the way of his aggrandizement, and this was enough to rouse his bitterest resentment. As he dared not give vent to his rancorous spirit in words, he was resolved to do so by deeds. Harbouring the most revengeful feelings towards this people,

* Numbers xxii, 22.

and regardless of their being under God's special protection, he craftily devised their ruin by placing temptation before them. The better to hide his intolerant hatred he concealed it under a veil of dissimulation and hypocrisy. How could the Israelites believe that he who had spoken these words, "Behold, I have received God's command to bless, and *He hath blessed, I cannot reverse it*",* would ever seek to harm them? Yet the malignant spirit of this ambitious man overpowered every consideration, and how greatly he misled them the following verse discloses, " Behold, these women caused the children of Israel *through the counsel of Balaam* to commit trespass against the Lord".† His hatred, however, far from stopping short at this point, only became intensified, and finally showed its extreme virulence in overt acts of hostility. Thus we find him openly siding with the Midianites in the war they waged against the chosen people whom he had so lately blessed! But mark the fate of this hypocrite, of him who, after emphatically exclaiming in reference to the Israelites, " may my last end be like theirs", yet sought by every possible device to destroy them body and soul! In that very war he perished, as we read, " Balaam also they slew with the sword". Such was the violent end of this obstinate, irascible, revengeful man. His last years were evidently a blank, as had been his ambitious hopes; no rich prize attended his acts of disobedience, but in its stead he incurred the disfavour of the King, and that which was indeed far, far worse, the just displeasure of the King of Kings.

Now, on turning to consider the character of the prophet Jonah, we find that he also on more than one occasion incurred God's anger by acting in direct opposition to His expressed will; but, as shown under the heading of Self-Discipline, this proceeded from want of self-control and due reflection, not from wilful disobedience, as in the case of Balaam. Naturally of a rash and impulsive temperament,

---

* Chap. xxiii, 20. † Chap. xxxi, 16.

he allowed himself to be carried away by the passion of the moment, and thus it was he fled to Tarshish instead of proceeding to Nineveh in accordance with the command of God. Now assuredly in thus acting he had no worldly purpose to serve, nor may we trace therein a spirit of defiance. Thence was God's anger easily appeased. As has been justly said, " the wrath of God is not a passion, but a principle ; it is the calm, deep, deliberate recoil of His nature from sin", and had Jonah wilfully and deliberately turned from the path of duty, we may hardly suppose that he would have been a second time entrusted with the important mission of announcing to the sinful inhabitants of Nineveh the overthrow of their city. But if we need additional evidence we have it in Jonah's own words, uttered in prayer just after the remission which God graciously accorded to the repentant nation. Seeking to justify his past conduct, he says, " When, O Lord, I was yet in my own country was not this my saying, therefore I fled unto Tarshish, for I knew that Thou art a gracious God and merciful, slow to anger, and of great kindness, and repentest Thee of the evil". Thus in the fulness of his faith he had foreseen what ultimately occurred, yet, instead of glorifying God for this marked proof of His mercy and loving-kindness, he allowed himself to feel aggrieved. The utter failure of his prophesy wounded his self-love, and " it displeased Jonah exceedingly ; he was very angry".* Indeed, such was the sensitiveness of his nature, or we will rather say, of his vanity, that mortification became the predominant sentiment of his mind, and he even besought God to withdraw from him the breath of life, saying, " It is better for me to die than to live". Self-love for the moment hardened his heart, and made him forgetful of the sympathy and love due to others. Pride overpowered pity, and roused a spirit of sinful repining, whereas a sentiment of gratitude alone should have predominated. Such unjust and wrathful feelings on the part of His servant dis-

* Chap. iv, 1.

pleased the Lord, and led him to put the question, "Doest thou well to be angry?" but meeting with no response, the All-Gracious took occasion to reprove him by a practical lesson as beautiful as effective in its moral teachings. Jonah had to undergo a trial that taxed his utmost powers of endurance, bringing with it such suffering as might well have softened his heart and induced a kindred sense of pity at the very idea of a dire calamity befalling an entire people. In pure waywardness he seated himself outside the city, "until he might see what would become of it. Now, God prepared a gourd, and made it to come up over Jonah that it might be a shadow over his head",* to protect him from the overpowering heat of the noon-day sun, "so Jonah was exceedingly glad of the gourd". But God ordained that on the next day it should wither, and Jonah fainted by reason of the sun's heat, and wished to die. Naturally infirm of temper, he lost all command of it under this vexatious ordeal, and when God interrogated him as before, this impulsive man replied, "I do well to be angry even unto death". Truly a rash and passionate exclamation; nevertheless we may not doubt that the gracious words further vouchsafed by the Lord quelled the discontented spirit which had inspired it, and that, like the gourd, it disappeared as suddenly as it had sprung into being.

With these two incidents before us we may, in conclusion, briefly contrast the conduct of Jonah and Balaam, for thereby we shall throw the character of each into bolder relief, and while making manifest the superior moral worth of the former, show that notwithstanding his higher qualities, his kindliness of nature, his faith and just appreciation of God's gracious attributes, he yet wrought evil rather than good on important occasions, owing to his sad infirmity of temper. If we look solely to acts, both were equally culpable, one proceeding to Tarshish, and the other following the King's messengers to the capital, in direct contravention to the will of

* Chap. iv, 6.

the Most High. But if we analyse the feelings which dictated their conduct, it at once appears in a far different light. Jonah only regarded the Supreme as a God of infinite mercy, and entertaining the firm conviction that in the greatness of His compassion the Lord would " turn away from His fierce anger and repent", he rashly concluded that the mission entrusted to him would be futile, and *therefore* could not bring himself to undertake it ! Balaam, however, showed no such faith in God's goodness; he simply pursued what he believed to be his own interest, and assuredly would not have resolved upon his journey but that he hoped in some measure to fulfil the wishes of Balak. He stopped not to consider how the King's views could be made compatible with the expressed will of the Supreme, who had thus spoken, " Thou shalt not curse the people, for they are blessed".* Nor could he abstain when in the presence of the King from acknowledging that there was " no enchantment against Israel", and that " he could not curse whom God had not cursed"; nevertheless he studiously refrained from blessing them, and it was only on the third time of " taking up his parable" that " his eyes opening, and seeing that it pleased the Lord to bless Israel", he no longer equivocated, but proclaimed, " Blessed is he that blesseth thee, and cursed is he that curseth thee".† He had at length discovered there was no alternative left him but to comply with God's will, and thereupon uttered a glowing peroration, prophesying Israel's happiness and greatness. He had eagerly sought to please the King, but being finally moved to incense Him by uttering words of ill omen, he received his dismissal, and had to return home without the honours he so greatly coveted. A marked difference is also observable in the proceedings of Jonah and Balaam when they were in transit to their respective destinations. Jonah would not allow his shipmates to suffer for his misconduct. No sooner did he perceive the sad consequences which his disregard of God's word was

---

* Numbers xxii, 12. † Numbers xxiv, 9.

likely to entail than, hoping to save the innocent, he resigned himself to meet a watery grave. He alone had erred, and God permitting, he alone would bear the punishment due to his rashness and folly. Turning to Balaam, we see in his acts only vindictiveness and passion. No consideration had he for either man or brute that thwarted his designs, and thence his inhuman treatment of the poor faithful animal he bestrode. Finally, when God in His good pleasure had brought them both to see the error of their ways, their course of action was totally dissimilar. Jonah, truly penitent, set himself at once to fulfil the mandate of the Lord; but, as we have seen, Balaam nourished so bitter a feeling of animosity towards God's people that he could even resolve to nullify his own predictions and resist the will of the Almighty, rather than forego the satisfaction of humbling and degrading them. Truly Balaam's proceedings were the reflex of a bad heart, while those of Jonah were due solely to a peculiarly sensitive mind. With the former there was *design*, he disregarded God's word even in his calmest moments, but *impulse* and passion alone led the latter into open acts of disobedience. Assuredly both were culpable, and while the one serves to warn us against over-sensitiveness and vanity, the other should induce us sedulously to cultivate the good dispositions of the heart, and uproot those baser passions which are the sure concomitants and promoters of ill *temper*.

DEATH.

Deut. xxxiv, 5, "*So Moses, the servant of the Lord, died there in the land of Moab, according to the word of the Lord.*"

If we measure life by the varied incidents which give it colour as well as by length of years, then was the life of the great legislator MOSES of most uncommon span. That it should have been thus long was the more remarkable, since throughout almost its entire duration, dangers menaced and perils beset his path. Indeed, the thread of his existence would have been violently snapped even before consciousness had dawned on his infant mind but for a miraculous deliverance. Interesting as is this historic period, with the occurrences which threatened to nip the fairest blossom of humanity in its very bud, we do not propose to comment thereon, since where there is no free agency there can be no practical lesson, no example. But when we proceed to consider the many stirring events wherein Moses distinguished himself, we must be struck by his intrepidity and his fearlessness. Manfully did he encounter and resolutely contend with ever-recurring perils and dangers. Truly, to the man of stout heart and firm faith, death has nought appalling. The call of duty and of honour sweeps away all base fear; and thus it was with Moses. It is this truism, then, that we have to trace, for assuredly as life is, so is death.

We pass over the forty years which carried him up to ripe manhood, a period spent in Egypt; for although we may infer that, if known as one of the despised and hated Hebrew race, Moses must have had many sworn enemies, or if regarded only as the favourite at the palace, he must not less certainly have raised up a host of envious and rancorous detractors, yet having no positive data whereon to rely, we know not how frequently he had to struggle with implacable and dangerous, because often covert foes. Turning, therefore, to the known facts of his history, we at once come to that incident which wrought so great a change in his condition. Moses had doubtless been on various occasions an eye-witness to the cruel treatment which the Hebrews, his brethren, experienced at the hands of the Egyptian taskmasters, without, however, indulging his angry emotions by any overt act of violence; but when an aggravated case of barbarity was afterwards presented before him, he allowed indignation to gain entire mastery, and in a fit of passion slew the vile and relentless oppressor. Now, by this deed of violence, which speedily became known, he must assuredly have revealed his extraction, and shown that in heart as well as by birth he was an Israelite. From this moment till the time he reached the land of Midian, whither he fled for safety, his life must have been in jeopardy, for, as we read, "when Pharaoh heard this thing he sought to slay Moses".* Escaping this extreme danger, it was only to fall into others hardly less critical, yet having this important difference, that he could face these with a bold front, while he must have cowered under the one just past. Fear ever attends a troubled conscience, and although his impulsive act originated solely in a generous sentiment and patriotic feeling, he must nevertheless have felt himself highly culpable, and therefore entertained a natural dread of after-consequences.

On reaching the land of Midian, we find in his very first act ample evidence of his willingness to risk his life for the good of others. He had seated himself near a well, when the daughters of the priest of Midian approached to water their father's flock, and at the same moment, shepherds came forth to drive them away, "but Moses stood up and helped them".† Well might the shepherds, re-echoing

* Exodus ii, 15.   † Exodus ii, 17.

those words which had sounded so ominously to the ears of Moses in Egypt, "Who made thee a prince and a judge over us", have resented the interference of an alien and a stranger, and sought to take his life. Indeed, their conduct towards the weaker sex augured most unfavourably in regard to their natural disposition, and showed them to be prone to strife and contention. Yet even this consideration did not prevent Moses from accomplishing the task he had undertaken. His chivalrous devotion to the weak and unprotected brought its own reward, for we find him receiving a hospitable reception under the roof of Jethro, and soon afterwards obtaining the hand of one of his daughters in marriage. Now, although he had been fortunate enough to secure a home, the change in his circumstances was of the most trying nature, but having alluded thereto under the heading of "Temper", it will here suffice to observe that he left a palace, with its luxuries and delights, for a desert life full of perils; he quitted a civilized land for one of semi-barbarism, and there had to undergo such toils, such privations and rebuffs, as called for the exercise of all his fortitude, patience, and power of endurance; nor may we doubt they were the more acutely felt that he had hitherto been a stranger to hardships and severe trials. For forty years he followed the occupation of shepherd, and wended his way by night and by day along desert paths, in ever close proximity to the wild beast and oft yet fiercer man, differing from himself in race, language, and worship. But at the expiration of this long term of years a marked change occurred, involving new and serious responsibilities. The trials and hardships, so resolutely, so manfully encountered for two score years, well fitted him to undertake the perilous and arduous duties with which he was now to be entrusted. He, the poor shepherd and friendless exile, was to become the messenger of God to the mighty Pharaoh. He was to be deputed to rescue his down-trodden brethren, and by extraordinary displays of power to effect their signal deliverance from the land of bondage.

And thus was his long and trying banishment brought to a close. Moses was passing with his flock at the "back part of the desert near Mount Horeb, when the angel of the Lord appeared unto him in a flame of fire out of the midst of a bush". There, standing on holy ground with feet uncovered, he received the command of the God of his fathers to enter on the gigantic task which he so ably, so courageously, so faithfully accomplished. That death often stared him in the face while engaged therein admits of no doubt, but it is equally certain that such had no terror for him. Was he not filling a post of duty as well as a post of danger? and could he, who had been deemed worthy of holding converse with the great Unseen, lack faith or resignation? No, truly, these proved an impenetrable coat of mail, and thus armed, he set himself to the task which had been confided to him from on High, resolutely confronting and successfully contending with the ensuing dangers. Now, of the many perils he incurred in the discharge of his glorious mission, the first was not the least imminent, for we find that after calling together the elders of Israel with the object of proclaiming the Lord's high will, he proceeded with his brother Aaron to the palace of Pharaoh, and presented himself unbidden before that stern and ruthless monarch, petition in hand. That this rash intrusion, so well calculated to rouse the ire of the tyrant, did not cost him his life must be attributed to the potent spell which high resolves and moral courage invariably exercise. Was not Moses, when preferring his claim for his suffering brethren before this mere king of earth, supported by the great King of Kings, the Supreme Ruler? Here, indeed, was his strength, and here also his safeguard. What but the noble daring of Moses, inspired by truth and trust in God (for this poor exile had no numerous retinue wherewith to enforce his demand) could have so overawed the proud tyrant as to induce him to hearken to the words of one so lowly. That the quiescence of Pharaoh was not dictated by fear of the

Supreme, we may feel well assured, since after hearing the request of Moses, thus couched in the name of the Lord, " Let my people go that they may hold a feast unto me in the wilderness",* that Ruler at once declared, " *I know not the Lord:* who is the Lord that I should obey His voice and let Israel go ?" So self-willed a monarch, and one so resolute in ignoring a higher Power, needed more than mere words to induce him to forego his own interests, and relent in favour of those whom he had so long oppressed. Thence ensued the several plagues of Egypt ; but neither threats nor miracles, the nation's certain ruin, nor the people's assured misery, were effectual in causing the hardened Ruler to yield obedience to the will of Omniscience, for though brought to bend at extreme junctures, he relapsed into indifference and impenitence† as soon as the penalty due to his obduracy was remitted. Such persistence on the part of Pharaoh, coupled with the wilful infliction of fresh cruelties on his bondsmen, as also their refusal to hearken unto Moses for "anguish of spirit", at times discouraged this faithful servant of God, for we read, " And Moses returned unto the Lord and said, Lord, wherefore hast thou so evil intreated this people ? why is it thou hast sent me ? For since I came to Pharaoh to speak in thy name he hath done evil to this people, neither hast thou delivered thy people at all."‡ And again, " Moses spake unto the Lord, saying, Behold, the children of Israel have not hearkened unto me, how then shall Pharaoh hear me ?" But notwith-

---

* Exodus v, 1.

† The word *impenitence* is used advisedly, since, on referring to chap. ix, 27, and chap. x, 17, we find that Pharaoh was brought not only to recognise God's hand, but also his own sinfulness, while yet obstinately refusing to act in accordance with the Divine injunction, for thus spoke he to Moses, " I have sinned this time ; the Lord is righteous and I and my people are wicked"; again, on a later occasion, he petitioned, " Forgive, I pray thee, my sin only this once more, and entreat the Lord your God for me".

‡ Exodus v, 22.

standing such depressing influences, Moses again and again bearded the inexorable monarch, and this with greater hazard of his life on each succeeding occasion. Indeed, each new miracle, which might well have humbled Pharaoh and softened his heart, only served to harden it and render the position of Moses more critical. As proof of this we have Pharaoh's own words addressed to this servant of God just before the miraculous visitation which finally brought about the deliverance of Israel. They run thus, ch. x, 28, "Get thee from me, *take heed to thyself,* see my face no more, for in that day thou seest my face *thou shalt die*".

With the exodus from Egypt uprose a host of new dangers to the great leader, for the very people whom he had succoured soon turned against him. Terrified at the appearance of Pharaoh, who with a numerous army had pursued and seemed about to overtake them, whilst the Red Sea was an apparent bar to their further progress, these broken-spirited slaves, losing all remembrance of past miracles, as also of what was due to their great chief, fell to murmuring, and even reviled him for effecting a deliverance which was to secure to them the blessed boon of freedom. Perilous, indeed, must have been the position of Moses at this juncture, nor did it promise to be less so in the future. Were it possible that the Lord should suffer them to fall into the hands of the incensed monarch, he would assuredly be the first to suffer death, or if, as he believed in the fulness of faith, a final deliverance from the oppressor should be secured through some new miracle, yet what had he to expect from a people who could thus turn against their Benefactor at the first appearance of danger? Surely the trials consequent on long and weary wanderings in the wilderness were no way likely to work a favourable change in their sentiments towards him, and but too much reason had he to apprehend repeated seditious risings. That these anticipations were unhappily verified, and that the great leader of Israel was equal to every emergency, is matter of history, and will be but briefly alluded to here, since having had our attention when treating of the *early Israelites,* under the heading of "*Obduracy*", and of the *character of Moses,* under the heading of "*Temper*". One thing is certain, that Moses' life must have been in constant jeopardy during the forty years of his leadership, there being no seditious movement in the camp which had not for its aim either to undermine and resist his authority, or to turn the people from their allegiance by electing princely rulers who would sanction the retracing of their steps to Egypt! A marvellous display of firmness, boldness and sagacity on the part of Moses was indeed requisite to quiet and appease a rabble hungering for bread, as was the case in the wilderness of Zin, or armed with stones ready to slay him when thirsting for water as at Marah; nor were these admirable qualities less serviceable to him when the people lapsed into idolatrous practices, and he forced them to drink water impregnated with dust ground from the golden calf at Mount Sinai; when they lusted after flesh at Taberah; when they obstinately refused to advance towards the land of the Anaks; and finally, when the whole congregation gathered themselves together against Moses and "chode with him". Now, had he in these instances been cowed before the irate multitude, or basely yielded to their unruly desires and idolatrous propensities, as did Aaron, his brother, such timidity or moral cowardice would surely have proved fatal. His contempt of death and resolute bearing whenever a point of duty was concerned, or a principle had to be enforced, could not fail to impress even the most seditious spirits and humble them into submission. Thus stemming every adverse influence on the one hand, and elevating the moral character of his people on the other, Moses was enabled to carry them through many terrible ordeals, and bring them in safety to the glorious land of promise.

But to secure this happy consummation, many were the personal sacrifices made by this noble-spirited chief, who, ambitioning nothing so much as the good of his people, unhesitatingly faced alike danger and death when such magnanimity could in any way subserve thereto. Indeed, Moses was prepared to make a still greater self-sacrifice to save his poor benighted countrymen from the consequences of their folly and sin, and truly he presents us with an instance of self-abnegation which finds no parallel in history. Not only had this spiritual hero conquered the fear of death when any such fear clashed with duty, but he could even face the dread thought of annihilation, and voluntarily yield up the blessed boon of immortality, if by so doing he might mitigate God's just resentment towards the fallen of His people! Here are his words: "Oh! this people have sinned a great sin, yet now if Thou, O Lord, wilt forgive their sin, and if not, blot me, I pray thee, out of thy book which thou hast written".* The magnitude of this self-devotion acquires additional proportions when we consider that Moses, having spoken face to face with the Deity, must have had as glowing a vision of heaven as might be vouchsafed to mortal eye. And yet, after this glorious sight, in the sublimest and purest spirit of philanthropy, he could, of his own free will, propose to erase his name from the great muster roll, and thereby himself close the entrance gate to that beatific region which lies beyond the grave! Brave, magnanimous soul, rich to overflowing with the sweet spirit of love—a love sublime, angel-like; a love generous, self-denying, self-sacrificing!

We now proceed to consider the incidents which mark the close of this great man's career, and well do they harmonise with those which preceded them. Eloquent as was his life, his *death* was no less so. Brightly as had shone forth every exalted virtue during his long and unrivalled course, they appeared to gain even additional lustre at the approach of the final hour. Moses had reached the venerable age of one hundred and twenty years with powers unimpaired, he

* Exodus xxxii, 32.

had set foot on the confines of the promised land, when the voice of the Lord was heard calling him hence. God spake, "Get thee up into this mount Abarim, and see the land which I have given unto the children of Israel, and when thou hast seen it, thou also shalt be gathered unto thy people".* The appeal he had previously made to the All-Merciful to be permitted to enter the "goodly land" had brought no favourable response, and he thus simply narrates the overthrow of his long-cherished hopes : "God was wrath with me for your sakes, and would not hear me".† No remonstrance, no murmur, was to be heard from this godly man. With the most perfect equanimity and resignation he received the Divine summons, and at once prepared for his final departure. It was at this solemn moment that the disinterestedness which had characterised his whole life became, if possible, yet more marked. Totally excluding all selfish and all family considerations, he directed his every thought to promote the future welfare of his people. He first besought aid and guidance from above, supplicating the All-Gracious in these words : "Let the Lord set a man over the congregation who may go out before them, and who may go in before them, so that the congregation of the Lord be not as sheep which have no shepherd". Full well he knew that upon the character of his successor would greatly depend the well-being of those whom he was about to quit, and therefore appealed to Him who alone can read the heart of man. And when Joshua had been nominated, Moses solemnly invested him with the command before the entire congregation, and laying "his hands upon him, gave him a charge as the Lord had commanded", further exhorting him as follows : "Be strong and of good courage, to do according to all the law, not to turn to the right hand nor to the left, so that thou mayest prosper whithersoever thou goest". Having thus publicly manifested his approval of their future leader, nobly ignoring the hereditary claim of kindred when it might

* Numbers xxvii, 12. † Deut. iii, 26.

prejudice the general well-being, he proceeded to counsel the people for their good, urging them to be humble-minded, to walk in the right way, to fear God, and then concluded his sublime exordium in these terms: " Set your hearts unto all the words which I testify among you this day, which ye shall command your children to observe to do, all the words of this law, for it is not a vain thing for you, *but it is your life*".* This duty accomplished, he prepared their minds for his approaching departure, and, as a final injunction, bid them reflect on God's unceasing love, mercy, and *justice*". Having thus warmed their hearts towards their heavenly Father, he proceeded to the last solemn act of blessing the people " after their respective tribes". Now, in order justly to estimate such blessing, let us consider the political and spiritual position which their leader of forty years' standing had attained in the eyes of the nation. In Deut. xxxiii we are told that Moses was *king in Jeshurun* " when the heads of the people and the tribes of Israel were gathered together, also that Moses, *the man of God*, blessed the children of Israel before his death". Surely a halo of glory surrounds a nation thus blessed, and well may the Israelites ever hold in glad remembrance the last prophetic words of their great law-giver, " Be happy, thou, O Israel, for who is like unto thee, O Jacob, saved by Jehovah, who is a shield to help thee, a sword to protect thee, and though thine enemies will betray, yet shalt thou ascend their high places".†

All doubts concerning the future welfare of his people being at an end, Moses, in accordance with the command of God, commenced the ascent of Mount Abarim, and though proceeding *alone* in this instance, as in that of Mount Sinai, was his step less firm *now*, *after* he had faithfully and zealously discharged the mission wherewith God had entrusted him, than at the period when his task had only just begun? Assuredly not. Full well he knew that a reward for past anxious toils awaited him in a glorious immortality, and

* Deut. xxxii, 46. † Deut. xxxiii, 29.

gladly must he have laid down his life even at the very moment that his worldly hopes were about to meet their fruition, particularly as by so doing he could furnish one more practical lesson to his people. The moral of this lesson may be traced in the culmination of his faith and in his *implicit belief in the immortality of the soul*, evinced by his calm departure for the ascent of Mount Nebo, step by step. Had the people believed that death of the body implied death of the soul, then indeed they would have failed to discern among God's gracious attributes that *justice* of which Moses had so repeatedly, so emphatically spoken. But they saw, as did their leader, a home beyond this world, and, though they long wept and mourned his loss, they became yet more impressed with this glorious and solemn truth, that at the very gates of death lies life everlasting.

Death, viewed through the eyes of faith and reason, bears a totally different colour and aspect to that which imagination, fear, and despondency lend it; the latter see only the funereal hue, the solemn ceremonial, the mortal remains, the chill, dark, resting-place of the defunct body—the former soar higher, and regard these only so far as they serve to convey sound moral and spiritual instruction; their gaze is fixed not on the grave, but on heaven. Now it is clear that, death being a dispensation of God, it must be absolutely wrong to encourage a morbid view or presiding dread of it; but, at the same time, altogether to shun the contemplation of that which is a practical reality and the law of our very being, cannot be right. Neither in thought nor act must we fear or court it. All that is demanded of us is to meditate thereon at suitable intervals, and seek to meet its approach with becoming fortitude and composure. Nor may we doubt that, if we judiciously conform to the first duty, the latter will follow almost as a natural consequence. Only let reason be supported by faith when engaged in the contemplation of death, and many a bright ray will descend to cheer us in the seeming darkness and gloom. We shall piously reflect that a dispensation which is universal cannot be an evil, and indeed that to the virtuous and God-fearing man it is a supreme good, since it allows him to crown a long life of laudable endeavours and progressive improvement by faith, by childlike faith; again, that death is a messenger of heaven, therefore a messenger of love, and should, like life itself, be recognised as a blessing coming from the Divine Hand, and that, far from being a spirit of darkness, it is truly an angel of light to him who has faithfully served his God and done life's duties manfully, cheerfully, and zealously. Thus it is assuredly impossible to consider death *abstractedly*—apart from its sombre appendages and gloomy associations—without arriving at the conclusion that both as a natural dispensation and as the final bourne of each man's pilgrimage it is truly a blessing. Thence it should be occasionally regarded at a distance, say through the pages of history and biography. These will enable us to form a correct impression of the benefits conferred by death under its various guises. Through them may we surely discern and trace God's goodness and loving kindness as displayed in this dark, mysterious agent. They markedly point to the fact that such an equilibrium as the general good demands, could not be secured without this visitant, and further, their teachings infallibly lead to the conclusion that those physical and moral laws which are essential to the well-being of the individual and to mankind, would be more frequently violated but for the terror which death is apt to inspire. Sad indeed would be the condition of mortals were death to stay its hand. Assuredly nought but misery could ensue. Chaos would reign where order now presides. Were this not self-evident, it might be exemplified by the perverseness of the generations before the flood, who through extreme length of days either lost sight of death, or, only seeing it in the dim vista of centuries, gave no thought to the final dread summons. Truly, all past experience teaches us that death

—the sharp-edged sword of justice to the evil-doer—ever hangs suspended by a slender thread, and only awaits God's good time to be made visible to the obdurate offender. Oftentimes, through the infinite mercy and goodness of the Supreme, it makes no marked advance till pain, debility, and sickness have acted as reminders and certain indicators of its approach, yet occasionally it gives no warning, but calls for instant surrender. How, then, will the tyrant stand aghast at the gaunt spectre, how will the despot's proud heart sink within him when death advances and claims sovereign sway, how will the worldly man, the man of the world, the evil-doer, tremble, as conscience, awakening at the approach of God's messenger, upbraids him for the wilful neglect of life's duties, for past misdeeds, and for a criminal persistence in evil courses. Nor will the impenitent sinner, the malefactor, the sceptic, be altogether proof to the change at hand in the dark hour of dissolution, which must surely appear *to them* a king of terror, a foreshadowing of the retribution which is justly due to their perversity. Now it is clear death renders an important service to mankind when it swallows up evil by calling away the sinner, when it delivers society and the world from the criminal and the oppressor. Nor is it less frequently a friend and benefactor to individual man, and, would we recognise this truth, we have only to reflect on the pitiable condition of the infirm and decrepit, who may be said rather to exist than to live, since alike incapable of performing life's manifold duties or participating in its enjoyments. Indeed, each day only further impairs their mental and physical powers, rendering them more helpless, more burdensome to themselves and others. Arrived at this point, it is death, not life, which is craved as a blessing, and truly prolonged existence would be more than a misfortune—it would be a curse. Again, death has occasionally proved itself a friend to the oppressed by delivering them with a mighty hand and ushering them through the gates of martyrdom to the land of liberty and peace. It has often brought ease and rest where before was great physical suffering or mental anguish, and led mortals to acknowledge this truth, that death becomes a blessing the moment life ceases to be such.

But it has been kindly ordained by Providence that even mere reflection on the exodus of life should work practical good. The contemplation of death checks all rash self-confidence, while the messengers which it oft sends in advance—debility, pain, and sickness—remind men that they are mortal. The fear it is apt to inspire leads to the preservation of health, and proves the best guardian of life. The thought of sudden dissolution, of a pestilential, violent, or ignominious death has brought many to forsake their evil courses and repent. Dread of the destroyer, the spoiler, has often reunited in bonds of affection those who have been estranged, and made even the most callous set a high value on that which was lightly esteemed till likely to be forfeited. Then the consideration that it spares no one, nor high nor low, but robs most from those who have most to lose, and most affrights those who have most to fear, tends to strengthen the conviction of that equality which exists among men. Finally, reflection of death humbles the proud, weans the heart from senseless enjoyments, checks selfish indulgences, and conduces to a virtuous and pious life.

Now, although death at a distance or in the abstract may be easily regarded as a blessing, though violent passions and false pride may set it at defiance, though fear of shame and dishonour occasionally exceed and overpower the fear of its dread presence, though excess of woe, of pain, of grief may, alas! induce some to court and even rush upon it, yet assuredly it is only the truly good man who can watch and await its arrival with calmness and resignation. Upheld by faith, and relying with implicit confidence on God's gracious Providence, he will mark its gradual approach without dismay or apprehension. That fortitude which is derived from virtue and piety will sustain him when death is brought closely home, either through the loss of those held most dear, or his own immediate danger. Truly only he who has walked with God during life, and sedulously sought to fulfil life's duties, will meet death without fear at any moment the Sovereign Ruler may appoint. The consciousness that we have not abused or made a careless use of the loan of time graciously accorded us, that we have striven to make God our friend by sedulously following His laws, coupled with the conviction that he exercises no unnecessary severity towards His creatures, can alone enable us to dispel all misgivings and calm the perturbed spirit. And surely we fall into a sad, a fatal error, when we flatter ourselves that at the final hour we may leap, as it were, into the reward of virtue; that though we have looked little beyond self-gratification, and pursued a devious course, we yet can reach the same goal as he who has followed the straight path of duty and of honour. But as we touch the final bourne we shall discover how sadly we have miscalculated, and surely find that precisely as we have lived so shall we die; we may not divide life and death. The latter is part of the former, though it be but an infinitesimal portion, and the character we have built up for ourselves will undergo no perceptible change at that moment when nature's forces, mental and physical, are touching their nearest point of exhaustion. Now, would men only recognise this truth, and act in accordance therewith, we should hear much less of, and believe much less in, death-bed repentance. All sacrifices to be efficient must be voluntary, not forced; but what can we cede, what relinquish, what forego of our own freewill in the mortal hour? Are we not *then* utterly powerless to show our appreciation of the truth by a radical reform? We may poignantly regret the past, *but* to repent and atone for the misdeeds which blot its pages demand that time which is slipping away—that life which is fast ebbing. Let, then, this consideration stimulate our good resolution while we have life before us. Why should we ever put off that preparation so essential for every mortal? why, ever looking to the future, neglect the most important hour which that future will inevitably bring? Such rash folly is surely only to be accounted for by that wilful blindness which permits weak and frail creatures to "believe all men mortal but themselves". They pretend to see long years before them, though unable to answer for the coming hour. Birthdays come and go; sickness stretches them on that couch whence they may never rise; Sabbaths of rest, sleep, the grave, each in turn speak of the final rest; further, they may see their fellow-mortals yielding up life's latest breath, and nevertheless remain nearly proof to all serious and all disquieting reflections as regards their own feeble tenure of existence. Thus time speeds onwards, and lo! the grim spectre death stands suddenly and unexpectedly before them. Unfamiliar with this apparition, terror seizes the mind and oft paralyses it; what, then, becomes of death-bed repentance? Truly, only they who have lived the life of the righteous may reasonably expect to die their death; only they who have set apart appropriate seasons for reflection on life here and hereafter, who have moulded their conduct so that mortality should earn its immortality, and sedulously sought to secure the protection of the Supreme, may hope to meet God's messenger, not only without terror, without dismay, but with such perfect resignation, such holy trust, as to call forth those sublime words of faith, "O grave, where is thy victory? O death, where is thy sting?" The good man, the man of piety and faith, looks forward to a world beyond the grave, and, far from trembling at the thought of the journey thither, seems to say with his latest breath, "fear not to follow me". In a word, he speaks as the heir of a glorious immortality.*

* It has been the object of the writer to impart a strictly practical character to each subject reviewed, excluding all that is controversial or doctrinal; and, desirous not to depart from this rule, he proposes treating the subject of "Death" with only the faintest reference to the im-

And, in conclusion, we are here led briefly to refer to the benefits and spiritual joy which a belief in immortality will surely impart, when such belief is the result of thorough conviction, not of mere sentiment. If it be not grounded on reason as well as on feeling and natural instinct, if it derives not its chief support from the inspired pages of Scripture, it will be nearly powerless for good, and possibly, alas! fail in cheering the drooping spirit at the supreme hour. But when this glorious belief is founded on mature reflection, then will it teach us to sow here that we may reap hereafter; to lay up such treasures as we may carry away with us; it will enable us to recognize in God's messenger a friendly summoner to the celestial abodes, and thence while we mourn the loved and esteemed ones who are taken from us, we yet shall not selfishly lament, but acknowledge in the fulness of religious trust that our loss is their gain. It will exalt our ideas, purify our aspirations, and induce us to train our minds and faculties for a higher state of being. It will throw many a ray of light over life's journey, and cast a golden hue over the terminus which would otherwise be dark and gloomy. It will enable us to bear with composure sickness, grief, and pain, by pointing to that abode where trials and sorrows are unknown. Impressed with a sense of an eternal beatitude beyond this world, each departure of a loved and respected friend or relative must necessarily wean us more and more from the breast of mother-earth, and send our heart to that far country whither has fled our heart's treasure. Further, to believe in immor-

mortality of the soul, since such may not be deemed purely practical. Nevertheless, standing in immediate connection with the present topic, and also having an important bearing on many others, it necessarily demands especial attention, and therefore cannot fail to form an appropriate sequel to this essay. It is this consideration which induces the author to conclude with a letter that enters at some length upon this all-important subject, without, however, trenching on purely speculative grounds. It was written some three years since, at the request of a beloved relative, now no more.

tality is to believe in man's responsibility and God's justice; in the fulfilment of man's highest aspirations and God's goodness; in a state of retribution, but also in God's infinite mercy and love. Now, assuredly none can disbelieve but such whose interest it is so to do, for leaving apart faith and revelation, instinct itself speaks aloud, as the records of even the most uncivilised nations prove. The obdurate sinner willingly ignores an after-state, because to him it can only be fraught with gloomy forebodings. He full well knows not only that he has never sought to attain the crowning reward of a virtuous life, but has violated every moral law and misspent that time wherewith he was intrusted. Thence he sees only an avenging God, and strives to shut from his gaze that which is too dreadful to contemplate. But strive as the wicked may, the moment must arrive when their wilful blindness can no longer be of any avail, and then by their very terror will they practically acknowledge their belief in immortality. Truly pitiable as must have been their former condition, it will be yet more abject at the approach of death. But what a different scene will the last hours of the good man present, and what a lesson! With him we see mighty hopes hastening to their fulfilment. He has shown us how we should live, and now he practically demonstrates how a man may die. Truly, as he peacefully slumbers into ever-lasting life, he is bequeathing to his descendants a golden legacy of faith—a lasting and solemn record of an unshaken belief in immortality.

PRECEPTS.—If life be a blessing, as surely it is, then must death be such, else Solomon would never have told us that "The day of death is better than the day of one's birth".* But in order to recognise this truth, we must have fulfilled life's duties and accomplished the purposes of our being. Does not Isaiah tell us that if we have dealt charitably and kindly towards our fellow-creatures, or, as he expresses it,

* Eccles. vii, 1.

ch. lviii, 10, " If thou draw out thy soul to the hungry and satisfy the afflicted" then " *thy righteousness shall go before thee;* the glory of the Lord shall be thy reward". And to the same effect, ch. xxv, 8, " *God will swallow up death in victory*". Further, we must have reflected seriously on life and death, or again and again conned over such verses as these, Eccles. ix, 2, " All things come alike to all, there is one event to the righteous and to the wicked"; or Psalm lxxxix, " What man is he that liveth and shall not see death". Then we have David's view thereon, when he says, Psalm xxxix, 4, " Lord make me to know mine end, and how frail I am. Behold, Thou hast made my days as an handbreadth, and mine age as nothing before Thee; verily every man at his best state is vanity". Again, Psalm cix, 23, " I am gone like the shadow when it declineth". Also Moses, the man of God, tells us, Psalm xc, 10, " The days of our years are three score years and ten, and if by reason of strength they be four score years, yet is their increase but labour and sorrow, for it is soon cut off, and we flee away"; while we further read in Psalm cxvi, 15, " Precious in the sight of the Lord is the *death* of his saints". Such considerations, culminating in this last glowing thought, will help to prepare us for the final change, and enable us to meet God's messenger not only with composure, but in perfect faith and holy trust. Nothing is more conducive to this state of mind than to mark how the pious of this earth have departed. With what calmness David, when the " day drew near that he should die, spake unto his son saying, I go the way of all the earth".* Truly, he knew naught of terror, but much of hope, as is amply demonstrated in very many of his beautiful Psalms. Thus we read, Psalm xxiii, 3, " Yea, though I walk through the valley of the shadow of death, I will fear no evil, for Thou art with me, Thy staff and Thy support shall comfort me". Well might he exclaim, Psalm xxxix, 7, " And now, Lord,

* 1 Kings ii, 2.

what wait I for? my hope is in Thee". Again, Psalm xxxvii, 37, "Mark the perfect man, and behold the upright, for the end of that man *is peace*". But though he was prepared to meet death, he nevertheless did not court it; indeed, he felt that the final hour was an all-important one in man's life, and, as proof of this, we find that, after declaring himself to be "a sojourner on the earth as all his fathers were", he entreated the Lord to hear his prayer, and then exclaimed, Psalm xxxix, 13, "Oh spare me, that I may recover strength before I go hence and be no more". Now, if even the righteous need strength in the mortal hour, how weak and desperate must be the condition of the wicked. This verse especially applies to them, Psalm civ, 29, "Thou, O Lord, hidest Thy face, they are troubled; Thou takest away their breath, they die and return to their dust". They will then at least be forced to acknowledge how weak they are without God's guiding Hand, and how sadly, how fatally, they have erred in believing in death-bed repentance. Many, indeed, are the Scripture passages which should discourage all such belief, for example we read, Eccles. viii, 8, "There is no man that hath power over the spirit to retain it; *neither hath he power in the day of death*". Again, Prov. xxix, 1, "He that being often reproved hardeneth his neck, shall *suddenly* be destroyed, and that without remedy". And again, Prov. x, 25, "As the whirlwind passeth, so is the wicked no more".

We would now bring Scripture to testify to the folly of the wicked, who, having just cause to fear death, yet persist in pursuing that course which most surely leads thereto. They are like the "scornful men" depicted by Isaiah, who says, chap. xxviii, 15, "We have made a covenant with death, and with the grave we are at agreement; when the overflowing scourge shall pass through it shall not come unto us". But mark how they are answered, verse 18: "Your covenant with death shall be disannulled, and your agreement with the grave shall not stand; when the overflowing scourge shall pass through, *then shall ye be trodden down by it*". Again, chap. i, 28: "The destruction of the transgressors and of the sinners shall be together, and they that forsake the Lord shall be consumed". Truly, it is not to the sinner, but to the godly "who dwelleth in the secret place of the Most High", that the Psalmist thus speaks, Ps. xci, 5: "Thou shalt not be afraid for the pestilence that walketh in darkness, nor for the destruction that wasteth at noon-day; a thousand shall fall at thy side, and ten thousand at thy right hand, but it shall not come nigh thee; only with thine eyes shalt thou see the retribution of the wicked". Again, Solomon remarks, Prov. xii, 28: "In the way of righteousness is life, and in the pathway thereof there is no death". Sickness, disease, and death are indeed in ever-close proximity to sin, as we read, in Prov. xi, 19: "He that pursueth evil *pursueth it to his own death*"; and again, Prov. ii, 18, "The house of the strange woman inclineth unto death and her paths unto the dead". Then we are told, in Ps. xxxiv, 21, "Evil slayeth the wicked", while Job declares, chap. xviii, 5, "The light of the wicked shall be put out, *destruction shall be ready at his side*". Numberless other passages to like effect might here be quoted, but let us rather select those verses which, while showing that vice is antagonistic to life, further demonstrate that a virtuous course of action is highly conducive to length of days. Thus we read, Eccles. viii, 13, "It shall be well with them that fear God, but it shall not be well with the wicked, neither shall he prolong his days"; and in Prov. iv, 23, "Keep the heart with all diligence, for out of it are the *issues of life*". Then, Job iv, 7, "Whoever *perished* being innocent? but they that sow wickedness reap the same; by the blast of God they perish, and by the breath of his nostrils are they consumed". And again, Ps. xxxiv, we are told that "the man that desireth life and loveth many days" must "*depart from evil and do good*". We have now finally to show the essential service which fear of death may render to the wicked and the all-important benefit death itself confers on the godly. The former oftentimes checks the sinner in his evil courses, as exemplified in Ps. lxxviii, 34: " When God slew them *then* they sought him, and they returned and inquired early after God". And if any reflections can increase the terror with which the impenitent regard the near approach of dissolution, they will be suggested by such verses as these, Prov. xi, 7, " When the wicked man dieth *his expectation shall perish*, and the hope of the evil-doer decay"; and chap. x, 7, " The name of the wicked shall rot, and the treasures of wickedness shall profit nothing". Then, returning to the latter consideration, does not death usher in immortality? If it be indeed the extinction of earthly hopes, is not the fruition of heavenly aspirations also due to it? Scripture emphatically answers in the affirmative. Each portion of the Holy Volume alludes more or less plainly to a future state, and points to immortality as the crowning reward of a truly virtuous life.

This fact being fully demonstrated in the latter pages of this book, it is only here necessary to give two or three quotations on the subject. David declares in Ps. xvi, 10, " Thou, O Lord, wilt not leave my soul in the pit, but thou wilt show me the path of life; in thy presence is fulness of joy, at thy right hand there are pleasures *for evermore"*. Again, in Ps. xxiii, 3, " God refresheth my languishing soul, and guideth me in the path of righteousness. Surely goodness and mercy shall follow whilst I live, *and then shall I rest for ever in God's eternal abode"*. And here are Solomon's words, Prov. xxiii, 18: " Envy not sinners, but be thou in the fear of the Lord all the day long, for *surely there is an hereafter, and thine expectation shall not be cut off"*. But belief in immortality is not enough, since it is easy for man to believe what he wishes; we must further take to heart this truth, that as we sow here we shall reap hereafter, for just in proportion as this conviction gains ascendency in our minds so shall we make surer and firmer strides in the paths of duty and virtue. And may we doubt that this fact was uppermost in Solomon's mind when he brought to a conclusion his beautiful and instructive lesson for all generations in the last two verses of Ecclesiastes? After briefly recapitulating the "whole duty of man", he proceeded to forewarn us that our actions, though past, are not for ever done with, but that as responsible agents we shall have to render an account of them to the Great Ruler of the Universe. Truly no more significant words on immortality, as well as on rewards and punishments, could possibly have terminated this moral lesson than the following, Eccles. xii, 14: "Fear God and keep his commandments, for *He will bring every work into judgment*, with every secret thing, whether it be good or whether it be evil".

EXAMPLES.—It is not to the death of the evil-doer we would here refer, else we might well allude to the ignominious end of the crafty and wicked Haman, the dishonoured termination of the sinful life of the vile Jezebel, to the violent deaths of the "disobedient prophet", the licentious Amnon, the plotting and selfishly ambitious Absolom, of the besotted Nabal, and the impenitent Zedekiah. Most of these had wrought incalculable ills in their immediate sphere or nation, and were still obdurately bent on perpetrating fresh wrongs, fresh crimes, when arrested by the hand of death. Now in each of these cases where was the opportunity for death-bed repentance, even could such have served to atone for past misdeeds? Had any of these sinful men a single calm, thoughtful hour wherein they might have sought to make their peace with God and give some faint token of contrition? Assuredly not; the sharp, *sudden* stroke of death precluded all such possibility, and thus they died as they had lived. What a sad but all-important lesson is here revealed, and easy would it be to trace each separate catastrophe, with its final results, to the criminal misconduct of the individual. Nor is retributive justice the only moral to be drawn from these violent deaths. However, not to dwell longer on this gloomy picture, we proceed to make a passing remark on one of a reverse character, viz., the last moments of the truly virtuous and pious, whose name is legion. In perfect trust have they ever resigned their spirit unto God who gave it, and calmly, peacefully awaited the final summons while fulfilling to the last the charities and duties of life. What sublime examples of parental love, of generous devotion, of self-abnegation, have they bequeathed to revolving generations of men. And from among the host of these noble spirits we may single out the worthy patriarch JACOB, who years before his death declared himself, in the presence of the mighty Pharaoh, to be but a pilgrim on the earth. We first find him exhorting and blessing his children, and, when this last duty was accomplished, peacefully retiring to his eternal repose, safe in the Hand of an All-disposing Power. Then we may note instances of voluntary self-sacrifice, dictated by pious and patriotic motives; for example, the youthful ISAAC, who would have yielded up his life, a willing martyr to faith and filial obedience. Again, we have DAVID, the ever-ready champion of his people, who even in old age exposed his life for his country's cause, and could only be induced to relinquish the post of danger at the entreaty of his loving subjects. And when the last hour of this pious, God-fearing monarch drew nigh, what a sublime, what a useful lesson did he therein practically inculcate. Like Jacob, he exhorted and then blessed his son; he charged him to build a temple to the Lord, for which he himself had "prepared abundantly";* he commanded the princes of Israel to help Solomon, saying, "Is not the Lord your God with you, and hath He not given you rest on every side? therefore set your hearts to seek Him, and build ye the Sanctuary of the Lord God".† Then he urged upon the Levites and the people the fulfilment of their several duties.‡ This done, he abdicated in favour of his son, and, after pro-

---

* I Kings ii, 2. † I Chron. xxii, 18. ‡ II Chron. xxii, 6.

fessing his faith in God's promises, 1 Chron. xxix, 28, "he died in a good old age, full of days, riches, and honour".* Truly, he had to the last fulfilled every duty, and, knowing how zealously he had sought to serve the Lord and benefit his fellow-creatures, was well prepared to quit this life for that other which had been ever before him, and of which he speaks in such glowing terms in so many of his beautiful Psalms.

Several other characters might call for a brief remark under this heading, nevertheless we will now give our attention exclusively to the two contemporaries, ELI and SAMUEL—alike prophets of the Lord—and contrast their lives and deaths, since such can hardly fail to furnish a highly instructive lesson. Like position and circumstances might well have dictated like conduct, but notwithstanding, their mode of action was essentially dissimilar, and as a natural consequence led to widely different results, both as regards themselves and the nation over which they long presided. Both holding the high and important position of judge, their example and their teachings could not fail to influence the moral character of the people, and in most instances determine their course of conduct. They had a wide field of labour before them, but were not alike capable of fulfilling their task, nor equally zealous in the discharge of their duties, thence greatly did they diverge in their mode of action, and frequently work in exactly opposite directions. Indeed, their characters differed in many essential points. Eli was evidently weak-minded, while Samuel was bold as a lion; the former was faint-hearted and unstable, the latter ever earnest in good. Assuredly in life as in death they had little in common. Two or three marked instances in the history of each afford ample evidence of this. The culpable neglect of Eli in the training of his sons, having been already alluded to under the heading of "Parental Affection," here calls for only a brief remark. It is sad to be told that "the sons of

* II Sam. xxiii.

Eli were the sons of Belial, they knew not the Lord";* more sad still to find that when made cognisant of their perversity, he, a priest of the Lord, stopped short at simple remonstrance, and "restrained them not";† but above all it is to be deplored that, knowing they "made themselves vile", and caused "the people to transgress", he yet allowed them to retain their high and important posts. Now, had the duty he owed to God been a paramount consideration to Eli, he would assuredly have dismissed his sons from the sacred office they desecrated by their profligacy. Had he held the welfare of the people as a matter of the gravest importance, he would never have permitted these gross, these shameless debauchees, to hold a post wherein they must inevitably exercise a most pernicious influence. But we do not even find that he sought to counteract their evil example; indeed, under his judgeship the nation was in a state of decadence, and so low had it fallen about the period of his death that it hovered on the very brink of ruin. The moral weakness of the Israelites soon produced political weakness, and their old enemies, the Philistines, were not slow to avail themselves of so favourable an opportunity for recommencing a deadly struggle with a people they both hated and feared. Nor, indeed, had they miscalculated, the Israelites being defeated with great slaughter. Surely then at least the High Priest might have exhorted the people, and called them back to their duty and their God; he might have inspired and cheered them to renewed exertions, while showing the one only way whereby they could retrieve past disasters. Such was not the case however, but he remained silent at this momentous crisis, and it is only too evident that he even absented himself from his post, as we find *his sons* delivering up the ark of God to the people on their simply demanding it! But under these circumstances the Ark could be no pledge or symbol of victory to the chosen nation, since even when overwhelmed with reverses they had

* 1 Sam. ii, 12. † Chap. iii, 13.

not endeavoured to win back God's love and protection. Had piety and not superstition led them to covet possession of the Holy Tabernacle—had they regarded it only in connection with an ever-presiding Providence and thus become inspired by a holy faith, they would assuredly never have succumbed before enemies who were so timid and doubtful of the issue as to exclaim, " Woe unto us ! God is in their camp, and who shall deliver us out of the hand of these mighty gods ?"* As it was, the Israelites were signally defeated, and no less than thirty thousand perished on the field of battle, while the Ark itself fell into the hands of the uncircumcised Philistines. And what of its late custodian and guardian ? No mention is made of him till all was lost; then we are told he " sat upon a seat by the wayside watching, for his heart trembled for the ark of God".† Now, undoubtedly Eli was not a bad man, his faults being rather those of omission than commission ; but these faults did not therefore prove the less fatal to himself or the nation that owned his sway. He had been forewarned in years long past of what would befall his house, " because of the iniquities which he knoweth"‡ regarding his sons; nevertheless he sought not to avert God's displeasure by dismissing them from their high office, and replacing them by others more worthy of trust. To this criminal *omission* we may easily trace many subsequent evils. Had he, the delegated keeper of the Ark, strictly guarded it, and only confided it to the hands of such as knew and served the Lord, it would have been held as a sacred deposit; or if taken to the field of battle with the object of making it a rallying point and stimulating the drooping spirits of the combatants, it would have remained in security, protected by undaunted, because faithful, servants of the Most High.

We now pass to the History of Samuel, all the incidents of whose life show him to have been a man of quite another stamp. But we may here remark that no less than twenty

---

* 1 Samuel iv, 8.   † 1 Samuel iv, 13.   ‡ 1 Samuel iii, 13.

years elapsed before the people began to recover from the moral degradation and political depression which had been the unhappy effects of Eli's weak rule. Truly a sad legacy had he left them in the harsh sway of the Philistines, coupled with the curse of idolatry! Though the Ark was restored, the Israelites were not able to throw off the yoke of the enemy, their hands and hearts not being strengthened by faith in the true God. But at the end of this long term of years the " House of Israel lamented after the Lord", and from that period onwards we may note a marked change in their moral and political condition. Samuel had doubtless been anxiously awaiting the first favourable opportunity of calling them to repentance, and we find him thereon addressing "the House of Israel, saying, If ye do return unto the Lord with all your hearts, if ye put away the strange gods from among you, and prepare your hearts unto the Lord, and serve Him only, then He will deliver you out of the hands of the Philistines".* Happily, they were open to counsel, for we further read, "Then the children of Israel did put away Baalim and Ashtaroth, and served the Lord only".† Thus much attained, Samuel well knew all else would be easy. And now mark how he proceeded. He first called the people together, bidding them fast and humble themselves before the Lord. He then prayed for them, and led them to declare in words of heartfelt repentance, "We have sinned against the Lord".‡ The next change that occurred was his elevation to the judgeship, and happy was it for the nation that they selected this resolute, wise, and righteous ruler. Under his sway all prospered; by his firmness and courage, the natural fruits of piety, he brought the people out of their distress, utterly routing the Philistines in several pitched battles. Further, he carried them with unvarying success through every ordeal, and finally raised the nation to a high pitch of glory. Yet this ultimate triumph cost many a struggle, for not only had he

* 1 Sam. vii, 2.   † Verse 4.   ‡ Verse 6.

F F

to deal with an obdurate people, but with men who had lost much of their elevation of character during their late humiliating state of vassalage. Indeed, in spite of all the influence he attained through his many admirable qualities, Samuel was yet at times powerless to overcome their wilful defection and perversity. Thus it was in the case of their persistent demand for a King. Though he expostulated and remonstrated, showing them that while the fulfilment of their desires would be in every way detrimental to their interests, they were also sinfully rejecting the Lord, that He " should not reign over them";* nevertheless they " refused to obey the voice of Samuel, and said, Nay, but we will have a king over us".† Still this ungrateful proceeding on the part of the entire nation could not deter the noble-hearted prophet from pursuing the course he had set himself, and we find him thus declaring unto the people, " God forbid that I should sin against the Lord in ceasing to pray for you, but I will teach you the good and the right way, only fear the Lord and serve Him in truth with all your heart".‡ He must have felt somewhat aggrieved, however, at their ingratitude to himself, since he at once called the people together that they might testify to his integrity during the period he had been their ruler, though far, far more grieved was he to witness their obstinate rejection of the Theocracy. Indeed, so criminal did he deem their conduct that he could not allow it to pass without reproof, and even called down upon them a mark of Heaven's displeasure. Nevertheless, he soon relented, and from that date onward served the state with his former indefatigable zeal. He even reproved Saul—the elected sovereign—on more than one occasion; he gave his invaluable aid in every emergency, helped to humble the Philistines and defeat the Amalekites, and condemned to death the ruthless and wicked Agag, thus fulfilling duties which of right belonged to this weak-minded and culpable King of Israel. Finally, Samuel

* 1 Sam. viii, 7.   † Ib., verse 19.   ‡ Chap. xii, 23.

anointed David as Saul's successor, and then only, having attained a venerable old age, he retired to a life of quiet and seclusion.

Now, having compared the lives of Eli and Samuel, we will briefly consider their deaths, and review some of the incidents connected therewith. And what a moral do they alike unfold! Samuel was reverenced to the last, and though he retired from his judgeship, and left the capital in order to pass his remaining days in tranquil privacy, we are told that on his death "*all* Israel gathered together and lamented him, and buried him in his house at Ramah".* They justly estimated the national loss, and fully recognised how greatly their growing prosperity and happiness was due to the sagacity, the firmness, the piety of this unselfish ruler, this undaunted champion of their rights, this faithful prophet and servant of the Lord. Well might the whole nation join in testifying their grief and offering grateful homage to his memory. Not so, however, as regards Eli. Though at the time of his death he was judge in Israel, and had been ruler for no less than forty years, we do not find that his tragic end called forth one token of regret or respect—indeed, no further mention is made of his name! Doubtless the people were too much engrossed with their own sorrows to bemoan the loss of one who had so ill-performed his duties, and proved himself utterly incapable of helping them by personal counsel, or through that Divine assistance which was ever graciously vouchsafed to each faithful prophet of the Lord.

In conclusion, we would strive to show by the light of Scripture how different must have been the state of mind and feeling of these two men at the approach of their final hour. As to Eli, he was wrapt up in sorrowful forebodings, momentarily awaiting the most sinister tidings both as regarded himself and the entire nation. The ominous words which had fallen from the youthful Samuel some twenty

* 1 Sam. xxv, i.

years before must have resounded in his ears, and he will have felt that they were now about to be fulfilled. Well might he tremble, for what had he done during that long period to avert God's displeasure, while had he not left much undone which would possibly have arrested the disasters now impending? Dark thoughts these in a dark, dark hour. What a world of woe in such sombre reflections, and heavily must they have weighed on his mind. But the culminating blow had yet to fall, the last faint spark of hope to be extinguished. The chilling dread was to be exchanged for heart-rending reality. Not only did the messenger from the field of battle tell of defeat and of his sons' death, but alas!—far sadder still—Eli learnt in the same hour that the Ark of God, which had been entrusted to his safe keeping, had fallen into the hands of the enemy. Then indeed all, all, was lost, and the feeble old man, with one groan, fell back from his seat and expired. Truly did such overwhelming calamities "bring down his gray hairs with sorrow to the grave". Now, let us turn from this sad yet useful lesson to the death of Samuel, which stands out in strong contrast therewith and is hardly less instructive. This faithful servant of the Lord could review his past life not only without regret, but with positive satisfaction. Deeply interested in the welfare of his people, he must have exulted in their growing prosperity, and rejoiced in the thought that, under God, he had been the instrument of their regeneration. Moreover, he could look forward and see with prophetic eye the glorious epoch which the accession of Saul's worthy successor would usher in. He had resided a long time with David, and, thoroughly appreciating the character of the future monarch of Israel, foresaw with unerring certainty that the good seeds he himself had sown, would burst forth in a golden harvest when the God-fearing David should sway the destinies of the nation. Yet all this was only a portion of his rich reward. He could also turn his mental eye inwards, and look back without a blush upon an unblemished career.

He had hearkened to the voice of conscience, and never wronged himself or others through selfish indulgence or unlawful pleasures. All his remembrances must have been sweet in death, for he will have seen in his good and virtuous deeds those golden links which unite a happy past with a glorious and blissful future. In a word, having zealously served his country and his God, when the solemn hour arrived, he had nought to depress, but much to raise his spirits. Prayer, which had been the source of his past strength, virtue, and fortitude, now proved his sure refuge, and through it, he will have opened for himself the gates of life eternal. Truly, we could not more pithily sum up the character and life of this wise and righteous judge, this pious, faithful servant of God, than in the words of the following Scriptural quotation: " Mercy and truth are met together, righteousness and peace have kissed each other",* while the concluding verse of the same Psalm is equally applicable to his death, " Righteousness shall go before him, and shall set us in the way of his steps". Assuredly every faithful servant of the Lord should strive to walk "in the way of his steps", and thereby earn for himself a happy life, a peaceful death, and a blessed immortality.

* Psalm lxxxv, 10.

LETTER ON IMMORTALITY.*

Dear ———,—In fulfilment of my promise, I gladly place before you some of the numerous Biblical quotations which refer to the all-important subject of immortality. They are culled from the various books of the Old Testament, and directly or indirectly bear testimony that belief therein has ever been the very essence of the Jewish Faith.

Referring, firstly, to the *Five Books of Moses,* we find that almost all relating to a future state is of a *practical* character; thus the *death of the righteous Abel* by the hand of his guilty brother, when considered in connection with the goodness of the Deity, affords ample evidence that this life is but the prelude to another and a better world. If death be annihilation, where was Abel's merited reward? God had no sooner testified His pleasure with the conduct of His pious servant than death befel him! Surely, were there no future state, this untimely fate must be considered a chastisement, and certainly not a recompense for his past virtuous life, thence we *must* believe in immortality if we believe in the justice and goodness of God. The *death of Moses* speaks no less forcibly to the same effect. For one inconsiderate act he was not only denied the privilege of entering the land of promise, but had to yield up his life at the very moment that his hopes were about to meet their fruition! If dissolution of the mortal frame were indeed synonymous with extinction of the soul or spirit, breathed by God into man, we should assuredly be unable to reconcile the fact of his departure from this world at such a moment with the gracious attributes of the Lord. Truly the great law-giver Moses in his death added to his other valuable

* See note p. 421.

teachings the all-important lesson that at the very gates of death lies life everlasting. The *translation of Enoch* to heaven without dying is not without its significance; indeed, it goes far to prove that another habitation does exist for the sons of men, and is reserved for the faithful servants of the Lord. Other practical examples might be adduced, but we will now select some quotations from the same five books which are scarcely less conclusive. Take the sentence, "Thou shalt *go to thy fathers* in peace";* also, chap. xxv, "He was *gathered unto his people*"; and what meaning may we attach to such words but the assurance of a future state? Indeed, when applied to Abraham, Moses, Aaron, Samuel, Jeremiah, and various others, it is evident that the *soul*, and not the *body*, is referred to, since not one of these was buried near his fathers, but *in distant sepulchres*, and in more than one instance lonely solitudes, far, far from the haunts of men. These words would otherwise be worse than meaningless; they would not even bear the high stamp of truth, in itself an utter impossibility, proceeding as they did from the God of truth. Again, in Gen. xlvii, we find Jacob alluding to the length of his *pilgrimage*, and averring before Pharaoh that the years of his life had been "few and evil". Now, the very word pilgrimage betokened his belief that this world was but a preparation for another, free from those trials which beset his path here on earth. Then among the divers laws given by Moses to the Israelites, we may note such expressions as these, Gen., "He who doeth this wrong *shall be utterly destroyed*", "that *soul* shall be cut off"; and again in Lev., "that *soul* shall be *utterly* cut off". Here death of the *soul* is threatened as a punishment, thereby clearly implying that a future world is reserved as a reward for the pious and virtuous. Then what is more significant and expressive of the belief in immortality among the Israelites than their impassioned words to Moses, "Behold, we die, we *perish*",† implying utter annihilation. Again, Moses

* Gen. xv, 11. † Numbers xvii, 12.

thus addresses the people,* "I call heaven and earth to record this day against you that I have set before you *life and death, therefore choose life*", &c. Now, since death befalls the virtuous no less than the evil-disposed and vicious, "life" evidently here implies life everlasting. Further, by the light of immortality alone could the people have understood the promised reward of Moses that "their days should be as the *days of heaven* upon the earth" would they but act in obedience to the Holy Law. And again, did not Moses clearly allude to a future life when, after imploring forgiveness for his people, he added, "Yet now if Thou wilt not forgive their sin, then *blot me*, I pray Thee, *out of Thy Book*". Surely, such words must convince us that a belief in immortality as well as future rewards and punishment was entertained both by the law-giver and his people.

It is true, however, that the Five Books of Moses speak less plainly and touch more lightly on this subject, this belief, than the Psalms or the prophets, but the reason is obvious; like prayer, it is an instinct, a craving of the human heart, and therefore, like it, was never especially "commanded". Further, Moses could not consistently set himself to impress a people, but lately emancipated from slavery, leading a wandering life and deeply engrossed in every-day cares, with the doctrine of prospective advantages in a future life, but this he knew full well, that when their minds became enlightened they would not only comprehend it, but would even grasp its full and high import. It sufficed that he had laid a foundation with ample materials to develop the superstructure into a fundamental principle in future generations. And as we pass onwards reviewing the various portions of Scripture, this truth openly reveals itself. We find that when once the Israelites had freed themselves from their enemies and established a powerful kingdom, then, and then only, were they enabled to dismiss the overwhelming cares of the moment, and turn their thoughts into loftier

---

* Deut. xxx, 19.

channels. Spiritual welfare was then considered as well as the well-being of the body. Of this we may feel convinced when we peruse the beautiful *Psalms of David*, which repeatedly revert to the immortality of the soul. These were written *for the entire people*, and had they not already entertained a well-grounded hope of a blessed hereafter, David's allusions thereto would have been totally unintelligible to them. How could they have comprehended such passages as these: Ps. xxiii, 3, "The Lord *restoreth my soul*"; Ps. cxix, 15, " God will *redeem my soul from the power of the grave,* he will receive me"; and Ps. xcvii, 10, " Ye that love the Lord hate evil, He *preserveth the soul of His saints";* and again, Ps. xxxvii, 37, "Mark the perfect man, for the end of that man is *peace*", such peace being the sure result of a firm belief in life eternal, for a holy trust ever banishes all fear, all doubts, all questionings. Then we have David's memorable words addressed to his *servants* on the death of his son," While the child lived I fasted and prayed, for who could tell whether God will be gracious to me that it may live, but now that he is dead, wherefore should I fast?. Can I bring him back again ? *I shall go to him*, but he will not return to me". Surely this answer alone would afford conclusive evidence of his faith in a world beyond the grave. Again, how may we construe the following words of Abigail to David if not persuaded that they allude to immortality : "The *soul* of my Lord shall be bound in the bundle of life with the Lord thy God",* thence showing that the belief not only animated the king, but had taken firm hold on the minds of the whole people. Although more worldly-minded, Solomon spoke no less forcibly or distinctly of a future state than did his father David. His words are not to be misunderstood, being entirely free from all ambiguity. Thus in Eccles. we read, " All go to one place, all are of the dust, and all turn to dust again ; who knoweth *the spirit of man that goeth upwards ?*" and chap. 12, " Man goeth to his long

---

* 1 Sam. xxv.

home; then shall the dust return to the earth as it was, and *the spirit will return unto God who gave it*". Then in Proverbs, which were especially adapted for the people, we read, chap. xi, " Righteousness *delivereth from death*"; also we are told, " When the wicked man *dieth his expectation shall perish*"; and again, " In the way of righteousness is *life*, and in the pathway thereof *there is no death*".

We now turn to the *Book of Job*, supposed to have been written in the time of Moses, and therein we find additional proof that the blissful hope of immortality was *then* a belief, a fixed trust. Thus we read, chap. xix, " And after this *body* is destroyed, out of my flesh shall I see God". Again, " God looked upon men, and if any say, I have sinned, then *will He deliver his soul, and his life shall see the light*".

A few practical incidents calculated to strengthen the belief in immortality may be here introduced; for example, when Elijah prayed to God that Zarephath's child's *soul* should come into him again, the Lord granted his request, and *" the soul came back unto him again, and he revived".* Then also the *translation of Elijah* himself clearly proves that there is another habitation for the sons of men.

Turning next to the *Book of Kings*, we find that in more than one instance *death was promised as a blessing, as a reward for virtuous conduct*, as in the case of that excellent monarch Josiah,* yet could this have been deemed such by monarchs in the zenith of their prosperity had they not firmly and fixedly believed in immortality?

And now we may add some quotations from the Books of the *Prophets*, written at various epochs, most of them in the reigns of the Jewish kings, but some few when a portion of the Israelites had become captives and exiles in the land of their enemies. Thus we read in *Isaiah* xxvi, 19, " The *dead* shall *live; awake* and sing ye that dwell in dust", etc. Again, chap. lv, 3, " Incline your ear and come unto me, saith the Lord, and *your soul shall live.* Let the wicked

---

* ii Kings xxii, 20.

man forsake his way and turn unto the Lord, and God will *abundantly pardon*". Next, extracting from *Jeremiah* xxii, 10, "Weep ye not for the dead, neither bemoan him, but weep sore for him that goeth away (into exile), *for* HE *shall return no more*". Then what words could be more significant of eternal life than the following of *Ezekiel*, chap. xiii, 19 : "Thus saith the Lord God, will ye pollute me among my people *to slay the souls that should not die?*" Again, speaking of a righteous man, chap. xviii, 9, "He hath walked in my statutes, and hath kept my judgments to deal truly, *he is just, he shall surely live,* saith the Lord". Also, alluding to the evil-doer, "When the wicked man turneth away from his wickedness that he hath committed, and doeth that which is lawful and right, *he shall save his soul alive*"; and again, chap. xxxiii, 15, "If the wicked restore the pledge, etc., *walk in the statutes of life,* without committing iniquity, *he shall surely live, he shall not die*".

Turning next to *Daniel,* we read, chap. xii, "And at that time thy people shall be delivered *every one that shall be found written in the Book,* and many of them that sleep in the dust shall awake, *some to everlasting life,* etc., and they that be wise shall shine as the brightness of the firmament, and they that turn many to righteousness *as the stars for ever and ever*". Then in *Hosea* xiii, 9, "O Israel, thou hast *destroyed thyself,* but in Me is thine help; *I will ransom them from the power of the grave,* I will *redeem them from death*". Lastly, in *Malachi* iii, "They that feared the Lord *spake often one to another,* and the Lord hearkened, and a *book of remembrance was written before him* for them that feared the Lord and that thought upon his name". Truly, a reiteration of the words of Moses, containing the same glorious promise to the good and righteous.

Profane History further yields ample evidence that the Biblical teachings of immortality were not lost upon the Jewish nation. During long years thousands died for their religion, and by their willing martyrdom not only proved their love and trust in the One sole God, but also practically demonstrated their belief in a future and happier state. To those who thus perished, death was not annihilation, but an entrance into realms of bliss. The *writings of the learned Israelites* of successive generations give additional testimony that this belief has never been extinct in the nation. And finally, as a conclusive proof that the immortality of the soul is, and ever was, an essential *principle* among the Jews, we need only turn to the *thirteen fundamental articles* of their faith, wherein this belief is clearly embodied. Now, had not Moses in his five books inculcated this doctrine, had it been a mere instinct or the offshoot of another creed, this tenet could not possibly have found a place there. Assuredly that which Moses taught or commanded, *and nothing else*, forms the basis of the Jewish Faith. To his teachings, then, is this belief due, and if it has in a measure grown and strengthened in successive generations, such is but the natural consequence of the increase of enlightenment, and the ever-growing supremacy of reason and Faith.

THE END.

BIOGRAPHICAL INDEX,

COMPRISING SIXTY-FIVE CHARACTERS IN ONE HUNDRED AND TWENTY PARTS.

	No. of Page.	No. of Parts or Subdivisions.
1. ABRAHAM	53, 62, 74, 85, 103	5
2. AARON	310	1
3. ABIGAIL	196	1
4. ASA	306	1
5. Amaziah	100	1
6. AHAB	396	1
7. Absolom	262	1
8. Ammon	61	1
9. BALAAM	398	1
10. BUILDERS OF BABEL	46	1
11. BOAZ	83	1
12. CAIN	31, 394	2
13. CALEB	122, 292	2
14. DAVID	15, 51, 69, 101, 152, 238, 283, 429	8
15. DANIEL	35, 51, 72, 178	4
16. Daniel's three companions.	72	1
17. Disobedient Prophet	139	1
18. EZRA	9	1
19. EVE	24	1
20. ESTHER	23, 341	2
21. ELI	73, 101, 430	3
22. ELIJAH	307	1

		No. of Page.	No. of Parts or Subdivisions.
23.	ELISHA	84, 265	2
24.	Esau	60	1
25.	GIDEON	121	1
26.	HANNAH	23	1
27.	HAMAN	50, 397	2
28.	HEZEKIAH	42, 139, 177	3
29.	Hazael	395	1
30.	Hannaniah	121	1
31.	ISAAC	85, 142, 156	3
32.	ISRAELITES, early	266, 288, 344	3
33.	ISRAELITES under Judges and Kings	281, 302, 360	3
34.	JACOB	60, 181, 202, 428	4
35.	JEREMIAH	328	1
36.	JEPHTHAH	197	1
37.	JOSEPH	51, 59, 140, 225, 245	5
38.	JOSEPH'S BRETHREN	228, 241	2
39.	JOB	43, 61, 101, 220, 339	5
40.	JONAH	73, 242, 398	3
41.	JOSIAH	120	1
42.	JOSHUA	122, 292	2
43.	Jotham	52, 155	2
44.	KORAH	292	1
45.	LOT	53, 103, 126	3
46.	MOSES	60, 260, 371, 406	4
47.	MORDECAI	124	1
48.	Miriam	35	1
49.	NEHEMIAH	82	1
50.	NOAH	37	1
51.	Nabal	395	1
52.	Naaman	395	1

BIOGRAPHICAL INDEX.

		No. of Page.	No. of Parts or Subdivisions.
53. Othniel	-	304	1
54. Phineas	-	291	1
55. Rachel	-	35	1
56. Ruth	-	257	1
57. Rebecca	-	83	1
58. Reuben	-	140	1
59. Rehoboam	-	100	1
60. Samuel	-	42, 430	2
61. Saul	-	36, 198, 396	3
62. Samson	-	28	1
63. Solomon	-	15, 29	2
64. Shunammite	-	23, 218	2
65. Simeon	-	394	1

ERRATA.

Page 11, line 3, *for* " Omnipotence" *read* " Omniscience".
Page 71, line 29, *for* " conceived" *read* " concerned".

T. RICHARDS, PRINTER, 37, GREAT QUEEN STREET, W.C.